The First Liberty

A HISTORY OF THE RIGHT TO VOTE IN AMERICA, 1619–1850

MARCHETTE CHUTE

☆

The First Liberty

A History of the
Right to Vote in America,
1619–1850

J. M. DENT & SONS LTD
LONDON

Printed in the U.S.A.
for
J. M. DENT & SONS LTD
Aldine House · Bedford Street · London

The quotation from William Meredith which stands
at the beginning of Part One is from "The Inventors"
on page 55 of *The Open Sea and Other Poems*, published
by Alfred A. Knopf Inc., in 1958, and reprinted by
permission

Designed by the Etheredges

ISBN 0 460 03969 5

FOR B.J.
A JEFFERSONIAN DEMOCRAT
AND MY JOY

Contents

Foreword

This book traces the right to vote through two and a half centuries. It opens with the events that led to the formation, in 1619, of the first representative assembly in America. It closes with the aftermath of the Dorr War, which took place in 1842 and marked the last major attempt to deprive the white American male of the franchise.

His right to vote is now so familiar a doctrine that it would be easy to believe that it always existed in America, but it did not. Five years after Thomas Jefferson wrote the Declaration of Independence, he estimated that more than half of the white men in Virginia who paid taxes and served in the militia were not permitted to vote; and when John Adams wrote a state constitution for Massachusetts to replace the old colonial charter, he did not expand the franchise. He narrowed it.

The majority of men in the late eighteenth century still believed that the vote was a privilege, to be conferred only upon those who possessed enough money or land to be politically reliable. A minority insisted that it was a right, and that a white man who lived under a country's laws was entitled to a share in its government.

When this victory was finally won in the middle of the nineteenth century, most of the people in the United States were still disfranchised. It took further generations of struggle before the right to vote was extended to all adult Americans. But at least a beginning had been made, and it is this beginning that *The First Liberty* records.

The quotations are all contemporary, but spelling and punctuation have been modernized; the sources will be found in the back of the book. With the exception of one volume in the British Museum, all the titles are obtainable in The New York Public Library, which is one of the most magnificent research institutions in the world. Without it, *The First Liberty* would not have been written.

M. C.

Part One

Language includes some noises which, first heard,
Cleave us between belief and disbelief.
The word America is such a word.

—WILLIAM MEREDITH

Chapter One

England was a passionate country in the seventeenth century. Arguments over government and self-government were conducted with a violence that was very unlike the normal temperament of the people, and the century was shaken by civil war and revolution.

It was during this period that the English colonies in America were born. With its left hand, as it were, England created a series of political units along the eastern coast of North America while it was conducting a strenuous political experiment at home, and it scattered the seeds of its own unrest on what might otherwise have been a conventional shore.

It was not the intention of the English colonizers to bring any such characteristics to America, and their plans, on paper at least, were quite orderly. What altered them was the pressure of forces in England itself. They were too new to be named or even recognized, but too powerful to be smothered by planning or good intentions, and it was from these forces that the future United States was born. Each colony shifted and turned in the hands of its creators, just as England itself was shifting and turning, and the transplanted Englishmen three thousand miles away behaved just as oddly as Englishmen were behaving at home.

The century opened with no sign of the coming storm. When Queen Elizabeth died in 1603, the strong Tudor line died with her and there had been brief fears of a return to earlier battles over the succession. The crown passed peacefully, however, to her Stuart cousin, King James of Scotland, who became James I of England, and every Englishman had the right to congratulate himself on so stable a political system.

There was every reason to believe that the new reign would be both peaceful and prosperous. The long, dragging war with Spain ended as soon as King James came to the throne, and so did the depression that had plagued the war years. England was caught up on a wave of business confidence, and men who had accumulated capital began to look around for profitable investments.

The moment had obviously come to reconsider a dream which had lain dormant during the war years for lack of money and shipping. It was the adventure that had made Spain rich—the discovery and colonization of the New World.

England was an island, and slow to be stirred by the winds of change that had swept over the Continent during the Renaissance. In the field of exploration the nation had been especially laggard, and the one real spark of imagination had been shown by the city of Bristol. Five years after Columbus discovered America, the businessmen of Bristol financed a Venetian seaman named John Cabot, and some of them sailed with him in the first English ship to cross the Atlantic Ocean. Cabot discovered a shore which he named "New Found Land" and believed to be the longed-for Cathay. The mariners of Europe soon found that it was not, and all that the merchants of Bristol gained from their investment was to open the international fishing grounds that made the banks of Newfoundland a meeting place for the ships of many nations during the summer season.

The next English thrust toward the eastern coast of North America was a long time in coming. In the meantime, the brilliant and indefatigable Spaniards, after repeated failures and much quarreling, had managed to make a permanent settlement there, naming their fort St. Augustine. Protestant England looked upon Roman Catholic Spain as its chief enemy, and patriotic Englishmen were well aware of the importance of getting a permanent foothold of their own on the eastern shore of the continent. Sir Humphrey Gilbert made an heroic attempt to found a colony, and when he was lost at sea his half-brother, Sir Walter Raleigh, took up the burden.

Nearly twenty years after the Spaniards founded their fort in Florida, Sir Walter Raleigh financed an exploratory expedition which landed on the shore of what is now North Carolina. The Island of Roanoke, with its dangerous shoals and hurricanes, could not be used as the basis of a permanent English settlement, but a scouting party brought back word of a huge bay to the north where even the largest ships could shelter in safety. Two years later, in 1587, a band of colonists sailed from England and headed for this "Bay of Chesapeake, where we intended to make our seat."

The men of the Renaissance were formal in their dealings with the wilderness, and thirteen men were entrusted with the seal of the city which, it was hoped, would rise on the shores of Chesapeake Bay. The City of Raleigh was to be governed by a corporation consisting of a Governor and twelve Assistants, and each man had been granted a coat of arms by the Office of Heralds since this was the usual way to reward "the virtuous, worthy and valiant acts of excellent men." There were seventeen women in the company, with good English names like Agnes Wood and Margaret Lawrence. Two of them were pregnant, and one of these—Eleanor Dare—was daughter of the Governor and wife of one of the twelve Assistants.

The company never reached Chesapeake Bay. Those in command became involved in the usual quarrels (faithful as their shadows to nearly all colonists) and the expedition was forced to settle temporarily at Roanoke. The Governor's granddaughter was born there in August, and she was christened Virginia after the land that Raleigh had named in honor of the Virgin Queen. Earlier in the same month an Indian named Manteo was also christened. He had come out with the expedition after living for three years in England and it was hoped that he would assume authority over the Indians living on Roanoke and on the neighboring island of Croatoan.

Governor White went back to England for supplies and then found that he could not return; war with Spain had broken out and England's ships were needed elsewhere. It was not until 1590 that he finally arrived back at Roanoke, and he was not alarmed to find it deserted. It had never been intended that the colonists should stay there permanently, and it had been arranged that they would leave behind them, carved on a tree or post, "the name of the place where they should be seated." The name that Governor White found carved was CROATOAN, and he was delighted. "I greatly joyed that I had safely found a certain token of their safe being at Croatoan, which is the place where Manteo was born and the savages of the island our friends." He was less rejoiced to find that the chests he had left buried in the sand had been dug up and despoiled—"my books torn from the covers, the frames of some of my pictures and maps rotten and spoiled with rain, and my armor almost eaten through with rust"—but he believed this to have been the work of enemy Indians "who had watched the departure of our men to Croatoan."

Governor White decided the following morning "to weigh anchor and go for the place at Croatoan, where our planters were." But the hurricane season had begun and a storm blew up on that dangerous coast. A prisoner of the winds, he tried to reach Trinidad. Then he tried with equal unsuccess to reach the Azores and finally arrived back in England late in October. As for the little band of men, women and children who had tried to establish the first English colony in America, they were never found or heard from again.

In 1589 Raleigh had assigned his rights in the City of Raleigh to a syndicate, and one of its members was that incorrigible optimist Richard Hakluyt. Hakluyt was convinced that it was England's destiny to colonize America, and his voice had been raised untiringly on the subject of what was called "western planting." Since the great geographer was also a clergyman, he signed himself Richard Hakluyt, Preacher, and he was so indeed. His sermons may have been commonplace, but his writings were a trumpet call to patriotic and adventurous Englishmen. Undisturbed by past failures, he was still hopeful when the new century opened and in fact had just published a greatly enlarged edition of his book of explorations.

Hakluyt had many allies, and three years after James I came to the throne the hard work of years became suddenly visible. On the tenth of April, 1606, the King approved a charter for the colonization of Virginia, and Richard Hakluyt, most suitably, was one of the eight men named in it.

Behind these eight names stood two distinct groups of massed capital, one in London and the other in the western ports of Bristol, Exeter and Plymouth, and the charter gave each group the right to attempt a settlement in America. The London group was authorized to attempt one in southern Virginia, to be known as the First Colony, and the other one was to attempt a Second Colony in northern Virginia, in the area later known as New England.

The responsibility for governing the two areas was vested in a board known as the King's Council of Virginia. This in turn was to choose two groups of thirteen men each to do the governing overseas, as had been done in the case of the City of Raleigh. They were not given coats of arms but each man had the right to be addressed as Captain and each group was to be given a seal as the sign of its local authority. Instead of being known as a Governor and his Assistants, they were to be called a President and his Council. It was an innovation that each of these two Councils was to elect its own President. He was to have "full power and authority, with the advice of the rest of the said Council, or the greatest part of them, to govern, rule and command."

The goal of the First Colony was Chesapeake Bay, and the three ships that were destined to found the colony of Jamestown went out that December. They reached the Bay late in April and a cross was set up on Cape Henry as a token that the land was claimed for King James. A sealed box of instructions had been kept secret until then, so that there would be no conflict of authority on board ship, and when it was opened it was discovered that there were only seven names listed to serve on the Council, instead of the thirteen that had originally been planned. It was upon these seven that the full responsibility for governing the First Colony would rest.

The charter had stated, rather smugly, that one of the reasons for colonizing Virginia was to "bring the infidels and savages living in those parts to human civility and to a settled and quiet government." Instead, it was the Englishmen who found it difficult to achieve a quiet government, whereas the Indians already possessed one. Their orderly system of minor rulers operated under a chief called Powhatan, and when one of these local princelings entertained the new arrivals they had to admit that he conducted himself "as though he had been a prince of civil government." It was the Englishmen who behaved otherwise.

This was not for lack of good advice, and the official letter of instructions which they carried with them had ended on a note of almost fatherly eloquence: "The way to prosper and achieve good success is to make yourselves all of one mind for the good of your country and your own, and to serve and fear God, the Giver of all goodness, for every plantation which our Heavenly Father hath not planted shall be rooted out." The men who founded Jamestown prayed morning and evening and heard two sermons on Sunday, but they found it impossible to be of one mind.

The quarreling had started even before the election for President, which was held in the middle of May. Captain Edward-Maria Wingfield was chosen by the majority of the seven men, and he promptly announced that he would not permit Captain John Smith to remain on the Council. Since their orders made it legal to depose the President "upon any just cause," all Captain Smith had to do was to get the majority on his side and he could then depose Captain Wingfield. Faction prospered in the already stormy atmosphere, and the First Colony rocked with the charges and counter-charges of the men who were supposed to be governing it.

Equally unlucky was the choice of a site, although here the instructions had been far more realistic. "You must take especial care that you choose a seat for habitation that shall not be overburdened with woods near your town, for all the men you have shall not be able to cleanse twenty acres a year. . . . Neither must you plant in a low or moist place because it will

7

prove unhealthful." Christopher Newport was in command of the three ships and he was an experienced and reliable man. He conducted a long, conscientious search, but in the end he sounded his trumpets and struck sail at a peninsula some thirty miles up the James River, in an area choked with trees, poisoned by marshlands, and with a water supply that was seriously contaminated. Yet the harbor itself was a good one, and because the peninsula was nearly an island it could be defended from possible attack by the Spaniards.

Moreover, Newport had obeyed a key point in his letter of instructions: "Have great care not to offend the naturals." The Indians were agriculturists, living in towns where grew "the goodliest cornfields that ever were seen in any country," and Newport could not run the risk of leaving his little group of Englishmen on land which the Indians wanted for their own use. Some of the Indians were already hostile, and Powhatan had tried to silence the murmuring by pointing out, "They take but a little waste ground, which doth you nor any of us any good."

Under the best of circumstances it would have been difficult to govern Jamestown, since no one knew how such a colony should be run. The problem was compounded by bad luck and bad judgment, but the root of the trouble lay in the fact that the seven men on the Council had such contempt for each other. Both sides committed to paper extensive reports of their own virtue and wisdom and of the extreme viciousness and stupidity of the opposition. According to the vigorous accounts of Captain John Smith and his supporters, it was he who saved the colony. According to the equally vigorous accounts of the opposition party, he nearly ruined it.

Perhaps some of the bitterness at Jamestown might have been prevented if Bartholomew Gosnold had lived. He had been from the first one of the most ardent backers of the project, and his courage and integrity were unquestioned. It was apparently his influence which kept that other country gentleman, Wingfield, his friend and neighbor in Suffolk, in the office of President. But Gosnold died in the sickness that struck Jamestown that first summer, and Wingfield's term of office ended nineteen days later.

Another great loss was the death of their minister, who had been able to mediate successfully between the warring factions. He was a Sussex man named Robert Hunt who remained cheerful in the face of personal disaster and who struggled to keep the Church of England alive in the wilderness. Captain John Smith, writing years later, had a vivid memory of Hunt's efforts. "I well remember, we did hang an awning (which is an old sail) to three or four trees to shadow us from the sun, our walks were rails of wood, our seats unhewed trees till we cut planks, our pulpit a bar of wood nailed to two neighboring trees. . . . Yet we had daily Common Prayer, morning and evening, every Sunday two sermons, and every three months the holy communion till our minister died."

Meanwhile the ships of the Second Colony had gone forth, carrying the same sealed instructions. These colonists built a fort in northern Virginia—in what is now Maine—at a site where the Androscoggin and Kennebec rivers meet to form the Sagadahoc. Again the minister conducted himself well. Again there sprang into existence what one of the backers denounced as "childish factions. . . . The President himself is an honest man, but old and of an unwieldy body and timorously fearful to offend." Again the men on the Council spent their time "dividing themselves into factions, each disgracing the other." There was almost no sickness in the Second Colony, and no one died that first year except the elderly President himself. At the same time, there was none of the fierce energy that heaved and churned in the tormented little colony of Jamestown.

The backers of both colonies were deeply disappointed. No doubt they had been unrealistic, dreaming of gold and silver in the south and even of cinnamon and nutmeg in the north, but the colonies were only kept alive by supply ships and sent no goods to England that were worth the sending.

The time came when the investors could accept no further drain on their resources. The men of the western ports admitted defeat, in spite of the ardor of Sir Ferdinando Gorges of Plymouth, who clung to his conviction that it was "a very excellent country." The men of London had more financial and political power and many conferences were held, including a "solemn meeting" at the house of the Earl of Exeter in the Strand. It was finally decided that there must be a complete reorganization and Sir Thomas Smythe agreed to be in charge of it.

Sir Thomas Smythe was one of the richest and most imaginative of the new breed of international businessmen, and his huge house in Philpot Street was the headquarters of mercantile operations that stretched over half the globe. He was the first Governor of the Levant Company, first Governor of the East India Company, Governor of the Muscovy Company, and head of the syndicate that sent Henry Hudson to explore the Arctic in search of a passage to Asia through the northern seas. Smythe was just back from a trip to Russia when the Virginia charter was planned, and he involved himself in the new project with his usual energy and optimism.

It was clear to Sir Thomas Smythe that the faltering experiment at Jamestown would have to be completely transformed. It would have to be cut free from its present control by the Crown and from its links with the western ports, and, above all, it would have to be refinanced. So expensive an undertaking could not be supported by a small group of private individuals; the only way to keep the venture alive was to follow the normal procedure of English businessmen when they needed a large amount of risk capital and to organize a joint-stock company.

It was decided that stock in the new enterprise would have a par value of twelve pounds, ten shillings, and a brilliant publicity campaign was launched to sell shares to the general public. An alluring prospectus, called *Nova Britannia,* pictured Jamestown as an earthly paradise, and the promoters played upon every patriotic, religious and financial instinct that the Jacobean public possessed. They even guaranteed, as a final inducement, that the names of all subscribers would be listed in the new royal charter for Virginia that King James had agreed to bestow.

This new charter was granted on the 23rd of May, 1609, and the names which march proudly across its pages constitute a cross section of middle- and upper-class England. Six hundred and fifty-nine private investors were listed, starting with earls, bishops and knights and proceeding to a medley of businessmen, gentlemen, ministers, professional men and widows. There were also fifty-six London Companies on the list, starting with rich ones like the Goldsmiths and working down through the Cooks, Plumbers and Upholsterers.

The charter announced that the name of the new corporation was "The Treasurer and Company of the Adventurers and Planters of the City of London, for the First Colony in Virginia." The Planters were those who went forth to Virginia, the Adventurers were those who stayed behind and adventured only their money, and the Treasurer was Sir Thomas Smythe. To assist him in governing the corporation, a large Council was also listed in the charter. This was made up of lords, bishops and other prominent and energetic men whose advice would be useful and whose names would be effective. The Lord Mayor of London, for instance, was a member of the Council, and he was in the position to deliver "a most worthy and pithy exhortation" to the powerful Grocers Company when it hesitated to invest its funds in the venture. Another member of the Council, Sir Edwin Sandys, wrote with special effectiveness to the Mayor of Southwark, urging his support of "an enterprise tending so greatly to the enlargement of the Christian truth, the honor of our nation, and benefit of English people."

Sir Thomas Smythe and his distinguished Council did not intend to accept any advice from the stockholders on the way they ran the Virginia Company. Or, as the charter put it less bluntly: "It is not convenient that all the Adventurers shall be so often drawn to meet and assemble as shall be requisite." Therefore, the right to make the laws was given in the charter to the Treasurer and his "careful and understanding Council," and the stock-holders gathered together only when the Treasurer, as chief executive officer, wished to summon them. They had the right of election but it was a rather meaningless one, since the current members of the Council served for life and had already been selected.

It was natural for Sir Thomas Smythe and his colleagues to design an organization over which they had full control, since it would be difficult enough to revive the languishing colony at Jamestown without interference from the stockholders. This was especially true since it was so easy to become a member of the Virginia Company. In most corporate bodies in England, the right to enter and to become "free" of the corporation was jealously guarded and therefore any man could be trusted with a certain amount of political power once he was inside. But in the case of the Virginia Company, anyone could become a freeman of the corporation by investing twelve pounds, ten shillings. This made him a member of what was described as "one body politic" but it did not give him any real share in its government.

The inherent difficulty in maintaining this program in the Virginia Company lay in the fact that a great many of the stockholders were members of the landed gentry. This was a class that refused to let itself be silenced, as the Tudors had already found in their dealings with the House of Commons. The subscription lists show that Sir Thomas Smythe was obliged to turn more and more to the gentry in his efforts to raise money for the ships and cattle and supplies that were so desperately needed at Jamestown, and the gentry set a price for their cooperation. As they stated formally in the next decade, "They would never have adventured in such an action . . . if in the regulating and governing of their own business their own votes had been excluded."

It was not possible to give them this voting power within the framework of the charter of 1609, but three years later a new one was written. This third charter for Virginia passed the seals in the spring of 1612, incorporating what "time and experience hath found to be needful," and among the various innovations was a new form of government for the Virginia Company.

The right to make the laws was taken away from the Treasurer and his Council. It was given instead to four quarterly Courts, or assemblies, which were to consist of the Treasurer, the Council and all the stockholders. These four meetings were to be styled "the four Great and General Courts of the Council and Company of Virginia." The voting was to be done by a show of hands, the decision of the majority was final, and it was this majority which now had "full power and authority" to govern the Virginia Company.

There was no provision to protect the larger investors. Each stockholder had one vote in the General Court, whether he owned one share or fifty and whether he were a haberdasher or a knight. This was, in fact, the same kind of voting equality that operated in the House of Commons itself. It was a point of real pride in the lower house of Parliament that each member had the power of a single vote and an equal right to make himself heard. "There is an equality amongst all, the lowest burgess being in that place of as good worth as the highest knight."

The Virginia Company had changed its earlier structure and was now "a government ruled by voices," but for the moment there was no real change in the way it was run. Sir Thomas Smythe was still in full command. The chief difference now was that he was obliged to cultivate the art of creating and keeping a majority, and although he was a member of the House of Commons, as his father before him had been, he was not temperamentally a parliamentarian. The greatest parliamentarian in England was a member of his Council, Sir Edwin Sandys, and when there was ultimately a test of strength between the two men in the Virginia Company, it was Sandys who won.

Meanwhile, Jamestown was operating under a system which had been imposed as soon as Smythe took control in 1609. It was clear that the original plan of a President and Council had been unworkable—"not powerful enough among so heady a multitude"—and a more normal one was substituted. The officials of the Virginia Company went to a great deal of trouble to find an experienced professional soldier to take the dual position of Lord Governor and Captain General of the colony, with two equally good men under him as Lieutenant General and Marshal. The dignity of the Lord Governor was maintained by fifty red-cloaked halberdiers, he sat on a special chair of green velvet in the church at Jamestown, and he headed a chain of command which involved every colonist in Virginia.

These laws were published in London in 1612 under the title of *Laws Divine, Moral and Martial,* and the moral ones were especially severe. They reflect a frontier society and a period in which mutilation and death were normal punishments for slight offenses, yet even so the penalties were remarkably high. A woman was liable to the death penalty if she stole flowers from the garden she was weeding, or a man if he butchered his own cow without official permission. Nor was anyone in Jamestown permitted to protest. It was punishable by death on the third offense to "utter unseemly and unfitting speeches" against those in authority or against official publications.

If provisions like these were seriously enforced, the people of Jamestown had exchanged their "first ragged government" for one of cold steel. Sir

Thomas Smythe himself expressed concern that such rigorous laws might prevent colonists from migrating to Virginia, and the Virginia Company needed able-bodied men in Jamestown just as much as it needed enthusiastic investors in England. Yet it was Smythe who authorized the London publication of the *Laws,* probably on the assumption that their severity would be modified by the common sense of the Lord Governor, and it was true that when the son of one of the investors left Jamestown in 1614 he was able to report that the severity of the laws was "now much mitigated."

Nevertheless, the government that had been decreed for Jamestown in 1609 was as unrealistic as the one that had been decided upon for the Company itself, and for the same reason. Both were dictatorial, and ran counter to the profound conviction of Englishmen that they had a right to a voice in their own affairs. The government of the Company itself had been changed by charter in 1612, giving the vote to the stockholders, and a few years later they gave the same privilege to their fellow Englishmen in Virginia.

The records of the Virginia Company for its earlier years are very incomplete, and the preliminary discussions on the subject are not extant. But on the 29th of April, 1619, the newly appointed Governor of the colony, Sir George Yeardley, arrived in Jamestown with an entirely new set of instructions. The colonists heard with "great joy" that many changes were to be made, and one of them gave the people a share in the government. Their representatives were to meet with the Governor and Council in a General Assembly, and it was this Assembly that would henceforth make the laws for Virginia, subject to the approval of the Virginia Company itself.

It might seem that members of the Company were only extending to the colony the rights they themselves possessed and that a General Assembly in Jamestown, consisting of Governor, Council and burgesses, was very like a General Court in London, consisting of Treasurer, Council and stockholders. This was not, however, the Company's own view of the matter. Instead, it designed the forthcoming meeting of the General Assembly at Jamestown to resemble as closely as possible the meetings of the English House of Commons. Even the salaried officials were not those of the Virginia Company—the Husband and the Beadle; they were those of the House of Commons—the Clerk and the Sergeant at Arms. At every point the intention seems to have been to make the General Assembly in Virginia a miniature version of the Parliament of England, and a great deal of careful planning must have gone into this extraordinary decision.

The General Assembly of 1619 met in Jamestown for five days at the end of July and the beginning of August, and a very able public official sent back the report to the Company. His name was John Pory and he had come out as Secretary, a post that John Donne, the poet, had coveted a few years earlier. Pory was connected by marriage with Governor Yeardley but he also happened to be qualified for the position. He had studied geography under Richard Hakluyt, who praised him highly, and since then he had spent several years in travel and as an attaché in foreign embassies.

Pory was inclined to regard Jamestown as an intellectual wasteland. He complained of "the solitary uncouthness of this place" and found his chief refuge in reading. Yet he was deeply interested in the first Assembly of what he called "our infant commonwealth," and the account he wrote of the five-day meeting is lit by his pride in it.

Pory had reason to be proud. The Englishmen who met together in that hot little frontier town conducted their parliamentary business as carefully and formally as if they had indeed been members of the House of Commons meeting in the ancient chapel of St. Stephen's in Westminster.

They convened in the wooden church, which had recently been rebuilt, and they did everything properly and in order. Governor Yeardley sat in the choir of the church and grouped around him were the six members of his Council of State, corresponding in that miniature assemblage to the monarch of England and his House of Lords. Directly in front of the Governor sat John Pory, who had been chosen as Speaker of the House. Next to him was the Clerk, while the Sergeant at Arms stood at the bar "to be ready for any service the Assembly should command him."

In front of them were twenty-two burgesses, elected by the people of Virginia to be their representatives. They had gathered to hear the opening prayer, but they could not serve until each member had taken the Oath of Supremacy which guaranteed that they were loyal members of the Church of England. In Westminster, it required the combined efforts of the Lord Steward and a dozen deputies to administer the oath to all the members of the House of Commons, but in so small an assemblage it did not take long for each man to answer to his name and to take the oath that made him an official, voting member of the Assembly. Together they would make the laws, which would then be ratified by the Virginia Company in London and stamped with its official seal.

The twenty-two burgesses represented eleven units of settlement, or "plantations," and there was some question whether the two representatives from Captain Martin's plantation should be permitted to remain. The influential and obstreperous Captain Martin held a special grant from the Company which gave him the rights of a lord of a manor and he was not willing to "submit himself to the general form of government as all others did." Therefore the Assembly decided not to admit the two delegates from Captain Martin's plantation, on the grounds that anyone who helped make the laws must be willing to submit to the will of the majority once they were made.

The next order of business was the formal address delivered by the Speaker of the House. John Pory had served in Parliament and he knew that the Speaker was expected to deliver an elaborate piece of rhetoric on this occasion, rich with the classical, historical and Biblical allusions so loved by the men of the Renaissance. He also knew that he was incapable of "long harangues," for he was ill and the July heat was lethal. He therefore contented himself with explaining briefly why they had come together and reading aloud the text of the orders that Governor Yeardley had brought with him.

These orders had been most carefully and thoroughly considered by the Virginia Company in London. They had been examined by a select committee, approved by the Council, discussed and approved in what was called a preparative court, and finally read and discussed in one of the quarterly General Courts and voted upon by raised hands. The Assembly in Jamestown was supposed merely to agree to it, or, as John Pory put it, the Company "did expect nothing but our assent thereunto."

It was not in the nature of Englishmen to give that kind of assent. The House of Commons usually held the afternoons open for committee work, and the Assembly at Jamestown at once formed two committees of eight men each to examine the document in detail. The committees worked three hours apiece that hot afternoon and decided on favorable reports. Then, on the following morning, after the full Assembly had conducted a thorough discussion of "the great charter of laws, orders and privileges, the Speaker put the same to the question and . . . it had . . . the general assent and the applause of the whole assembly."

One of the delegates died on Sunday. The rest worked on, the sickness increasing, and the following Wednesday Governor Yeardley, who himself was ill, decided to end the session. The laws which they had agreed upon had not yet been engrossed on parchment in the correct parliamentary manner, but John Pory promised to attend to this final detail himself.

He closed his report with an apology to the members of the Virginia Company, "hoping their courtesy will accept our poor endeavor, and their wisdom will be ready to support the weakness of this little flock." He had no reason to apologize. The first representative assembly in the New World had behaved in a fashion which any parliamentarian would have admired.

There was one aspect of the business, however, in which the procedure was unlike that of the House of Commons, and that was the way in which the representatives to the assembly had been elected.

For the past two centuries in England, elections to the House of Commons had been based upon a single principle: no man could take part in the voting for representatives unless he had enough property and social standing to make sure that he would be reliable. This principle applied to the voting for both kinds of representatives in the House of Commons, those that were sent by the counties of England and those that were sent by the incorporated towns.

All county voting operated under a single standard—simple, uniform and very restrictive—which had been established by an Act of Parliament in 1430. The preamble to the Act explained that a "very great and excessive number of people" had been voting in the county elections, each of them claiming "a voice equivalent . . . with the most worthy knights and esquires." It was to be feared that this would result on election day in "manslaughters, riots, batteries and divisions" and the obvious way to avoid disorder was to limit the right to vote. From that time forward, no Englishman could vote in a county election unless he owned a freehold property with an annual value of forty shillings. He must, in fact, be prepared to swear to the sheriff by the holy evangelists that his freehold was actually worth that sum.

The law of the forty-shilling freeholder was very difficult to apply. A great deal of land was held by copyhold or leasehold rather than by freehold, and it took an experienced lawyer to make his way through the snarled and ancient thicket of land tenures to find the exact status of his client. Moreover, the freehold could be in something other than land—a church pew, for instance.

The application of the Act might be confusing but the principle was clear, since a freehold was an infallible sign of independence and respectability. The freeholders were the men who in Chaucer's day had been called franklins, yeomen who were often richer than the lord of the manor and who could safely be trusted with the vote.

In the case of voters in the incorporated towns—the boroughs—the standard was much less consistent. Sometimes the qualifications of the voters were specified in the borough charter, sometimes they were the result of local custom, and sometimes they were the result of a special decision in the House of Commons. However, in practice the right to vote always went to the more prosperous and stable members of the community.

As soon as a borough had been given its charter by the Crown, it was an incorporated body politic, possessing its own seal and the sole right to accept or reject applicants for membership. The privilege of being "free" of this corporation was sometimes inherited. Usually it involved some kind of training or the payment of a fee. But always it went to reliable townsmen who were qualified to take part in local government, and it was these men who sent the burgesses to the House of Commons.*

Throughout the sixteenth century, the power of the House of Commons rose steadily in England, but it was not the power of the common people. It was only the men of property who could be entrusted with the vote, and below that level, voiceless, were the majority of the inhabitants of England.

It was therefore curious that the Virginia Company imposed no property restrictions when it authorized elections for the Assembly at Jamestown. The Governor's proclamation apparently merely stated that the two burgesses from each plantation were to be chosen by the inhabitants. In English usage this word sometimes meant householders—meaning those who were heads of households and therefore men of property—but this does not seem to have been the meaning here.

In subsequent elections in Virginia, not only free men without property but also servants were permitted to vote, and this seems to have been so even in the first Assembly. On the last day of its meeting, the question had come up who was to pay for the work that had been done by the Speaker, the Clerk and the Sergeant at Arms. In England, these officials were paid by the Crown, but the Virginia Company had not supplied any money for the purpose. Therefore, it was decided to tax the people. "It is fully agreed at this General Assembly . . . that every man and manservant of above sixteen years of age shall pay into the hands and custody of the burgesses of every incorporation and plantation one pound of the best tobacco, to be distributed to the Speaker and likewise to the Clerk and Sergeant of the Assembly according to their degrees." Because money was scarce in Virginia, tobacco was used as legal tender, and since this tax was imposed on all males over sixteen it seems probable that all of them were voters.

This was a very casual voting procedure, but there were various reasons why it might have seemed justified. For one thing, the burgesses in the Assembly had relatively little power since the right to make the laws rested, by royal charter, with the General Court of the Virginia Company in

---

* The corporation voted as a unit, and it was quite possible for a single individual to be the whole of the corporation. It was even possible for the individual to be a woman, as was the case of the incorporated town of Aylesbury. "I, Dame Dorothy Packington, widow, late wife of Sir Thomas Packington, knight, lord and owner of the town of Aylesbury . . . have chosen . . . Thomas Lichfeld and George Burden, esquires, to be my burgesses of my said town of Aylesbury. . . . In witness whereof . . . I have set my seal."

London. It was in part because the early House of Commons had relatively little power in England that the voting requirements had remained so casual up to 1430. It could also be argued that in so small a community as Jamestown and its environs, each man had a direct stake in the general welfare whether or not he possessed property, and in any case it was so fluid a society that a man could become rich in a very short time.

A few years earlier, the first experimental consignment of Virginia tobacco had been shipped back to England and it was immediately clear that the colonists had found a cash crop. The tobacco was not of high quality at first, but it required little capital and less skill and there was always a market waiting for it. When Pory arrived in Jamestown in 1619 he noted that one tobacco planter had cleared the astonishing sum of £200 in a single year. The wife of a man who had been a collier in England was now sporting a "beaver hat with a fair pearl hatband and a silken suit" and even the "cowkeeper here . . . on Sundays goes accoutered all in fresh flaming silks." In a land where social forms could dissolve so quickly, it might well have seemed meaningless to apply the English principle of the forty-shilling freeholder.

It would also have been difficult to persuade skilled labor to migrate to Virginia if there was a policy of disfranchisement. The Virginia Company had sent some Poles to the colony because of "their skill in making pitch and tar and soap-ashes" and the question of their political rights had come up for discussion in a meeting of the Company during that same July of 1619. "Upon some dispute of the Polonians resident in Virginia, it was now agreed (notwithstanding any former order to the contrary) that they shall be enfranchised and made as free as any inhabitant there whatsoever."

Some men were disturbed by the laxity of the situation, and one of the most vocal was a stockholder in the Virginia Company whose name was John Bargrave. Captain Bargrave was convinced that the Virginia Company had made a serious mistake in permitting such a casual franchise in the colony, and he was equally convinced that the root of the trouble lay in the voting equality within the Company itself. A company "governed by popular voices" had been permitted to transfer a similar pattern to its colony, "and it is a shame that the common weal of Virginia . . . should be governed so." Bargrave became so emotional that he even decided that it was no accident but a deliberate plot which had resulted in this "profuse throwing out liberty among the planters. . . . They did it knowingly and wittingly against the sovereignty of England, extreme liberty being worse than extreme tyranny."

Captain Bargrave had no objection to the existence of a representative assembly in Jamestown. What he disliked was the freedom that was being permitted in the voting for delegates. He wrote several treatises on the way he thought Virginia should be governed, and there is extant a very elaborate scheme which he worked out for the franchise. He embedded it in an ideal constitution which was full of those classical allusions so dear to the contemporary heart. The constitution included many things, including a President who served by the month, but its basic purpose was explicit: "The mouth of equal liberty . . . must needs be stopped."

In Bargrave's ideal Virginia there were to be two orders of colonists. The first order consisted of all former servants, of all men who held land as tenants, and of all men who had only enough money to get themselves overseas. None of these would be allowed to vote.

Bargrave set up the second order—"them we call our citizens"—by "dividing them into five degrees," each with its own kind of political power. The lowest degree was that of Commoner. Such men were rich enough to bring two men apiece overseas and could therefore be trusted with the election of lesser officials, such as highway surveyors. The highest degree was that of the Patriot, and such men were rich enough to bring over three hundred men apiece. Only Patriots were to be permitted to serve on the governing Council, make the laws and be eligible for the rotating office of President.

The plan was constructed, as Bargrave said, to "suppress popular liberty," and was highly ingenious, since it based political power on property and at the same time recognized the basic English principle of representation. Since citizenship was so carefully restricted, it would be safe to let all citizens vote. "We may for these reasons give them the elections of their own governors . . . which all free subjects do naturally desire." The plan was also specifically constructed to counteract the danger that the men of Jamestown might try to set up an independent government, and each member of Bargrave's governing Council was to take an oath that every law which was passed was for "the uniting of Virginia to the crown of England."

Bargrave worded his constitution as though it had been issued by the King, and whether or not James I saw it, he would have agreed with its basic contention that the control of the colony should be taken away from the Virginia Company. Things had been going from bad to worse from the royal point of view, and the trouble dated from 1619. This was the year in which Sir Edwin Sandys took the control of the Company away from Sir Thomas Smythe, and King James considered Sandys to be his enemy.

Sir Edwin Sandys was a member of the gentry, a class that had become increasingly critical of the way King James was governing his kingdom. During the previous century, the Tudors had been obliged to accept this class as allies, and now its members in the House of Commons had begun to talk of "the true and ancient liberties of the House" as though these had existed from the dawn of English history.

The conviction of such men that there was a partnership between the people and the Crown was alien to the current theory of a Christian monarchy, and it frankly baffled King James when he arrived from Scotland to be crowned. As he said to the Spanish ambassador, in apology for the difficulties he continued to have with the House of Commons: "I am a stranger and found it here when I arrived, so that I am obliged to put up with what I cannot get rid of." Queen Elizabeth had managed to keep the House of Commons under reasonable control by a remarkable combination of tact, firmness and guile, but James had never learned the practical art of political maneuver. The House, on the other hand, had been working out for itself an increasingly efficient way of operating, especially through committees, and by now it was attracting the services of some of the most talented men in England.

Sir Edwin Sandys had been a fairly quiet and conservative member of the House under Queen Elizabeth, but he rose to immediate prominence in the first Parliament under James. Sandys respected the monarchial system, but he was deeply convinced that Englishmen possessed certain natural rights which no monarch could abridge or destroy. When he spoke in favor of a free trade bill in the Parliament of 1604, it seemed reasonable to pitch his argument in part on what he called "Natural Right. —All free subjects are born inheritable, as to their land, so also to the free exercise of their industry. . . . Merchandise being the chief and richest . . . it is against the natural right and liberty of the subjects of England to restrain it into the hands of some few, as now it is."

Steadily, respectfully and eloquently, Sir Edwin Sandys and his political associates thwarted the will of the King, and the climax came in 1614, during the brief session which was known as the Addled Parliament because it passed no laws. James was in chronic need of money and he attempted to use the device, quite normal in Europe, of levying a special customs duty on certain goods at the ports. This undercut the most precious of all parliamentary privileges, and the Commons set itself under Sandys' leadership to destroy the King's plan. If an English monarch were to be permitted to raise money without Parliament, he would next think himself free to "make laws without Parliament," and the result would be slavery.

During the debate on the subject, Sir Edwin Sandys delivered a speech that came close to sedition. He said that the King of England ruled by consent of the people, "and with reciprocal conditions between King and people." Anything else would be tyranny, and the people had the right to revolt against a tyrant. This last was hinted at discreetly in a Latin quotation, "pronounced at length" as a member of the audience noted.

The infuriated King did not summon another Parliament for seven years, and Sir Edwin Sandys had a great deal of extra time to devote to the Virginia Company. His open quarrel with Sir Thomas Smythe began when he served on the audit committee and decided, rightly or wrongly, that Smythe had been mishandling the accounts. It is quite possible that so busy a man, and one involved with so many organizations, took an occasional shortcut in the interests of efficiency, but Sir Edwin Sandys decided, characteristically, that Smythe was trying to create "a perpetual dictatorship."

Sir Thomas Smythe did not run for the office of Treasurer of the Company in 1619, but he put up his own candidate and expected him to be elected. Instead, the Sandys faction made common cause with another powerful bloc of votes within the Company. A law was suddenly passed, stipulating that all election of officers must be by secret ballot, and when the votes were counted under this new method Sir Edwin Sandys was the Treasurer of the Virginia Company. It was at this point that King James began to have grave doubts about the way the Company was being run.

When election time came around again the following year, it was plain that the new Treasurer would be reelected, and James decided to interfere. He had no intention of letting the Virginia Company be controlled by the "principal man that had withstood him" in the Addled Parliament. The stockholders of the Virginia Company proved equally stubborn. The royal charter of the Company gave them the right to choose their own officers and they considered the King's attempted interference "a great breach into their privilege of free election."

The problem was finally solved by electing the Earl of Southampton instead. The man who in his youth had been Shakespeare's patron was deeply interested in colonization. He had financed two exploratory expeditions to America before Jamestown was founded, and he became an ardent supporter of the Virginia Company.

The election of the Earl as Treasurer was a victory for Sandys, since the two men had been on the same side politically during the Addled Parliament; Sandys headed the opposition to the King in the House of Commons while Southampton headed a similar but more informal group in the House of Lords. The Earl had neither the time nor the inclination to burden himself with administrative details, so that the affairs of the Company remained firmly under the control of Sandys and his voting majority.

The Virginia Company was now split into two irreconcilable factions, and the tone was reminiscent of the one that had existed at Jamestown in the days when Captain John Smith had battled with his opposition. Now, as then, each side sincerely believed that it had supplied every good thing that was being done for the colony, and that the other side was bent on ruining it.

Sir Edwin Sandys was an idealist, and like many idealists he had the fault of believing that he was always right. Moreover, in spite of his hard work and devotion, he lacked both tact and administrative ability. The bedeviled Company sank deeper and deeper into debt, with its leaders assuring each other that God would not forsake Virginia and sending out more and more colonists to a country which could not support the ones it had.

Final disaster came in 1622. The Indians had been watching the English settlers spread out over what had once been their own cornfields, and decided to destroy them all. In the massacre, over three hundred and fifty colonists died. Sandys had been suppressing some of the letters of complaint he received from Virginia, but no one could hide the magnitude of the March disaster.

Company elections were held two months later and again the Sandys majority held firm. Again the King tried to influence the vote, protesting, however, that he had no wish "to infringe their liberty of free election," and again the stockholders, by a huge majority, voted the royal candidates down. The minutes of the meeting noted that "His Majesty seemed not well satisfied," which was a profound understatement.

The members of the Company pushed on against what were now beginning to be hopeless odds. "We conceive it a sin against the dead to abandon the enterprise." They did their best to put on an assured front and in November gave an official feast. John Donne, now Dean of St. Paul's, delivered the sermon on this occasion and prayed that the Lord would "bless them with disposition to unity and concord." The prayer was not answered. By now the two factions were quarreling openly on the streets of London and in the Royal Exchange.

In April of 1623 the Sandys majority drew up a formal document to explain its policies. This was in answer to an equally formal document by the opposition which had made some very serious charges. "They allege that the government as it now stands is democratical and tumultuous. . . . Their allegation is a slander, for the government is not democratical." The word was a shocking one in monarchial England, and Sandys and his party made haste to reject it. It was true that the government of the Company had "some show of a democratical form," but this had been unavoidable; the financing had come about through the "purses of many" and such men would not have consented to invest their money "if in the regulating and governing of their own business their own votes had been excluded." Moreover, those that "cry out against democracy and call for oligarchy" had not been able to show that this would produce a better form of government.

The Privy Council thought otherwise. After due deliberation, it decided that the basic fault of the Virginia Company lay in the charter of 1612 which gave the power to the stockholders and that its defects could only be remedied "by reducing the government into the hands of a fewer number of governors." This meant that the charter would have to be abandoned, and the stockholders refused to do it. They sent a crisp statement of one sentence to the lords of the Privy Council to inform them that only nine stockholders had voted to surrender the charter; "all the rest (being about threescore more) were of a contrary opinion."

The Court of King's Bench promptly issued a *quo warranto*. This was a demand to show cause why the charter should not be surrendered and was the first step toward its dissolution. The stockholders voted Company funds to hire the best lawyers they could get. They fought all winter and in the spring turned for help to the House of Commons. King James told Parliament not to interfere.

The General Court of the Virginia Company had its usual quarterly meeting in April of 1624, and the Earl of Southampton was elected Treasurer by a large majority. In June a preparative court was held to arrange for the next meeting of the stockholders, but with this entry of June seventh the minutes cease. The charter had been revoked, the Virginia Company ceased to exist, and the strange experiment in self-government was ended.

What did not come to an end was the equally strange little seedling the Company had planted in America; the miniature parliament that had been authorized at Jamestown did not go out of existence when the charter ceased.

The men of Jamestown had watched the long battle in England in a state of real anxiety, for they were naturally partisans of Sir Edwin Sandys. A group of commissioners who were sent to Jamestown early in 1624 to investigate conditions found the colony much more prosperous than had been expected and the members of the Assembly furious, having worked themselves up to "the highest pitch of spleen and detraction" against Sandys' enemies in England. They felt that Sir Edwin had given them the Assembly and that if his power were to be destroyed they might lose representative government.*

---

* Sandys made a list of the contributions his administration had made to the welfare of the people of Virginia, and one of the items was "the liberty of a General Assembly being

No one knew what might happen to the colony now that it was no longer the property of the Virginia Company, and the Assembly wrote two cautious letters to King James, hoping he would not authorize any arrangement that would lead to "tyranny." No decision had been made when James died the following year and his son ascended the throne as Charles I.

King Charles issued a proclamation stating that his father had dissolved the Virginia Company because it was not suited to a monarchial system, being "ruled by the greater number of votes and voices." He announced that he intended to place the government of the colony under a royal council in England and a subordinate council in Jamestown. Under this plan, of course, the General Assembly would vanish.

It did not intend to vanish. The current Governor of the colony was Sir Francis Wyatt, elected by the stockholders just before the Company was destroyed, and Wyatt was a strong ally of representative government. On his own responsibility he authorized local elections, and when the General Assembly met in Jamestown in May, 1625, it drafted a careful petition to the Crown.

Three years later, King Charles needed local support for a new tobacco policy and he himself authorized the calling of a General Assembly. When the King's little colonial parliament in Jamestown sent in its report, it spoke of "our former General Assemblies" in a tone which clearly implied that they were now traditional. And so they were. King Charles did not try to interfere with their existence, and each year the principle of representative government became more firmly entrenched in what had once been called the First Colony.

Meanwhile, the backers of the Second Colony to the north had long since given up hope, with the single exception of Sir Ferdinando Gorges of the port of Plymouth. He enlisted the energetic services of Captain John Smith, who had lost interest in Jamestown after his term as President had ended in his being sent home in disgrace. Smith, with his passionately colonizing eye, saw a great future for settlers in the excellent fishing to the north, and when Gorges sent him there to make a survey Captain John Smith gave northern Virginia a new name—New England. Sir Ferdinando Gorges was greatly strengthened by Smith's able report and by the excellent map he made of the region, and he managed to interest a new group in the idea of colonizing the area.

granted them." This was not strictly true, since Sir Thomas Smythe was still Treasurer when the decision was made, but Sandys was an unfailing supporter of the principle of self-government and certainly one of the main forces behind the reforms that were granted so suddenly in 1619.

In 1620 this group was given a royal charter. It was organized as "The Council established at Plymouth in the county of Devon for the planting, ruling, ordering and governing of New England in America," and two years later Gorges issued a prospectus in which he advertised for colonists. In this he made it very clear that the colonial policy which had been inaugurated by the Virginia Company in 1619 would be continued. "All men by nature . . . do most willingly submit to those ordinances or orders whereof themselves are authors" and therefore New England would also be given representative government. "The general laws whereby that state is to be governed shall be first framed and agreed upon by the General Assembly of the states of those parts." The enthusiastic imagination of Sir Ferdinando Gorges even rushed ahead to the days when there might be great towns in the New England wilderness, and these too would send "their deputies or burgesses to this public Assembly" where they would have "voices equal with any the rest."

Nothing came of this dream of a parliament in New England, since the newly formed Council of New England failed in its efforts to colonize the land, but the same principle was followed in the next effort at colonization. In 1623, Sir George Calvert was given a royal charter to colonize part of Newfoundland, to be named Avalon. Included in this charter was a clause that the laws were to be made with the advice and consent of the freemen duly assembled for the purpose. (This did not mean freemen in the sense of members admitted into a corporation, since Avalon was not a corporation; it meant men who were not servants.)

The same gift of representative government made its appearance in subsequent charters. In 1629 Sir Robert Heath was given a royal charter for land south of Virginia, to be named Carolina, and the charter specified that the laws were to be made with the "counsel, assent and approbation of the freeholders." The following decade, Sir Edmund Plowden got a charter for another large tract on the coast, north of Virginia, and named it New Albion. Here too the laws were to be made "with the counsel, approbation and assents of the free tenants," and a later prospectus for New Albion spelled the matter out with more precision. Every year in the month of November the Governor of New Albion and his Council of State, constituting the upper house, and "thirty burgesses or Commons," constituting the lower house, were to meet to pass laws and levy taxes, "and without full consent of lord, upper and lower house, nothing is done."

All these were ghost parliaments, existing only on paper. It was extremely difficult to establish a permanent colony in America, and none of these brave dreams materialized. Only one man found the strength to keep on in the face of failure, and that man was Sir George Calvert.

Calvert had been a Secretary of State, but he left government service in 1625 when he became a Roman Catholic. He had just been created the first Lord Baltimore, and he threw his considerable energies into an attempt to build up his two-year-old colony of Avalon. He brought his wife and most of his family out to Newfoundland in 1627, intending to make it his home, and found to his horror that the winters were interminable, no green thing appearing before May. Moreover, there was the usual sickness. "My house hath been an hospital all this winter . . . fifty sick at a time, myself being one, and nine or ten of them died. Hereupon I have had strong temptations to leave all proceedings in plantations and, being much decayed in my strength, to retire myself to my former quiet."

Instead of retiring into quietness, Lord Baltimore was possessed by a new vision. Some of the land surrounding Chesapeake Bay was still available for colonization, and it might be possible to establish there a refuge for gentlemen of his religion. King Charles sympathized with this point of view for he had married a Roman Catholic—the pretty Frenchwoman whose name was Henrietta Maria but whom he called Mary—and in her honor the new province was named Maryland. Lord Baltimore was still nursing his charter through the complicated and expensive details of chancery procedure when he died in April of 1632. The charter was granted two months later and bore the name of the second Lord Baltimore, his equally dedicated son Cecilius.

The founding of Maryland was unique in the annals of colonization, since nearly everything went according to plan. There was no echo of the series of wild disasters and recoveries that had rocked Jamestown. Young Lord Baltimore was determined to avoid quarrels, and when he drafted a letter for the guidance of the first shipload of colonists he laid special stress on "unity and peace." He walked a narrow path of good will, since the gentlemen who went out were Roman Catholics and the indentured servants who went with them and made up the majority were Protestants. The only solution to the problem was extreme courtesy, and this was extended equally to the authorities at Jamestown—who were only seventy miles away and displeased to have newcomers on Chesapeake Bay—and to the Indians. The town of St. Mary's was built on land which was bought from the local Indians, who were allowed to stay until they had gathered in their crops. The Indians had been delighted to make the sale, since their present location exposed them to raids from the Indians of Delaware Bay, and a priest who accompanied the expedition to Maryland was deeply impressed by them. "They are generally so noble, as you can do them no favor but they will return it. . . . If these were once Christian, they would doubtless be a virtuous and renowned nation." Even the site that was chosen for St. Mary's was superb. It stood on a high bluff on the Potomac River, free from swamps and marshes, and with its tall trees so well spaced that a coach and four horses could have been driven among them.

The one thing that did not go according to plan was the way Maryland was governed. The charter contained the usual clause that the laws were to be made "with the advice, assent and approbation of the freemen of the same province, or the greater part of them," but there was no thought that Maryland should indulge in those "democratical" tendencies which Captain Bargrave had deplored in Virginia. Sir Edmund Plowden, who held the same kind of charter, wrote with satisfaction to his young friend Cecilius Calvert on the aristocratic nature of their two provinces. They were, said Sir Edmund proudly, "principalities and county palatines . . . with all regalities fit for men of honor and . . . not fit for a mean corporation." A business corporation like the group which had founded Virginia could not be expected to follow the nobler procedures that would characterize Maryland and New Albion.

By the terms of his charter, Cecilius and his heirs were the "true and absolute lords" of the country, and he possessed not only the control of all branches of the government but the privileges of royalty itself. His only obligation to the King of England was to set aside for the Crown one-fifth of all the gold and silver to be found in the province and to make an annual gesture of fealty by bringing two Indian arrows to Windsor Castle during the week of Easter.

No one had paused to consider how an absolute lord would fare when he tried to work with a representative assembly, and the arrangement had been blithely included in charters of this kind with no thought of how it would operate in practice. Lord Baltimore had the distinction of being the first proprietor of a colony who had to struggle with this problem, and his determination to be polite was put to a severe strain.

It had been assumed that the men of Maryland would wait for their lord's bidding before they gathered themselves together as legislators. They did not pause for a bidding, and only a year after the colony was founded they gathered together in an unauthorized assembly and passed a whole series of laws. There is no record of the activities of this assembly of 1635, since it had no legal right to exist, and when an authorized assembly was finally called together, three years later, it was made clear to its members that all the laws that had been passed in 1635 were void.

The new assembly met in January of 1638 and Lord Baltimore sent over the text of the laws he wished its members to ratify. His younger brother

Leonard was serving as his Lieutenant Governor, and he was obliged to send back to England a report that was unsuited to the eyes of an absolute lord. "The body of laws you sent over . . . I endeavored to have had passed by the assembly at Maryland but could not effect it."

In imitation of the House of Commons, the little Maryland assembly met each morning at eight. The group was mixed enough to include a carpenter and a mason, and they all took their duties with passionate seriousness. When Leonard Calvert suggested a temporary adjournment of the assembly, they "demanded the reason why it should be adjourned, and said they were willing to leave their other business to attend it."

The Lieutenant Governor finally decreed an adjournment to the end of the month, and those irrepressible parliamentarians promptly asked for the "privilege of parliament men for their persons." This was the privilege of not being subject to arrest in private suits while Parliament was in session, and the men of the House of Commons had achieved it just after King James came to the throne. In 1604, a member of the House had been imprisoned for debt to a goldsmith, and his colleagues had promptly declared this illegal and imprisoned the goldsmith instead. The House said proudly, but quite unhistorically, that it was operating here on "an ancient ground" and in 1624 the burgesses in the General Assembly at Jamestown successfully claimed the same privilege.

The General Assembly of Maryland was supposed to take a subordinate position in a rigidly structured feudal society. This it refused to do. It behaved in exactly the same way as the General Assembly of Virginia, and both of them modeled themselves tenaciously on the House of Commons in England.

Other European nations had succeeded in planting colonies along the same coastline, but none of them brought with them the political institutions they had developed at home. The Spanish in Florida tried to transplant the *cabildo,* the ancient institution of the town council, and make it part of the way in which St. Augustine was governed, but it withered and died in that alien land.

It was only the English who brought with them a commodity as portable and as sturdy as their muskets or their seeds: the conviction that they had a right to share in their own government. This was what Sir Edwin Sandys had in mind when he talked of the natural rights of Englishmen. The principle had neither clear rules nor defined limits but its force was irresistible, and by 1640 it had created two parliaments in the wilderness on the shores of Chesapeake Bay.

Chapter Two

On a Friday morning in May, in the year 1623, Captain John Bargrave unburdened himself on a subject which was, at the moment, dear to his heart. This was the anti-monarchial nature of the activities of Sir Edwin Sandys and the damage they threatened to do in colonial America.

Sandys' first offense, according to Bargrave, was the change of government he had permitted at Jamestown. "If the charter which by Sir Ed. Sandys his means was sent into Virginia (in which is a clause . . . that they shall have no government put upon them but by their own consents) and his other proceedings in those businesses of the plantations (especially such as concern government) were looked into, it would be found that he aimed at nothing more than to make a free popular state there."

Sandys' second offense, according to Bargrave, was of a similar nature. He had been trying to help some members of a religious sect called the Brownists—"those Brownists by their doctrine claiming a liberty to disagreeing to the government of monarchs."

Bargrave's first charge may not have been correct, but the second one certainly was. Sir Edwin Sandys had worked hard and successfully to make it possible for a group of Brownists to reach America. They had sailed only three years earlier, on a freighter called the *Mayflower*.

It was a fair description to call the Brownists anti-monarchial in their views. It was for this reason that their founder, Robert Browne, had been imprisoned thirty-two times in the days of Queen Elizabeth. He finally changed his views, but his followers did not and several of them were executed.

The Brownists did not consider themselves anti-monarchial and did not understand why the government called them seditious. They believed that since the Church of England had retained so much that was Roman Catholic both in its structure and its ceremonies, devout Protestants had the right to withdraw and form self-governing congregations of their own. In a period when Church and State were one, this was almost the equivalent of saying that an Englishman had the right to withdraw from the monarchial system if he chose, and Queen Elizabeth executed men like Penry, Greenwood and Barrow because they were a clear threat to her sovereignty.

From their own point of view, the Brownists were merely trying to reestablish primitive Christianity, before what they considered "popish and antichristian stuff" had entered into it. Not Robert Browne but the Apostles themselves had been the "beginner of this way," and they were convinced that their reforms would serve only to strengthen the kingdom. As John Penry explained to one of the ministers of Queen Elizabeth just before his execution: "Far be it from me, my lord, that I should move you to attempt that which shall bring inconvenience unto the peaceable estate of Her Majesty's crown, seeing the establishing of the truth and the abolishing of corruptions shall be always found to carry undoubted stability with it." Such men did not realize that their doctrine involved the destruction of the whole system of authority and control upon which the State rested, and that claiming the liberty to disagree was, as Captain Bargrave said, anti-monarchial.

Bargrave was also correct in pointing out how much help Sir Edwin Sandys had given them by aiding one particular group to reach America. In 1617 two of its leaders, John Robinson and William Brewster, wrote Sandys and thanked him for the "singular love . . . great care and earnest endeavor" he had shown their congregation. Robinson was its minister and Brewster one of its elders, and the letter continued in language that was unusually strong for such sober people: "Under God, above all persons and things in the world, we rely upon you, expecting the care of your love, counsel of your wisdom, and the help and countenance of your authority."

Sandys was remarkably liberal in his religious opinions; he could assist an extreme Protestant sect like the Brownists and at the same time refrain from hating their greatest enemies, the Roman Catholics. In 1621 the House of Commons was swept by an especially intense wave of anti-Catholic hysteria, and its members vied with each other in suggesting vicious and degrading punishments for an elderly Catholic barrister whose only crime had been a verbal indiscretion. It was Sandys, almost alone, who set himself against what was really mob action in the House and pleaded for moderation.

He was also a man of great personal kindness, and in the same year in which Robinson and Brewster sent him their letter of thanks he received a somewhat similar one from Virginia. It was written by John Rolfe, who had recently visited England with his wife, Pocahontas, and their little son; Rolfe wanted to express his gratitude to Sandys, "whom I have found a father to me, my wife and child, and will ever acknowledge it with the best gratefulness my heart and pen can offer."

In the case of Elder William Brewster, Sir Edwin had a special reason for showing kindness, since the Brewsters had served members of his family for two generations. In the same year in which William Brewster's father was made bailiff of the manor of Scrooby, Sandys' father became Archbishop of York and received the manor as one of his official residences. Later he leased Scrooby to his elder son Samuel, and William Brewster in his turn succeeded his father as bailiff.

Brewster was educated at Cambridge and had hoped to have a diplomatic career; he went abroad with his patron and returned to England wearing "a gold chain." But the patron lost favor at court, and when Brewster's father became ill he went home to work as his deputy, assuming all his father's offices when he died. These included a recent appointment as Master of the Post, a responsible position since Scrooby was on the Great North Road. As bailiff of the manor, Brewster had the responsibility for governing all the villages which lay in the Archbishop's local jurisdiction, and he made his home in the manor house along with his wife and his son Jonathan.

Brewster named his second child Patience and the third one Fear—by which he meant the fear of the Lord—and the names echo the way his life was turning. Cambridge was the mother of most of the religious radicalism in England, and Penry, Greenwood and Barrow had all been educated there before the government hanged them as Brownists. Brewster himself grew increasingly radical, more and more convinced that salvation could be attained only by separating from the Church of England. Like-minded people began to meet with him in the manor house, and one of these was a well-to-do boy named William Bradford. His uncles had been hoping to turn him into a farmer, but the ardent, Bible-reading youngster was drawn to Scrooby by the passion of his desire to worship God truly.

Later generations called this passion "Puritan" but it was not exclusively so; it was shared by very conservative members of the Church of England. There was Nicholas Ferrar, for instance, who was Sandys' deputy in the Virginia Company and who was driven by the same longing to serve God that consumed Brewster and Bradford. When Nicholas Ferrar was a small boy, he had gone into his father's garden one cold night, thrown himself on the ground, "and with extreme perplexity of grief, sobs, sighs and abundance of tears earnestly with all his strength humbly begged of God that He would put into his heart the true fear and care of His divine Majesty that he might know how he must serve Him." Ferrar ultimately became a deacon in the Church of England, living a life of such intensity of devotion that just before he died he destroyed three hampers of books he had loved and begged God to forgive him for all the time he had misspent in reading them. This yearning for salvation was a legacy from the Middle Ages, rendered still more intense and exhausting by the emphasis on individual responsibility which had come in with the Reformation.

The word "Puritan" was a nickname introduced early in the reign of Queen Elizabeth to describe men of this special intensity who had no intention of leaving the Church of England but who wanted to purify it. They had hoped that when Elizabeth succeeded her Roman Catholic sister Mary she would set up a state church which would be wholly Protestant, being unable or unwilling to realize that the new queen could not impose so violent an alteration upon a divided country. She set the Church on what came to be called the middle way, retaining ancient symbols like the cross and the wearing of the surplice, and locking the institution of the bishops into her system of government so securely that they could not be removed.

At first the men who were called "Puritan" tried only to rid the Church of England of its ancient ceremonials, but toward the end of the Queen's reign they made a daring attempt to undercut the authority of the bishops by introducing in some parts of England the presbyterian model. Elizabeth struck with annihilating fury, well aware of the danger to her throne of any such notion.

Since Puritan was an abusive nickname and greatly disliked, these reformers preferred to be known as Non-conformists. They did not wish to conform to some of the present practices of the Church of England, but they were in all other respects her faithful sons. They never doubted that a compulsory state church was necessary to the safety and happiness of the realm, and they were horrified by the Brownists, who believed in self-governing local congregations. As William Bradford said regretfully, men who were themselves being persecuted for their religious opinions dealt "very rigidly and roughly" with the Brownists.

The Brownists in turn disliked their own nickname, partly because Browne had recanted and returned to the Church of England. They preferred to be called Separatists, and in their turn they condemned more radical sects, such as the Anabaptists or the Family of Love, who seemed to be unwilling to acknowledge any kind of authority or order. The Family of Love, for its part, was convinced that it had chosen the one sure path to salvation and did not wish to be confused with any other movement. "The people of the Family of Love . . . do utterly disclaim and detest all the said absurd and self-conceited opinions and disobedient and erroneous sects of the Anabaptists, Browne, Penry, puritans, and all other proud-minded sects and heresies whatsoever."

King James was much less systematic in his religious persecutions than Queen Elizabeth had been, partly because he lacked her efficiency. Nevertheless, it was an act of real courage on the part of the little group which had been meeting in the manor house at Scrooby when it took, in 1606, the final, irrevocable step of separation from the Church of England. As William Bradford put it, "The Lord's free people joined themselves (by a covenant of the Lord) into a church estate, in the fellowship of the gospel, to walk in all His ways . . . according to their best endeavors, whatsoever it should cost them."

There were two of these Separatist or Brownist congregations in the district, harried by their neighbors and running an increasing risk of being noticed by the government. In the following year, therefore, they decided to leave England and go to the Netherlands. Religious emotion was quite as intense there as elsewhere, but political control was decentralized, and hardly half the people in the great Province of Holland belonged to the Church. As an English tourist put it, "One neighbor knows not, nor cares not much, what religion the other is of."

Both the Brownist congregations had difficulty in leaving England, since it was illegal to sail without a license, but both of them finally managed to reach Amsterdam. The capital of Holland was a very beautiful and cosmopolitan city, so unlike "their plain country villages . . . as it seemed they were come into a new world." There was liberty of conscience in Amsterdam, and freedom of the press, and other refugee English congregations had already established themselves there.

The bonds of fellowship which had tightened under persecution in England were much more difficult to maintain in the relaxed atmosphere of that great city. One of the two Brownist congregations was destroyed by the factionalism that usually plagued splinter groups of this kind, and the people from Scrooby might have gone the same path if it had not been for their remarkable minister. John Robinson was a man of great patience, wisdom and courtesy of mind, and he kept his little congregation together. Nevertheless it seemed wise to leave Amsterdam to avoid "contention" and the following year they moved to Leyden.

Here living conditions were much less attractive. Leyden was a heavily industrialized city, chiefly dependent on the textile industry, and the housing problem was aggravated by what a distinguished visitor to its University called contemptuously "the vile medley of races immigrating hither." From the point of view of the people of Scrooby, the great advantage of living in Leyden was that there was always work for untrained men. William Bradford, for instance, became a weaver and Jonathan Brewster made ribbons.

Jonathan's father had a particularly hard time of it during those early years in Holland, since his upbringing had not fitted him for manual labor. Eventually William Brewster went into publishing and tutoring and became relatively prosperous, specializing in teaching English to Germans and Danes. William Bradford also settled down prosperously. He sold his inheritance in England and invested the money in a house in Leyden that was worth over a thousand guilders. He married when he was twenty-three and the following year he was formally enrolled as a citizen of Leyden.

The congregation prospered sufficiently to be able to buy a large house where their minister, John Robinson, could live and preach. Sympathizers joined them from England, one a London businessman named John Carver who became a deacon. They lived together "in peace and love and holiness and many came unto them from divers parts of England, so as they grew a great congregation. And if at any time differences arose . . . they were . . . nipped in the head betimes. . . . Or else the church purged off those that were incurable and incorrigible." This was done by majority vote, and all other decisions were handled in the same manner.

Many of the members of the congregation became citizens of Leyden, and they were well liked by their Dutch neighbors. But they grew increasingly uneasy, that small company of the Lord in a city of strangers. Their children were beginning to follow Dutch ways, and they feared "the great licentiousness of youth in that country." Moreover, Holland might cease to be a refuge, since the twelve-year truce between the Netherlands and Spain was drawing to its close.

The congregation investigated several possibilities overseas and finally decided that the best plan would be to go to Virginia. This meant that the Virginia Company had to give them a patent, and there was one great obstacle to the Company's approval. The Leyden group could not take the Oath of Supremacy, acknowledging King James the head of the one true

Church and themselves as members of it. The rule had been designed to keep Roman Catholics out of Virginia, but it applied with equal force to Brownists.

It was here that they needed the help of Sir Edwin Sandys, and he gave it freely. At his suggestion, Robinson and Brewster drew up a statement which was very carefully worded and gave a deliberately vague acknowledgment of the authority of the Church of England. The Council of the Virginia Company accepted this, and Sandys even went so far as to try and get a special ruling from the Archbishop of Canterbury. George Abbot was so easygoing a prelate that he was sometimes considered a Non-conformist, but his tolerance did not extend to anyone outside the Church of England, and Sandys was unsuccessful here, as Captain Bargrave noted with special satisfaction. Sandys also approached King James indirectly through one of the Secretaries of State, and the King said he would let the would-be colonists "enjoy their liberty of conscience under his gracious protection in America." In other words, he would not officially authorize their going but he would let them alone if they did.

In 1619 the Virginia Company was shaken by its battle over leadership, and even after Sandys was elected Treasurer he had trouble consolidating his position. The situation made the Leyden group very anxious, and Robert Cushman, who was their agent in England, sent them a full report of the situation: "Sir Thomas Smythe, when he saw some part of his honor lost, was very angry and raised a faction to cavil and contend about the election, and sought to tax Sir Edwin with many things. . . . It is most like Sir Edwin will carry it away, and if he do, things will go well in Virginia."

Sir Edwin did carry it away, and the following month the Virginia Company granted the Leyden group the patent that gave it the right to settle in Virginia. It was made out to John Wincop, chaplain of the Countess of Lincoln, "a religious gentleman . . . who intended to go with them." In the end it was never used, since the Leyden group did not have enough money to equip an expedition, and its leaders entered into another round of anxious negotiation. This time it was with a group of investors who had acquired their own patent from the Virginia Company and were looking for colonists to send out. This group of about seventy men, called John Peirce and his Associates, had been operating for some time as an unincorporated partnership and had acquired the patent in February of 1620 as an investment. The Associates agreed to equip the Leyden group, after a great deal of arguing and under terms that both sides considered unfavorable.

There was also a great deal of discussion within the congregation at Leyden, since the trip to America meant a huge leap forward into the unknown. In the end, the majority of the members of the congregation decided to stay in Holland, and only thirty-five people undertook to make the voyage to Virginia. John Robinson was not one of them, since he could not separate himself from the bulk of his congregation, but he hoped to come later. The leadership for the little group of travelers therefore passed to William Brewster, John Carver and young William Bradford, who was taking his wife with him but did not risk the trip for his little son John.

It was Bradford who said of this small group: "They knew they were pilgrims." Nearly all Christians thought of life as a pilgrimage, but these were Pilgrims in a special sense and they deserved the title that posterity bestowed upon them.

Since the Pilgrims were so small a group, most of the colonists for the venture were supplied by the London investors, and Bradford calls these other colonists the "strangers." Both groups were to meet at Southampton, the strangers in their chartered freighter, the *Mayflower,* and the Pilgrims in their own ship, the *Speedwell.* The *Speedwell* turned out to be unseaworthy, and when they finally managed to leave England from the port of Plymouth both groups were crowded into the *Mayflower.* It was owned by Thomas Goffe, one of the investors in the venture, and it had been taken from the Mediterranean wine trade to make the Atlantic crossing.

The *Mayflower* left England only after a long and bitter period of confusion and quarreling. In August, Robert Cushman wrote a friend, "If ever we make a plantation, God works a miracle, especially considering how scant we shall be of victuals, and most of all ununited amongst ourselves."

This last point was of crucial importance since the Virginia Company had decided earlier in the year to give the holders of all Company patents the temporary right of self-government. The General Court had voted in February, during a meeting at Sir Edwin Sandys' house near Aldersgate, that all patentees should "have liberty, till a form of government be here settled for them . . . to make orders, ordinances and constitutions . . . provided they be not repugnant to the laws of England."

A group which was not united within itself could not make laws for its own government, and no one was more aware of this than John Robinson. He could not leave his congregation in Leyden to go with the Pilgrims and guide them, but he composed a letter for them to read before they set sail for America. It was a remarkable letter, and its subject was self-government.

Robinson opened with a discussion of self-control. He warned that they would find in each other "continual occasion of offense" and that touchiness was a luxury they could not afford—"as men are careful not to have a new house shaken with any violence before it be well settled and the parts firmly knit."

Normally it would have been the responsibility of the properly constituted authorities to keep the peace, but in this case no outside authority had been set over them. "You are to become a body politic, using amongst yourselves civil government, and are not furnished with any persons of special eminency above the rest." There would be no governors except those "which yourselves will make choice of for that work." Therefore the selections must be made wisely, not only "in choosing such persons as do entirely love and will diligently promote the common good, but also in yielding unto them all due honor and obedience."

He closed by turning their thoughts to God, with that loving eloquence that made him so beloved by his congregation. "My daily incessant prayers unto the Lord, that He Who hath made the heavens and the earth, the sea and all rivers of waters, and Whose providence is over all His works, especially over His dear children for good, would guide and guard you in your ways, as inwardly by His spirit, so outwardly by the hand of His power."

When the *Mayflower* finally managed to leave England on the 16th of September, 1620, it headed for an area just within the northern limits of the jurisdiction of the Virginia Company. The Dutch were of the opinion that they controlled this area, since Henry Hudson had been in their employ the year he explored the river that bore his name, but the Virginia Company had always disregarded this contention and the Pilgrims hoped "to find some place about Hudson's River for their habitation." They expected to stop first at Jamestown, since it was customary for holders of Company patents to report there, and they carried with them a letter from Sir Edwin Sandys to Governor George Yeardley, asking him to "give them the best advice he could for trading in Hudson's River." But the *Mayflower* did not reach America until the ninth of November, much too late to go first to Virginia, and Captain Christopher Jones made a landfall at Cape Cod.* An attempt to head southward to the Hudson River was beaten back by the winds, and it was clear that the people on the *Mayflower* would have to make a settlement where they were, before the worst of the winter came upon them.

---

* This was a familiar piece of ground to English mariners, and named by Bartholomew Gosnold when he discovered it eighteen years earlier. Captain John Smith tried to rename it Cape James in loyal recognition of his monarch, but the old name of Cape Cod still clung. Smith also renamed the Indian villages in the area, and in the handsome map of New England which he published four years earlier (which had been given wide distribution) the curved hook of the Cape pointed inward to a string of English names along the coast—such as London, Oxford and Plymouth.

At this point the Pilgrims found themselves faced with a difficult political problem. All the land in this northern area was under the control of the newly formed Council of New England, whose charter had not yet passed the seals when the *Mayflower* left England. As a result the colonists were no longer members of a body politic, since this status had been conferred upon them by an organization which had no jurisdiction in the north.

Some of the men on the *Mayflower* were quick to seize this opportunity. They announced "that when they came ashore they would use their own liberty, for none had power to command them, the patent they had being for Virginia and not for New England, which belonged to another government." William Bradford called such behavior mutinous, but it was not. There was no longer any authorized government to mutiny against.

The Pilgrims were in the minority on board the *Mayflower,* but they constituted the one group that knew exactly what it wanted and they moved with great political skill. They drew up, in careful official language, the remarkable document that is known as the Mayflower Compact, which re-created them as a body politic, and in some fashion they persuaded all the adult male colonists on board ship to sign it:

> In the name of God, Amen. We, whose names are underwritten, the loyal subjects of our dread sovereign lord, King James . . . having undertaken for the glory of God, and advancement of the Christian faith, and the honor of our king and country, a voyage to plant the first colony in the northern parts of Virginia, do by these presents, solemnly and mutually, in the presence of God and one another, covenant and combine ourselves together into a civil body politic . . . and by virtue hereof do enact, constitute and frame such just and equal laws . . . as shall be thought most meet and convenient for the general good of the colony, unto which we promise all due submission and obedience. In witness whereof we have hereunto subscribed our names at Cape Cod, the eleventh of November . . . 1620.

Forty-one men signed the Compact, and less than half of them were Pilgrims.

In time the Mayflower Compact acquired a great symbolic importance, and it came to be hailed as an example of early democracy at work. It was not so intended. It was a device, and a remarkable one, to control the majority of the men on the *Mayflower,* so that the minority, the men of the church in Leyden, could maintain the idea that had brought them to America. From now on, the government of the future colony was the one which the Pilgrims wished it to be, and their deacon, John Carver, was the Governor of them all.

Two years after the Mayflower Compact was signed, the full text was published in London, as part of a packet of papers which had been sent back to England to advertise the colony and to show how orderly its founding had been. On this occasion it was made clear that special circumstances had made the device necessary: "Observing some not well affected to unity and concord, but gave some appearance of faction, it was thought good there should be an association and agreement, that we should combine together in one body and to submit to such government and governors as we should by common consent agree to make and choose."

"Faction" was a terrifying word in the seventeenth century. It meant a difference of opinion, and this was the one thing that the Pilgrims were determined to avoid. They had avoided it in Holland, having "joined themselves (by a covenant of the Lord) into a church estate," and they had avoided it again by joining in a covenant with men who were not of their congregation, into a civil estate.

The members of this newly created body politic searched along the coast looking for a place to live, while their families waited on shipboard at Cape Cod. They finally decided to settle at the Indian village that was named Plymouth on Captain John Smith's map. It was empty now, a place of graves and deserted fields, and in the promotion material which he prepared to advertise New England, Smith pointed out how providential this situation was: "It seems God hath provided this country for our nation, destroying the natives by the plague . . . for they had three plagues in three years successively near two hundred miles along the sea coast."

Plymouth had the advantage of ground that was already cleared and of a good water supply, but the colonists were forced to carry from some distance the wood they needed to build their houses. Moreover, there was no harbor, and it was a slow and difficult business to unload supplies from the *Mayflower,* now anchored a mile and a half off the shallow shoreline.

By this time the deaths had begun, increasing at a terrifying rate as the winter advanced, and it was not easy for Governor John Carver to keep control. "In these hard and difficult beginnings they found some discontents and murmurings arise amongst some, and mutinous speeches . . . in other; but they were soon quelled and overcome by the wisdom, patience and just and equal carriage of things by the Governor and better part, which clave faithfully together in the main."

Elections were held in March, since that was the official beginning of the year, and John Carver was returned to office. He died in April, stricken while he was working in the fields, and they buried him "in the best manner they could, with some volleys of shot by all that bore arms." William Bradford was elected Governor in his place, and took office as soon as he had recovered from his own illness.

When the *Mayflower* sailed back to England in the spring, it carried an application for a patent from the owners of the land. Or, as Sir Ferdinando Gorges put it, "They hastened away their ship, with order to their solicitor to deal with me, to be a means they might have a grant from the Council of New England's affairs to settle in the place, which was accordingly performed." The Council had its own elaborate plans for the government of New England, but in the meantime it gave the men of Plymouth a temporary patent, dated the first of June, 1621, which conferred upon them the right to settle the land and make the laws.

Now that the colony was under the "authority of those thrice-honored persons, the President and Council for the affairs of New England," it was much easier to advertise for settlers. To assist this process the Pilgrims had sent the packet of papers which were published in 1622 by John Bellamy, a young Londoner who specialized in New England material. The little book is sometimes called *Mourt's Relation* since George Morton, their London agent, signed the Address to the Reader, but its actual and proud title was "A Relation or Journal of the beginnings and proceedings of the English plantation settled at Plymouth in New England, by certain English Adventurers, both merchants and others. With their difficult passage, their safe arrival, their joyful building of, and comfortable planting themselves in the now well-defended town of New Plymouth."

There is almost no mention in the *Relation* of the agony and the near disasters that attended that "comfortable planting," and the book gives the general impression that no Englishman could do better than to follow the first colonists to New England. "We have here great peace, plenty of the Gospel, and many sweet delights and variety of comforts." Any Londoner who might wish to read the eloquent letter John Robinson had sent to his flock, or the text of the Mayflower Compact, or the story of the first Thanksgiving, had only to buy a copy of the little book in Bellamy's shop near the Royal Exchange.*

John Pory stopped off to visit Plymouth in this same year of 1622, and he was greatly impressed by what he saw. In a letter to the Earl of Southampton he praised the excellence of the location, the size of the lobsters and the

---

* All colonial promoters were well aware of the importance of advertising, and in 1621 the Virginia Company decided to "have a fair and perspicuous history compiled" which would give a full account of all the worthy men, past and present, who had helped to found Jamestown. The stockholders approved the idea warmly, but Virginia was always less successful than New England when it came to promotion and the book was never written.

virtue of the inhabitants, and he added a wish that the people in Virginia could be as well behaved. Pory liked the intellectual atmosphere at Plymouth, and in a letter to Bradford he added a grateful postscript on the subject of books.

The one group of men who found it impossible to give wholehearted approval to the colonists at Plymouth were the investors who had sent them there. John Peirce and his Associates sustained a great shock when the *Mayflower* returned to England without any cargo, and one of them wrote a letter whose discourtesy is a measure of his financial disappointment. "I know your weakness was the cause of it, and I believe more weakness of judgment than weakness of hands. A quarter of the time you spent in discoursing, arguing and consulting would have done much more." Governor Bradford replied very temperately under the circumstances, pointing out that the investors had risked a good deal of money but the colonists had risked their lives.

Another cause for discontent among the Associates was the increasing suspicion that the colony was a Brownist undertaking. The investors included many shades of religious opinion, and the Pilgrims had ardent allies among them. They also had ardent detractors, and the meetings began to be tumultuous, with "great combats and reasoning, pro and con."

The uneasiness of the investors increased as the result of a shipload of colonists which arrived at Plymouth in July of 1623. The colonists had paid their own passage overseas, which was known as going out on one's Particular, and the Associates had sent a courteous letter along with them: "They will be a strengthening to the place and good neighbors unto you. . . . Let it not be grievous unto you that you have been instruments to break the ice for others who come after with less difficulty; the honor shall be yours to the world's end."

Before the year was over, some of the Particulars were back in England, where they presented an indignant list of complaints to the Associates. They seem to have overestimated the delights of migration, since they had visualized good schools and plenty of beer and had not expected wolves and mosquitoes. The Pilgrims retorted rather acidly: "They are too delicate and unfit to begin new plantations and colonies, that cannot endure the biting of a mosquito. We would wish such to keep at home till at least they be mosquito-proof." To counteract the "vile and clamorous reports" which the Particulars were spreading, the Pilgrims hurried into print a second promotion pamphlet, written by Edward Winslow and called *Good News from New England,* which John Bellamy published in 1624.

The Particulars who remained in Plymouth colony signed a written agreement. It was a kind of Mayflower Compact in reverse, since they agreed to submit to all the laws of the community but at the same time accepted the fact that they would be permitted no share in the making of them. The only contribution which the Particulars were permitted to make to the political life of the colony was that they would be taxed; every male among them over sixteen was to pay a bushel of grain or its equivalent "towards the maintenance of government and public officers of the said Colony."

This arrangement seemed wholly reasonable to the original settlers. If the signers of the Mayflower Compact permitted shiploads of newcomers to have the vote, they would themselves be outvoted. This would be a risk to them all, but a real disaster to the men of Leyden. They had come three thousand miles and endured sickness and famine to establish a Separatist colony in the wilderness, and if they lost political control they would also lose the right to worship in their own fashion.

The Pilgrims did not possess a church of their own. William Brewster, as their elder, had the right to expound Scripture and to preach on Sundays, but only their ordained minister, John Robinson, had the right to administer the sacraments. As long as he remained in Holland there was no way to take communion in Plymouth colony, and the children who were being born there could not be baptized. When the Associates inquired what the Pilgrims intended to do about the situation, the Pilgrims could only answer, "The more is our grief." They intended to do nothing, hoping against hope that Robinson would be able to join them.

The Associates could not wait indefinitely. They could not ask Christian Englishmen to go to a colony which gave them neither holy communion for themselves nor baptism for their children, and they solved the problem by sending out a minister of their own choosing. He arrived in 1624 on the *Charity,* accompanied by his wife and a large family, and his name was John Lyford.

The Pilgrims had been hoping that the *Charity* would bring butter and sugar instead. However, they resigned themselves to the presence of the Reverend John Lyford, since he assured them that he was in full sympathy with what they were trying to do.

What happened afterward is chiefly reported in the passionate words of Governor Bradford, who became convinced that Lyford was a spy, a marplot and an enemy of God's people. Moreover, Lyford had found allies among the Particulars and was sending back letters to England that plotted the colony's ruin. One of these letters is extant, and to an outsider the tone sounds reasonable enough. Lyford reported what was no less than the truth, that the religious life at Plymouth was under the control of those who were "the smallest number in the colony" and that more orthodox Protestants were "destitute of the means of salvation."

Lyford also reported that the Pilgrims wished only Brownists to inhabit the colony and that if men came over who were "not of the Separation" they were unwilling to welcome them. This was a charge which the Pilgrims denied indignantly, "for they were willing and desirous that any honest men may live with them, that will carry themselves peaceably and seek the common good." However, they were not prepared to let anyone else judge what the "common good" might be, for if they were to permit that, they might better have remained in Leyden.

The Reverend John Lyford was a Non-conformist; he considered "the Church of England to be a true church, although in some particulars . . . defective." Inevitably, one Sunday, he took the final step and called "a public meeting apart on the Lord's Day" so that one group in Plymouth colony met as Separatists under Elder Brewster and another met as members of the Church of England under the Reverend John Lyford.

Governor Bradford was roused to instant action. He already had a complete file of Lyford's letters, since he had rowed out personally to the ship to obtain them before it left for England. He called a public meeting, and the letters from Lyford and his allies were read aloud to prove that they were plotting a complete change "in church and commonwealth."

One of the gravest charges leveled against Lyford at this meeting was that he had said the Particulars should be given the vote and should have "voices in all courts and elections." The Particulars themselves, taxed to help pay for a government in which they had no voice, naturally agreed with him and there had been many "private meetings and whisperings." No one knew better than Governor Bradford that if the plan succeeded, political power would shift from that outnumbered group of which he was the leader.

Faced with a series of formal public accusations, the Reverend John Lyford gave in. He had a large family and no other means of employment and, bursting into tears, he promised to reform. A short time later, however, he was again writing to England, complaining of the irregularity with which his wages were being paid and the fact that he was not being permitted to exercise his calling.

The Pilgrims did not dare defy the London investors by disposing of the minister they had sent. The matter was solved when Lyford's wife announced that they had been forced out of Ireland because her husband "had a bastard by another woman." This providential news made it possible for Bradford to get rid of him, and Lyford went farther up the coast to settle with a group of Particulars who had found Plymouth intolerable.

The one remaining chink in the armor of the Pilgrims was their relationship to the investors, and in 1626 they managed to solve this problem also. Their representative had a meeting in London with the very dissatisfied Associates, who agreed to sell "all and every the said shares, goods, lands, merchandise and chattels to them belonging" in return for £1800 to be paid in a series of installments. Bradford and Brewster combined with six other colonists and four friends in London to make the necessary payments, and the ownership of the colony now rested with these twelve. They in turn chose the men in Plymouth they considered worthy to join in the partnership—"all amongst them that were either heads of families, or single young men, that were of ability and free and able to govern themselves with meet discretion, and their affairs, so as to be helpful in the commonwealth."

In January of 1630, the Council of New England gave the men of Plymouth the right to incorporate "for the better government of their affairs," but in fact the colony had been behaving like a corporation from the beginning. The "courts and elections" from which the Particulars had been barred were evidently like those in any corporation, and the officials they elected to assist Governor Bradford went by the usual corporation title of Assistants. In a letter to the London investors, Bradford assured them that no one was allowed to vote in Plymouth who was under the legal age of a voter in England; "neither do we admit any but such as are above the age of twenty-one years." Once admitted, all such men had the rights of freemen in a corporation, and Bradford made it clear that everything was being done in an orderly English fashion.

The formal incorporation that was granted the colony in 1630 was an official recognition of the principle of exclusion upon which the colony was already based. The charter of incorporation which was conferred by the Council of New England gave Bradford and his colleagues the right to set up the standards for "receiving or admitting any to his or their society." This right of entry was guarded with special care by corporations which had the responsibility for civil government, and if a mistake in judgment was made and the wrong kind of man admitted it was possible to vote for expulsion.*

No official records were kept of the Plymouth corporation until 1633, a year in which Edward Winslow was Governor. Then they open with the names of all the freemen, including those of the Governor and his Assistants,

---

* In the case of the corporation that governed the English town of Warwick, one of the members was of a "self-liking and resolute opinion, ruled by the loose lines of liberty, without respect or regard of the law of God or man." This independence included his refusal to wear the long dark gown that was considered essential to the dignity of the members, and in the end he was expelled from the corporation.

now increased to seven men and known as the Council. The subsequent records list the names of the new members who had been "admitted into the freedom of this society." Each one took the oath as a freeman of the corporation and it was this carefully controlled group that made the laws.

Bradford was usually elected Governor, and he presided over a colony which was governed very much as Robinson's congregation had been governed in Leyden. Differences of opinion were "nipped in the head betimes," anyone could be purged if he "were incurable and incorrigible," and Plymouth could continue in the peace that was born of the absence of all dissenting opinion.

Chapter Three

Two years after the Pilgrims reached America, the Council of New England issued an advertising prospectus. Sir Ferdinando Gorges had written the little book and in it he announced proudly that "we have settled, at this present, several plantations along the coast." There was, in fact, no settlement within the Council's jurisdiction in 1622 except the little group at Plymouth, but his enthusiastic imagination was already dreaming of great towns in New England which would send burgesses to a representative assembly.

Sir Ferdinando Gorges had some reason for optimism. The Council of New England consisted of forty men of great distinction, and by 1622 all its initial difficulties seemed to have been solved. The Council issued its prospectus, bought some office furniture, hired a staff, and prepared for a flood of applications from would-be colonists.

None came, for the Council of New England had nothing whatever to offer, and the following year the whole inflated structure collapsed. A ceremony was held in June at the royal palace at Greenwich, where illustrious patentees drew lots to divide up the only asset they possessed—the land. The royal favorite, Buckingham, could not attend, and King James drew his lot for him in a ceremony that was as dreamlike as the whole arrangement had been.

The charter itself still remained in existence, giving the Council of New

England the right to govern a land it had failed to people, and when the Duke of Buckingham was assassinated the Earl of Warwick became the new President. It was Warwick, for instance, who signed the patent of incorporation which the Council gave Plymouth in January of 1630.

By this time, however, another little seedling had put down roots in New England. One of the Council's early patents had been given to a group of investors in the town of Dorchester, in western England, who were hoping to establish a colony on Cape Ann, and the project had been conceived by a man as enthusiastic and energetic as Gorges himself.

His name was John White and he was a minister in Dorchester. He had full control of "the purses of his parishioners, whom he could wind up to what height he pleased on important occasions" and he persuaded them to invest more than three thousand pounds in the Dorchester Company to colonize Cape Ann. The Company was an unincorporated association, like the London group which had financed the Pilgrims, and John Humphrey, who was one of White's parishioners, served as its treasurer.

The minister's plan was a reasonable one. Cape Ann was already inhabited in the summer by the men who went out on the fishing boats, and he wanted to send out men who would stay there through the winter. They would put up houses, plant corn, have their own minister and form a permanent colony, which would be financed by profits from the fishing.

The first winter was nearly disastrous, for, as White said ruefully, the settlers, "being ill chosen and ill commanded, fell into many disorders." Then a friend of White's said he had a brother in New England who might be willing to assume the management of the Cape Ann colony, and Humphrey, as treasurer of the organization, wrote and asked him to take charge.

The brother's name was Roger Conant. He was one of the Particulars and he left Plymouth because he disliked the form of government. Conant moved his family north to Nantasket, which jutted out into what was later to become Boston Harbor. Also at Nantasket were other "religious and well-affected persons who had lately moved out of New Plymouth on account of their dislike of their principles of rigid Separation," and among them was the Reverend John Lyford. He was asked to be the minister of the struggling colony on Cape Ann, and Conant was asked to be its superintendent.

Roger Conant did his best; but the land on the Cape was not fit for farming, the shipping was mismanaged, and in 1626 the Dorchester Company was bankrupt. As a last generous gesture, it offered all its colonists free transportation back to England, and Lyford refused, preferring to go south to Virginia. Conant also refused, but he had no intention of leaving New England. Instead, he offered to take the cattle that had been shipped over the previous year and to attempt a settlement at the northern end of Massachusetts Bay in the deserted Indian village of Naumkeag.

The Reverend John White, rejoicing to find in Conant a spirit as valiant as his own, collected the money for even more cattle to be sent out and decided to intensify his efforts in England. He managed to infect a great many well-to-do Englishmen with his enthusiasm, and the greatly expanded organization managed to get a new patent from the Council of New England. The Earl of Warwick, as President of that nearly defunct body, issued this patent in March of 1628 after making sure that Gorges approved. It gave the new group the right to colonize an area running three miles north of the Merrimack River to three miles south of the Charles.

One of the men in whose name this patent was issued was John Endecott, a man of great executive ability who was one of White's parishioners in Dorchester. He was sent out to govern the colony, replacing Roger Conant, and arrived in June of 1628. The old Indian name of Naumkeag was abandoned soon after he assumed control, and the rapidly growing town on Massachusetts Bay received the new name of Salem.

Endecott had a cousin by marriage whose name was Matthew Cradock —a London merchant who was deeply interested in the new venture and pushing hard to expand it. The following February Cradock sent a letter to Salem in which he told Endecott that the organization, "much enlarged" since his departure, was going to send out a large shipment of colonists and livestock that spring.

He did not tell Endecott his most important news, but within the month it was common knowledge. While Cradock and his associates had been working out the plans for the spring fleet, they had been working with equal energy on a still more difficult matter—a royal charter which would free them from their dependence on the Council of New England. This charter was obtained on the fourth of March, 1629, and Cradock was able to announce officially in his next letter that the company was now "a body politic, with ample power to govern and rule all His Majesty's subjects that reside within the limits of our plantation." The new corporation was entitled The Governor and Company of the Massachusetts Bay in New England, and Matthew Cradock was named in the charter as Governor.

The man who succeeded him in this office said of this particular charter: "It is well known that these patents are not drawn by any direction from the King or State, but by some counsellor-at-law whom the patentee employs, and allowed by the Attorney General." The terms of the charter were approved by the Attorney General and signed into existence by King Charles because the men who were backing it were sufficiently rich and influential to get the terms that best suited their purpose. Cradock spoke feelingly of the fact that the document had been obtained "with great cost, favor of personages of note, and much labor," and this must indeed have been so. Any charter was expensive, and this one destroyed the rights of the Council of New England in a large area.

The backers were a miscellaneous group drawn from various parts of England. Nine of them had been investors in the Plymouth venture and were still hoping to spread the Gospel and make money in New England; one of these was Thomas Goffe, owner of the *Mayflower,* and he was named in the charter as Deputy Governor of the new Company. Another group came in through the Reverend John White's efforts, and the treasurer of the extinct Dorchester Company, John Humphrey, was named in the charter as one of the Assistants. Others came in through an influential group of people in Lincolnshire, and most of the rest were Londoners.

Unlike the other charters that King Charles was granting in the New World—those of Avalon, New Albion and Carolina—this was a businessman's charter. The Massachusetts Bay Company was set up as a joint-stock company and it was modeled very closely on the structure of the now defunct Virginia Company, except that the chief executive officer was called a Governor instead of a Treasurer. The Governor, the Deputy Governor and the eighteen Assistants were all listed in the charter and it was their responsibility to conduct the normal business of the Company in the monthly courts or assemblies. Four times a year, as with the Virginia Company, there were to be "four Great and General Courts," to which all the stockholders, or freemen of the Company, would be admitted. By majority vote, these General Courts would make the laws for the Company, and in the spring meeting elect the officers, for, as its charter proudly stated, the Massachusetts Bay Company was a "body politic and corporate in deed, fact and name" and it would remain so as long as it possessed the charter.

Unlike their counterparts in the Virginia Company, the stockholders of the Massachusetts Bay Company showed very little energy, and in spite of the best efforts of the officers there was a poor attendance at most of the meetings. There was no sign of the tumultuous activity on the lower levels which had characterized the brief career of the Virginia Company, and it may have been this lack of energy which explains the curiously paternalistic way in which the Massachusetts Bay Company decided to run its colony in New England.

The decision was an odd one because it went counter to everything that had been learned about managing a colony in America. In 1619 the colonists of Virginia were given a representative assembly, and ever since then each owner of a royal charter had extended the same privilege. From Newfoundland to Carolina, the members of English colonies had the right to assist in their own government.

The owners of the Massachusetts Bay charter decided otherwise, and set up a Council instead. Thirteen of "the most wise, honest, expert and discreet persons resident upon the said plantation" were to "have the sole managing and ordering of the government and our affairs there." As a gesture toward the men who had originally settled Salem, they were to be permitted to choose two men on the Council. Three more were to be appointed by Governor Endecott, who would himself be a member, and the remaining seven—the majority—were sent out by the Company in the spring fleet. This group, to be called The Governor and Council of London's Plantation in the Massachusetts Bay, was put in control of what was to be "an absolute government," and at the meeting of the General Court in London, after the fleet had sailed, the whole arrangement was obediently ratified.

This was an astonishingly old-fashioned approach to the problem of governing a colony. It was, in fact, a reversion to the method that had been used when Sir Walter Raleigh sent out his ill-fated Council of thirteen, or the one that had been used with equal lack of success at Sagadahoc and in the early days at Jamestown. Yet no doubt it seemed a practical and business-like arrangement in the eyes of a group of men who had also thought it desirable to ship out to Salem "divers paper books." These were to be used by overseers whom Governor Endecott would appoint, and in them precise track would be kept "of the daily work done by each person in each family" that had been sent out at Company expense.

It is easy to sympathize with the anxiety of the Massachusetts Bay Company, for the huge sum of £2400 had been invested in the spring fleet. It set out for Salem in April of 1629, carrying a duplicate of the Company charter and a silver seal for the use of the Council. There was a large number of colonists and cattle, and each of the three ships had a minister. Also in the company were two prominent gentlemen of Essex, the brothers John and Samuel Browne, who would serve with the ministers on the Council. The fleet bore the hopes of the Massachusetts Bay Company that the colony would be obedient, energetic, God-fearing and make a great deal of money for the investors.

It was difficult to gather together any collection of God-fearing Englishmen of this generation without some sort of explosion, and in this case it was brought about by a difference of opinion between the Browne brothers and the ministers. The fuse and the dynamite traveled together to Salem, and all that was needed to set them off was the heady atmosphere of New England.

It had been difficult enough to find suitable ministers, since those who were willing to go to New England were usually Separatists. The Reverend John White, in this year of the climax of his beloved project, was determined to avoid any taint of Separatism, with its attendant suspicion of being anti-monarchial, and he was careful to point out what he called the "great difference between Separation and Non-conformity." The Massachusetts Bay Company took equal precautions. A fourth minister, Ralph Smith, had been granted passage before it was discovered that he was a Separatist, and the Company sent Endecott a warning about him: "Unless he will be conformable to our government . . . suffer him not to remain within the limits of our grant." He was not conformable, and he was accepted as the minister of Plymouth colony, its first since John Lyford.

Whatever the private religious convictions of some of its members might be, the Massachusetts Bay Company could not risk antagonizing the English government or the vast majority of its own stockholders by employing a minister who was not a member of the Church of England. At a Company meeting in March the name of Francis Higginson was suggested, and John Humphrey went down to Leicestershire to interview him. He also wanted to get a report on him from the famous Leicestershire minister Arthur Hildersham, who was a prominent Non-conformist and a vigorous foe of Separatists.

Francis Higginson was also a Non-conformist, and had strong personal reasons for refusing the offer; he was not well, and one of his eight children was a cripple. A year earlier he would probably have turned Humphrey down, but in 1628 the religious climate of England underwent a sudden change. George Abbot, the easygoing Archbishop of Canterbury, had lost his authority to a five-man commission headed by the Bishop of London, William Laud.

Laud was an idealist who had dedicated himself to a vision of the Church of England, sealed up and made perfect, from which all differences of opinion in matters of ritual would be forever banished. He envisioned Church and State supporting each other in holy harmony, and he had the full support of King Charles, who was an idealist also. With the King's complete and ardent approval, William Laud set out to enforce an absolute uniformity upon all the ministers in the Church of England, and Non-conformists who had been conducting their modified services quite peacefully under Abbot suddenly found themselves called to account.

One of these ministers was Francis Higginson. He was expecting to be deprived of his office and had already prepared his farewell address when John Humphrey arrived in Leicestershire in 1629 with the offer from the

Massachusetts Bay Company. Hildersham advised Higginson to accept it, and he did. He felt "that New England might be designed by Heaven as a refuge and shelter for the Non-conformists against the storms that were coming upon the nation, and a region where they might practice the church reformation which they had been bearing witness unto."

The voyage was a long and difficult one, and the little crippled daughter died on the way. Yet Higginson was caught up by the excitement of seeing so many new things and he was especially impressed by the whales. "Those that love their own chimney corner, and dare not go far beyond their own town's end, shall never have the honor to see these wonderful works of Almighty God."

The three ministers who went out with the fleet had all declared themselves "to be of one judgment and to be fully agreed on . . . how to exercise their ministry." They did not agree. The three thousand miles of ocean had a profound effect on Higginson and on Samuel Skelton of Lincolnshire; they did not affect the third minister, Francis Bright. Bright remained orthodox and went back to England; Higginson and Skelton moved across the gulf that lay between Separatism and Non-conformity and established a Separatist church in Salem. On the 20th of July, they testified to an inward calling from the Lord and an outward calling from the congregation, and by the laying-on of hands Skelton was ordained pastor and Higginson teacher.

This could not have been done without the consent of Governor John Endecott, but he also was leaning toward Separatism. During the epidemic the previous winter in which his wife had died, Plymouth colony sent over its own physician to be of assistance. Governor Endecott wrote Governor Bradford that he and Dr. Fuller were in agreement on "the outward form of God's worship." After Higginson and Skelton arrived, they also "consulted with their brethren at Plymouth," and the result was the creation of a Separatist church at Salem. The congregation was a self-created association— "a company of believers . . . joined together in covenant to walk together in all the ways of God"—and this company had ordained its own minister.

The two Browne brothers were devout members of the Church of England and they were appalled. John Browne was a lawyer and one of the original Assistants named in the Company charter, and he and his brother Samuel were furious that the two ministers should so openly defy the wishes of the organization that was employing them. The quarrel was referred to the Council, of which all four men were members, and the Council split.

John Endecott, as Governor of Salem, had the last word and he decided in favor of the ministers. He accused the Brownes of behavior "tending to mutiny and faction" and shipped them back to England. There they lodged an angry protest with the Company, which in turn sent out anxious letters to Endecott and the two ministers on the subject of "rash innovations begun and practiced in the civil and ecclesiastical government."

By this time, however, the Massachusetts Bay Company had little leisure to worry about innovations in New England. It had itself been shaken by a much greater explosion, one that was altering the whole nature of the organization. The cause was a public event that had taken place in March in this same year of 1629, and again it was the religious question—the greatest source of energy in that age—which set the fuse burning.

King Charles had come to the throne four years earlier with a great many misconceptions about the power of the King of England. A year after his accession, he was obliged to issue an edict in which he threatened to punish all those who, "for the satisfying of their unquiet and restless spirits, and to express their rash and undutiful insolencies, shall wilfully break that circle of order which, without apparent damage to Church and State, may not be broken." It was a circle of order which gave very little power to representative government, and what King Charles was interpreting as insolence was to the men of the House of Commons a legitimate protection of their rights.

William Laud had embittered an already complicated situation by introducing a doctrinal dispute. He was in favor of a position which softened the doctrine of predestination and which was called Arminianism by its foes. King James and Archbishop Abbot had both opposed it vigorously, since predestination was considered fundamental to the Protestant position in its battle against Roman Catholicism, but Laud had the support of King Charles and he set about to make the Church of England Arminian.

The political risk of Laud's position was that it made it possible for his enemies in the House of Commons to evoke the ancient specter of popish tyranny as a threat to English rights and liberties. "What good will they do any man . . . that resolves to live and die a freeman and not a slave, if Popery and Arminianism, joining hand in hand as they do, be a means . . . to bring in a Spanish tyranny amongst us?"

The House of Commons demanded specific religious safeguards before it would turn to the question of authorizing money for the use of the Crown, and Charles decided to impose taxes without its consent. This was what his father had tried to do, and the effort had evoked the speech of Sir Edwin Sandys in the Addled Parliament. The situation was much more dangerous now. King Charles did not have his father's easygoing temperament, and a very overheated emotional atmosphere had been allowed to develop.

In January of 1629 a Member of Parliament reported the seizure of his goods because he had refused to pay tonnage and poundage, a tax which had not been authorized by the House of Commons. A small group of radicals became convinced that the House must take a stand, even against the King himself, and they found their leader in Sir John Eliot, a member of the gentry from the West Country. Late in February he and eight others held a meeting at a tavern called the Three Cranes. Parliament was in recess, but they worked out the strategy they would pursue when it reconvened on the second of March.

The government found out about the plan and made one of its own. As soon as prayers had been read on opening day, the Speaker of the House delivered a royal message that they were to adjourn until the tenth. Sir John Eliot said that one of the fundamental liberties of the House was the right to adjourn itself. He and his colleagues were determined not to leave the room, "like sheep scattered," until they had at least left behind them some sort of testimony.

The scene that followed was an extraordinary one for law-abiding country gentlemen. They held the weeping Speaker of the House in his chair so that he could not leave it as the King had commanded him to do. They ordered the Sergeant at Arms to lock the door and bring them the key, and when he quite properly refused they did it for him. Outside the locked door, the Gentleman Usher of the Black Rod called out royal instructions, but he went unheeded.

After some confusion, a list of three resolutions drawn up by Sir John Eliot was read aloud to a chorus of *Yea's*. The first stated that anyone who tried to introduce "Popery or Arminianism or any other opinions disagreeing with the true and orthodox Church shall be reputed a capital enemy to this kingdom and commonwealth." The second stated that any supporter of the tax of tonnage and poundage was an enemy to England, and the third stated that anyone who paid such a tax, "not being granted by Parliament, he shall likewise be reputed a betrayer of the liberties of England and an enemy to the same." The House then adjourned itself to the tenth of March, just before the Captain of the Guard set himself to break down the door, and the following day the men who had met at the Three Cranes were all arrested.

On the tenth of March, King Charles formally announced the dissolution of Parliament, addressing himself exclusively to the House of Lords. He blamed the recent disaster on "the malevolent dispositions of some ill-affected persons of the House of Commons," whom he characterized as vipers. The King saw no reason why he should resign himself to the existence of so untidy and insolent an institution, and he made up his mind to rule without it.

Six days earlier, on the fourth of March, the Massachusetts Bay Company had received its charter, and it seemed to many anxious Englishmen that God had suddenly opened a way of escape for them. The Protestant religion, "sealed by the blood of so many martyrs" in the days of the Roman Catholic Queen Mary, seemed again to be threatened. Perhaps it might once again be saved by an organized exodus of the faithful and their families—not to wait across the English Channel as they had then but to sail across the Atlantic Ocean and establish a holy commonwealth in New England.

No one knows who first conceived the idea of turning the Massachusetts Bay Company, which was a business organization, into an instrument to build a New Jerusalem. It seems clear, however, that the primary influence came neither from Dorchester, which had set the colony in motion, nor from London, which had sustained it. The new impulse came from Lincolnshire, and one of its leaders was an ardent young clergyman named Isaac Johnson.

Johnson was a wealthy man but, unlike the Londoners, he had not come into the venture to make more money. "When this plantation began, Mr. Isaac Johnson said more than once that he was resolved to spend and be spent in this business." He kept his word, and when he died the following year he had already paid out the huge sum of five thousand pounds.

Johnson had estates in four counties but his home was in Lincolnshire. Six years earlier he had married the Lady Arbella Clinton, the sister of the young Earl of Lincoln, and had thus become a member of one of the most influential of the great Non-conformist families of England.

Arbella's mother, widow of the third Earl of Lincoln, already had her own connections with America, since the John Wincop who had hoped to accompany the Pilgrims was a chaplain of her household. The redoubtable Countess had eighteen children, of whom the present Earl was the eldest son, and he had delighted her by marrying a woman of whom she warmly approved. This was Bridget, daughter of Lord Saye and Sele, another Non-conformist nobleman. The old Countess of Lincoln wrote a book which she dedicated to her daughter-in-law, because of the "very great esteem" in which she held her.

Bridget, the young Countess of Lincoln, was one of the leading spirits in the group of Non-conformists who gathered in Lincolnshire that spring to discuss New England. Their meeting place was Sempringham, a fine house on a hill about twenty miles distant from the Earl's main seat at Tattershall.

The idea that was conceived at Sempringham was to transfer the government of the Massachusetts Bay Company to New England and to transfer with it, in one vast migration, as many English families as were

55

willing to go. This involved two difficult operations which would have to be performed simultaneously: getting control of the Company away from the London investors, while at the same time finding members of the gentry who would be willing to lead the exodus into New England.

The Reverend John White was immediately enthusiastic and began casting about for ministers; at the commencement at the University of Cambridge early in July, they were being lined up in answer to "Mr. White's call." Matthew Cradock may have been less enthusiastic but he was willing to go along with the idea and in fact presented it at the next meeting of the General Court as his own. "Mr. Governor read certain propositions conceived by himself, viz. . . . to transfer the government of the plantation to those that shall inhabit there, and not to continue the same in subordination to the Company here, as now it is." Cradock admitted that the step was a radical one, but he pointed out that it would encourage "persons of worth and quality" to migrate to New England.

On July the 28th, which was the same day that Cradock was addressing the General Court in London, a large meeting was held in Sempringham. One of the Londoners who attended it was a friend of Isaac Johnson's whose name was Emmanuel Downing, and he brought with him his brother-in-law, a country gentleman named John Winthrop. They had come to Sempringham together the day before, and Winthrop had narrowly escaped drowning when his horse stumbled into a bog.

If the new plan were to succeed, Winthrop was precisely the kind of man that was needed. He was a Non-conformist, he was a member of the gentry with a large circle of devoted friends, and at the moment he had no occupation. He had recently lost his position as an attorney in the Court of Wards and Liveries and was living quietly on his estate in Groton.

When Parliament ceased to exist that March, Emmanuel Downing wrote his brother-in-law a full account of its last hours. In one long, breathless sentence he described to Winthrop the weeping of the Speaker, the barring of the door and all the rest of the fateful activities. Two months later Winthrop was himself in London and he wrote his wife, Margaret, his hope that the Lord would "provide a shelter and a hiding place for us and ours." Then he evidently discussed the matter at some length with Emmanuel and Lucy Downing, for in June he wrote Margaret Winthrop: "I am still more confirmed in that course which I propounded to thee, and so are my brother and sister D."

On the eighth of July, Isaac Johnson wrote Downing a letter from Sempringham, sending his regards to John Winthrop and "expecting you both here ere it be long." They both arrived for the meeting on the 28th of

July, which lasted longer than was expected. On the eighth of August, Mrs. Downing wrote to her nephew in Holland that Winthrop and her husband were still at Sempringham.

The program was in difficulties, for the meeting of the General Court in London had been inconclusive. After a great deal of debate over Cradock's proposal, no decision was reached and it was finally voted to refer the matter to the next meeting of the General Court, at the end of August. In the meantime, everyone was to write down his reasons for or against the proposition.

Nothing delighted an Englishman of the period more than an opportunity to set his reasons forth in an orderly manner on paper, and the letters flew about England. Those of the Sempringham group had two objectives: to present the project as an orderly and devout endeavor and to persuade prominent men—John Winthrop in particular—to head the planned exodus.

The first problem was dealt with in a much copied paper called "General Considerations." It gave a glowing picture of what godly men might achieve in America, and indicated four reasons why earlier colonists had failed:

1. Their main end and purpose was carnal and not religious.
2. They aimed chiefly at profit and not at the propagation of religion.
3. They used too unfit instruments, a multitude of rude ungoverned persons. . . .
4. They did not stablish a right form of government.

A second document which circulated almost as widely (there is even one version extant in the handwriting of Sir John Eliot) presented the reasons why John Winthrop ought to be willing to go.

Winthrop was under pressure from some of his neighbors in Suffolk not to take part in the venture. He was shortly to become a grandfather, and as one of them pointed out, "Plantations are for young men." Moreover, in such dangerous times, he was needed in England. On the other hand, Winthrop was aware that many men who were interested in the venture refused to leave without him. Moreover, the whole bent of his vigorous nature inclined him to accept the challenge of a kind of work which he would never, under King Charles, be permitted to do in England. Sir John Eliot was in prison as the price he paid for defying the King, and he stayed there until he died. The document which he copied out about Winthrop was a shortened version, but it contained a truth to which Eliot could himself bear witness: "If he let pass this opportunity, that talent which God hath bestowed upon him for public service is like to be buried."

The 28th of August had been set as the day when the General Court of the Massachusetts Bay Company was to meet and render its final decision. By that time Winthrop had made up his mind, and two days earlier he and eleven of his colleagues met together at Cambridge to exert a pressure on the General Court which they hoped would be decisive. They set their names to what is called the Cambridge Agreement, which promised that they would all leave for Massachusetts Bay by the first of March. "Provided always that before the last of September next the whole government together with the patent for the said plantation be first by an order of Court legally transferred and established to remain with us and others which shall inhabit upon the said plantation."

The General Court met in London on the 28th with this paper before it, and again found itself deadlocked. If it voted for the plan, the Massachusetts Bay Company would cease to exist in England. If it voted against the plan, it would have to assume the responsibility for having blocked an influx of educated, wealthy and powerful men into the colony and could probably hope for no more emigrants to Massachusetts Bay.

The meeting broke up without a decision, time at its heels, and two committees were scheduled to meet at seven o'clock the following morning. One committee represented the business interests that were fighting to stay in control of the Company and the other was headed by Isaac Johnson and Sir Richard Saltonstall. Saltonstall was the nephew of a former Lord Mayor of London, and both he and Johnson had signed the Cambridge Agreement. It was the responsibility of the two committees to argue the matter to a conclusion and present a report to the General Court, which would meet at nine.

It was the second meeting of the General Court in two days, and there was what the minutes call "a long debate." Cradock was not present, and the Deputy Governor, Thomas Goffe, finally put the matter to the vote. "As many of you as desire to have the patent and the government of the plantation to be transferred to New England, so it may be done legally, hold up your hands." Only twenty-seven men were present, a fraction of the total membership of the Company. The majority held up their hands and in so doing changed the whole future history of New England. The committee which was set up to investigate the legality of moving the charter to New England found nothing in the text of the document to prevent it, and the plans that had been made at Sempringham moved on to fulfillment.

John Winthrop did not attend these August meetings of the General Court, and he was almost certainly not yet a member of the Company. His name first appears in the minutes when he was put on a committee in the middle of September. The following month an election of new officers had to be held, since Matthew Cradock did not intend to go to America, and John Winthrop was chosen as the new Governor of the corporation. The other nominees for the office were Saltonstall, Johnson and Humphrey, but it was Winthrop, the newcomer, who received the most votes.

The same day he wrote his wife that he had been called "to a further trust in this business of the plantation than either I expected or find myself fit for. . . . I never had more need of prayers. Help me, dear wife." Margaret Winthrop, who was a remarkable woman, wrote back her encouragement, and Winthrop was able to say gratefully, "Blessed be God, Who hath given me a wife who is such a help and encouragement to me in this great work, wherein so many wives are so great a hindrance to theirs."

Winthrop had grown up in a family whose members loved each other and did not hesitate to say so. As a result he made friends effortlessly and kept them, and the gift was a great help to him in his new office. As Governor, he was obliged to make a speech in December on the vexed question of how to divide up the Company stock. The speech is artful and persuasive, constructed with a lawyer's logic but above all affectionate. In his first draft he had written, "I see . . . in your faces, my associates, that you will declare your consents by a cheerful holding up your hands." He then crossed out the word *associates* and put in *friends* instead.

The new Governor did not let the weight of his responsibilities worry him. As he had once said, "It is a policy of Satan to discourage us from duty by setting before us great appearances of danger, difficulty, impossibility, etc." Armed by the absolute conviction that he was doing God's work, Winthrop plunged into the complex details of organization. The deadline for getting freight on board the ships was the 20th of February, 1630, and throughout England families sold their homes and gathered their possessions for the great migration.

Two meetings of the Massachusetts Bay Company were held in March. The first was at the port of Southampton, and the second was on board the flagship, which had been renamed the *Arbella* in honor of Isaac Johnson's wife. The Company now consisted only of officers, and there were still changes to be made. John Humphrey, for instance, had replaced Thomas Goffe as Deputy Governor and then decided he could more usefully remain in England for the time being. Therefore he in turn was replaced as Deputy Governor by Thomas Dudley, a forceful and experienced individual who had served as steward to the Earl of Lincoln and who was one of the signers of the Cambridge Agreement. Dudley's son-in-law, Simon Bradstreet, had been the Company secretary since February, and "at a Court of Assistants aboard the *Arbella*" he took the oath of an Assistant. So did William Coddington, another Lincolnshire man, and they joined the handful of officials like Winthrop, Saltonstall and Johnson who now made up the whole of the Massachusetts Bay Company.

A famous minister of Lincolnshire, John Cotton, journeyed down to Southampton to give the travelers his blessing. Both Dudley and Coddington had been his parishioners, and there would be many empty pews in Cotton's beautiful church in Boston, eighteen miles from Sempringham. He chose for the text of his farewell sermon the Lord's promise to David: "I will appoint a place for my people Israel, and I will plant them, that they may dwell in a place of their own and move no more." Southampton was not the only port from which the ships were leaving, and there were so many of them that it was almost like a piece of England breaking away.

The exodus was openly a religious one and many people suspected it of being a Brownist undertaking. In April, the *Arbella* was at Yarmouth, a village on the Isle of Wight, having been delayed by contrary winds, and the leaders issued from Yarmouth a manifesto "to the rest of their brethren in and of the Church of England, for the obtaining of their prayers and the removal of suspicions and misconstructions of their intentions." The signers made clear that they were all loyal sons of the Church, "ever acknowledging that such hope and part as we have obtained in the common salvation, we have received in her bosom."

While the fleet was still at sea, the Reverend John White also rushed into print to defend his beloved project from the charge of Separatism. He described to his readers the whole history of the project from its beginnings with the Dorchester Company, and he pointed out to them that "the joint asseveration of so many godly men" on the *Arbella* could indeed be trusted.

The *Arbella* arrived in Salem the middle of June and all the ships made the crossing successfully. But the time that followed was a desperately hard one and there was a heavy mortality. The Lady Arbella died in August, and Isaac Johnson survived his "dearly beloved wife" by only a month.

The following March, Thomas Dudley wrote a letter to Arbella's sister, Bridget, Countess of Lincoln, in answer to the letters she had sent him. He composed it "by the fireside upon my knee" since his household did not yet have a table. Dudley did not gloss over the difficulties or the heavy mortality, but he made it clear that the people of Massachusetts Bay refused to be discouraged. Their neighbors in Plymouth had survived a similar period of testing, and they would do the same.

Dudley noted that some ill-wishers had been spreading "false and scandalous reports against us, affirming us to be Brownists in religion and ill-affected to our state at home." He assured Bridget that there had been no changes "either in ecclesiastical or civil respects since our coming hither, but we do continue to pray daily for our sovereign lord the King, the Queen, the Prince, the royal blood, the Council and whole state as duty binds us to do."

Dudley did not mention a difficulty which he and the other officials had encountered as soon as they arrived in Salem. There was already a church there, organized on Separatist principles and with the Reverend Samuel Skelton as its ordained minister. Skelton refused point-blank to administer the sacraments to Winthrop, Johnson, Dudley and Coddington when they arrived, since they would not repudiate the Church of England, and he also "denied baptism unto Mr. Coddington's child." The only sacraments Skelton would administer were to those who came from Separatist congregations in England. When John Cotton heard of this, he was horrified. The two ministers had been friends in Lincolnshire, and Cotton wrote him regretfully, "I am afraid your change hath sprung from New Plymouth men."

A month after the *Arbella* landed, Winthrop, Dudley and Johnson brought a church of their own into existence in Massachusetts Bay and they took pains to make it clear that they were not renouncing the Church of England. They ordained John Wilson as their minister "only as a sign of election and confirmation, not of any intent that Mr. Wilson should renounce his ministry he received in England."

Nevertheless, the three thousand miles of ocean had the same effect upon them that it had had on Skelton and Higginson, if to a lesser degree. For this church also was a church of the Separation, in the sense that it was based on a covenant and under the full control of its own congregation.

Three years later John Cotton arrived in New England, and he became the chief apologist of the system he had once condemned. It was Cotton who gave it the name of Congregationalism. After some preliminary confusion it settled down in a middle way "betwixt presbytery as too rigorous, imperious and conclusive, and Brownism as too vague, loose and uncertain," and all the churches of Massachusetts Bay followed the Congregational model.

It was not easy for John Winthrop to explain this development to his friends in England. As he wrote to Sir Simonds D'Ewes in 1633, "Both our practice and judgment differ from yours; but I suppose we should soon be agreed if you were here to see the state of things as we see them." In his next letter to D'Ewes, Winthrop attributed the change to "clearer light and more liberty." It could also be attributed, in part at least, to the width of the Atlantic Ocean.

Sir Simonds D'Ewes was not in a position to argue the point as vigorously as he would have liked, since the current state of affairs in England was making it increasingly difficult for moderates like himself to maintain their position. William Laud became Archbishop of Canterbury in 1633, and the power he had wanted for so long was at last in his hands. He at once availed himself of the whole formidable machinery of church discipline to impose absolute conformity in the Church of England, or, as D'Ewes put it in his anguish, to cause the liturgy "to be poisoned by idolatry and superstition."

Whatever oddities of church structure might be permitted in Massachusetts Bay, it was at any rate a haven from Laud, and in 1634 Sir Simonds D'Ewes made a reverent note of how much the population was increasing there. "I could not but wonder withal at God's providence, that this year, especially in the springtime, put into the hearts of so many godly persons, as well women as men . . . to go into New England."

John Humphrey had remained in England to create favorable publicity for the colony, but instead it was being created by Archbishop Laud. He was making England so uncomfortable for Non-conformists that they took their families and left for Massachusetts. "About thirty ships this summer already," Winthrop wrote exultantly to D'Ewes on a July day in 1635.

Not all of them came for religious reasons. There was a depression in England, especially in the cloth-producing counties, and from the first the skillful publicity for the colony had emphasized that a way of escape lay open from the poverty that threatened so many Englishmen. It was pointed out that in Massachusetts Bay they could buy a quart of milk for a penny and that the mosquitoes were really no worse than those in the Lincolnshire fens.

There was also a wonderful harbor, and into it stretched a neck of land that was free not only from mosquitoes but from those other two great drawbacks of New England—rattlesnakes and wolves. It was true that it lacked trees and pasture, so that its inhabitants had to get their wood from the nearby islands and leave their cattle inland. But the location was so excellent that its inhabitants were sure that it would some day rival the great port of Boston in Lincolnshire, and they named their little town Boston also.

By the time Boston was six years old, shopkeepers had begun to make their appearance, and the Reverend John White was sorry to hear it. He had hoped that this "holy society" would maintain a rustic innocence in which the worldliness of retail commerce would have no part. There was also in Boston "costliness of apparel and following new fashions," and the elders of the church of Boston were asked to help in combating it. This idea failed, as

Winthrop noted regretfully, because "divers of the elders' wives, etc. were in some measure partners in this general disorder."

The chief characteristic of the Massachusetts Bay colony was energy, and it would have been a difficult place to govern under the best of circumstances. Winthrop's problem was greatly complicated by the fact that the only government that existed was the one that had been designed to run a business organization in London. He and his colleagues had hoped to set apart a nation for the Lord, and their zeal was very like that of the men of Israel when they returned from captivity in Babylon; but the men of Israel had not tried to govern through a joint-stock company.

When Winthrop had been elected Governor of the Company, it had not been by the stockholders in general but by the relatively small group into whose hands the operation of the Company had fallen. Or, as the Reverend John White put it approvingly, it was "not the multitude, but all the men of best account amongst them," who elected him to be the leader. By the time the Winthrop fleet left England, this group was smaller still and consisted only of officers.

When the Court of Assistants gathered on the 23rd of August, 1630, for its first meeting in America, there were nine men present—Governor Winthrop, Deputy Governor Dudley, Bradstreet as Secretary and six Assistants. At the next meeting of this Court, in September, twelve men were present, and John Endecott took the oath of an Assistant. After this, attendance fell off in the Court of Assistants, and it was decided the following year that less than nine men would be considered a quorum.

On October the 19th, 1630, the first General Court was held—the quarterly meeting that was authorized to make the laws for the Company. This time only eight men were listed as present—Winthrop, Dudley, Bradstreet and five Assistants. However, it was one of the functions of the General Court to admit new members, and they had before them a list of more than a hundred names "of such as desire to be made freemen."

At this point Winthrop was faced with a real political dilemma. Eighth on the list, for instance, was Roger Conant, the original founder of Salem and a man of eminence who could not legitimately be refused entrance to the Company. On the other hand, Conant had left Plymouth colony because he disliked the religious restrictions there; once he had entered the Company and had the right to help elect the officers and make the laws, it was not likely that he would give his support to the holy commonwealth that Winthrop and the rest of his small band of present members were determined to create.

The only solution was to adjust the charter so that the long list of men who were petitioning for entrance would not have the right to make the laws once they were inside. Nor should they have the right to elect the Governor, since this also would be reserved to the present little group: "For the establishing of the government, it was propounded if it were not the best course that the freemen should have the power of choosing Assistants when they are to be chosen, and the Assistants from amongst themselves to choose a Governor and Deputy Governor, who with the Assistants should have the power of making laws and choosing officers to execute the same. This was fully assented unto by the general vote of the people, and erection of hands."*

The next meeting of the General Court took place on the 18th of May, 1631, and a hundred and eighteen men took the oath of freemen. They were displeased to discover that they could only elect an Assistant if there was a vacancy, and it was agreed to make an adjustment. "For explanation of an order made the last General Court, holden the 19th of October last, it was now ordered with full consent of all the commons then present that once in every year, at least . . . it shall be lawful for the commons to propound any person or persons whom they shall desire to be chosen Assistants, and if it be doubtful whether it be the greater part of the commons or not, it shall be put to the poll."

This was not an "explanation." It was an outright retreat, although a minor one, and it took no prophet to foresee what would happen. The right to admit new members rested with the voting majority, and this majority was no longer the small group made up of Winthrop and his friends. Those comfortable and propertied Englishmen had left their homes and come into the wilderness in pursuit of a dream. Like the men of Israel they were building a nation for the Lord, and they could not stand by and see it destroyed by "unfit instruments."

Again a very agile mind went to work and again a solution was found: a postscript was added to the "explanation." In order that "the body of the commons may be preserved of honest and good men, it was likewise ordered and agreed that for time to come no man shall be permitted to the freedom of this body politic, but such as are members of some of the churches within the limits of the same." Any corporation had the right to set up its own standards for admitting new members, and henceforth this was to be the standard for the Massachusetts Bay Company. No one could join it unless he was already a member of one of the churches in Massachusetts Bay.

---

* Since these are the minutes of a corporation, the "people" means those corporation members who were present and voting.

It was not easy to become a church member. A man was not expected to apply until he had received some inward conviction of salvation—that goal which was the focus of so many doubts and such tormented longing that when it finally arrived it was almost an earthquake of the spirit. Then the applicant was examined by the church elders to make sure that he was not self-deceived. If the elders approved his application it was then presented to the whole membership of the church and voted on by raised hands. The Congregational churches were "very strict in their admissions to church-fellowship, and required very signal demonstrations of a repenting and a believing soul before they thought men fit subjects to be entrusted with the rights of the Kingdom of Heaven."

From now on, in Massachusetts Bay, only those who had attained in this manner the rights of the Kingdom of Heaven would have any political rights on earth. Nothing could be done about the one hundred and eighteen freemen who had just been admitted, but behind them the door swung firmly shut, to be opened only to those who had already passed successfully through an even narrower door.

It seemed for the moment that the government of Massachusetts Bay had settled down to an acceptable, practical arrangement. The freeman voted annually for the Assistants, and the Assistants chose a Governor and Deputy Governor from among themselves. It was the privilege of this group, which was now beginning to be known as "the magistrates," both to pass the laws and to make sure that they were executed.

Within the year the system was in trouble. The magistrates levied a tax on all the towns of the Bay, which in the case of Watertown amounted to eight pounds, and the men of Watertown refused to pay it on constitutional grounds. They were led by their minister, whose name was George Phillips. He was a good friend of John Winthrop, who had in fact advanced the money for his passage on the *Arbella*. In January of 1632 Phillips and the other leaders in Watertown gathered the people together and told them "that it was not safe to pay moneys after that sort, for fear of bringing themselves and posterity into bondage." They based their argument on the fundamental English conviction that a tax was tyrannical unless it had been voted by the representatives of the people.

Governor Winthrop summoned them to Boston to answer for their behavior, and there was "much debate" before Phillips finally gave in. Winthrop pointed out with a lawyer's ingenuity that the people of Watertown were mistakenly thinking in terms of the kind of corporation that governed an English borough. "The ground of their error was, for that they took this government to be no other but as of a mayor and aldermen, who have not power to make laws or raise taxations without the people. . . . This government was rather in the nature of a parliament," since the freemen elected the Assistants annually. Bemused, perhaps, by that magic word *parliament,* the rebels at Watertown ceased their opposition and Winthrop forgave them graciously for their presumption. Or, as he put it, "their submission was accepted, and their offense pardoned."

Winthrop had a conviction of the divine right of magistrates which was not unlike King Charles' conviction of the divine right of kings. He believed with the full force of his passionate nature that it was the will of God that the top men in the community should do the governing. "We should incur scandal, by undervaluing the gifts of God, as wisdom, learning, etc. . . . if the judgment and authority of any one of the common rank of the people should bear equal weight with that of the wisest and chiefest magistrate."

Winthrop had the full support of his fellow magistrates, and some of them were more narrow than he. There was a rumor in May of 1632 that the freemen were going to insist on the right of electing the Governor themselves. When one of the Assistants heard of this he "grew into passion and said, that then we should have no government . . . and protested he would then return back into England." Winthrop, however, was willing to make this concession, and in the next General Court the freemen voted him into his usual post as Governor.

The political restlessness of the freemen increased, and two years later, in 1634, it reached its climax. The meeting of the General Court was scheduled for May, and in April a delegation of two men from each town made a formal demand to be permitted to see the charter. Thus they discovered that the right to make the laws belonged to the whole General Court instead of to the magistrates, and they asked Winthrop for an explanation. He gave it smoothly. "He told them that, when the patent was granted, the number of freemen was supposed to be (as in like corporations) so few, as they might well join in making laws." Under the present circumstances, however, so many freemen had entered the corporation that this would be impossible. However, he was willing to consider a compromise. A committee of the freemen might be formed annually to suggest revisions in the laws the magistrates had made, "but not to make any new laws."

The freemen had no intention of accepting this compromise. Instead they planned a revolt and organized it with great efficiency. They introduced the secret ballot, the same weapon that the stockholders of the Virginia Company had used to break the political domination of Sir Thomas Smythe, and when the smoke of battle had cleared away their victory was complete.

John Winthrop was no longer Governor. He was reduced to the rank of an Assistant, and Thomas Dudley was elected Governor instead. All the rights which the charter had given the General Court were declared into law: "None but the General Court hath power to make and establish laws. . . . None but the General Court hath power to raise moneys and taxes. . . . There shall be four General Courts held yearly . . . not to be dissolved without the consent of the major part of the Court." As for Winthrop's point about the unwieldy size of the assembly, this was answered by turning it into a representative body. The freemen would attend the General Court only for the May elections. At the other three General Courts, they would be represented by the delegates they had chosen from each of the eight towns.

Thus, in Boston, on the 14th of May, 1634, representative government came to the colony of Massachusetts Bay as it had come, fifteen years earlier, to the colony of Virginia. Both parliaments came into existence through the will of a corporation, and in both cases the motive force was the determination of Englishmen to have a share in their own government.

John Winthrop kept his temper better than Sir Thomas Smythe had done after a similar public defeat, and his characteristic courtesy did not desert him. "All things were carried very peaceably . . . and the new Governor and the Assistants were together entertained at the house of the old Governor, as before."*

Winthrop was no longer at the head of the government, but he had no reason to fear that the holy commonwealth was in danger. As long as the rock of a church franchise remained, the voters of Massachusetts—the freemen—could be trusted to behave in an orderly manner.

What no one realized was that this rock rested on a very precarious base. It rested on the will of a series of local congregations, and over none of these did the government have any control.

Every church in Massachusetts Bay was a self-contained unit, governed by the will of its own congregation and jealously determined to maintain complete independence. On one occasion when Winthrop was Governor, a congregation could not agree about a matter of church government. "Being much divided about their elder, both parties repaired to the Governor for assistance." They made it clear to Winthrop, however, that he was not coming to them with any political authority but only as a member of a neighboring congregation. The churches did not even share a common voting procedure, as a visitor from England noted. "In Boston, they rule . . .

---

* The new Governor, Thomas Dudley. had quarreled bitterly with Winthrop several times over the past years. After one such battle, Winthrop made so graceful a conciliatory gesture that Dudley himself capitulated: "Your overcoming yourself hath overcome me."

by unanimous consent, if they can. . . . In Salem, they rule by the major part of the church: You that are so minded, hold up your hands; you that are otherwise minded, hold up yours." The base of the whole operation, as the Englishman pointed out, was that each church had "power of government in and by itself."*

It was a system which worked only so long as there was fundamental agreement among the churches. Suddenly, and very violently, it became clear that there was not, and the rift that developed among the churches in the Bay nearly split the colony in two.

The trouble was caused, curiously enough, by Winthrop's own church of Boston. Its congregation possessed the most distinguished churchman in America after John Cotton arrived from Lincolnshire to be its minister, and many of his admirers came overseas to be near him. Among these was a Lincolnshire family named Hutchinson, and Anne Hutchinson later testified that she left England solely on Cotton's account. "When our teacher came to New England it was a great trouble unto me. . . . There was none then left that I was able to hear, and I could not be at rest but I must come hither."

Mrs. Hutchinson could not be at rest in New England, either. Like all Christians she wrestled to know the will of the Lord, but unlike most of them she found it through "an immediate revelation . . . by the voice of His own Spirit to my soul." Carried to its logical conclusion, this would mean that there was no need for churches at all. Even if it were not carried to extremes, it evoked the ancient dispute over salvation through faith or through works—that dispute which so quickly conjured up the specter of heresy.

It was always dangerous to introduce a theological dispute into an intensely religious atmosphere, as William Laud found out when he tried to modify the doctrine of predestination. In this case there was an equal emotional risk, for Anne Hutchinson was a very remarkable woman. Quick-witted and well read, she possessed the magnetism of a great preacher, and the church of Boston began to sway in the wind of her eloquence. Even John Cotton became in a sense her disciple, and so did a new and distinguished member of the church of Boston, Henry Vane.

---

* Where there was no church, there could be no machinery of civil government either. The town of Marblehead, for instance, had a population of fishermen, and no church had ever been gathered there. Since it had no church members it had no freemen, and therefore it could not elect a constable, nor was any local man eligible to serve in that office. Therefore the General Court passed special legislation. Because of the lack of "freemen at Marblehead . . . the inhabitants of Salem shall have liberty to commend some honest and able man, though he be not a freeman," to serve as constable in that politically powerless community.

Vane was an aristocratic young Englishman who had saddened his father and astonished his friends by deciding to migrate to New England. "Sir Henry Vane . . . hath as good as lost his eldest son, who is gone into New England for conscience' sake. . . . No persuasion of our bishops, nor authority of his parents, could prevail with him." The young man's travel license permitted him to stay only three years, but he evidently intended to "lead the rest of his days" there. In November of 1635 he was admitted to membership in the church of Boston. He became a freeman the following March, and in May was elected Governor.

The heresy called Antinomianism had already achieved a majority in the church of Boston and it was now anchored in the government itself; Mrs. Hutchinson had the support of the Governor of Massachusetts Bay as well as the minister of its greatest church. In temperament, they were the followers and she was the leader in the fierce battle that was now raging between the church of Boston and all the other churches of the Bay. Vane was only twenty-four and unaccustomed to the rigors of such warfare. At one point he burst into tears and suggested that he should go back to England. The church of Boston forbade him to leave and so he remained at his post, "an obedient child to the church."

Only one member of the church of Boston stood in open opposition to Mrs. Hutchinson, but that one was John Winthrop. He was her match in strength and stubbornness, and he was not going to permit the fabric of the colony to be destroyed. When the General Court met in May of 1637 for the annual elections, both sides fought hard for political control. There were "fierce speeches, and some laid hands on others" and "there was great danger of a tumult that day." Nevertheless, when the votes were counted, Vane had been defeated and Winthrop was once more the Governor of Massachusetts Bay.*

When the General Court met in November, it had before it a long list of freemen who were not fit to share in the government because they had tried to change it. Fifty-eight of the names were from Boston, for Mrs. Hutchin-

---

* Back in March of 1636, Winthrop had achieved an earlier victory when the General Court passed a law against the spread of heresy. No new church could be formed in the Bay without the consent both of the magistrates and of the majority of other churches, and if a church dared to form itself illegally, its members would not be "admitted to the freedom of this commonwealth" and could never have the vote. The goal for which Winthrop was striving was that no man could have political power in Massachusetts Bay unless he were orthodox in his religion, and at the end of August in 1637, a synod of ministers was called together to decide what was orthodox. The synod discovered that eighty-two mistakes in doctrine had been spread about the country, "some blasphemous, others erroneous and all unsafe." In the name of safety, all eighty-two were condemned.

son had built up a large following there, especially among the merchants. Henry Vane had gone back to England, Cotton had publicly admitted his error, and her followers could now be disarmed and deprived of their vote.

The leaders, who included Mrs. Hutchinson's brother-in-law, were banished from Massachusetts Bay, for, as Winthrop put it, they "were so divided from the rest of the country in their judgment and practice, as it could not stand with the public peace that they should continue amongst us." Banishment was a normal weapon for a corporation to use and had a long tradition behind it. It was, in fact, the usual way to dispose of any undesirable element.

The General Court examined Anne Hutchinson in November, and that heroic woman conducted herself with a vigor and spirit that made her all the more intolerable. The Court could not banish her immediately, since the heavy snows made travel dangerous, and so it "committed her to a private house, where she was well provided." By this time, nearly all her sympathizers had left the church of Boston, and those that remained voted in the spring for her excommunication. She left town so unshaken in her opinions that she sent back to the church a formal admonition of her own, pointing out its sins.

The Reverend Hugh Peter, who was currently the minister of the church of Salem, was one of the most vigorous of those who attacked Mrs. Hutchinson and he put the case against her in a single sentence: "You have stept out of your place; you have rather been a husband than a wife, and a preacher than a hearer, and a magistrate than a subject; and so you have thought to carry all things in church and commonwealth as you would."

Church and commonwealth cast her forth and sealed itself into a tight partnership behind her. As Winthrop reported contentedly to the Earl of Warwick: "The ministers have great power with the people, whereby through the good correspondency between the magistrates and them, they are the more easily governed." The freemen continued to press successfully for more power in the General Court, but since they were all members of orthodox Congregational churches there was no danger that they would try to shake the base of the structure as Mrs. Hutchinson's party had done. John Winthrop had good reason to believe that the last threat to his holy commonwealth was now removed.

He was mistaken. It was, in fact, growing increasingly difficult to maintain a system of government in which so many prominent men, especially merchants, were deprived of political power because they were not Congregationalists. The more prosperous the colony became, the more difficult it was to justify such a rigid standard. The unrest increased and finally, in 1646, a determined effort was made to widen the franchise in Massachusetts Bay.

The movement was headed by Dr. Robert Child, who was one of the most valuable and public-spirited men in the Bay. He had a degree from Cambridge and another from Padua, and he was spending a large part of his fortune in an effort to make New England self-supporting. He was one of the chief backers of the mining projects developed by Winthrop's eldest son, John Winthrop the Younger, and when he went back to England for a visit he made himself "very very useful" to the colony. Nevertheless he could not vote in Massachusetts Bay; he was not a Congregationalist but a Presbyterian.

Robert Child and six others drew up a petition which was presented to the General Court when it met in May of 1646. None of the signers could vote except Samuel Maverick. He was an Episcopalian, but he happened to belong to that earlier group of over a hundred who had been admitted as freemen just before the church franchise went into effect. Maverick was willing to risk his own welfare in an effort to help others, for during an epidemic of smallpox among the Indians, he and his wife and servants "went daily to them, ministered to their necessities, and buried their dead, and took home many of their children." The toll was as high as thirty in a single day, but Maverick did not falter in this act of compassion and conscience.

The petition to the General Court was written with great care, and the tone was courteous. The seven signers declared that they were not aiming "at novelty and disturbance, but at the glory of God," and that while those at the helm had the authority, "those who are under decks" could see the leaks. The charter on which the government of the colony rested had promised that the settlers would have the "liberties and immunities of free and natural subjects . . . as if they . . . were born within the realm of England," and to permit none but Congregationalists to vote was therefore a denial of the charter. Throughout the colony there were men who led orderly and useful lives, served in the wars against the Indians, paid heavy taxes, and still were not permitted to vote. The situation led to "too much unwarranted power and dominion on the one side, and of perpetual slavery and bondage to them and their posterity on the other . . . which is intolerable. . . . We therefore desire that civil liberty and freedom be forthwith granted to all truly English, equal to the rest of their countrymen."

The petition was circulated with great thoroughness, copies of it even reaching the West Indies. It amounted to a public appeal to the conscience of mankind, and in Massachusetts Bay it had a particular attraction to the young.

71

John Winthrop was head of the committee that was set up to draft a reply to the Child petition, and it took all his skill as a lawyer to answer so eloquent an appeal to the fundamental liberties of Englishmen. By listing the laws of Massachusetts Bay and the provisions of Magna Carta in parallel columns, he proved to his own satisfaction that all the fundamental liberties of Englishmen had been scrupulously observed. As for the right to vote, this was not universal in England either. "Their deputies are chosen for all the people but not by all the people; but only by certain freeholders and free burghers in shires and corporations." In Massachusetts Bay the same principle was maintained. "Our deputies are chosen for all the people but not by all the people, but only by the company of freemen according to our charter." Every corporation had the right to set up its own standard of admission, and while the one that had been set up in Massachusetts Bay might be unusual it was not on that account illegal.

The measured tone of Winthrop's reply hid real terror. If Robert Child had his way, the principle upon which the colony had been founded would collapse, and Winthrop was correct in calling the petition a blow at "the very life and foundation of our government." At the November meeting of the General Court, Child was fined the huge sum of fifty pounds for daring to present a petition which attacked the authority of the present government and which therefore was "tending to sedition." He was fortunate that his petition did no more than tend, since sedition had been made a capital crime in Massachusetts Bay at the beginning of that decade. "If any man . . . shall treacherously or perfidiously attempt the alteration and subversion of our frame of polity or government fundamentally, he shall be put to death."

Robert Child spent the winter in close confinement and was obliged to write a letter to John Winthrop the Younger, asking for the return of forty pounds he had lent him. He remarked bitterly, "Your father (I thank him) hath been the especial occasion of my stoppage here and imprisonment," but he signed the letter "your loving friend," for the members of the Winthrop family did not lose friends easily. The following May, the Child faction made a determined effort in the General Court to influence the elections. "Great laboring there had been by the friends of the petitioners to have one chosen Governor who favored their cause." But the majority held firm, and John Winthrop was again elected Governor of Massachusetts Bay.

Winthrop was nearly sixty now, still clinging to the policy upon which he had built the colony and finding it increasingly difficult to do so. In this same spring of 1647 he received a letter from the Reverend Hugh Peter, who had been such a tower of strength to him in the Hutchinson affair and who was now in England. Hugh Peter had discovered in England a loosening undercurrent of toleration, and he urged Winthrop to be less rigid. "Be tender towards those that . . . would live quietly under your government; not that I love errors . . . but what will you do with men dissenting?"

To Governor Winthrop, this kind of advice was a sure path to disaster. Like King Charles and Archbishop Laud, he believed that it was still possible to maintain the medieval ideal of a union of Church and State—that perfect circle of order from which all differences of opinion would be forever excluded.

Winthrop built his holy commonwealth on the rock of a church franchise. He saved it from erosion from within, in the Hutchinson case, and from bombardment from without, in the Child case; and when he died, only a few months after King Charles himself, his agile mind and dedicated spirit had created a structure whose chief characteristic was an absolute rigidity.

Chapter Four

The colony of Massachusetts Bay was only part of New England. The enormous energy released by the migrations could not be held within such rigid limits and some of the men who left England in the 1630's ended up in the wilderness, outside the jurisdiction both of Plymouth and of Massachusetts Bay.

There were no authorized governments in the wilderness, and so the Englishmen created them. In the space of two years—from 1638 to 1640—seven such governments were set up in New England, seven written compacts created and signed by men to whom self-government seemed as natural as breathing. These compacts varied as much as the men who wrote them, but they all had the same quality of self-imposed order.

The largest group of Englishmen to break away from Massachusetts Bay settled in Connecticut, and the government they shaped for themselves owed a great deal to that remarkable man the Reverend Thomas Hooker.

Hooker had a profound sense of the importance of the individual, and this was one of the reasons for his success as a preacher. "Each ear that heard him said, He spoke to me." Unlike many ministers, he was not unduly impressed by the loftiness of his position, and a story is told of him that shows how little he valued his own importance. He accused a youngster with a bad reputation of having damaged some property, and when the boy denied the charge the Reverend Thomas Hooker lost his temper. The boy then compounded the offense by insubordination. He walked off, remarking, "Sir, I see you are in a passion. I'll say no more to you." Hooker investigated, found that there was no real case against the boy and told him so. He also told him that he himself was at fault. "Indeed I was in a passion . . . and I am truly sorry for it. And I hope in God I shall be more watchful hereafter."

Hooker arrived in Massachusetts Bay in September of 1633, on the same boat as his friend John Cotton. Laud had made England intolerable for them both, and, as Cotton put it, there was little "service my self and brother Hooker might do . . . in prison." Cotton became minister of the church at Boston and Hooker became minister of the church at Newtown, which was already filled with followers of his who had arrived earlier from England.

Almost at once a certain amount of political unrest began to be noticed. "After Mr. Hooker's coming over, it was observed that many of the freemen grew to be very jealous of their liberties." Hooker did not agree with Governor John Winthrop that government should be confined to a few men at the top. He believed, as he showed later, that political responsibility should be shared among the many.

The people of Newtown had another cause for unrest. Newtown was as rich as Boston, and since it had been originally intended as the seat of government it was beautifully laid out on the banks of the Charles River. But the town limits had been set too narrow, and the inhabitants did not have enough room to pasture their many cattle. Therefore, the spring after Hooker arrived, they were given the right to move somewhere else within the jurisdiction of Massachusetts Bay.

The men of Newtown first thought they might go northward and settle along the Merrimack River. Then they investigated to the southwest and were greatly attracted by the green fields along the lower reaches of the Connecticut River. Since this was outside the jurisdiction of Massachusetts Bay, the people of Newtown petitioned the General Court in September of 1634 for the right to leave.

John Winthrop moved at once to block the petition. He had lost the office of Governor in the spring but he was still an Assistant, and the Assistants held a veto power over the freemen in the General Court. The majority of the Assistants voted against the Newtown petition, the majority of the freemen for it. This meant that the petition had failed. Winthrop and the other magistrates were determined to keep the veto power, "considering how dangerous it might be to the commonwealth, if they should not keep that strength to balance the greater number of the deputies."

The arguments over this right of the veto roused such fury that the

General Court disbanded temporarily so that all the churches of Massachusetts Bay could conduct a day of fasting and prayer on the subject. When it met again the following week, John Cotton delivered a speech in support of the veto. "Mr. Cotton had such an insinuating and melting way in his preaching, that he would usually carry his very adversary captive after the triumphant chariot of his rhetoric." This occasion was no exception. One of the elders of Newtown apologized for his rudeness to one of the Assistants, and Newtown accepted defeat for the time being.

The following year the whole situation changed. In the autumn of 1635 John Winthrop the Younger arrived from England bearing a commission which gave him the right to govern Connecticut for a year and which empowered him to build a fort at the mouth of the Connecticut River.

This area was under the control of the Council of New England, which was defunct for all practical purposes. But the President of the Council, the Earl of Warwick, still had the seal in his possession, and he could still issue patents that gave the right of settlement. No one had been supervising his activities, and the Earl seems to have become increasingly lighthearted about the strict legality of his proceedings. He was, moreover, always glad to oblige his friends.

The Earl of Warwick was a Non-conformist and so were two of his friends, Lord Saye and Sele and Lord Brooke. It was the daughter of Lord Saye and Sele—Bridget, Countess of Lincoln—who had been one of the moving forces behind the Winthrop migration, and the situation of the Nonconformists was now much worse than it had been in 1629. Laud had become Archbishop of Canterbury, and Sir John Eliot was dead in the Tower.

In 1632, the Earl of Warwick gave a patent for land in Connecticut to a group of eleven men headed by Lord Saye and Sele and Lord Brooke, and three years later they sent over John Winthrop the Younger as Governor. His instructions were to build a fort named Saybrook at the mouth of the Connecticut River, and he brought with him men, equipment and £2000 for preliminary expenses. The fifty men with young Governor Winthrop were first to build lodgings there "for their own present accommodations" and then "such houses as may receive men of quality."

One of the members of this group of eleven patentees was John Hampden, a very distinguished parliamentarian who had been Sir John Eliot's closest friend. It was for Hampden's use that Eliot copied out in prison the list of reasons for the Winthrop migration. Also a member of the group was another distinguished parliamentarian, John Pym. Men like

Hampden and Pym had been silenced now that King Charles refused to call Parliament into session again, and men like Lord Saye and Sele, members of the House of Lords, had been silenced also.

The group of patentees sent the authorities of Massachusetts Bay a paper entitled "Certain proposals made by Lord Saye, Lord Brooke and other persons of quality, as conditions of their removing to New England." It was apparently Lord Saye and Sele who wrote the proposals, since it was with him that John Cotton corresponded on the subject.

It was the plan of the patentees to create a parliament of "two distinct houses" in Connecticut. The upper house would consist of "the Right Honorable the Lord Viscount Saye and Sele, the Lord Brooke . . . and such other gentlemen . . . as they, before their personal remove, shall take into their number." Future members of the upper house would be chosen in America "by the consent of both houses" and it was from this upper house that the Governor would be chosen. The lower house would consist of freeholders, elected by the people to be their deputies, and both houses would have the right of veto. It was Lord Saye and Sele's intention to set up a permanent aristocracy in Connecticut, for although he was a foe of King Charles he had never had any thought "of leveling the ranks and distinctions of men." In fact, one of the reasons why that noble lord disliked Archbishop Laud was that he was "a man of mean birth."

It was left for the Reverend John Cotton to explain to Lord Saye and Sele why the government of Massachusetts Bay did not consider the proposals acceptable. They would produce a secular government in Connecticut, and it was "the will of the Lord Jesus" that all New England should be a theocracy. "Nor need Your Lordship fear . . . that this course will lay such a foundation, as nothing but a mere democracy can be built upon it. . . . Church government is justly denied (even by Mr. Robinson) to be democratical, though the people choose their own officers and rulers."

It was clear to John Cotton that a government which was formed according to the will of God could not be democratical. "Democracy I do not conceive that ever God did ordain a fit government either for church or commonwealth. If the people be governors, who shall be governed?" He was sure, however, that a satisfactory agreement could be worked out between Lord Saye and Sele and those whom he called the "leading men amongst us."

In the end the patentees changed their mind and did not come to Connecticut. It is possible that the reason was their lack of agreement with the men of Massachusetts Bay, but it seems more likely that what influenced them was the political situation at home. For an opportunity presented itself in 1635 to make a public protest against the policy of the government, and both John Hampden and Lord Saye and Sele availed themselves of it.

In an effort to raise money, King Charles had extended to the inland counties a tax in support of the navy that was already being paid by the coastal areas. Since Parliament was not in existence, the taxation was unauthorized and set up a dangerous precedent; or, as Sir Simonds D'Ewes put it, "this taxation was absolutely against law and an utter oppression of the subjects' liberty."

The Earl of Warwick, Lord Saye and Sele and John Hampden all refused to pay what was called ship money, and the government decided to make a test case of Hampden. He was a very rich man, with property in a dozen parishes, but it was on the basis of a twenty-shilling tax on one of his estates that the sheriff's writ was issued in August of 1635.

The trial was conducted before the twelve judges of the Court of Exchequer, and the Attorney General presented the case for the Crown. When Hampden's lawyer made his final presentation the speech was awash with precedents stretching back to the Danes, but the heart of the problem was not a technical one: it concerned the right of the King to tax an Englishman without his consent. Hampden's lawyer even went so far as to declare that the House of Commons had the right to tax only "because each subject's vote is included in whatsoever is there done."

The Attorney General said that this was a ridiculous argument, since King Charles was not obliged to consult his subjects' pleasure in the methods he took to finance the navy. "Surely this argument is made by the people, or to please the people; what will the consequence of it be, but the introducing of a democratical government when every man shall be his own defender." The word *democratical* conjured up visions of all that was unruly and undesirable, but the principle that was being discussed was nothing so radical as that. It was rooted in a conviction about English government so basic that it was now believed it had been guaranteed by Magna Carta four centuries before.*

The twelve judges of the Court of Exchequer gave their decision in 1638, and John Hampden lost the case by the narrow margin of a seven-to-five ruling. The long trial had roused a great deal of public excitement, and

---

* Article Twelve of Magna Carta said only: "No scutage nor aid shall be imposed in our kingdom, unless by the common council of our kingdom, except for the ransoming of our body, for the making of our oldest son a knight, and for once marrying our oldest daughter," but by now this was being interpreted as a sacred shield against taxation without representation.

Hampden was now a famous man. There was no reason why Hampden and Pym and Lord Saye and Sele should bury themselves in Connecticut, since there was now a very real hope that they could institute reforms in England itself.

It was three years earlier, in 1635, that they had sent John Winthrop the Younger to build houses for "men of quality" at Saybrook and given him a commission as Governor of Connecticut; and one of his first responsibilities had been to reach an agreement with settlers from Massachusetts Bay who had been moving without authorization into the lower reaches of the Connecticut River.

In the same month of October in which young Governor Winthrop arrived in New England, there had been an especially large migration of this kind. Sixty people, including "women and little children," set out on the two-week journey to the Connecticut River through the wilderness, in spite of the fact that winter was coming on. They may have been residents of Newtown, for a migration was being planned there; when Thomas Hooker's future son-in-law arrived in Newtown this same month of October, he found "many houses empty and many persons willing to sell." Or they may have come from the towns of either Dorchester or Watertown, both of which were also planning migrations to the Connecticut River.

A formal letter was sent to the people of Dorchester, signed by John Winthrop the Younger, by the Reverend Hugh Peter, and by young Harry Vane. They had come out on the same ship, and Lord Saye and Sele and his colleagues had therefore chosen them all to act as agents. The letter stated that "full power, right and authority" in the Connecticut area rested with the Saybrook patentees, and it demanded assurance that the people of Dorchester would "submit to the counsel and direction" of the Governor already chosen for Connecticut.

The letter was specifically addressed to Roger Ludlow, who had served vigorously in the Massachusetts Bay government since its beginnings and who disliked the current political atmosphere. It was of the utmost importance that men like Ludlow should not be permitted to settle in the Connecticut River area unless they were willing to state by what "right and pretence they have lately taken up their plantations within the precincts forementioned and what government they intend to live under."

By March of 1636, it had become clear that some sort of temporary formula would have to be agreed upon. The situation was that certain "noble personages and men of quality . . . by virtue of a patent do require jurisdiction of the said place and people, and neither the minds of the said personages (they being writ unto) are as yet known, nor any manner of government is yet agreed on." The General Court of Massachusetts Bay therefore set itself up to act as an agent "on the behalf" of both parties, and on March the third it created a commission to govern Connecticut. This commission was to operate for the space of one year, unless before that time some other plan of government had been worked out "with the good liking and consent of the said noble personages."

The commissioners were all chosen from the migrating towns, and one of them, of course, was Roger Ludlow. They were given the right to call together "the said inhabitants of the said towns to any convenient place that they shall think meet, in a legal and open manner, by way of Court," and the first of these assemblies met on the 26th of April, 1636, with Ludlow presiding.

The court was "holden at Newtown" since they brought the old names with them to the Connecticut River, but the Reverend Thomas Hooker had not yet arrived. It may have been the illness of his wife that was causing the delay, but the end of the following month he left Massachusetts Bay at the head of a mass migration. "His wife was carried in a horse litter; and they drove one hundred and sixty cattle, and fed off their milk by the way." The town they left behind them was renamed Cambridge, and became the home of Harvard College.

In February of 1637, which was one month before the authority of the commissioners expired, the three towns on the Connecticut River changed their names. Newtown became Hartford, Watertown became Wethersfield, and Dorchester became Windsor. By this time it was clear that the distinguished patentees in England were not coming to Connecticut after all. Young Winthrop's commission as Governor had not been renewed, and one of the inhabitants of Saybrook complained that they were left "like so many servants whose masters are willing to be quit of them."

To the men of the three river towns this was no cause for lament, and they immediately held what Hooker called "the time of our election." They chose the men who would govern them the following year, and when the assembly met at Hartford on the first of May 1637 it was called the General Court. But the six men were in fact the same ones who had attended the previous meeting, and Ludlow, as usual, presided.

Their proceedings were very orderly. Anyone who talked to the man next to him while the Court was in session was fined a shilling, which was double the sum imposed for similar misbehavior when the Massachusetts Bay Company met in London. Nevertheless John Winthrop the Elder found the people of Connecticut difficult neighbors after he himself recaptured the office of Governor of Massachusetts Bay, chiefly because of the Connecticut habit of referring decisions to both "the magistrates and people" instead of to the magistrates only.

In 1638, Governor Winthrop made a list of the mistakes which the river towns had made, and he attributed them to "two errors in their government: 1. They chose divers scores men, who had no learning, nor judgment, which might fit them for those affairs. . . . 2. By occasion hereof, the main burden for managing of state business fell upon some one or other of their ministers."

The minister upon whom this responsibility fell with special weight was Thomas Hooker, and in August of this same year Winthrop wrote Hooker a long letter on the subject of the government of Connecticut. As Winthrop put it, "I expostulated about the unwarrantableness and unsafeness of referring matter of counsel or judicature to the body of the people. . . . The best part is always the least, and of that best part the wiser part is always the lesser."

Hooker thought otherwise, and in his answer he stated a point of view that was, in Winthrop's eyes, political heresy. Hooker was willing to leave matters of small consequence to the judgment of the few; but "in matters of greater consequence, which concern the common good, a general council chosen by all, to transact businesses which concern all, I conceive . . . most suitable to rule and most safe." Nor did Hooker believe that it was safe to let the magistrates, when they acted in their capacity as judges, move without some sort of check upon their behavior. He reminded Winthrop that the Apostles themselves had been imprisoned because the magistrates thought their preaching was a danger to the state. "I must confess, I ever looked at it as a way which leads directly to tyranny and so to confusion, and must plainly profess, if it was in my liberty, I should choose neither to live nor leave my posterity under such a government."

The three river towns had no intention of following Governor Winthrop's advice, but they were well aware that the present arrangement was a makeshift one. At the end of May, in this same year of 1638, they had written Massachusetts Bay to announce that they had decided to draft "some rules, articles and agreements by which we may be regulated." Their purpose was to "join hearts and hands . . . to defend our privileges and freedoms" and what they had in mind was a written constitution.

Two days later, on May the 31st, the Reverend Thomas Hooker addressed a meeting of the Connecticut General Court. The sermon survives only in the brief notes taken by one of the listeners, but Hooker made himself very clear. His text was from the Book of Deuteronomy: "Take you wise men, and understanding, and known among your tribes, and I will make them rulers over you." The Reverend John Cotton would have used this text to justify the power of the magistrates, but Hooker used it to proclaim the power of the people. "The choice of public magistrates belongs unto the people, by God's own allowance. . . . They who have the power to appoint officers and magistrates, it is in their power also to set the bounds and limitations of the power and place unto which they call them. . . . Because the foundation of authority is laid . . . in the free consent of the people." The heart of the sermon lay in its close: "To persuade us, as God hath given us liberty, to take it."

They took it. On the 14th of January, 1639, the three river towns of Connecticut voted into existence the first written constitution in America, and they called it the Fundamental Orders. The text makes its appearance in the book that was being used to record the minutes of the Court meetings. It follows ten blank pages, and with it the hard work of the past nine months became suddenly visible:

> Forasmuch as it hath pleased the Almighty God by the wise disposition of His divine providence so to order and dispose of things that we, the inhabitants and residents of Windsor, Hartford and Wethersfield, are now cohabiting and dwelling in and upon the River of Connecticut and the lands thereunto adjoining; and well knowing . . . that to maintain the peace and union of such a people there should be an orderly and decent government established according to God . . . do therefore associate and conjoin ourselves to be as one public state or commonwealth.

The form of the government was not unlike the one they had left behind them in Massachusetts Bay. There was to be a Governor, Deputy Governor, six Assistants, and two General Courts each year to which each of the towns sent delegates. The Governor could not, however, succeed himself, and if he failed to call the General Court together the freeman could call it without him. It was the General Court which had "the supreme power of the commonwealth" and it alone could levy taxes or admit freemen.

It was on this last point that Connecticut differed so greatly from Massachusetts Bay, for it rejected the idea of a church franchise. Only the Governor had to be a "member of some approved congregation," and there was no such restriction on the Assistants or the freemen. The river towns took "a larger compass, as to their freemen, than the Massachusetts had done . . . for where a government is founded on the consent of the people, it will be necessary to extend the favor of a civil freedom to many who otherwise might be looked upon not so capable, at least not so worthy thereof."

Even in Connecticut, however, the consent of the people did not mean all the people. Men could become freemen, or be chosen deputies, only if they had first "been admitted inhabitants by the major part of the town wherein they live," so that no man was free to exercise political rights unless he had first passed through the gate of an earlier majority decision.

The right of a town to admit or refuse applicants was traditional, and it had come over to New England as a matter of course. As early as February of 1637 the three river towns had set up a system of fines to prevent violations. "It is ordered that no young man that is neither married nor hath any servant, and be no public officer, shall keep house by himself, without consent of the town where he lives . . . under pain of twenty shillings per week. It is ordered that no master of a family shall give habitation or entertainment to any young man to sojourn in his family but by the allowance of the inhabitants of the said town where he dwells under the like penalty of twenty shillings per week." Without the consent of the majority of the admitted inhabitants, no unattached man could live in a Connecticut town either by himself or in another man's household, and it was therefore relatively easy to keep out anyone who might be politically undesirable.

Another way to avoid dissension was the one that Hooker used in his own congregation. It was difficult to maintain harmony under the voting system of the Congregationalists, and when any question came up that might divide Hooker's church, he would dampen it down "by delaying the vote until another meeting." The members of his church lived "in great peace together all the days of Mr. Hooker," and there was only one excommunication in the fourteen years he lived in Hartford. Hooker's talents as a peacemaker were so valued that Massachusetts Bay paid his expenses to attend the synod on heresy after the Hutchinson affair and to serve as one of the moderators. Winthrop and Hooker were on the same side here; it was only on the subject of civil government that their views differed so profoundly.

The Reverend John Cotton agreed with Winthrop on civil government; it must be a theocracy founded on a church franchise. It was therefore a special joy to Cotton when one of his closest friends in England, the Reverend John Davenport, helped create a settlement in Connecticut which was wholly based on the will of the Lord.

John Davenport had been interested for some time in the colonization of New England. He was active in the group that formed the Massachusetts Bay Company, and its first Governor, Matthew Cradock, was a member of his London congregation on Coleman Street. He assisted the Reverend John White in screening the names of the first group of ministers to be sent overseas by the Company, but under the pressure of Laud's activities he became increasingly radical in his religious point of view. Cotton and Hooker had escaped prison by fleeing England, and Davenport finally decided also to come to New England.

His congregation in Coleman Street was composed chiefly of wealthy Non-conformists who were also successful businessmen, and chief among them was a merchant named Theophilus Eaton. He was a very forceful and well-educated man with some diplomatic experience and had been an Assistant of the Massachusetts Bay Company from the time it was formed. It was only a month before Winthrop's departure that Eaton decided to remain behind.

He and Davenport were close personal friends, and they worked out plans for a migration that would set up a great trading center in New England. Their expedition arrived in Massachusetts Bay in the summer of 1637, when the furor over Anne Hutchinson was at its height, and they "viewed many places" in both the Plymouth and Massachusetts Bay jurisdiction where they might settle. During the nine months they remained in the Bay they quietly recruited devout families who would be suited to take part in their dream of a city of God for businessmen in the wilderness, and the following March they set sail for the place they had finally chosen.

The land was on the Connecticut coast some twenty miles west of Saybrook, and it was not really theirs to take. The Council of New England had suddenly revived and it had ousted the Earl of Warwick from his very lax presidency, prying the seal loose from him with some difficulty. Then its members drew lots a second time for the distribution of the land, and again as unrealistically. This time the land was divided among eight noblemen, with this particular part of Connecticut passing under the jurisdiction of the Earl of Carlisle. Then the charter was surrendered to the King, so that by the time that Eaton and Davenport settled in the place of their choice it was under the direct control of King Charles. This was, however, a point to which the settlers paid no attention.

They named the settlement New Haven and designed it to be a great commercial city. It was laid out with rigid precision in the form of a square divided into nine smaller squares. Unfortunately this design had no relation to the harbor upon which the city would have to depend, and the elaborate houses were built with the same lack of realism. Eaton's, which had twenty-one fireplaces, was shaped like the first letter of his name, while the Reverend John Davenport's was given the shape of a cross.

The houses of New Haven were still unfinished on the fourth of June, 1639, when the colonists gathered in Mr. Newman's barn to decide upon their form of government. Seventy men were gathered there, and the minutes of the meeting were recorded, very suitably, in the blank pages of a merchant's day book. A preliminary draft had been tentatively drawn up for their approval, but Davenport pointed out that they were "free to cast themselves into that mould and form of commonwealth which appeared best for them." The draft was divided into sections, and each section was read aloud by Mr. Newman and then voted upon by a show of hands.*

The vote was unanimous until Mr. Newman reached Section Five, which was on the subject of the franchise and which specified that "free burgesses shall be chosen out of the church members." They only would have "the power of choosing magistrates . . . and the power of making and repealing laws." At this point one of the seventy men arose and said "that free planters ought not to give this power out of their hands."

He got no support from the rest. One man said that he had been studying the Bible before he came to the meeting, and his reading of the Book of Deuteronomy had convinced him of the necessity of a church franchise. Another said that the eloquence of his colleagues had convinced him. "He came doubting to the assembly, but he blessed God, by what had been said, he was now fully satisfied that the choice of burgesses out of church members . . . is according to the mind of God." Each section was worded as a query until it was approved; and Mr. Newman was now able to write down, as an order, that all future residents would have to agree to the principle of a church franchise before they could be permitted to settle in New Haven.

The quotation from the Book of Deuteronomy which had been so convincing came from the seventeenth chapter: "One from among thy brethren shalt thou set king over thee." Theophilus Eaton was elected as their first ruler, and he was almost literally a king. He held the office of chief magistrate of New Haven until the town united with several other settlements to become the colony of New Haven. He then became the Governor of New Haven and held that office until he died.

Theophilus Eaton ruled an absolute theocracy. The jury system was not permitted in New Haven, and those who were hanged in Oyster-shell Field for their crimes died because the Book of Leviticus decreed that they should. The Reverend John Davenport ruled the church with equal severity. It was

---

* The Virginia Company used this same method when it voted, section by section, on the text of the defense drawn up by the Sandys administration. A John Davenport had become a freeman the year before, and this may very well have been the same man who was in Mr. Newman's barn. He was a curate of St. Lawrence Jewry at the time of the vote in the Virginia Company, and it was a short time later that he left to become vicar of St. Stephen's in Coleman Street.

customary in New England to permit an excommunicate to listen to the sermon as long as he did not make himself conspicuous, but in New Haven, "where Master Davenport is pastor, the excommunicate is held out of the meeting, at the door, if he will hear, in frost, snow and rain." It is some satisfaction to know that when Anne Eaton, the Governor's wife, was excommunicated for her heretical opinions, the event at least took place in April.

There were now four godly governments in New England: Plymouth, Massachusetts Bay, Connecticut and New Haven. They all practiced corporation voting and were orderly communities, even though they disagreed over what the voters' qualifications should be. As early as 1637, John Winthrop had been trying to work out some kind of a confederation for mutual defense against the Indians and to solve other joint problems, and he finally achieved his goal in 1643. The New England Confederation was formed, calling itself the United Colonies, and an annual president was elected by rotation from each of the four member colonies.

The United Colonies had many excellent reasons for joining together, but there was one reason which could hardly be mentioned in the Articles of Confederation. This was the deplorable fact that in the midst of these godly communities—west of Plymouth, east of Connecticut and New Haven, south of Massachusetts Bay—there was an area penetrated by the long fingers of Narragansett Bay and inhabited by heretics. The area was considered "the drain or sink of New England," and one of the great advantages of the Confederation in the eyes of its members was that the disruptive communities of Narragansett Bay would not be permitted to join.

The first of these heretical little communities had been founded by a young English minister named Roger Williams who arrived in Massachusetts Bay less than a year after John Winthrop. He and his wife came in midwinter, after what had been a "very tempestuous passage," and he proved to be as tempestuous as the weather itself.

By one of those sudden leaps of the mind to which Roger Williams was subject, he had cut short a very promising career in England to embrace an extreme Brownist position with all its risks. As Williams put it: "Mr. Penry, Mr. Barrow, Mr. Greenwood followed the Lord Jesus with their gibbets on their shoulders, and were hanged with him and for him, in the way of Separation," and he was willing to travel the same road wherever it might lead him.

In England he had been under the loving patronage of Sir Edward Coke, and he later wrote the daughter of that great jurist to describe the bitterness of his departure from England. "Your dear father was often pleased to call me his son; and truly it was as bitter as death to me when Bishop Laud pursued me out of this land, and my conscience was persuaded against the national church and ceremonies and bishops, beyond the conscience of your dear father. I say it was as bitter as death to me, when I rode . . . to take ship . . . and saw Stoke House, where the blessed man was; and I then durst not acquaint him with my conscience and my flight."

Williams consulted his conscience when he arrived in Massachusetts Bay in February of 1631, and he found he could not accept an offer from the church of Boston. "I durst not officiate to an unseparated people, as, upon examination and conference, I found them to be." The one church that met his own rigid standards was the one that Skelton and Higginson had established at Salem. Higginson had died the previous summer and Williams took his place, with Higginson's widow selling him the house. He stayed only a short time and then went to Plymouth, where he served as assistant to their newly acquired Separatist minister, Ralph Smith.

Governor Bradford noted reluctantly that Roger Williams "began to fall into some strange opinions." He wrote a little treatise to prove that all charters and patents were useless, since the land did not belong to the monarchs of England but to the Indians. He also attacked King Charles through quotations from the Book of Revelation which proved that he was supporting "the religion of antichrist." The Governor of Plymouth loved Roger Williams, since it was impossible not to love a man who was at the same time so ardent and so gentle, and Bradford noted helplessly in his journal: "I hope he belongs to the Lord and that He will show him mercy."

After he returned to Salem, Roger Williams served for a time under Skelton, and after Skelton died he was ordained by the congregation. He developed a devoted band of followers, especially among women, and the General Court of Massachusetts Bay grew increasingly uneasy. Williams was still vigorously proclaiming that every church in the Bay, except Salem's, was "full of antichristian pollution" and that no one in the commonwealth had a right to the land on which he lived, since it should have been purchased from the Indians. He had also taken a third position, one which destroyed the base on which the government rested; for Williams maintained that the power of the magistrates was a civil power only and gave them no authority over the conscience of the individual.

The General Court hoped it would not be obliged to move against Williams, and it asked the Reverend Thomas Hooker, who was still at that time the minister at Newtown, to reason with him. The two had already argued together one day in England when they rode to a meeting at Sempringham, along with the Reverend John Cotton. Williams had not changed his opinion on that occasion, and he did not change it now.

The General Court decided on banishment, on the basis that Roger Williams had "broached and divulged divers new and dangerous opinions against the authority of magistrates." The matter was clumsily handled, perhaps because Winthrop was not serving as Governor that year, and the authorities suddenly changed their minds. They decided to ship Williams back to England instead because there was a rumor that he "had drawn above twenty persons to his opinion, and they were intended to erect a plantation about the Narragansett Bay, from whence the infection would easily spread."

On a cold January day in 1636, Roger Williams escaped from Salem and into the wilderness. He left behind his wife and their two little daughters—Mary, who had been born in Plymouth, and the baby, born in Salem and characteristically named Freeborn. Thirty-five years later, Williams could still remember that winter journey and the coldness of the snow, "which I feel yet."

He and his little band of followers settled first at Seekonk, near the head of Narragansett Bay and on the east bank of the Seekonk River. They did not know that this side of the river was in the Plymouth jurisdiction and lost the chance of the first year's harvest before they discovered their mistake. Then they moved across the river and founded a permanent settlement which they named Providence. Two years later, in 1638, a son was born to Roger Williams and he was named Providence also.

Five men had settled with him at Seekonk and followed him across the river to Providence, and it was by these six that the town was governed. The arrangement ceased to be practical as the town grew, and Williams wrote Winthrop to ask his advice. The two were close friends, in spite of the differences of opinion between them, and Williams apologized for writing him so often: "I sometimes fear that my lines are as thick and over-busy as the mosquitoes . . . but . . . your love will cover."

John Winthrop had not yet won back the Governorship when Williams wrote him for advice about the management of Providence, so that the date of this particular letter must be 1636 or 1637. "The condition of myself and those few families here planting with me, you know full well. . . . Hitherto, the masters of families have ordinarily met once a fortnight and consulted about our common peace, watch and planting; and mutual consent have finished all matters with speed and peace. Now of late some young men, single persons (of whom we had much need) being admitted to freedom of inhabitation, and promising to be subject to the orders made by consent of the householders, are discontented with their estate and seek the freedom of vote also, and equality."

The problem was similar to the one that had been encountered by the first-comers at Plymouth after the Particulars arrived and threatened their political control, and Roger Williams proposed to solve it in the same fashion. He included in the letter to Winthrop the text of two proposed agreements, one to be signed by the householders of Providence and the other by the young men who did not have the vote and could not be permitted to have it.

The text of the householders' agreement was not unlike that of the Mayflower Compact: "We whose names are hereunder written . . . do . . . promise each unto other, that for our common peace and welfare (until we hear further of the King's royal pleasure concerning ourselves) we will . . . subject ourselves . . . to such orders and agreements as shall be made by the greater number of the present householders, and such as shall be hereafter admitted . . . into the same privilege and covenant."

The second agreement, the one to be signed by the young unmarried men, later became the first entry in the book of the town records of Providence, and this text differs very little from the draft that Roger Williams sent to Winthrop: "We whose names are hereunder, desirous to inhabit in the town of Providence, do promise to subject ourselves in active or passive obedience to all such orders or agreements as shall be made for public good of our body in an orderly way by the major consent of the present inhabitants, masters of families, incorporated together into a town fellowship, and others whom they shall admit unto them."

Underneath the text of the agreement, and just before the signatures, is a vital phrase which was remembered too late to be included in the body of the text: "only in civil things." Roger Williams had not abandoned the principle for which he had fought so vigorously in Massachusetts Bay, and the men who governed Providence claimed no control in matters of religion.

If Roger Williams had been a less unusual man, he would have made Providence a refuge for extreme Separatists like himself. Instead he really believed in freedom of conscience and he created something that was unheard-of in New England. He established Providence as a refuge for all "persons distressed for conscience," whatever their religious opinions might be.

Later on, Williams wrote one of the most important books of the seventeenth century in defense of this position, and it was bitterly attacked by John Cotton. Cotton said that there were two "great questions of this present time. . . . How far liberty of conscience ought to be given to those that truly fear God" and to what extent it ought not to be given "to turbulent and pestilent persons that not only raze the foundations of godliness but disturb the civil peace." Cotton believed that freedom of conscience would inevitably be followed by anarchy in government, and most of his contemporaries agreed with him. Roger Williams, on the other hand, was convinced that there was no surer path to destruction than "that body-killing, soul-killing and state-killing doctrine of . . . persecuting all other consciences and ways of worship."

He would have none of it in Providence. In fact, before he and his companions crossed the river from Seekonk they made a pact among themselves that anyone who betrayed this principle would lose the privilege of taking part in the government and would no longer have the right to vote in town affairs.

One of the men in this original group was Joshua Verin, late of Salem, and in the spring of 1638 he broke the compact. His wife, Jane, had been attending religious meetings in the house of Roger Williams, and Verin tried to prevent her going there. He had thus deprived her of the right to follow her own conscience in religious matters and therefore had no further right to help govern Providence.

One of the householders said that there was another way of looking at the situation. Verin was obeying the Biblical injunction that wives must be subject to their husbands. He thus did what he did "out of conscience; and their order was that no man should be censured for his conscience." In spite of this ingenious argument, the majority vote went against Verin and the decision was duly entered in the town records: "It was agreed that Joshua Verin upon the breach of a covenant for restraining of the liberty of conscience shall be withheld from the liberty of voting till he shall declare the contrary." Or, as Williams put it regretfully in a letter to Winthrop, they had been obliged to "discard him from our civil freedom" and permit him no further share in the government of Providence.

Two years later, the town had grown sufficiently so that some rudimentary form of representative government was needed, and a board of five arbitrators was elected to hear disputes. They promptly found themselves in the hottest argument in the long and contentious history of Providence. It was caused by one Samuel Gorton, who arrived with what Roger Williams called "his poison" to split the town in two. In fact, one of the arbitrators, William Arnold, said he would sell out and leave Providence if Gorton were allowed to remain.

Samuel Gorton was an extraordinary man. A religious eccentric, notable even in that great age of eccentrics, he had worked out a religion which almost no one could understand. As one of his followers put it, his books "were written in heaven, and no one could read or understand them unless he were in heaven." It seemed natural to Gorton to name one of his daughters Mahershalalhashbaz, or to announce in prophetic tones, "We are come to put fire upon the earth, and it is our desire to have it speedily kindled."

In his political views, however, Gorton was a conservative. He was so conservative, in fact, that he believed no government could exist in New England unless it had been specifically authorized by King Charles. This naturally made him very unpopular, since he refused to live peaceably under an unauthorized government, and he had been harried out of several New England settlements before he arrived at Providence in the winter of 1640-41. Since the land had been bought from the Indians instead of having been granted by King Charles, it was Gorton's opinion that the town had no right to exist. Its inhabitants were all there illegally—the voting householders and the disfranchised young men alike—and he threw in his lot with the young men.

The problem was to find some way to suppress Samuel Gorton without seeming to suppress liberty of conscience. As William Arnold put it despairingly, they say "that we are persecutors, and do persecute the saints, in not receiving of them into our town fellowship." Roger Williams sent an anxious letter to Winthrop on the subject of Gorton. "Some few and myself withstand his inhabitation and town privileges. . . . Yet the tide is too strong against us." Williams had bought one of the smaller islands in Narragansett Bay and named it Patience. He thought seriously of going there to live if Samuel Gorton had his way in Providence.

Williams had foreseen that this kind of difficulty might arise, and a few years earlier he had asked Winthrop if he would be justified in requesting a private veto: "Whether I may not lawfully desire this of my neighbors: that as I freely subject myself to common consent, and shall not bring in any person into the town without their consent, so also that against my consent no person be violently brought in and received." He finally decided not to request this privilege, but he must have longed for it when Providence was being torn apart over the question of Samuel Gorton.

In November of 1641 there was an armed riot. The town had tried to impound some cattle belonging to Francis Weston, because he had not paid a claim against him for fifteen pounds, and the Gorton group rallied to combat what they said was tyranny. They attempted a rescue by force, and matters deteriorated to the point where the men of Providence were obliged to write an imploring letter to the men of Massachusetts Bay. "Lend us a neighbor-like helping hand . . . and ease us of our burden of them."

Roger Williams did not sign this letter. His instinct was always for peace, and the problem ended when Gorton left town with eleven of his followers and established a settlement of his own. It was just south of Providence on Narragansett Bay, and after many vicissitudes Gorton named it Warwick in honor of the Earl who helped him secure title to the land. His enemies had been convinced that he and his followers wanted "no manner of honest order or government," but in fact Gorton behaved in an exemplary manner as soon as he found himself under the accredited authority of his mother country.

As for Roger Williams, he lived forty-seven years in Providence, trying to keep the peace in that argumentative community. "It hath been told me that I labored for a licentious and contentious people. . . . But, gentlemen, blessed be God . . . for His wonderful providences, by which alone this town and colony, and that grand cause of truth and freedom of conscience, hath been upheld."

The year in which he founded Providence was 1636, and it was in this same year that the controversy over Anne Hutchinson had erupted. In that year also her husband's brother-in-law, the Reverend John Wheelwright, arrived in Massachusetts Bay with his wife and five children, and he at once took up her cause. The following January he delivered a sermon which the General Court denounced as seditious and which became the central point of the bitter political battle that followed.

When the forces of conservatism triumphed in November of 1637, John Wheelwright was one of the many who were banished. Like Roger Williams before him, he traveled in winter, and he himself said that it was wonderful he survived "the deep snow in which he might have perished." Unlike Roger Williams he went northward, crossing the Merrimack River and into what is now New Hampshire.

Twenty families followed Wheelwright into exile and when he established Exeter in 1639 the compact of government that was drawn up was signed with thirty-five names. "Considering with ourselves the holy will of God and our own necessity that we should not live without wholesome laws and civil government among us, of which we are altogether destitute, [we] do in the name of Christ and in the sight of God combine ourselves together." An Englishman could never, in fact, be "destitute" of government. He carried about with him an unquenchable determination to form yet another body politic, always on paper and always signed.

Meanwhile another group of Anne Hutchinson's followers had also left Massachusetts Bay and had also signed a document proclaiming themselves to be a body politic. This was a very distinguished group of people, mostly belonging to the merchant class and members of the church of Boston, and their first idea had been to settle in Long Island or even to go as far south as Delaware Bay. Dr. John Clarke, a prominent physician, was one of their number, and as he put it, "We were now on the wing, and were resolved, through the help of Christ, to get clear of all and be of ourselves."

They finally decided on Narragansett Bay, and Roger Williams helped them to buy land from the local Indians. Their purchase was the largest island in the Bay, the Island of Aquidneck, and they named their settlement Pocasset. By this time they had written and signed their political agreement:

> We whose names are underwritten do here solemnly, in the presence of Jehovah, incorporate ourselves into a body politic, and, as He shall help, will submit our persons, lives and estates unto our Lord Jesus Christ, the King of Kings and Lord of Lords, and to all those perfect and most absolute laws of His given to us in His holy word of truth, to be guided and judged thereby.

There were nineteen signatures on this agreement, and twelve of these were of former members of the church of Boston. One of the twelve was William Hutchinson, Anne's husband, who was a well-to-do merchant and apparently a rather gentle individual. Even his wife's most bitter enemies characterized him as "a very honest and peaceable man of good estate." During the same month of March in which this compact was signed, Anne Hutchinson was excommunicated by the church of Boston, and a short time later she joined her husband at Pocasset.

The most vigorous man among the exiles on Aquidneck Island was another Boston merchant, William Coddington. He had been an Assistant before the Winthrop fleet left England, and it was his child that the Reverend Samuel Skelton had refused to baptize. Coddington had built the first brick house in Boston and had prospered greatly, but when Anne Hutchinson went on trial before the General Court he spoke in her defense. When the vote was taken, only two men were "contrary minded" and one of them was William Coddington.

Coddington tore up his life by the roots and left with the others. As he later wrote John Winthrop, "I was not willing to live in the fire of contention with yourself (and others whom I honored in the Lord) having lived seven years in place of government with you. But chose rather to live in exile, and to put myself upon a sudden removal, upon fourteen days times, to a place without housing (choosing rather to fall into the hand of God). . . .

What myself and wife and family did endure in that removal, I wish neither you nor yours may ever be put unto."

William Coddington and his fellow exiles signed, on the seventh of March, 1638, their agreement to live by the laws of Jehovah, and it resembled very closely the government which that other devout merchant Theophilus Eaton set up the following year at New Haven. Coddington and Eaton were very much alike, successful and vigorous businessmen who were sure they knew what was best for everyone. They differed in matters of theology, but they were very close on questions of government. Both were convinced that the Bible was the "perfect rule for the direction and government of all men" and that they themselves were best fitted to be the governors. Theophilus Eaton ruled New Haven from the first, and William Coddington was quite willing to accept the same responsibility at Pocasset.

Since there had been judges ruling in Israel, there would be a judge at Pocasset, and Coddington was at once elected to the office. There would be no juries there, since none were mentioned in the Bible, and Coddington would be the chief and only magistrate. In the middle of May he presided over the first town meeting, and its first recorded act was to protect the principle of exclusion that was so vital to the existence of any body politic: "It is ordered that none shall be received as inhabitants or freemen, to build or plant upon the Island, but [such] as shall be received in by consent of the body."

In the nature of things, most of the people who applied for admission to Pocasset were "of Mrs. Hutchinson's judgment and party," flocking there now that she herself had arrived. They were people of spirit, and they did not wish to remain under the rule of a single magistrate, however benign it might be.

The following January, Coddington was obliged to submit to a modification of his power. Three men, to be called Elders, were to assist the Judge in his duties and they were to be elected by secret ballot. Coddington survived this challenge by getting his own followers elected Elders, but he was threatened by another law passed at the same time. The townsmen of Pocasset were given the power to veto the rulings that the Judge and the Elders made.

At this point a new element arrived to complicate matters still further. Samuel Gorton made his first appearance in Narragansett Bay. He had been banished from Plymouth in December after a violent altercation, and he and his devoted family waded through snow up to their knees to reach a haven in Pocasset. Once he was there, he contributed to the bitterness that had developed between the Coddington and Hutchinson factions, and things became "very tumultuous."

In April, William Coddington took sudden action. In one large and majestic gesture he left Pocasset, taking with him the town records and the deed to Aquidneck Island. The whole of the government went with him— the Secretary and the three Elders—and so did four sympathizers. The nine went to the southern part of the Island, where there was a magnificent harbor, and named their new settlement Newport.

The nine created the written compact by which Newport would be governed even before they chose their new location. "It is agreed by us whose hands are underwritten, to propagate a plantation in the midst of the Island or elsewhere . . . and that our determination shall be by major voice of Judge and Elders, the Judge to have a double voice." Coddington, of course, was the Judge, and all the rest except the Secretary became Elders. At a town meeting on the 16th of May they drew a line across Aquidneck Island to separate the settlement at Newport from the misguided people at Pocasset.

Meanwhile, the people of Pocasset had written out a compact also and it was signed by thirty-one people, the first name being that of William Hutchinson. The second was Samuel Gorton's, and the document as a whole shows the hand of that determined constitutionalist. The signers acknowledge themselves to be the subjects of His Majesty King Charles, and it is "in his name" that they unite themselves into a body politic. The laws of England, not those of the Bible, would henceforth be their guide, and jury duty made its first appearance on Aquidneck Island. The office of Judge was retained, but it was the gentle William Hutchinson who was elected to it, and he was to have seven Assistants. At the first quarterly meeting, the people of Pocasset gave their town a new name, and it became Portsmouth.

It was not a very practical arrangement to have two governments on an island only sixteen miles long, and within the year Portsmouth and Newport staged a reunion. In March of 1640 they established still another form of government, the fourth in two years. This one was clearly a compromise, consisting of a Governor, a Deputy Governor and four Assistants. Coddington was elected Governor, William Hutchinson became one of the Assistants, and Samuel Gorton did not attend the meeting.

The following March there was a General Court which lasted three days and was attended by sixty freemen. They voted to get themselves a seal (that invariable proof of sovereignty) and decided that it should bear a sheaf of arrows and the motto *Amor Vincit Omnia*—Love Conquers All. They strongly reiterated the principle of freedom of conscience that Roger Williams had proclaimed at Providence, and it was "ordered, by the authority of this present Court, that none be accounted a delinquent for doctrine."

The General Court also defined its government: "It is ordered and unanimously agreed upon, that the government . . . is a democracy or popular government; that is to say, it is in the power of the body of freemen orderly assembled, or the major part of them, to make or constitute just laws by which they will be regulated." It was characteristic of the people of Narragansett Bay to choose a term which was so shocking to the sensibilities of the rest of New England. As John Winthrop explained, "A democracy is, among most civil nations, accounted the meanest and worst of all forms of government; and therefore in writers it is branded with reproachful epithets, as *Bellua mutorum capitum,* a Monster, etc., and histories do record, that it hath been always of least continuance and fullest of troubles."

Aquidneck Island acquired the nickname of "the island of errors" and it seemed clear to religious conservatives that the "great strife and contention in the civil state" of the islanders must be due to their unsound religious position. It was certainly true that Mrs. Hutchinson found no peace there, and after her husband died in 1642 she moved out of New England entirely.

Samuel Gorton also found that he could not live under the new government of Aquidneck Island. He refused to accept Coddington's authority, denouncing the justices as "just asses." Banished from Aquidneck, he went to Providence, where he made Roger Williams equally unhappy until Providence finally managed to get rid of Gorton also.*

When Gorton and his followers were at last able to settle peacefully in their own town of Warwick on Narragansett Bay, they practiced there as a matter of course the same sort of political exclusion that existed everywhere else in New England. The town orders of Warwick specify the method to be used: "That inhabitants after they are propounded shall be received or rejected by papers or beans."

There were now three units of government in existence in the Narragansett Bay area—Warwick and Providence on the mainland, and on Aquidneck Island the arrangement between Newport and Portsmouth. The New England Confederation, with its four units of government, considered the ramshackle and heretical collection in their midst to be a real threat to law and order, and it was clear to the people of Narragansett Bay that, little

---

* Temperaments like Gorton's were not peculiar to the free air of the New World. The records of the English town of Warwick ring with the deeds of a similar individual, Richard Brook. He called his fellow burgesses "gorbellied churls, gouty wretches, crafty knaves and other names" and was finally expelled from the corporation.

as they liked the prospect of cooperating with each other, they would have to consider forming some kind of a confederation of their own.

What was first needed was official authorization to occupy the land, and Roger Williams went back to England to get a charter for the area. He came back with it triumphantly, "a free charter of civil incorporation and government." It gave the people of the area "full power and authority to rule themselves" and they were to be known "by the name of the Incorporation of Providence Plantations."

Too late for inclusion in the charter, the people on Aquidneck Island suddenly decided to give it a new name. Characteristically, they could not decide precisely what the form should be, but it was either the "Isle of Rhodes or Rhode Island." Advocates of the first form could trace it back to Verrazano, who first explored the territory and noted an island about as large as the Isle of Rhodes. Advocates of the second could quote a later explorer, Adrian Bloch, who wrote in his ship's log that "in this bay there is to be found a little red island," or, in his native Dutch, *roode eylandt*.

The charter gave the people of Narragansett Bay the right to set up whatever form of government was approved by the majority, but the question was a difficult one to decide. After a great deal of wrangling, the four towns finally managed to send delegates to an assembly which met in Portsmouth in 1647, with Roger Williams as one of the delegates from Providence. It was not, however, until three years later that the towns finally hammered out the document by which they agreed to be governed. There was to be a President, elected by secret ballot, and four Assistants, one from each town. A man from Warwick was elected President, and Roger Williams was the Assistant from Providence.

None of the four towns was willing to give up its sovereignty and the quarrels continued. In the eyes of the rest of New England this was only to be expected, since Providence Plantations had publicly embraced those twin enemies of orderly government—religious toleration and political democracy. They had formally stated, "All men may walk as their consciences persuade them, every one in the name of his God," and "The form of government established in Providence Plantations is democratical."

The first statement was true. The second really was not, for the structure of the four towns was not "democratical." In each case a closed society had been created by the first men to arrive. They were the ones who owned the land, and they had therefore the right to enter into what Roger Williams called the fellowship of the vote. All future voters had to be admitted one by one into this propertied fellowship, by the consent of those already inside.

The principle of exclusion was a normal one for any Englishman of the period. When Roger Williams drafted the text of a submission to be signed by the young men who were disfranchised, when Coddington authorized as the first official act on Aquidneck the acceptance or rejection of applicants for town membership, when Gorton set up a government at Warwick which excluded by paper ballots or by beans—each one of them was behaving like a normal man of the seventeenth century.

They were ahead of their day in being willing to accept the principle of diversity in religious life, but the same principle applied to political life was still beyond their reach. In all that strange medley of self-constituted governments, formed by men who had been quite free to set up whatever kind they wished, no one doubted that the principle of exclusion was the only reliable way to set up a body politic.

Chapter Five

When Captain Bargrave drafted a proposed constitution for Virginia, he designed it so that it would "without charge of garrisons tie Virginia in a dependency on the Crown." The Crown never had any reason to doubt the loyalty of Virginia, or of Maryland either. It was New England which it mistrusted, for, as one of the royal chaplains put it, the area was a "receptacle of discontented, dangerous and schismatical persons."

William Laud was well aware of this situation and set himself to correct it as soon as he had the authority. Three years after the Winthrop fleet set sail, Laud became Archbishop of Canterbury, and the following year he was made the head of a newly created executive agency, the Commission for Foreign Plantations. The chief foe of the people of Massachusetts Bay now had the right to ensure their "ease and tranquility" by appointing their Governor, making their laws, and punishing the disobedient "by imprisonment or other restraint, or by loss of life."

The men of Massachusetts Bay went at once on the alert. The General Court levied a heavy tax to be spent on arms and fortifications, and it established a commission "for the managing and ordering of any war that may befall us." The following March the powers of the commissioners were extended; they were permitted to imprison anyone they considered an enemy of the commonwealth, and the General Court even added that final sentence of open war: "It shall be lawful for the said commissioners to put such persons to death."

The men of Massachusetts Bay assured themselves that this was not an act of open defiance. They were merely taking reasonable precautions to "defend our lawful possessions." They had many sympathizers in England, eager to oppose Laud in any way they could, and when John Humphrey arrived in New England in 1634 with his wife, Susan, the sister of the Lady Arbella, they brought with them guns and ammunition that had been subscribed in England.

The English government decided not to use force against Massachusetts Bay but to take away its charter instead. The Attorney General filed a *quo warranto,* as had been done in the case of the Virginia Company, and with the same result. The Court of King's Bench ruled in 1637 that the charter was void, and the following year Laud's Commission wrote Governor Winthrop that he was to send the document back to England on the next ship.

John Winthrop had no intention of parting with the charter. Instead he wrote a letter which was very respectful but which nevertheless contained a thinly veiled threat of organized revolution against the Crown. "If our patent be taken from us . . . the common people here will conceive that His Majesty hath cast them off, and that hereby they are freed from their allegiance and subjection and thereupon will be ready to confederate themselves under a new government."

New England might well have been invaded the following year if Laud had not decided to aim first at a nearer target. He had always felt that to draw Presbyterian Scotland into the arms of the Church of England would be "a great service to the Crown, as well as to God Himself," and this very impractical ambition was one of the reasons King James had consistently refused to advance him. James knew his countrymen well and, as he said, there was no way to make "that stubborn kirk stoop more to the English pattern."

William Laud and King Charles, those ardent idealists, found themselves involved in two unsuccessful wars with Scotland in which nothing was achieved except that Parliament had to be called into session to pay for them. Once it was called, the King found himself sinking into a political quagmire in which all thoughts of reforming Scotland, or New England either, had to be abandoned.

A small but brilliantly organized group of men in Parliament decided that they could force through a series of reforms in Church and State, and its leaders were that "pack of discontented noblemen and gentlemen . . . Saye,

Hampden, Pym and others," some of whom had once thought to end their days at Saybrook. The genius among them was John Pym, who believed that "they had now an opportunity to make their country happy, by removing all grievances and pulling up the causes of them by the roots." Pym had two great allies—the religious pressure that had been increasing in violence the more Laud tried to suppress it, and the conviction that King Charles had been trying to destroy English liberties.

The Long Parliament came into existence on the third of November, 1640, and it set itself to undo what the King had done. In December, for instance, the House of Commons voted unanimously that the decision of the judges against John Hampden in the ship-money case was void, and in January the House of Lords ordered that all the documents on the case "be razed cross with a pen," as though they had never been.

By November of 1641, John Pym considered himself strong enough to draft the Grand Remonstrance, which was a long, jumbled and occasionally very unjust indictment of the way King Charles had been behaving. The text came up for discussion on the 22nd of November, and the men of the House of Commons began debate at nine in the morning. At dusk candles were brought in, and at midnight they were still debating. In the end Pym was victor by the narrow margin of eleven votes, and the Remonstrance was presented to King Charles on the first of December as an example of the affection borne by the House "to the public good of this kingdom and His Majesty's honor."

Charles knew treason when he saw it. On the third of January he instructed the Attorney General to impeach Pym, Hampden and three other members of the House of Commons. The following day he arrived in person to arrest them, an act of such idiocy that Queen Elizabeth would have shuddered in her grave. The Speaker of the House, who was traditionally the servant of the Crown, fell to his knees and said that he could not obey him. "I have neither eyes to see, nor tongue to speak in this place, but as the House is pleased to direct me, whose servant I am here."

John Hampden was normally a gentle man, but from that day forward he was "much altered . . . seeming much fiercer." It became increasingly difficult to maintain any area of compromise, and on the final question of who had the right to control the militia, King and Parliament broke. The fourth of July, 1642, Parliament set up a Committee of Safety which included Hampden, Pym and Lord Saye and Sele, and the following month Charles declared war.

In its own eyes Parliament was now the ruler of England, and a year later it struck its own seal. It was honestly believed that the battle was not against his sacred Majesty but only to rescue him from evil advisers; even so the choice whether to follow King or Parliament was a desperately hard one to make. Family after family split on which side to choose in England's civil war. Sir Oliver Cromwell, once a stockholder in the Virginia Company, fought for his King, while his nephew, who was also named Oliver, followed John Pym.

In the American colonies there was no such pull of conflicting loyalties. The two southern colonies of Virginia and Maryland were wholeheartedly on the side of King Charles, while the New England colonies embraced with equal passion the cause of Parliament.

Massachusetts Bay got its first news of the war from two fishing boats, and the heavy flow of migration to the colony dried up instantly. In fact, it turned and began to flow in the opposite direction. A month after King Charles declared war, the first class was graduated from Harvard College and seven of the nine young men went back to England. There were also many New England enlistments in the Parliament army, and a single regiment had four officers from Massachusetts Bay—Lieutenant Colonel Israel Stoughton, Major Nehemiah Bourne, Captain John Leverett and Ensign William Hudson.

When Governor Bradford finished writing his history of Plymouth colony, he looked back in wonder on the changes that had taken place in England. "Little did I think that the downfall of the bishops . . . had been so near, when I first began these scribbled writings. . . . Hallelujah!" One of the first acts of the Long Parliament had been to imprison the Archbishop of Canterbury on the charge of high treason, and Laud remained in the Tower for four years. At one point someone in the House of Commons suggested that he should be shipped over to New England. This was considered, even by his bitterest enemies, as "so horrible" a punishment that it was rejected, and in 1645 Laud died on the scaffold instead.

Many prominent New England ministers like Cotton, Hooker and Davenport were invited back to England to help rear a true Christian church on the ruins of the old. All of them refused and in any case they would have been outnumbered, since Parliament had no thought of setting up individual congregations on the Separatist model. The goal for which the English Nonconformists had been striving was a Church of England as absolute as before but stripped of all remnants of popery and, above all, no longer governed by bishops. A synod of churchmen and laymen, called the Westminster Assembly, set the pattern for the new order, and in January of 1645, by Act of Parliament, the Church of England became Presbyterian.

In theory, since Parliament had the right to govern the state it also had the right to "establish church government and to set up the true religion," but in fact Parliament had attempted an impossibility. The air was thick with pamphlets shouting contrary religious opinions, delivered with all the greater passion for having been so long denied. The ministers joined the chorus, for "all pulpits were freely delivered to the schismatical and silenced preachers who till then had lurked in corners or lived in New England." Such men were not Presbyterians. Most of them were those who had once been called Brownists or Separatists but who were now going "under the new name of Independents." More radical than the Independents were a series of small sects, each one passionately convinced that it possessed the whole truth as revealed in the Bible and all of them determined to be heard.

When Roger Williams came to England in 1643 to get a charter for Narragansett Bay, he arrived in the midst of this religious ferment. He saw a perfect opportunity to set the ax at the root of the tree and wrote that remarkable book, *The Bloody Tenet,* which was published the following year. In it Williams advocated the separation of Church and State and condemned "the bloody tenet of persecution for cause of conscience."

Parliament ordered the book to be burned, for it struck at the base of all civil order. A Presbyterian minister, the Reverend Thomas Edwards, described religious toleration as "the grand design of the Devil . . . the most compendious, ready, sure way to destroy all religion, lay all waste, and bring in all evil." Government was upheld by a perfect union of Church and State, and the only alternative was chaos.

Yet, as the Reverend Hugh Peter wrote: "What will you do with men dissenting?" When Hugh Peter lived in Massachusetts Bay, he had been a foe of dissenters and one of Winthrop's chief allies in the Hutchinson case. But after he returned to England he became an army chaplain, and his opinions changed. As the Reverend Thomas Edwards put it, "The two things that have poisoned him are his being in the army and his converse with some wicked politicians of these times."

The chief of these "wicked politicians" was Oliver Cromwell, and Hugh Peter became his chaplain. Cromwell was an Independent and at first, if Roger Williams is to be believed, the Independents were as intolerant as the Presbyterians. But Cromwell needed the best fighters he could find, and he was quite willing to welcome members of the sects. He reproved an officer who rid himself of a subordinate because he might have been an Anabaptist, and when he formed the New Model Army he permitted in it every shade of Protestant opinion. The Reverend Richard Baxter, who was a very distinguished and eloquent minister, became an army chaplain because he hoped to keep the soldiers from religious radicalism, and Baxter noted with bitter disapproval that Cromwell "headed the greatest part of the army with Anabaptists, Antinomians, Seekers or Separatists at best; and all these he tied together by the point of liberty of conscience, which was the common interest in which they did unite."

It was this New Model Army which won the Battle of Naseby. It was fought in June of 1645 and broke the military power of the King. After that, Parliament with its Presbyterian majority remained theoretically in control, but in fact it was the army with its freedom of conscience that now held the balance of power. The dream of religious conformity was over in England.

It did not occur to King Charles that this could be so. He clung to his vision of a perfect relationship between Church and State, and in August of 1646 the imprisoned monarch was confidently writing his eldest son: "The chiefest particular duty of a king is to maintain the true religion, without which he can never expect to have God's blessing. . . . Be constant in the maintenance of the Episcopacy."

King Charles kept his mind clear by the simple device of closing his eyes to the changes that had been taking place in England. His subjects were less fortunate, and now that the fighting seemed to be ended the dominant emotion was confusion. George Downing wrote a letter to his uncle, John Winthrop, in America, and he gave an excellent description of the current state of mind: "While the common enemy was unsubdued, there was some kind of agreement, all knowing that if he prevailed, all without distinction should be swallowed up in the common fate; but when he began to be very low, then every one bethinks himself, what have I fought for all this while, why have I so deeply engaged myself in this unnatural war?"

This was particularly true of the foot soldiers in the New Model Army. They had left their homes to fight against tyranny, and at first they had believed it was the tyranny of King Charles. But now they sat around with nothing to do while their superiors argued over what to do with the imprisoned King, and they began to feel that they were in fact the victims of an older tyranny than his. This was the class of Englishman whom an Independent newspaper contemptuously called "the hobnails and clouted shoes," and since they did not have the vote they had never had any say in the government. They were fit to fight for England, but they were not fit to help make the laws, and it began to seem that they were fighting to save an England which would be no better and freer after the war than before it had begun.

This vague sense of injustice was brought into focus by a series of inflammatory pamphlets which were being written in London by a group of political radicals, and the Reverend Richard Baxter considered this skillful London propaganda one of the main causes of the current unrest. "A great part of the mischief they did among the soldiers was by pamphlets, which they abundantly dispersed, such as R. Overton's . . . and some of J. Lilburne's." Since the soldiers had no fighting to do and spent so much time "in their quarters, they had such books to read when they had none to contradict them."

These pamphlets were distributed by a new political party—nicknamed the Levelers by its enemies—which was blazing like a brief and brilliant comet across the sky of England, and they were written by its three leaders: Richard Overton, William Walwyn and John Lilburne.

Lilburne was a former army officer and one of England's greatest propagandists. He had had a tempestuous career before he joined forces with Overton and Walwyn and had been fighting repression wherever he found it. Lilburne appealed from the King to the House of Lords, from the House of Lords to the Commons, and finally from the House of Commons to the people. Each time that he was whipped and imprisoned, his voice grew stronger and his point of view more radical.

It was when Lilburne was in prison in 1646 that he formed his alliance with Walwyn and Overton, and out of this alliance the Leveler party came into existence. Walwyn was a very different sort of man—grandson of a bishop, son of a country gentleman and himself a wealthy silk merchant of London. He was the kind of man with whom the authorities have always found it difficult to deal, for he was a true practicing Christian and willing to sacrifice both money and position in an attempt to bring freedom to England. The third member of the triumvirate, Richard Overton, was a lively, mocking skeptic, with little respect for tradition and a fierce hatred of tyranny.

At first, Walwyn and Overton had defined freedom as religious freedom and worked hard for toleration. Two months before the Battle of Naseby, Overton published a characteristic pamphlet describing the trial of Mr. Persecution, and the members of his fictional jury included Walwyn and that current idol of the reformers, Roger Williams.

When John Cotton attacked Williams' doctrine of religious toleration, he said that if men began to dissent in religious matters they would begin to dissent in civil matters also. The prophecy came true in England. In the heated political atmosphere that followed the Battle of Naseby, the leaders of the Leveler party became more radical by the month, more and more convinced that the common people of England had political rights that were being violated. For "the only and sole legislative law-making power is originally inherent in the people and derivatively in their commissions chosen by themselves by common consent and no other. In which the poorest that lives hath as true a right to give a vote, as well as the richest and greatest."

These were heady words, read by voteless men in the army quarters where, as Baxter said, there was no one to contradict them. The brilliantly written pamphlets of the Levelers acted like fire on dry grass, and each one proclaimed more strongly than the last the basic rights of all Englishmen.

Normally, the army leaders would have ignored the opinions of the rank and file, but in the spring of 1647 the situation was not normal. Parliament had tried to disband the New Model Army, realizing what a threat it was to its own political power, and officers and men made common cause against any such attempt. On the fifth of June an extraordinary thing was done. A General Council was set up to which every regiment sent representatives, with decisions to be reached by a majority vote.

This kind of voting was not new in the army, but up to now it had involved only the officers. The army council consisted of the general staff and the regimental commanders and they conducted their meetings somewhat in the fashion of a New England church, through discussion and a final decision by the majority. Two years earlier, for instance, there was a debate over the taking of Bristol. "A council of war being called and all the colonels present, after a long debate whether to storm Bristol or no, it was put to the question and resolved in the affirmative."

The General Council that was formed on the fifth of June, 1647, was a very different thing, for it consisted of two officers and two common soldiers from each regiment. This was done because there was no other way to maintain a united front against Parliament. It was an unheard-of gesture to let common soldiers elect representatives, and a very risky one, since the men they chose would almost certainly be the radicals who were already working closely with the Levelers in London. However, as a newsletter from army headquarters said frankly, these were the men "who now in prudence we admit to debate . . . considering the influence they have upon the soldiers."

The foot soldiers were the lowest rung in the army hierarchy, but they showed that instinct for orderly government that seemed to be bred in the bone of Englishmen. Each man taxed himself fourpence so that his company could send two delegates to a general meeting, and this representative body in turn elected delegates who were empowered to represent both the foot soldiers and the more aristocratic cavalry at the debates of the General Council.

Back in May, John Lilburne had issued a pamphlet which sketched out his ideal for Parliamentary elections: "Each county equably and proportionally, by the common consent of the people, to divide itself . . . so all the people (without confusion or tumult) may meet together in their several divisions, and every free man of England, as well poor as rich . . . may have a vote in choosing those that are to make the law, it being a maxim in nature that no man justly can be bound without his own consent." This was the principle under which the General Council of the army was put together, and to many men it seemed a portent of what might some day happen in Parliament.

Secure in the support of the London Levelers, the army radicals were swept by a wave of excitement in which anything seemed possible. With the instinct to get something down on paper that was so characteristic of the period, they drew up a list of reforms which they wished to see introduced. It was a kind of constitution for England, and they called it *An Agreement of the People.*

When the Reverend Richard Baxter read the document he was horrified. "The thing contrived," he said darkly, "was an heretical democracy." This was not really true, for the tone of the *Agreement* was moderate. Article One, for instance, suggested a reform of the franchise, but it merely asked that voting districts be more fairly apportioned. This was a reform that was long overdue, since the membership of the House of Commons did not reflect shifts in population and the rise of cities.

On the 29th of October, 1647, the General Council tried to decide whether the *Agreement* should be accepted, and the debate turned instead into a long and eloquent discussion of the right to vote. The speeches were taken down in shorthand by William Clarke, who was secretary of the General Council and assistant to John Rushworth.* The record of the debate disappeared among the Clarke papers and was not rediscovered until the end of the nineteenth century, so that no one knew until then how ardently the revolutionary army had concerned itself with the rights of man.

It was called the Putney debate because it took place in the village of Putney where the army currently had its headquarters. This was a strategic point halfway between the King in his stately imprisonment at Hampton

---

* Rushworth had been appointed secretary to the Commander in Chief and the Council of War when the New Model Army was organized, and a better man could not have been chosen. Even before the war broke out he had kept a record of the important events of those revolutionary days. He attended Hampden's trial and took it down in shorthand, and he did the same when King Charles tried to arrest the Five Members. Rushworth made no secret of his sympathies and called the King's abortive attempt to invade the House of Commons "the greatest violation of the privileges of Parliament that ever was attempted."

Court and the Parliament sitting in increasing frustration at Westminster. The army leaders were living with different families in the village—General Fairfax with the High Sheriff, Lieutenant General Cromwell with a Mr. Bonhunt, and so on. They held their meetings in the village church, sitting around the communion table, and opened them with a sermon from the Reverend Hugh Peter, who was Cromwell's chaplain, or from some other minister. Like the men of Massachusetts Bay they were God-driven, seeking to do the Lord's will in England, and they prayed as other men might breathe.

Oliver Cromwell acted as chairman of the meeting on the 29th of October, since the Commander in Chief, Sir Thomas Fairfax, was ill and could not be present. Cromwell had promised that there would be "a liberal and free debate," but he was not sympathetic to a theoretical idealism that would not work in practice. "It is not enough to propose things that are good in the end. . . . It is our duty as Christians and men to consider consequences." The aim, the end, of the *Agreement* was reform, but the consequences would nevertheless be disastrous unless "the spirits and temper of the people of this nation are prepared to receive and to go on along with it."

Cromwell's chief ally in support of this position was Henry Ireton. Ireton was an officer in the cavalry under Cromwell and since the preceding summer had been his son-in-law. The two men shared the same general view of government, but Ireton's was a lawyer's mind—quick, tenacious and logical—and he had no difficulty in dealing with abstractions.

Ireton emerged as the chief spokesman for the higher-ranking officers present, those members of the gentry who were fighting to save an England they loved and who hoped to return to an unchanged world, freed only from any threat of tyranny by the Crown. Ranged against these gentlemen were men like Edward Sexby. Sexby was a private in the army and entitled to speak out because of authorized election by his fellow privates. Such men had no desire to go back to the kind of England they had known before the war; they wanted a better one.

There was one man among the high-ranking officers who wanted it for them, and that was a colonel named Thomas Rainsborough. His father had refused a knighthood, and he himself had had a distinguished career. In the fleet he bore the title of Vice Admiral, and in the army he had served with such courage that he was singled out in the dispatches. He won special praise at the capture of Bristol, for "he had the hardest task of all at Pryor's Hill Fort, attempted it, and fought three hours at it." His "resolution was such that notwithstanding the inaccessibleness and difficulty, he would not give over." Israel Stoughton of Massachusetts Bay served under him for a time as

Lieutenant Colonel. Stoughton also was a very stubborn man, and he must have been delighted with his commander.

Colonel Rainsborough had made it clear, in a discussion the day before, that he was not interested in what was practical but in what was right. "Let the difficulties be round about you—have you death before you, the sea on each side of you and behind you . . . are you convinced that the thing is just, I think you are bound in conscience to carry it on." Ireton thought otherwise, and the two emerged as the chief antagonists in the debate that took place in Putney Church on the 29th of October.

The plan had been to read the whole of the *Agreement of the People* aloud and then debate each article, but they never got beyond the first one. This was the attempt to reform apportionment in the House of Commons and it contained the phrase "the people of England." Ireton, with his lawyer's mind, had no intention of approving a phrase behind which a well-known Leveler doctrine might be lurking and he challenged it. If "the meaning is, that every man that is an inhabitant is to be equally considered and to have an equal voice . . . then I have something to say against it."

What Ireton had to say ultimately took up many pages of Clarke's transcript, and he said it with brilliance, eloquence and absolute conviction. He was defending the ancient principle which restricted the vote to men of property, and he knew that he had on his side all the forces of history, tradition, public opinion and common sense. He could afford to feel a mild contempt for radicals who believed that political equality could really exist in a sane world, and he would have had an easier time of it that day if Thomas Rainsborough had not been his chief antagonist.

Rainsborough stated his position to Ireton at once, in a single sentence that contained the gist of all the coming centuries of struggle and reform. "Really I think that the poorest he that is in England hath a life to live, as the greatest he; and therefore truly, sir, I think it's clear that every man that is to live under a government ought first, by his own consent, to put himself under that government."

"Give me leave to tell you," said Ireton in prompt rebuttal, "that if you make this the rule I think you must fly for refuge to an absolute natural right, and you must deny all civil right." It was civil right that concerned Ireton, the actual problems of real government, and he in his turn put into a single sentence the position that future generations would use to defend the principle of property in connection with the vote. "I think that no person hath a right to an interest or share in the disposing of the affairs of the kingdom, and in determining or choosing those that shall determine what laws we shall be ruled by here—no person hath a right to this, that hath not a permanent fixed interest in this kingdom." This interest was possessed in county voting by the forty-shilling freeholders and in borough voting by members of the corporation—"that is, the persons in whom all land lies and those in corporations in whom all trading lies. This is the most fundamental constitution of this kingdom . . . which if you do not allow, you allow none at all." As for equality, Ireton pointed out with some pride that the forty-shilling freeholder had the same vote as a man worth ten thousand pounds. This, to Ireton, was wholly satisfactory and involved as much political justice as he wished to consider.

To Colonel Rainsborough it was not satisfactory and no justice at all. If an Englishman entered the war against the King and spent so much in the effort that he was no longer worth forty shillings a year, he would be disfranchised, and it would be his zeal for liberty that had disfranchised him. "Neither by the law of God nor the law of nature" could a man be justly deprived of his right to help elect "those who are to make the laws for him to live under, and for him, for aught I know, to lose his life under." In Rainsborough's opinion, there was one unshakable political fact: "The foundation of all law lies in the people."

Ireton, on the other hand, was interested in safety, and safety lay in exclusion. No one should possess the right to vote unless he had a "permanent interest in the kingdom," and Ireton told his antagonist that any other principle would result in the abolition of property rights altogether. If the theory were once to be admitted that "we are free, we are equal, one man must have as much voice as another," then there was nothing to prevent the idea from being pushed a step farther. "By that same right of nature . . . by which you can say, one man hath an equal right with another to the choosing of him that shall govern him—by the same right of nature, he hath the same right in any goods he sees."

Rainsborough's answer was the plea that has been forced on every reformer in history: "I wish you would not make the world believe that we are for anarchy."

Cromwell interposed to say that of course no one believed that Colonel Rainsborough was for anarchy; nevertheless, the rule he was trying to apply would tend to anarchy and "must end in anarchy." What else could occur if the vote were given to men who had no stake or interest in the country except "the interest of breathing"? Cromwell was enough of a revolutionary to approve of the execution of his King fifteen months later, but he was not enough of a revolutionary to agree that government should exist by the consent of the governed.

Colonel Rainsborough said bitterly, "I would fain know what we have fought for." Apparently it was to perpetuate a political system "which enslaves the people of England—that they should be bound by laws in which they have no voice at all."

The debate wore on all afternoon. Many voices were heard on both sides, and again and again Rainsborough returned to the question of simple justice which seemed to him to lie at the heart of the whole matter. "I still say, what shall become of those . . . that have ruined themselves by fighting and hazarding all they had? They are Englishmen. They have now nothing to say for themselves." Rainsborough was himself a man of property, with a voice in the government, and he intended to use it to speak for the disfranchised, the voiceless. "I would fain know what the soldier hath fought for all this while. He hath fought to enslave himself, to give power to men of riches, men of estates, to make him a perpetual slave."

Cromwell was willing to admit that there might be a certain injustice in restricting the vote to the forty-shilling freeholder, and he said that a cautious enlargement of the franchise might be possible. "Perhaps there are a very considerable number of copyholders by inheritance that ought to have a voice." Ireton, for his part, was very willing to support a more equal distribution of seats in Parliament. "I will agree with you, not only to dispute for it, but to fight for it." What neither man could agree to was the basic doctrine for which Rainsborough was fighting. It was summarized that day at Putney by John Wildman, a young lawyer and a civilian who was there to serve as a link with the Leveler party in London. "Every person in England hath as clear a right to elect his representative as the greatest person in England. I conceive that's the undeniable maxim of government: that all government is in the free consent of the people."

The Reverend Hugh Peter suggested that a small committee might be set up to discuss the question of the franchise and come to an amicable settlement, but this attempt at peacemaking was ignored. Tempers continued to rise, and on the subject of the vote an agreement was farther away than when the meeting had begun. Finally Rainsborough suggested that "the army might be called to a rendezvous and things settled," since it was possible that if all the regiments were gathered together the *Agreement of the People* would be accepted by acclamation.

The rendezvous of the army took place at Corkbush Field, some thirty miles outside London, on the 15th of November. Many of the soldiers arrived with copies of the *Agreement* stuck in their hats and backed by the slogan in capital letters, ENGLAND'S FREEDOM, SOLDIER'S RIGHTS. Rainsborough brought with him a petition to present to the Commander in Chief, Sir Thomas Fairfax. In it, soldiers and officers stated that they saw no hope "of settling the foundations of freedom, but by entering into this *Agreement."*

General Fairfax, conservative and honorable man that he was, viewed the whole thing as a kind of temporary madness. In his report to the House of Lords, he explained that most of his unfortunate and misguided soldiers gave in as soon as they were "informed of their error" and that only one of the regiments required discipline. "I . . . drew out divers of the mutineers, three whereof were presently tried and condemned to death; and, by lot, one of them was shot to death at the head of the regiment. . . . I do find the same regiment likewise very sensible of their error . . . and indeed, I do see that the London agents have been the great authors of these irregularities."

The General was within his rights, for in the army at large any difference of opinion was indeed mutiny and to be punished as such. Fairfax expressed confidence that Rainsborough would avoid such errors in the future, and no doubt he would have done so, since he was no mutineer. In any case he was killed the following year, unarmed and heroically resisting capture, and no high officer came forward again as a champion of the people.

It was the custom to refer to "a leveling, anti-monarchial spirit . . . in the army," but that was to confuse two entirely different things. Cromwell might be briefly forced into an uneasy political alliance with the Levelers, but he had no sympathy whatever with their dreams of reform. Yet Cromwell and other like-minded gentlemen were growing increasingly anti-monarchial. In 1648 King Charles managed to precipitate a second civil war, and after it was over it seemed that there was only one way to ensure peace in England. The King must die, "and monarchy must die with him."

The Presbyterians had a large majority in Parliament and they would never have consented to the death of their King. Cromwell and the army did not dare to act without Parliament's consent, and the only answer was to station Colonel Pride at the door and permit no Presbyterians to enter. The remnant of the Long Parliament that survived Pride's Purge set up a special court of justice to try the King, and on a winter day in January, 1649, Charles Stuart was condemned to death "as a tyrant, traitor, murderer, and a public enemy."

The King met his death with serene dignity, secure in the knowledge that he had been a faithful son of the Church. "This is my second marriage day . . . for before night I hope to be espoused to my blessed Jesus." He brought with him to the scaffold a small piece of paper—notes for the speech he wished to deliver—so that he could explain to his subjects the nature of liberty. The liberty of Englishmen was "not their having a share in the government; that is nothing appertaining unto them. A subject and a sovereign are clean different things."

After the King was dead, the House of Commons dissolved the House of Lords and ruled alone. In theory England was now a commonwealth ruled by the Long Parliament and its servant, the Council of State. In practice the army was the one real political force in England and Oliver Cromwell was now Lord General of the army.

Shortly before the revolution, Cromwell had been discussing the question of reforms in Church and State with two colleagues in the House of Commons, and he made a very revealing remark. "I can tell you, sirs, what I would not have; though I cannot, what I would." When he finally decided that he did not want a monarchy, he destroyed it, but he could not decide what kind of a government to set up in its place.

Early in 1653, the Long Parliament decided to dissolve itself the following autumn, which meant a general election, and each Wednesday was devoted to the difficult subject of the election machinery. In any such election, Cromwell's supporters would have been outnumbered and he could therefore not permit it to take place, for he knew that God had chosen him to guide England. On the 20th of April, 1653, he dissolved the Long Parliament in a very emotional speech, and the following morning some humorist fastened a notice on the door of the Parliament House: "This House is to be let, now unfurnished."

To replace Parliament, Cromwell hit upon a device that would have pleased the late John Winthrop. Each self-governing congregation in England was told to submit a list of suitable men, from which Cromwell and his colleagues would choose members for a new representative assembly. Since only the Independents and sects like the Baptists had these congregations, the virtue and godliness of the assembly would ensure its reliability.

The assembly did not prove to be reliable at all. In fact, after only one meeting it voted to call itself a parliament and to move back into the empty Parliament House. One of its members was a London leather merchant named Praisegod Barebones (he himself spelled it Barbon) and it was nicknamed the Barebones Parliament.

An energetic minority showed itself so determined to impose reforms that in September Cromwell dissolved this Parliament also. He did not intend to permit any changes in the social or judicial structure in England, and he was struggling with the nearly insoluble problem of preventing any major alterations while at the same time making it impossible for monarchy to return.

The Commander in Chief could hardly continue to dissolve parliaments at the rate of two a year, and it was clear that England would have to be governed in an orderly fashion through a written constitution. In December of this same year of 1653, the army drew up such a document. It turned the Commonwealth into a Protectorate and was called the *Instrument of Government*. Cromwell was named in the document as Lord Protector, and he took the oath of office immediately.

The details of government were worked out with great care. Parliament was to assemble the following September, and after that once every three years. It was to pass laws and levy taxes, and all the voters in England were to have the same qualification: each man was to possess two hundred pounds in real or personal estate. Anyone who had been on the wrong side in the revolution was not to be permitted to vote for the first twelve years, and Roman Catholics were permanently disfranchised.

The following September, the first Parliament to meet under the new constitution duly assembled itself. It was Cromwell's opinion that its members had gathered to ratify the *Instrument,* but in their own opinion they had gathered to discuss it. They began by objecting to some of the sweeping powers that had been conferred upon the Lord Protector, and Cromwell was obliged to inform them that while it was certainly "a free Parliament" it was not that free. After this rebuke they contented themselves with altering details, such as changing the franchise back to the forty-shilling freeholder. But Cromwell could not work successfully with this Parliament either, and on the 22nd of January, 1655, he dissolved it. England was again without a representative assembly.

Cromwell tried another device. He divided the country into districts to be governed by godly major generals and found this to be both unpopular and very expensive. Cromwell's foreign policy was expensive also, and in September of 1656 he finally called another Parliament. In this one he managed to come to terms with the strongest political force in England outside the army—the property owners who wanted peace and stability—and they offered him the crown. When he refused it they confirmed him as Lord Protector, and an almost regal ceremony took place on a June day in 1657. The Earl of Warwick, who was a close friend of Cromwell's, robed him ceremoniously in purple velvet and ermine. The Lord Protector held in his hand twin symbols of power: a golden scepter modeled closely after the one King Charles had held, and a sword.

Cromwell died the following year, and any hope that the government might be permanent died with him. It dissolved into warring factions, and the only rock which remained was that there was still representative government in England. General Monk, who was Commander in Chief of the army in Scotland, arrived in London in February of 1660, and he admitted back into Parliament the men that Colonel Pride had excluded more than a decade earlier.

This Parliament blotted from the record the fact that it had been dissolved by Cromwell, so that the Long Parliament was still theoretically in existence. Then it dissolved itself after ordering general elections. The new Parliament assembled at the end of April, 1660, and requested the late King's eldest son to return from exile as Charles II.

Thus ended the brief dream that God would remake England in His holy image. What was called, sometimes in derision, the Good Old Cause made its final appearance in the heroic behavior of the men who were executed for the death of the King. One of these was the Reverend Hugh Peter, one-time minister of the church of Salem and member of the committee to manage Harvard College, late chaplain of Oliver Cromwell and foe of monarchy. He had worried that he might show fear, since the death was the horrible one of hanging, drawing and quartering. He did not, and neither did any of his companions.

The first to die was Major General Harrison. He met his fate as serenely as King Charles had done, and he "sent his wife word that that day was to him as his wedding day." Harrison felt no regret for his part in the death of the King. "I have many a time sought the Lord with tears to know if I have done amiss in it, but was rather confirmed that the thing was more of God than of men."

The strength of such men lay in their conviction that they served God, and it was this that gave the Puritan Revolution its terrifying energy. When the long and bitter struggle was over and the House of Stuart had returned to the throne, it was still not clear where political sovereignty really lay in England. It would take a second revolution in that tormented century before the question was finally decided. But the Restoration of 1660 brought with it a different political atmosphere, and neither King nor Parliament believed any longer that they moved under direct instructions from the Lord.

Chapter Six

Some men found it easy to adjust to the changed atmosphere of the Restoration, and one of these was Winthrop's nephew, George Downing. He had been serving as ambassador to the Dutch, and he moved as easily as a cat into the same position under Charles II. Downing was a member of the first class to graduate from Harvard College, and he explained smoothly that his New England education had inculcated principles which he could now "see were erroneous." Assisted by such cooperative powers of reasoning, he returned to The Hague after the Restoration and King Charles gave him a knighthood.

Downing was a trade expert, and his attitude toward the Dutch did not change. He was convinced that their control of the seas was a threat to England, and he did everything he could to undercut their naval and commercial power. He had the support of an influential group in England which was headed by James, Duke of York. The King's only brother was Lord High Admiral and an ardent advocate of naval and colonial expansion.

Four years after the Restoration, this group had its way. King Charles gave his brother a charter for a huge area on the eastern coast of North America. It was done quickly and in secret, for all this land was owned by the Dutch and called New Netherland.

The Dutch claim to New Netherland dated from 1609. This was the year in which Henry Hudson, commissioned by the Dutch East India Company to find a passage to India, had sailed up the Hudson River. A small trading company was given rights to the area and in time began to think of colonization. It informed the Dutch government that there was "residing at Leyden a certain English preacher" who was prepared "to plant there a new commonwealth." This was John Robinson, temporarily blocked in his efforts to get English financing for the Pilgrims and willing to consider a Dutch offer instead. The trading company was willing to accept him, and petitioned the government to give him safe passage and protection.

The petition was rejected for political reasons. The twelve-year truce with Spain was almost at an end, and the United Provinces of the Netherlands were planning to set up a huge armed mercantile corporation whose purpose was to seize Spain's colonial possessions and cut off the source of its wealth. The corporation was named the West India Company and received its charter in 1621.

New Netherland was a very small part of this vast and complicated project and it was not mentioned in the charter. It was, however, absorbed into its general system of government. Five "chambers of managers" were set up to represent the capital that had been put into the venture by five of the Dutch Provinces, and a board of nineteen Directors in Amsterdam handled the administrative details.

The nineteen Directors were sure they knew what was best for the little colony which was founded on the island of Manhattan at the mouth of the Hudson River. The fort that was built there was named New Amsterdam, and the Directors specified the exact dimensions of every building that was erected. Equally rigid were the instructions they sent their Governors. The Directors were businessmen, not politicians, and they wished to have a businesslike organization that would bring in a great deal of money to the shareholders. This had also been the chief purpose of the English corporations that founded the colonies of Virginia and Massachusetts Bay, but they had changed as circumstances changed and grown from within. The men at the head of the Dutch West India Company remained stolid, conservative and motionless.

It was not easy to colonize New Netherland, since the Directors found that their countrymen were reluctant to migrate to America. "The colonizing such wild and uncultivated countries demands more inhabitants than we can well supply, not so much through lack of population, in which our Provinces abound, as from the fact that all who are inclined to do any sort of work here procure enough to eat without any trouble." There was no depression in the prosperous Province of Holland to drive men from their homes, nor was there any religious persecution in that comfortable country. The forces that had served to populate New England did not operate in New Netherland, and two decades later the land was still relatively empty.

Another attraction that New England could offer was the fact that its people were all under some form of representative government, while the people of New Netherland were bound in absolute obedience to the Governor sent out by the Company. In their own country the Dutch had a long tradition of political liberty, and they grew increasingly restless under the restrictions they encountered overseas. Finally, in 1649, a brilliant and energetic lawyer of New Amsterdam named Adriaen van der Donck drew up a Remonstrance which was an attack on the whole policy of the Company. His name was at the head of eleven signatures, and he and two others risked a charge of sedition by going back overseas so that they could present it personally to the authorities.

The petitioners had a list of eight complaints, and the first and most important was "unsuitable government." They wanted some form of representative government set up instead, so "that those interested in the country may also attend to its government and keep a watchful eye over it." They especially recommended to the attention of the Company the political system that was so successful in New England. "Each colony hath its Governor, and neither patroons, lords nor princes are known there; only the people." "Few taxes are imposed, and these only by general consent." "The Governor and Deputy are chosen annually by the entire province, although some have been continued from the beginning until this time. Nevertheless, the people have a new election every year and have power to make a change."*

It was a further source of irritation to men like Adriaen van der Donck that when New Englanders moved into New Netherland they were accorded special political consideration. Groups of New Englanders had been particularly attracted to Long Island, which had the "fairest soil in New Netherland," and they had been allowed to settle there under very favorable circumstances. The Company's sixth Governor, Willem Kieft, gave each such group

---

* The remark about some of the governments having remained unchanged "from the beginning" was very well informed; some of the New England leadership was almost stationary. Theophilus Eaton was Governor of New Haven every year until he died. William Bradford was Governor of Plymouth for thirty-three terms, with John Alden and Miles Standish as his almost equally permanent Assistants. The men of Connecticut made an attempt to break this pattern by inserting in the Fundamental Orders a law that no magistrate could be "chosen for more than one year," but they elected John Haynes their Governor every alternate year, which was as often as they could do it legally. Nevertheless the point made in the Remonstrance remained correct; the people had "power to make a change." Moreover, it was the delegates of the people, and not the Governors, who levied taxes.

a charter in return for an oath of allegiance. It was a pattern that had been used in Holland for incorporated manors, and none of the Dutch towns on Long Island was permitted so generous an arrangement.

The most energetic of these privileged English towns was Gravesend, which was founded by a former resident of Massachusetts Bay whose name was Lady Deborah Moody. The daughter of a Member of Parliament, she came to Salem after she was widowed and made heavy investments in land. But she disagreed with the church of Salem on the subject of baptism, and as John Endecott said to Winthrop, she was "a dangerous woman." On her way south, Lady Moody stopped at New Haven. There she contributed to the religious unrest of Governor Eaton's wife, who, like herself, was eventually excommunicated.

The Dutch were willing to permit almost any kind of religious dissent and had already given sanctuary to that other vigorous excommunicate, Anne Hutchinson, who lived for a time on Long Island before she moved to the mainland to live on what is now Pelham Bay. It was a source of satisfaction to her enemies in New England that she was near the "place called by seamen and in the map Hell-gate." She was massacred there in the course of a war with the Indians that Governor Kieft had foolishly provoked. Lady Moody in her house on Long Island escaped unharmed, since there were forty men to protect her.

Two years later, in 1645, Lady Moody and her associates founded the town of Gravesend near Coney Island, and the charter they were given by Governor Kieft gave them the right "to erect a body politic and civil combination amongst themselves as freemen of this province." This gave them no rights in connection with the government of New Netherland itself; their authority was purely local. Lady Moody and her associates were entitled to suggest candidates for the town sheriff or *schout* and for the town magistrates.

This seems to have been the only case on record in colonial America in which a woman became a freeman. Lady Moody maintained a very cordial relationship with Governor Kieft and also with his successor, Peter Stuyvesant. It was against Governor Stuyvesant that Adriaen van der Donck addressed his petition in 1649, and Lady Moody and her associates in Gravesend sent a letter to the nineteen Directors in Amsterdam with assurances of loyalty. "For we are as a young tree or little sprout now, for the first time shooting forth to the world, which, if watered and nursed by Your Honors' liberality and attention, may hereafter grow up a blooming republic."

The letter was composed by George Baxter, one of the magistrates of

Gravesend and the owner of a striking literary style. He had been Kieft's English secretary and was retained in that post under Stuyvesant. One of the advantages of Baxter's brand of rhetoric was that it could be turned in the contrary direction if the occasion demanded, and a few years later he turned it.

In December of 1653 a convention gathered on Long Island. It consisted of delegates from four Dutch and four English towns and was called to discuss problems that concerned them all. George Baxter composed the Remonstrance which the eight Long Island towns sent Governor Stuyvesant, listing the privileges which they felt were owing them in return for their allegiance.

The first asked for representative government: "We humbly submit that it is one of our privileges that our consent, or that of our representatives, is necessarily required in the enactment of such laws and orders."

Governor Stuyvesant was furious. He told them that they were wholly unfit for representative government. "Each would vote for one of his own stamp—the thief for a thief." He jeered at the Dutch towns for letting Baxter compose the manifesto. "Is there no one among the Netherlands nation expert enough to draw up a remonstrance . . . that . . . an Englishman is required to dictate what ye have to say?" Stuyvesant was secure in the conviction that he was invulnerable, for "we derive our authority from God and the Company, not from a few ignorant subjects." The Company naturally agreed with him. Its Directors branded the whole thing as "faction and sedition" and voted to send over extra arms and ammunition to bring the men of Gravesend to their senses.

Two years later Gravesend really did commit sedition. Baxter and his associates hoisted the flag of England over their little town in a ceremony which included the reading, three times, of a statement that Baxter had drawn up: "We, individuals of the English nation here present, do, for divers reasons and motives, as free-born British subjects, claim and assume unto ourselves the laws of our nation and republic of England over this place."

Adriaen van der Donck had warned, when he presented his own Remonstrance six years earlier, that unless his recommendations were heeded there would be no need to reform the colony, "for the English will annex it." Men of his kind nevertheless continued their pressure and they finally succeeded in getting a representative assembly in New Netherland. The bankrupt Company needed help in voting taxes and authorized Stuyvesant to call a General Assembly, which met in the City Hall of New Amsterdam in April of 1664. There were Dutch delegates from twelve political units.

It was too late. A month before, Charles II had signed the charter giving the whole area to the Duke of York. Warships had been secretly dispatched by way of Boston, and when they sailed into view in August, George Baxter was on board. So was John Winthrop the Younger, the current Governor of Connecticut, and he was one of the English signers of the Articles of Capitulation. They were drawn up in Stuyvesant's farmhouse in an agreement with the residents of New Amsterdam; Governor Stuyvesant himself refused to sign them.

Not a shot was fired, and after more than half a century of Dutch rule the land passed to the English as quietly as a leaf falling. The terms of surrender were extremely generous, and a population which already consisted of eighteen nationalities found little difference in its way of living except that the oath of allegiance was now to King Charles. In the next decade the province was briefly reconquered by the Dutch and named New Orange. Then the English retook it, and both city and colony settled down to the permanent name of New York.

The Duke of York's charter gave him absolute control over the province, "to correct, punish, pardon, govern and rule," and, like Governor Stuyvesant, James was determined to accept no assistance from the people. He was deeply interested in the territory he had acquired and attended conscientiously to its affairs; but he really believed with the full force of his limited intellect that it was dangerous to give the people any say in the laws by which they were governed. One of his Governors suggested that it would be wise to call a General Assembly, which the people were "desirous of in imitation of their neighbor colonies," and the Duke of York turned the suggestion down firmly—"nothing being more known than the aptness of such bodies to assume to themselves many privileges which prove destructive to, or very oft disturb, the peace of the government wherein they are allowed."

James Stuart had learned nothing from his father's execution and his own long years of exile except that the people must be kept down at all costs. In his opinion, any attempt at compromise was a clear sign of weakness. His older brother, on the other hand, had a very different point of view. Charles II had come back from exile determined to avoid any direct confrontation with Parliament on the subject of its rights, and he ruled as much as possible by indirection and guile, never letting himself be trapped into a direct test of power.

Moreover, the new King had a remarkably easygoing temperament, at least at the beginning of his reign. He startled his ministers by the casual way he granted colonial charters, especially in New England.

On the third of May, 1662, King Charles gave a charter to Connecticut. This was partly through the efforts of John Winthrop the Younger, who was now the annual Governor of Connecticut since the General Court had repealed the law that made it impossible for him to succeed himself. He arrived in England in 1661 with a petition from the Court asking that Connecticut be granted a charter, and the elderly Lord Saye and Sele threw his influence behind it.

The charter gave Connecticut exactly what it wanted. The colony was now a "body corporate and politic . . . by the name of Governor and Company of the English colony of Connecticut." There was the usual corporation setup of a Governor, Deputy Governor and twelve Assistants, and the assembly was to meet twice a year, in May and October, as it did already. It had full power to elect its own officers and make its own laws, and in fact the charter merely gave official authorization to what Connecticut already possessed.

It did more, for it gave Connecticut jurisdiction over the neighboring colony of New Haven. New Haven had lost its one real source of political energy when Theophilus Eaton died five years earlier, and for a time it struggled feebly against being swallowed up by Connecticut. After 1664, the alternative was to be swallowed up by the Duke's province of New York, and a year later New Haven chose the lesser of two evils and joined Connecticut, formally abandoning its religious qualifications for voting.

Next door was Rhode Island, small, tough and contentious. Rhode Island already had a charter but it was a useless one, having been given by Parliament and not by the Crown. Dr. John Clarke was serving the colony as its extremely able agent in England, and a year after Connecticut got its charter, the King granted a similar one to Rhode Island. Coddington, Williams, Gorton and the rest were joined in "a body corporate and politic . . . by the name of The Governor and Company of the English colony of Rhode Island and Providence Plantations," and they were given the same power as Connecticut to rule themselves.

The Rhode Island charter had one extraordinary innovation. Clarke had asked in his petition that the colony be permitted the "lively experiment, that a most flourishing civil state may . . . best be maintained . . . with a full liberty in religious concernments." This wording was incorporated in the charter itself and was not at all popular with the King's ministers. But, as Roger Williams noted exultantly, they could do nothing to prevent its passage. "They crouched against their wills in obedience to His Majesty's pleasure."

In this same year of 1663, King Charles granted yet another colonial charter, but not in New England. This one concerned the vast stretch of land to the south which his father had granted to Sir Robert Heath and which had been named Carolina. The old charter was inoperative because the land had never been settled, and in March of 1663 Charles made a new one. He granted Carolina to eight Proprietors, men who had been of service to him or who were old friends.

Like Heath's charter, the new grant carried the stipulation that the laws were to be made with the "advice, assent and approbation of the freemen of the said province." Two years later, the eight Proprietors amplified and extended this point by issuing the "Concessions and Agreements," which went into greater detail on the subject of a representative assembly. As the ghostly grant to Sir Edmund Plowden had put it thirty years earlier, men were moved to become colonists "by the love of gain and the sweetness of liberty," and since Carolina was dangerously near Spanish Florida it was necessary to make liberal concessions.

It seemed for a time that the long years of political experimentation in both England and America were ended. After a series of false starts and furious local battles, the principle that the people had the right to help make the laws was established in every English colony in America with the single exception of New York. Each colony had its representative assembly, just as England had its House of Commons. Here too the relationship was a peaceful one. The propertied English gentlemen who were elected to the House of Commons had developed a moderately successful working relationship with a monarch who was both agile and affable, and it seemed that the old days of fierce hopes and great changes had faded into nothing more than a half-remembered dream.

What remained was a great deal of paper discussion on the subject of ideal governments. Even in these quieter times the subject exerted a strong fascination, and one of the most influential books was a volume that had been published during Cromwell's Protectorate. This was James Harrington's *Oceana,* a detailed account of the way England might change into a perfect commonwealth, and this lively, literal account of a dream government found its way to the bookshelves of almost every political theorist in England.

Oceana was based on a theory which, in the eyes of Harrington's admirers, ranked with Dr. Harvey's discovery of the circulation of the blood. Most people believed that the late rebellion had been caused either by the mismanagement of the King or by the willfulness of his people, but Harrington detected a more fundamental reason and one which had been operating for more than a century. After the Wars of the Roses the wealth of England, and especially the ownership of land, was no longer concentrated in the hands of the King and the members of the House of Lords; it had begun to flow into the hands of the men who made up the House of Commons. This had caused the late war, which was a struggle for sovereignty, and the war had been won by the side which possessed the most property and therefore the most power.

When Harrington remade England in his imagination and christened it Oceana, he made sure that the land was so widely distributed that no man could be tempted to revolution and he used the same principle in connection with the vote. Like Captain Bargrave, he considered the franchise to be of great importance—"this equal sap from the root" that moved upward through the whole of the government—and, like Bargrave, he withheld the vote from those who had no property.

Harrington divided the people into servants and freemen, and he made a careful distinction between them. "Freemen are such as have wherewithal to live of themselves; and servants, such as have not." He then arranged his freemen on elaborate levels of power according to the amount of property they were allowed to possess. He divided his commonwealth of Oceana into political units such as tribes and parishes, and he even went so far in this creation of a brave new world to calculate the exact cost of ten thousand wooden ballot boxes in ten thousand parishes.

Harrington really believed that his elaborate scheme would work, and he tried hard to get Cromwell to sponsor it. He dedicated the book to the Protector, since he had the power "to set up a government, in the whole piece at once, and in perfection," and he seems to have been really astonished that Cromwell failed to avail himself of the opportunity.

What *Oceana* did succeed in doing was to exert a great deal of influence on the men of the Restoration whose charters gave them the right to govern whatever parts of the American coastline were still untenanted. The illusion of being able to create a perfect government began to shimmer in front of them, and the first to fall victim to this dream were the eight Proprietors of Carolina.

It had been very difficult to persuade colonists to settle in their vast domain, even in spite of the liberal terms of their "Concessions and Agreements," and at the end of the decade they had almost nothing to show for six years of possession. It began to look as if the new Proprietors would fail as Sir Robert Heath had failed before them.

They were fortunate, however, to have as one of their number Anthony Ashley Cooper, who had been created Baron Ashley at the King's coronation and who was shortly to become the Earl of Shaftesbury. Lord Ashley was a specialist in colonial affairs, and he had no intention of letting Carolina go by default. On an April day in 1669 he called his fellow Proprietors together and persuaded them to change their policy. He convinced them that they would have to contribute the money to outfit ships and recruit colonists in England, and he moved with such energy that by the first of August the ships were ready to sail.

Lord Ashley was a brilliant politician, perhaps the greatest of his day, and he was fascinated by theories of government. He set himself to draft an ideal constitution for Carolina, and he had the assistance of an even more brilliant individual who was living in his household: John Locke.

Locke had intended to be a doctor but he could not narrow his attention into the formal work that was necessary to get a degree. While he was in Oxford he met Lord Ashley, and the two men took to each other immediately. The following spring Locke moved into Ashley's town house in the Strand, where a room was fitted out for his use. There were shelves for his books and equipment for his chemical experiments, and under so brilliant and versatile a patron even Locke found enough to do.

The year of 1668 was typical of the variety of Locke's activities. He superintended the operation that saved Lord Ashley from a nearly fatal illness. He was elected a Fellow of the Royal Society. He opened the negotiations which ended in the marriage of Ashley's only son to a highly suitable heiress. He wrote a book on economics, his patron having just been made Chancellor of the Exchequer. He collaborated with the distinguished physician Dr. Sydenham on a book which was intended to be a review of the whole subject of medical therapy. And in this year also he became the secretary of the eight Proprietors of Carolina.

As soon as Lord Ashley's plan had been approved at the April meeting in 1669, he and Locke set out to draft a constitution for the colony. The final draft was of course in Locke's handwriting, as secretary, but much of the act of creation seems to have been his also. Sir Peter Colleton, who was a brother of one of the eight Proprietors, wrote Locke to praise "that excellent form of government in the composure of which you had so great a hand." It was dated the 21st of July, named the Fundamental Constitutions, and was intended to be "the sacred and unalterable form and rule of government of Carolina forever."

The Fundamental Constitutions are reminiscent of Captain Bargrave's ideal constitution for Virginia, possibly because both documents are dominated by the same purpose. Bargrave had tried to set up a government which would, as he said, "suppress popular liberty," and he did it by dividing the colonists into rigid compartments based on the amount of money each possessed. The Carolina constitution had for its purpose, as stated in the preamble, to "avoid erecting a numerous democracy," and this was to be achieved by dividing the colonists into equally rigid compartments based on the amount of land they owned.

The doctrine behind this division of land came from Harrington, who had proved that land was power. Ashley and Locke set up a hereditary nobility which would not be permitted to sell its land to the people. As Harrington said, England had stood firm "until the Statute of Alienations broke the pillars, by giving way to the nobility to sell their estates."

There was to be no breaking of the pillars in Carolina, and the whole intricate structure was intended to be as permanent as stone. At the top of the pyramid were the eight Proprietors, with a voice in every parliament. Just below them were the nobility, with their titles taken from German and Indian rulers. There was to be one landgrave and two caciques in each county, and two-fifths of all the land in Carolina would be held by these upper orders in perpetuity. Below them came the freeholders, who could send one delegate to parliament from each precinct, and only a freeholder who possessed at least fifty acres of land would be allowed to vote. The final page of the document was devoted to the important subject of social procedure. Eleven "rules of precedency" explained everyone's exact social standing and decreed that a landgrave came just beneath the younger son of a Proprietor.*

The constitution was greatly admired in England, where it was hailed as "the noble government which deep wisdom had projected for Carolina." It had a much less successful reception in the colony itself, and the Proprietors were forced to make concession after concession, each one increasing the political power of the freeholders. By the end of the century, the delegates of the people had won the right to initiate legislation and to meet separately as the Commons House of Assembly, in all things "imitating the House of Commons in England as nigh as possible." The hopeful model for a perfect society was in fact never ratified, and it was a deep disappointment to the Proprietors that the Assembly had "so disrespectfully refused our excellent Constitutions."

Two of the eight Proprietors of Carolina had an equally unsatisfactory experience elsewhere, for they were the joint owners of a colony to the north that was named New Jersey.

These two proprietors—Lord Berkeley and Sir George Carteret—were

---

* Locke himself was created a landgrave in 1671 but he never went to America. At this point in his infinitely varied career he was caring for Lord Ashley's infant grandson, the product of the marriage he had so successfully negotiated. The baby was left in his charge in 1671 while the family was away for the summer, and it was in this year that Locke began work on his masterpiece, the *Essay Concerning Human Understanding*.

both close friends of the Duke of York and had formed the major part of the subcommittee of the Council for Foreign Plantations which had advocated the conquest of New Netherland. Even before the English ships arrived at New Amsterdam, the Duke of York had deeded part of his new possessions to his two friends, and the grant was named in honor of the island of Jersey from which the Carterets came.

Both men had fought valiantly for the King in the late war. The island of Jersey, which Sir George Carteret defended, was the last stronghold to surrender to Parliament. Lord Berkeley had tried to defend the city of Exeter, and the poet Robert Herrick hailed his conduct on that occasion as "just and itchless." In the years of exile that followed, Berkeley had been very close to the Duke of York, and when James became head of the navy after the Restoration he made Berkeley one of the three commissioners on the Navy Board. Carteret became treasurer of the Board, and James saw a great deal of them both. He gave them New Jersey in June of 1664, and in spite of various pressures he never took it back. James was a narrow man and in many ways a stupid one, but he could not be accused of faithlessness to his friends.

The following February, Berkeley and Carteret issued a document called "Concessions and Agreements" which was designed to attract a flood of colonists to the area. It had the same name as the document that they and their fellow Proprietors in Carolina had issued six weeks earlier, and the text was the same also. It was widely distributed throughout New England and attracted some colonists who joined the Dutch settlers that were already there. In 1668 a General Assembly was held at Elizabeth Town, which had been named in honor of Lady Carteret, but the hopeful vision of the two Proprietors that New Jersey would soon be filled with "cities, towns, villages, boroughs or other hamlets" failed to materialize.

On the 18th of March, 1674, Lord Berkeley gave up his rights in New Jersey, selling them to a friend of his, Edward Byllynge, for a thousand pounds. In so doing he profoundly influenced the future development of the colony, for Byllynge was a Quaker.

The Quakers currently occupied the position in England that had been endured earlier by the Brownists, and every effort was made by other Christians to torment them out of existence. No Quaker was executed in England, but over four hundred of them died in the prisons into which they were herded during recurrent bouts of persecution.

In New England, Quakers were hanged, and when the General Court of Massachusetts Bay executed Mary Dyer it likened itself to the head of a family trying to keep out a carrier of plague. "The father of the family . . .

may withstand the intrusion of such infected and dangerous persons, and if otherwise he cannot keep them out may kill them." John Endecott was Governor that year, and when Charles II inquired into the reason for the series of hangings, Endecott offered a slightly different explanation. "The Quakers died not because of their other crimes . . . but upon their . . . incorrigible contempt of authority. . . . They would not be restrained but by death." Roger Williams achieved what was perhaps the greatest moral victory in the whole of his long life when he clung to his doctrine of religious liberty in a time of fear. He refused to expel the Quakers from Providence, although he believed, as he told them, that they acted under "the spirit and power of Satan."

George Fox, the founder of the Society of Friends, made a tour of the colonies early in the 1670's and on his way north from Maryland he was very much impressed by the "wilderness country . . . and wild woods" he passed through in New Jersey. With so much land lying empty, and with so many Quakers in England dying in prison or subjected to ruinous fines, the obvious solution was a mass migration to New Jersey, and this became feasible as soon as the Quaker, Edward Byllynge, bought Lord Berkeley's rights for a thousand pounds.

Since Byllynge was bankrupt at the time, the money was advanced to him by another English Quaker, John Fenwick. The two men quarreled and the question of who owned the rights became so confused that responsibility was finally assumed by three trustees, also Quakers, who were chosen for the purpose. The three trustees pacified Fenwick with an outright grant of a tenth of the land and then set up a joint-stock company to sell the rest, with first refusal going to Quakers. Before any of this could be achieved, the trustees first had to persuade Sir George Carteret to agree to a diagonal line running across New Jersey, so that he retained full rights to East Jersey and the Quakers controlled the West.

This complicated task was achieved with "no little labor, trouble and cost," and it was only achieved at all because one of the three trustees was William Penn.

Penn was now in his thirties, and in an abnormally influential position for a Quaker. This was chiefly because his father, Sir William Penn, had been one of England's most distinguished admirals and also a very close personal friend both of King Charles and of his brother James. Admiral Penn was knighted at the Restoration and made a commissioner on the Navy Board, so that he and the Duke of York saw a great deal of each other.

When Charles rode through London in his coronation procession on an

April day in 1661, Sir William Penn and his colleagues in the Naval Office had comfortable seats upstairs in a flagmaker's shop near the triumphal arch that had been dedicated to the navy. Sir William's son was at Oxford University, but the Admiral brought him down to London for so special an occasion, and this was probably the first time that young William Penn saw the royal brothers. Samuel Pepys was there too, for he was also a member of the Navy Board, and a brilliant one. Pepys was wearing a new velvet coat and greatly enjoying the wine and cakes, and he remarked with satisfaction that "both the King and the Duke of York took notice of us" as they rode by below in the glitter and the gold.

Two years later William Penn was expelled from Oxford for religious radicalism, and his troubled father sent him off to France. When he came back, very much the fashionable young gentleman in pantaloon breeches, he showed great ability in helping to administer his father's large estates in Ireland. It was there that he became a Quaker, and he endured repeated imprisonments for the sake of his faith.

When Sir William Penn lay dying, he sent an urgent message to his two friends, King Charles and the Duke of York, asking them to watch over his son and not to let his prison record be held against him. Some years later, Penn returned to court in an effort to get George Fox out of prison, and when the Duke of York heard that he was in the crowded antechamber he came out immediately. James had not seen his friend's son for eight years, but, as Penn wrote gratefully, "he was pleased to take a very particular notice of me, both for the relation my father had had to his service in the navy, and the care he had promised him to show in my regard upon all occasions." The Duke agreed at once to Penn's request and asked his brother that George Fox be released.*

When Penn entered the New Jersey tangle as a trustee, he succeeded in doing what no other Quaker could have done. It was through the Duke of York that Sir George Carteret was persuaded to sign the deed in which he relinquished all his rights to West Jersey. English Quakers, mostly small businessmen, bought up the shares, usually investing in a seventh for fifty pounds, and the wilderness that George Fox had once traveled began to fill slowly with their homes.

To govern these people, an extraordinary document was drawn up in

---

* The Duke of York himself belonged to a religious minority, for six years earlier he had become a Roman Catholic. He told Penn that in his younger days he had approved of religious persecution, but since then "he had seen and considered things better, and he was for doing to others as he would have others do unto him."

London and called the "Concessions and Agreements of West Jersey." Posterity gave Penn the credit for writing it, but a contemporary said that it was of Byllynge's "preparing." This would account for the radical nature of the document, for Byllynge had seen service under General Monk in Scotland and was one of the many revolutionists who had dreamed of turning England into a perfect commonwealth. Just before the Restoration, Byllynge had published a pamphlet which owed a great deal to the old Leveler doctrines and which listed thirty-one reforms that would provide a new constitution for England.

The "Concessions and Agreements of West Jersey" turned the control of the government over to the people, and an eloquent letter signed by Penn and Byllynge and their colleagues explained why this was being done. "We lay a foundation for after ages to understand their liberty as men and Christians, that they may not be brought in bondage but by their own consent; for we put the power in the people, that is to say, they to meet and choose one honest man for each propriety, who hath subscribed to the Concessions; all these men to meet in an assembly there, to make and repeal laws, to choose a governor or a commissioner and twelve assistants to execute the laws during their pleasure; so every man is capable to choose or be chosen."

It was an impressive experiment—too impressive, in fact, to work. A few years later Byllynge betrayed it and tried to impose himself on the population as their Governor. There was a fierce battle for control, and the London Quakers tried to settle the matter through arbitration. The majority of the arbitrators, including George Fox himself, decided in favor of Byllynge, and it was hoped that this majority decision would "extinguish all feuds, animosities, prejudices, heartburnings, passions, strife and divisions." It did not. Not even the Quakers could found a colony quietly in America.

East Jersey, on the other side of the diagonal line, remained in the possession of Sir George Carteret until he died. This was in 1680, and since he was bankrupt, the property was sold at auction. Twelve men bought it, eleven of them Quakers and again including William Penn. By this time, however, Penn was deeply involved with a huge colonization project of his own and could not give his full attention to the management of this new piece of land. Some Quakers in Scotland showed interest, and in 1683 the Duke of York signed yet another patent for the area, adding twelve more Proprietors to the original twelve. Half of them were Scottish and again most of them were Quakers.

Apart from Penn, the most distinguished man among the twenty-four Proprietors of East Jersey was Robert Barclay, a Quaker of Scotland. He was a fine scholar, a gentleman and, like Penn, a friend of the Duke of York. Barclay took formal charge of the East Jersey colonization, and, as the promotion material pointed out, so aristocratic an individual would never "be guilty of anything that is base or unbecoming a gentleman."

East Jersey already had a General Assembly, the one that had met in the early days at Elizabeth Town. The twenty-four Proprietors dreamed, however, of a much finer and more elegant form of government and designed one for the occasion. Like the elaborate and ill-fated model that had been drawn up to govern Carolina, it was named the "Fundamental Constitutions" and it too was a child of *Oceana.*

Political power was tied tightly to the ownership of land, and the rights of the twenty-four Proprietors were to be contingent on the amount of property they held. "Lest any should squander away their interest, and yet retain the character of the government that belongs to property, and thence be capable to betray it as not being bound by interest, there must be a suitable quantity retained; otherwise the title in the government extinguishes in him and passes to another, to be elected by the Proprietors, that dominion may follow property and the inconveniency of a beggarly nobility and gentry may be avoided."

Like the Proprietors of Carolina, the Proprietors of East Jersey believed proudly that their frame of government would remain in force forever. But it met the same ignominious fate as the one in Carolina, for the Assembly refused to accept it. It began to seem impossible that any of these theoretical constitutions could ever take root on American soil.

The one man who was sure it could be done was William Penn. He had been given a huge grant of land stretching from New York to Maryland and covering the whole area west of the Jerseys, and he set to work at once to design a frame of government that would be worthy of it.

The land was named Pennsylvania in honor of his father, and ostensibly it was in payment of a debt that the Crown owed Admiral Penn for his services. In fact, it was a mark of the love the two Stuarts bore his son. The Duke of York not only ceded his own rights to the area but the following year, over the protests of his agent, he added a piece of land south of the Jerseys so that Penn could have direct access to the ocean. This land on Delaware Bay was the only part of Penn's property that had any population to speak of, having first been settled by a Swedish development company and then captured by the Dutch. The Duke of York transferred it to Penn by a feudal grant, and part of the payment was "one rose at the feast of St. Michael the Archangel yearly, if demanded."

The charter for Pennsylvania passed the Great Seal on Saturday, the fourth of March, 1681, and it gave William Penn rights which were almost as absolute as those which had been granted Lord Baltimore of Maryland. As Penn said exultantly, "after many waitings, watchings, solicitings and disputes in Council, this day my country was confirmed to me under the great seal of England, with large powers and privileges, by the name of Pennsylvania . . . in honor of my father. . . . I shall have a tender care to the government, that it be well laid." Early in April he wrote to the scattering of inhabitants, "You shall be governed by laws of your own making," and he set himself to work out an ideal government for them.

Since Penn was a member of a bitterly persecuted minority, he had given a great deal of thought to the subject of the abuse of power. He had faced unjust imprisonment in Newgate and had defended himself with a lawyer's skill and an Englishman's passionate sense of his rights, and he was fully aware of the opportunity that presented itself in Pennsylvania. "As my understanding and inclination have been much directed to observe and reprove mischiefs in government, so it is now put into my power to settle one." Moreover, it was his special ambition to achieve what he called a holy experiment, the founding of a place of refuge where men of all religions, and not Quakers only, could live together in peace.

If ardor, idealism, intelligence and wide reading could have assured a perfect form of government, Penn would have achieved it in Pennsylvania, and to all these he added the willingness to accept a great deal of advice. His papers contain a whole series of drafts of his own and other men's suggestions, the latter carefully annotated by him.

One of those he turned to for advice was Algernon Sidney, a close friend who was famous for his anti-monarchial views. When Sidney tried to win a seat in the House of Commons during the bitter elections of 1679, Penn campaigned for him in a pamphlet called "England's Great Interest in the Choice of This New Parliament; Dedicated to All Her Freeholders and Electors." Penn gave twelve suggestions on how to cast a vote wisely. If these had been followed they would have brought men like Sidney into Parliament, and in fact he lost by a very close margin. Penn was deeply interested in Sidney's views, and in a meeting at Penn's house the two men had "a considerable argument" over the exact form of government that should be created for Pennsylvania.

Benjamin Furly was another friend of Penn's whose opinion he valued. Furly was an English Quaker who had moved abroad to extend the family business and who was now living in a fine house in Rotterdam. There he conducted his flourishing shipping business, built up a superb library, wrote controversial books and found time to serve as Penn's agent in Europe to promote the colonization of Pennsylvania. This promotion was done very thoroughly, and more than fifty books and pamphlets circulated in English, French, Dutch and German to proclaim the glories of living in Pennsylvania.

Benjamin Furly was an idealist. He dreamed of a Pennsylvania that would really be a new land, with all the injustices of the Old World at last removed, and he even advocated the establishment of an income tax there so that the helpless could be protected. He wanted "a certain part of every man's gain . . . brought into a common treasury" to be used for the education of children, the care of the sick, and the housing of orphans and the elderly.

Penn sent Furly a preliminary draft of government which he had worked out and called "The Fundamental Constitutions of Pennsylvania." There was a space at the end for the colonists to sign, and a preamble which expressed Penn's conviction that the chief end of government was "the virtue, peace and prosperity of the people." Penn divided his proposed government into twenty-four articles, and while he took several of his devices from *Oceana,* such as the voting division into tribes, he was much more idealistic than Harrington would have considered safe.

The heart of the document was Article Three. This accepted wholeheartedly the principle of representative government, for which all the colonies had labored and which by now had been achieved everywhere except in New York. "Since it hath been the judgment of the wisest men, and practice of the most famous governments in all ages, as well as that it is the most natural, reasonable and prudent in itself, that the people of any country should be consenting to the laws they are to be governed by, therefore I do . . . hereby declare . . . that there shall be held once every year . . . an Assembly . . . duly chosen by the freeholders of this country to serve as their deputies to consult, debate and resolve and in their names to consent to the enacting or abolishing of laws *and whatever is the privilege of an English House of Commons."* This last must have seemed very important to Penn, for he underlined it.

After he had sent this draft to Furly, Penn changed his mind about the government of Pennsylvania. His anxious paternalism and the practical problems involved in settlement began to get the better of him, and he finally decided that he had been trusting the people more than he should. It might be wiser and safer to give the power of making the laws to the Governor and his Council. The Council could be elective, so that the people would feel they were participating in the government, but the people's delegates in the Assembly would have no legislative power except to give "assent and approbation" to the laws that the Governor and Council had decided upon. This Assembly would not be the miniature House of Commons that Penn had formerly envisioned. It would instead be an obedient shadow, assenting to the plans of its betters.

It was this form of government that Penn finally decided to use, and he published the text in London in 1682 as the "Frame of Government of Pennsylvania." In a long and somewhat defensive preamble, Penn pointed out that it was very difficult to frame a perfect government, "there being nothing the wits of men are more busy and divided upon," but that any form of government would work if the people themselves were virtuous. To assist them to be virtuous, a series of laws were appended which had been agreed to in England and which echoed the noblest Quaker idealism. They also echoed the Quaker mistrust of Restoration excesses, and there were to be no "stage plays, cards, dice, May-games, gamesters, masques, revels, bull-baitings, cock-fightings, bear-baitings and the like" permitted in Pennsylvania.

When Benjamin Furly read this final draft of Penn's government he was deeply disappointed. "I far prefer thy first draft to this last. . . . Indeed, I wonder who should put thee upon altering them for these, and as much how thou couldst ever yield to such a thing." Especially troubling was the destruction of the article which, as Furly said, had given the Assembly "the power of making and abolishing all laws, and whatsoever is the privilege of an English House of Commons." Penn's new plan for the Assembly was, in Furly's opinion, "a divesting of the people's representatives . . . of the greatest right they have," and he was convinced that the new arrangement was unworkable. "For the people of England can never . . . be dispossessed of that natural right of propounding laws to be made by their representatives."

Penn, for his part, was very proud of what he considered the correct balancing of political power in Pennsylvania. In his eyes, it was "the very root of the constitution" that the Assembly should be "not a debating, mending, altering, but an accepting power."

Penn had also given a great deal of thought to the capital city of his province, which he named Philadelphia, the City of Brotherly Love. His colonists must be successful businessmen if the city were to prosper, and he avoided the mistake that had been made by the people of New Haven when they set up a grid pattern that had no relation to the harbor. Penn knew the shipping would be crucially important, and his surveyor locked the grid design into the water frontage. The Delaware River, which separated Penn's land from the Jerseys, was navigable for oceangoing vessels, and Penn located his city at the point where that "glorious river" met the Schuylkill.

Penn's surveyor laid the city out on a magnificent scale. High Street ran the full length between the two rivers, with Broad Street intersecting it at the central square, and both of them were wider than any street in London—a hundred feet each. The others, Chestnut, Walnut, Cranberry and the rest, were fifty feet wide, and town lots were distributed with great astuteness. By 1685 the handsome brick houses of the Quaker merchants had begun to spring up along the broad thoroughfares, and Penn rejoiced that there were now more than eight thousand inhabitants in his colony. Penn was equally delighted with the local Indians, whom he treated with his usual courtesy. "They have some great men amongst them, I mean for wisdom, truth and justice."

It was only in his political planning that William Penn abandoned his usual combination of idealism, optimism and commonsense and clung too closely to what seemed to him safety. He had restricted the powers of the Assembly because of his fear of pressure from the people, and Benjamin Furly had warned him that he was laying "a certain foundation for dissension amongst our successors."

There was no need, however, to wait for successors. The dissension occurred immediately, and the rest of Penn's life was darkened by his futile efforts to keep the Assembly in its place.

Penn made his first visit to his people in 1682 and everything seemed to be very peaceful. He was able to report the following year that two Assemblies had been held, both with "concord and dispatch." The second of these approved a revised Frame of Government after several weeks of arguing, and it was engrossed on parchment in April of 1683 as the law of the land. The Assembly had failed to get any official extension of its powers, but outwardly it had already begun to model itself on the House of Commons. It achieved a Speaker immediately, although Penn had not intended this to happen, and within the year it was also appointing its own Clerk.

At the end of the decade the House of Stuart lost its power in England, and Penn lost his province. It was taken over briefly by the Crown and during this period the Assembly pushed vigorously and successfully for more political control. The province was returned to Penn in 1694, but when a Governor of his choosing arrived in Pennsylvania, the Assembly refused to vote any supplies until their recent gains in power were incorporated in a new constitution. Governor Markham was obliged to agree to one, and it strengthened the political power of the Assembly at the expense of the Council.

The suffrage law was changed at the same time, so as to strengthen the control of the gentry and of the merchant class. It was clear by now that

Philadelphia was going to be one of the most prosperous cities in the American colonies, and the men of property wanted to make sure that political power stayed in the right hands. The original requirement for voting in the city was the payment of scot and lot, which was a local tax on householders. The new arrangement was that the voter in Philadelphia must own property worth fifty pounds.

William Penn paid another visit to his province in 1699 and tried hard to check the growing power of the Assembly. He was still clinging to his theory that Pennsylvania was ruled by the Governor and the Council, and that the Assembly was only a consenting power. His chief opponent was David Lloyd, whom he had sent out in 1686 to be his Attorney General. In the London office of Penn's lawyers, Lloyd had merely been one capable man among many. In America, he became an ardent Quaker and an even more ardent champion of the political rights of the Assembly.

In 1701, Penn capitulated. He abandoned all the hopeful devices he had borrowed from Harrington and all his theories about the power of the Council. He signed the Charter of Privileges, and with it the Council ceased to exist as a political power. The lower house took its place and was given all the "powers and privileges of an Assembly, according to the rights of the freeborn subjects of England and as is usual in any of the king's plantations in America." This was what Penn himself had first intended and then decided not to bestow. It was now the law of the land, for, as Benjamin Furly had told him, the people would not be content with anything less.

The Assembly hailed the new constitution as a charter of freedom and it remained an object of pride and delight to its members. Fifty years later they decided to commemorate the anniversary of their victory and commissioned a great bell to be hung in the new State House, the largest public building in the colonies. It was cast in London and its motto came from the Book of Leviticus: "Ye shall hallow the fiftieth year and proclaim liberty throughout all the land unto all the inhabitants thereof."

Penn did not buy peace by signing the Charter of Privileges. The men of the Assembly now turned their attention to the powers of the Governor, and a few years later Penn was writing, almost incredulously, of "those three preposterous bills, foolishly as well as insolently presented him by David Lloyd, the last Assembly." Penn did not want to punish his people but only to guide them. "As a father does not use to knock his children on the head when they do amiss, so I had much rather they were corrected and better instructed than treated to the rigor of their deservings." They did not seem to understand "the just order and decency of government and that they are not to command but to be commanded according to law and constitution of English government."

The steady encroachment on the power of the Governor forced Penn's secretary, James Logan, to warn in 1709 that if such behavior continued unchecked it would make Pennsylvania "decline into a state very little, if at all, distant from a democracy." He did not accuse the Assembly of having any such intentions, but "to such as value and would support an English constitution, all appearances that tend to its subversion beget a real uneasiness; such know that the people alone must not be vested with the sole . . . power in legislation here."

In 1710 Penn wrote a general letter from England to his old friends in Pennsylvania, reminding them how hard he had worked to draft a perfect constitution for his beloved province: "Before any one family had transported themselves thither, I earnestly endeavored to form such a model of government as might make all concerned in it easy." Since then he had permitted changes but he had always striven to maintain a "due proportion of the parts," and it was this that the Assembly seemed determined to destroy. "Seeing the frame of government ought to be . . . well proportioned . . . nothing could be more destructive to it than to take so much of the provision and executive part of the government out of the Governor's hands and lodge it in an uncertain collective body. . . . I cannot think it prudent in the people to crave these powers."

What Penn called "an uncertain collective body" was, in the eyes of men like David Lloyd, the cornerstone of the rights of Pennsylvania. The Assembly did not represent the whole of the people, any more than the House of Commons represented all the men in England, but it was based on the principle of representative government. It was this that Furly had called a natural right and that George Baxter of the Long Island town of Gravesend had called "the law of Nature." Against this stubborn and fundamental conviction nothing could make any headway in the English colonies, neither the paternalism of William Penn nor the autocracy of the Duke of York.

The Duke had given in to this pressure in 1683, only a short time after Pennsylvania was founded. The colonists of New York said that it was a "right belonging to every freeborn Englishman that there be a General Assembly called once a year," and finally James capitulated. He still believed, like former Governor Stuyvesant, that such a concession was a threat to the peace and order of government, but, like Stuyvesant, he needed help with the taxes.

There was now an unbroken line of these representative assemblies along the eastern coast of North America, each one brought into existence by a determination that was characteristically English. There was nothing like it in the colonial areas where the Spanish ruled, or in the huge stretches of land now under the control of the French. Here there was no question of who should vote, for there was no one to vote for. Instructions came from overseas, and the function of the local residents was to be obedient.

It was only the colonial English who refused, persistently and whole-heartedly, to live under a government in which they had no share and who forced into existence a series of representative assemblies. Each colony traveled by a different route but each one ended with the same achievement, and the result was a phenomenon which astounded the other colonizing powers. As a French-Canadian writer said in the middle of the following century, "No nation but the English is capable of such *bizarreries*—which, nevertheless, are a part of the precious liberty of which they show themselves so jealous."

Chapter Seven

The General Assembly of New York enacted the Charter of Liberties on the 30th of October, 1683, marking the sixty-fourth year that these little parliaments had been meeting in America. The first one had met in the summer of 1619 at Jamestown, and it was still meeting there.

By now, however, Virginia had settled into a much more conservative pattern of government. There was no longer any need for men like Captain Bargrave to worry about what he called "the mouth of equal liberty," for little by little the threat of this had disappeared.

When the first assembly met at Jamestown, it decided that "every man and manservant of above sixteen years of age" was to be taxed to pay for the salaries of its officials. This apparently meant that all such colonists had been permitted to vote, and the practice was definitely continued of giving the vote to menservants. The assembly decided in 1646 to levy a fine on voters who failed to put in an appearance on election day, and it specifically exempted voters if they were servants. "What freeman soever, having lawful summons of the time and place for election of Burgesses, that shall not make repair accordingly, such person or persons, unless there be lawful cause for the absenting himself, shall forfeit one hundred pounds of tobacco for his non-appearance, freemen being convenant servants being exempted from the said fine."

It was an astonishing gesture to permit servants to vote. Even the

Levelers, battling for a wider franchise in England, had been reluctant to push their reforms as far as that. As William Petty, who was one of the Levelers in the debate at Putney, explained: "I conceive the reason why we would exclude apprentices or servants . . . is because they depend upon the will of other men and should be afraid to displease."

The Assembly that met in Jamestown in 1646 saw no risk in continuing to let servants have the vote, and it also passed a very just and farsighted treaty with the Indians. It was presided over by Sir William Berkeley, who had once been a young courtier and playwright in London.* He had been Governor of Virginia for five years now, and his liberal and enlightened policies had made him enormously popular. After the revolution in England ended with the death of King Charles, Berkeley refused to recognize the new government. He told the men of the Assembly in 1651, "Do but follow me, I will either lead you to victory or lose a life which I cannot more gloriously sacrifice." The following year, however, he was forced to surrender to Parliament and left America, taking his Council with him.

For the remainder of the decade there was neither Governor nor Council in Virginia, and the House of Burgesses governed alone. They were men of property and wanted to consolidate their power, and in 1654 they passed an Act which sharply narrowed the franchise. It took the vote away not only from servants but also from former servants who were now free.

The Act of 1654 was very unpopular, and two years later the Assembly adjusted it. "We conceive it something hard and unagreeable to reason that any persons shall pay equal taxes and yet have no votes in elections. Therefore it is enacted by this present Grand Assembly that so much of the Act for choosing Burgesses be repealed as excludes freemen from votes." The vote was given back to those who had served their time and were now freemen, but men who were still servants remained excluded.

In the year of the Restoration, Sir William Berkeley returned as Governor of Virginia, still ardently concerned with the welfare of the country, but seeing it from the point of view of a man grown older, more rigid and more cautious. He was no longer the liberal young man who had presided over the Assembly of 1646, and order had become very important to him. The House of Burgesses, which was composed of equally conservative men of property, agreed with him, and Berkeley kept it in power by the simple expedient of not calling any elections.

---

* A play of his called *The Lost Lady* was revived after the Restoration, and Pepys did not like it. His judgment may have been affected by the fact that he had unwisely chosen to sit in the cheaper section and was seen by "four of our office clerks which sat in the half-crown box."

It was this Assembly which, in 1670, again disfranchised the freemen, and the wording of the Act echoes very closely the famous disfranchising Act which had been passed by Parliament in 1430, limiting the vote in England to the forty-shilling freeholders. This Act had maintained that "manslaughters, riots, batteries and divisions" were certain to ensue if "people of small substance, or of no value" were allowed to vote, and the Virginia Assembly of 1670 used the same argument. "Whereas the usual way of choosing Burgesses [is] by the votes of all persons who having served their time are freemen of this country, who having little interest in the country do often make tumults at the election . . . and whereas the laws of England grant a voice in such election only to such as by their estates real or personal have interest enough to tie them to the endeavor of the public good, it is hereby enacted that none but freeholders and housekeepers . . . shall hereafter have a voice in the election of any Burgesses in this country."

The Act was passed at a time when political unrest was increasing in Virginia. The government clung to an illusion, common to many governments, that if the discontent remained voiceless it would somehow cease to be discontent. The government was mistaken.

The trouble in Virginia had its roots back in the days when the colonists discovered a quick cash crop in tobacco and decided to lavish all their attention on a single commodity. Sir Edwin Sandys had struggled in vain against "the inordinate, excessive planting of tobacco," and Governor Berkeley was instructed by King Charles II to put "some restraint upon the planting of tobacco." This concentration upon a single crop not only made the economy vulnerable to bad weather or a shift in prices but it also kept the colonists sprawled out over large tracts of soon-exhausted land. In Virginia, the Indians lived thriftily and compactly in towns that sometimes included as many as five hundred families, while the English spread themselves thinly and greedily over more and more land. The 1670's were a time of bad weather, falling prices, heavy taxes and increased hatred of the Indians by the colonists. Berkeley himself said he was trying to govern a country where "six parts of seven at least are poor, indebted, discontented and armed."

In the summer of 1674, Berkeley welcomed the arrival of a young relative by marriage. Nathaniel Bacon was the son of a rich Suffolk squire, and he had been sent out to Virginia with £1800 and the hope he would settle down. Berkeley soon appointed him to the group of prominent men who made up the Council, for, as he told Bacon quite truly, "Gentlemen of your quality come very rarely into this country."

Nathaniel Bacon does not seem to have been very interested in government, since he attended only three meetings of the Council. What interested him was the tobacco plantation he had bought in Henrico County, some fifty miles upriver from Jamestown, and he was furious to discover what a privileged position the Indians occupied in Virginia. Those who disliked Governor Berkeley were convinced that he protected the Indians so that he could become rich by trading with them, and Bacon decided that these "protected and darling Indians" had no right to "the benefit and protection of the law."

Governor Berkeley refused to authorize an expedition against the Indians, and Bacon decided to go without authorization. He headed a wildly popular expedition which succeeded in slaughtering all the inhabitants of an unsuspecting Indian town, and Bacon's neighbors, eagerly believing every rumor, hailed him as a savior. "There were said to be above two hundred of the English murdered by the barbarous Indians . . . and yet no course was taken to secure them till Mr. Bacon went out against them."

Virginia had found its hero, and Governor Berkeley could not withstand the sudden surge of popular excitement. He was forced to call an election, something he had not done for fourteen years, and he did not try to invoke the disfranchising Act of 1670. As a result, not only was Bacon elected unanimously to be one of the two Burgesses from his county, but the whole House was taken over by the reform party. "At this new election (such was the prevalency of Bacon's party) that they chose instead of freeholders, free men that had but lately crept out of the condition of servants."

Berkeley told the people to present a list of grievances with their new representatives; "and supposing I, who am head of the Assembly, may be their greatest grievance, I will most gladly join with them in a petition to his most sacred Majesty to appoint a new Governor of Virginia."

The Assembly accepted this bid for peace, and there seems to have been a real effort to achieve a workable compromise. The first Act which was passed was a declaration of war against the Indians, with Bacon as Commander in Chief, but it was made very clear that this did not apply to all Indians, since "we ought not to involve the innocent with the guilty." The fourth Act prohibited "unlawful assemblies and rebellion," but a general pardon was issued for all previous misbehavior, while Act Seven widened the franchise. "Be it enacted . . . that the Act . . . which forbids freemen to have votes in the election of Burgesses be repealed, and that they may be admitted together with the freeholders and householders to vote as formerly in such elections." All these Acts were signed into law on the 25th of June, 1676, by Sir William Berkeley as Governor and Thomas Godwin as Speaker of the House.

Contemporaries called it Bacon's Assembly, although he seems to have had little interest in social reform and none in compromise. Yet he was the one who had pulled the cork out of the bottle, and he was "the darling of the people's hopes and desires." Inevitably he became the symbol of the Assembly's desire for social reform, although, as Bacon himself pointed out, he was not an advocate of "leveling" and all he had ever wanted was to protect Virginia from the Indians. "We find them all alike, neither can we distinguish this fatal undistinguishable distinction of the Governor, who only for the gain sake has so bridled all the people that no man dare to destroy the Indians . . . until I adventured to cut the knot, which made the people in general look upon me as the country's friend."

Armed with his commission as Commander in Chief, Bacon went off to fight the Indians. He and his friends were now so completely in control that Berkeley said bitterly at the beginning of the following month, "Three young men that have not been two years in the country absolutely govern it: Mr. Bacon, Mr. Bland and Mr. Ingram." When Berkeley tried to raise a militia against them, it refused to march.

Bacon, in his turn, issued a Declaration in the name of the people in which he gave the Governor four days to surrender or be branded a traitor. Both men, already hot-tempered, were by now almost crazed with fury, and the violence of the warfare increased. In September Bacon burned Jamestown so that it could not be used as a fort. The church and the state house went up in flames, and one of Bacon's followers, who had a large house there, set it on fire himself "with all its wealth and a fair cupboard of plate."

The war ended as suddenly as it had begun. Bacon died the following month of dysentery and the rebellion petered out, leaving Berkeley in a murderous rage. He dealt out so many death sentences that Charles II was said to have remarked that "the old fool has hanged more men in that naked country than he had done for the murder of his father."

In the official records, Bacon took his place beside Cromwell as an enemy of all lawful government. Unofficially he became an increasingly romantic figure, with his youth, his good looks and his early death. The English playwright, Aphra Behn, who was seven years older than he was, wrote a play in which Bacon was everything that a hero should be. She even supplied him with an Indian queen to adore, since "no hero ought to be without his princess." Bacon expires onstage after announcing that she was the "dear prize for which alone I toiled"—an ironic finale for a play about a man who hated all Indians with so impartial a fury.

The next Assembly in Virginia could not meet at Jamestown since the capital was in ashes. It met instead at the Governor's nearby plantation of

Green Spring and started picking up the pieces. The laws of the previous Assembly were repealed, and then most of them were promptly reenacted. The Act which was not reenacted was the seventh, the one that had widened the franchise.

When King Charles sent instructions to Berkeley on how to deal with the rebellion, he recommended that future assemblies in Virginia be "elected only be freeholders, as being more agreeable to the custom of England." The Assembly did not dare to be quite so extreme, and it did not want to take the vote away from householders. It went back instead to the Act of 1670, which had restricted the vote to freeholders and householders, and from that time on the voice of the landless was stilled.

In Maryland, next door to Virginia, there was the same pattern of restriction, unrest and ultimate repression. Two months after Virginia passed its disfranchising Act of 1670, Lord Baltimore issued a writ to the sheriffs of Maryland telling them not to accept any man as a voter unless he had at least fifty acres of land or a personal estate of forty pounds sterling.

At the time of Bacon's Rebellion, some of the men of Maryland staged one of their own, and a list of grievances drawn up by sixty Maryland colonists included the fact that the freemen had been deprived of their vote. The ringleaders were hanged, their attempts at reform were dismissed as seditious, and the Governor and Council took pains to point out that the restriction on the franchise was reasonable. "What man in England can be admitted to the election of Parliament that hath not a visible estate in lands or goods?" In 1678, Lord Baltimore's writ to the sheriffs was made into law by the Assembly, and Maryland, like Virginia, officially silenced those who had neither land nor money.

In New England also the franchise had become increasingly allied with the possession of property. Massachusetts Bay still clung to its church franchise, but under pressure from England it had agreed to modify it slightly in 1664 so as to admit those who had enough property to be assessed a tax "of ten shillings." New Haven, which also had a church franchise, had vanished into Connecticut; and in Connecticut the first General Court to meet after the granting of the royal charter decided that a voter must have taxable property worth twenty pounds. Later in the decade the colony of Plymouth forbade the vote to anyone who was not a freeholder with a taxable estate of the same amount.

The colonies in the middle area took it for granted that there should be a property qualification for voters. Penn's frame of government for Pennsylvania in 1682 gave the vote in Philadelphia to those who paid a municipal tax in the town, and the constitution of East Jersey which he and twenty-three fellow Proprietors wrote the following year was even more detailed. A voter in East Jersey must own fifty acres of which ten were under cultivation; or a house and three acres in town; or "a house and land only hired, if he can prove he have fifty pounds in stock of his own."

It was left for the province of New York, in this same year, to take the final step that swung an American colony into precisely the pattern of voting in England. The Assembly that the Duke of York had authorized so reluctantly met in 1683, chose a Speaker, and wrote a constitution which it called the Charter of Liberties and Privileges. The Charter specified that "every freeholder within this province and freeman in any corporation shall have his free choice and vote in the electing of representatives." "By freeholders is understood everyone who is so understood according to the laws of England"— that is to say, the forty-shilling freeholder—while the corporation freemen were the men of business who lived in either Albany or New York City and who were to have the same rights as their colleagues in English boroughs.

This was the arrangement that Colonel Ireton had defended so skillfully during the Putney debate thirty-six years earlier. These were the "persons in whom all land lies, and those in corporations in whom all trading lies," and because they had "a permanent fixed interest" in the country they could be trusted with the vote.

The Charter of Liberties and Privileges was sent to England for the Duke of York's approval and it could hardly have arrived at a worse time. The whole tone of the government had changed, and when William Penn returned to England in 1684 he noticed a great difference. The King and the Duke of York received him graciously. "Yet I found things in general with another face then I left them; sour and stern and resolved to hold the reins of power with a stiffer hand than heretofore."

The reason was that England had just undergone an attempted revolution. The same forces which had gathered against the King's father had coalesced again, driven by the knowledge that when the King died his Roman Catholic brother would succeed to the throne. They had been led with fierce brilliance by the Earl of Shaftesbury, formerly Lord Ashley and still the patron of John Locke.

Shaftesbury had found it very easy to whip up anti-Catholic hysteria in England. Ever since the days of the last Catholic ruler in England—Queen Elizabeth's elder sister whom the Protestants called Bloody Mary—popery and tyranny had prowled hand in hand in the minds of most Englishmen. Shaftesbury could evoke the same fears that John Pym had once played upon, along with Pym's other weapon of mob violence.

For three years, Shaftesbury and his followers tried to drive through

Parliament an Exclusion Bill which would make it impossible for James, as a Roman Catholic, to mount the throne of England. They increased their numerical strength in three savagely fought elections, and it was almost as though the old days of the early 1640's had come again. It was John Hampden's son Richard who moved to bring in a bill in the House of Commons "to disable the Duke of York to inherit the imperial crown of this realm," and when it finally passed, a whole procession of jubilant parliamentarians carried it through the streets accompanied by the Lord Mayor of London and the aldermen.

Shaftesbury might be a second Pym, but Charles II was not in the least like his royal father. He maneuvered and conciliated and waited until the anti-Catholic fury that had been raging with such disgraceful violence burnt itself out. Then he held his next Parliament at Oxford, where there were no London mobs, and had it so completely under his control that he was able to dissolve it in seven days. The King's financial support was coming from France and in any case he had the support of most of the country gentlemen of England, who had no wish to turn back the clock to the destructive days of the 1640's.

Shaftesbury was sure that the liberties of England were in mortal danger, and his followers turned to thoughts of revolution. The plot failed. Shaftesbury escaped to the Continent, where he died two months later, and the others were disposed of in the traditional fashion.

Among those who died on the scaffold was Penn's friend, Algernon Sidney, who was beheaded in December of 1683. Sidney's chief crime was that he had written a paper called *Discourses Concerning Government* which was clearly seditious; it maintained that government rested directly on the consent of the people and that a king could be removed from the throne if he were a tyrant. Sidney had not tried to publish the manuscript, but extracts were read at his trial and it was because of its statements that he died. The Duke of York was delighted by the death of a man whom he characterized as a rebel and republican, and so was Judge Jeffreys, who presided over Sidney's trial and gave a brisk summary of the *Discourses:* "This book contains all the malice and revenge and treason that mankind can be guilty of; it fixes the sole power in the Parliament and the people."

King Charles would also have liked to be able to behead the city of London. That ancient and mighty corporation possessed almost complete independence through the series of charters it had won from English kings, and throughout the seventeenth century it was a center for dissent and anti-monarchism. It was chiefly because of the power of London that Charles I had lost the war, and Charles II decided that he would tolerate it no longer now that he was at last strong enough to behave like a true Stuart.

A year after the Oxford Parliament, the corporation of London was served with a *quo warranto,* inquiring by what warrant London claimed its ancient liberties and privileges. The startled corporation gathered together its legal defenses, as the Virginia Company had done in the days of the first of the Stuarts. It fought for a year, and as uselessly. Final judgment was pronounced against the city of London on the fourth of October, 1683, and a new, subservient charter was drawn up instead. All over England the rights of other boroughs with royal charters were crumbling in the same fashion— lost under *quo warrantos* or given up voluntarily now that London had fallen.

King Charles had two purposes in view. He wanted to make sure that the boroughs would no longer be able to send men to Parliament who opposed his policies, and he wanted to modernize and centralize the English government. Across the Channel his friend and supporter, the great King Louis XIV of France, had instituted a brilliantly successful government of royal absolutism which was beginning to serve as an admired model for other European monarchs. Everywhere the ancient institutions of representative assemblies were losing their authority, and England was one of the few countries that was lagging behind in what seemed to be the march of progress, clogged by an antiquated system of government which stood for what Englishmen persisted in calling their liberties. Charles II had always known that he was the anointed King of England. It was only now, with his political opponents silenced or dead, that he was free to behave like one.

The same situation, and the same opportunity, existed in America. The vast French holdings, which were extending steadily westward over the Continent, were efficiently administered from France, with absolute control by the royal officials. The English holdings, on the other hand, consisted of a string of untidy and quarrelsome little colonies, founded upon no practical basis whatever and resembling each other only in the stubborn determination with which they had all insisted upon representative government.

The most uncooperative of them all was Massachusetts Bay, and ever since Charles II ascended the throne, the English authorities had been arguing with that prickly colony. A report that Edward Randolph made in 1676 put the matter in a nutshell, by quoting a conversation he had had with the current Governor of Massachusetts Bay: "He freely declared to me that the laws made by Your Majesty and your Parliament obligeth them in nothing but what consists with the interest of that colony, that the legislative power is and abides in them solely to act and make laws by virtue of a charter from Your Majesty's royal father."

The obvious solution was to dispose of the charter; now that London had fallen, there was no need to trifle with Massachusetts Bay. However, King Charles preferred to avoid difficulties when he could, and when the writ of *quo warranto* arrived in Boston late in 1683 it was accompanied by one last offer of compromise.

Many of the colonists wanted to accept the King's offer and so did some members of the upper house in the legislature. Ranged against them, however, were the members of the lower house—the House of Deputies—and the King's latest move increased their popular support. For instance, an influential churchman named Increase Mather, who was John Cotton's son-in-law, had not taken any interest in politics up to now. But when the question of the *quo warranto* was debated in Boston town meeting, Increase Mather spoke eloquently against submission.

The final decision was to fight the King in the courts, and Massachusetts Bay hired an attorney for the purpose. The Crown shifted its attack to another kind of writ, one that did not require the defendants to make an appearance, and in October of 1684 the Court of Chancery was able to declare the charter void.

Now that Massachusetts Bay no longer possessed a charter, Charles pushed ahead with his plan to modernize New England. He and his brother James met with the Privy Council in December and decided to put New England under a Dominion. It would be ruled by a royal Governor, with a royal Council to assist and advise him, and there would be no representative assembly.

The Privy Council had been petitioning for years against granting so many colonial charters, and the idea of a single government for the area had much in its favor. It was the idea of destroying the principle of representation that was so unwise, and yet only one member of the Privy Council protested. This was Lord Halifax, who said that Americans would not be inclined to submit to taxation unless they themselves had voted for it. He added that he would not "like to live under a king who should have it in his power to take at pleasure the money out of his pocket."

Halifax was a moderate. He had tried vainly the year before to secure leniency for Algernon Sidney, and he had no better success in his efforts to secure a representative assembly for the Dominion. Such was the King's rigidity by this time, or what William Penn called his sternness in holding the reins of power, that it was his plan to send over Colonel Percy Kirke as

Governor of the Dominion. Kirke had been acceptably strict as Governor of Tangier and he knew how to obey orders.

Charles never saw the fulfillment of his dream for New England. He died two months later, on the sixth of February, 1685, and his brother ascended the throne as King James II.

It would have been difficult to find a more unsuitable man to rule England than the former Duke of York. He had never swerved from his basic conviction that any representative assembly was a threat to orderly government, and he really believed that the whole duty of a good subject was to obey. As Bishop Burnet said of the new King: "He has a strange notion of government, that everything is to be carried on in a high way, and that no regard is to be had to the pleasing the people." Unlike his brother, James was also a man of real innocence. He believed that good intentions were sufficient in a monarch and that no attention need be paid to political realities.

On the third of March, less than a month after James ascended the throne, the question of what to do with his province of New York came up for discussion. Its Charter of Liberties and Privileges was still waiting to be ratified, but that was of course out of the question. It was a time for destroying charters, not for granting them. The question to be considered by the Lords of Trade was what to do about New York under the new circumstances, and the obvious answer was to make it part of the new Dominion.

The Lords of Trade constituted a subcommittee of the Privy Council, and it was composed of men who were experts on colonial affairs. Its members made up a well-balanced and able group, with a great deal of experience, and it was their responsibility to draft a workable plan for the Dominion. They recommended to King James that the Governor and Council be chosen by the Crown, but they also recommended that the Dominion should have a representative assembly.

James disliked this suggestion exceedingly. It was similar to the one that the Governor of New York had suggested to him, and on this earlier occasion, as Duke of York, James had given in with the greatest reluctance. Now he was no longer Duke, but King, and he did not need to give in to anyone.

The Lords of Trade asked the Attorney General for an opinion, and the Attorney General said that it would not be legal to govern in the colonies without a representative assembly. Nevertheless, no one could persuade King James to change his mind, and in the final plan for a Dominion he had his way. There was no assembly. The royal Governor General and his royally appointed Council were to govern alone.

The General Court of Massachusetts Bay refused to accept the plan. It "abridged of their liberty as Englishmen, both in the matter of legislation and in the laying of taxes." The General Court seemed unaware of the fact that it had legally ceased to exist as soon as the charter was declared void. It planned to have its next meeting in October in the usual way. It did not, and the minutes of the Company of Massachusetts Bay, after having been kept for more than half a century, ceased.

The Governor who presided over the last days of the General Court was Simon Bradstreet. He was now in his eighties, and the last surviving member of the group of officials who had come over with the Winthrop fleet in 1630. He had served steadily as an Assistant, and since 1679 he had been Governor.

Bradstreet was a moderate who believed in accommodation with England, and he was therefore offered a seat on the new royal Council. He refused, on the familiar grounds that a government without a representative assembly was contrary to Magna Carta, and it proved difficult to find men for the Council who would work together successfully. The members from Plymouth Colony showed their contempt for the members from Rhode Island, and the landowning interests from Massachusetts Bay fought with the merchant interests from the same colony. It made no real difference in any case, since they had no political authority. They were there only to give advice, and the final word rested with the new Governor.

This was not Colonel Kirke after all, for his services were needed at home. Therefore the King appointed Sir Edmund Andros, who had already served him intelligently as Governor of New York. William Penn admired Andros and would have liked to have his services in Pennsylvania. "If I had a place worthy of his care, I would give him ten thousand acres of land and the command of three counties and use him always as my friend." Yet even Penn had to admit that Andros had the fault of "sometimes an over-eager and too-pressing an execution of his powers."

The powers which Andros now possessed as Captain General and Governor in Chief of the Dominion resembled very closely those of the royal viceroys in the Spanish colonies. It was an error to suppose, however, that this made the New Englanders as obedient as the Spanish, or "that the judgment against their charter made them cease to be Englishmen." They were, as Edward Randolph had warned repeatedly, a "people who will not be forced."

In July of 1687, Andros put the new government to its first real test by setting out to levy taxes. He sent warrants to every town in New England, with instructions to choose local commissioners to levy a tax of a penny on the pound, and the first defiance came from the town of Taunton in Plymouth Colony. Its residents said that the tax was illegal and evoked a statute of Edward I that "taxes shall not be imposed without consent of the Commons."

In the colony of Massachusetts Bay, nearly every town in Essex County refused to obey the warrants and the most dramatic defiance came from the town of Ipswich. Led by its minister, the Reverend John Wise, the people at their town meeting voted unanimously against compliance, "considering that the said Act doth infringe their liberty as freeborn English subjects of His Majesty . . . that no taxes shall be levied on the subjects without consent of an Assembly chosen by the freeholders."

Governor Andros moved promptly. He arrested twenty-eight men in Essex County for being "factious and seditious" and in October the six from Ipswich were put on trial. John Wise led the defense, appealing to Magna Carta, and when he lost he was punished by a heavy fine. Andros then prohibited the holding of town meetings more than once a year, to prevent their being used for seditious gatherings, and felt justified in sending an optimistic report back to England.

In this same October, Connecticut lost its charter, and Andros rode to Hartford to inform the people that their former government had ceased. The following April, New York and the two Jerseys were gathered into the embrace of the Dominion, and it seemed to have been hoped that in time all the English colonies in America would be included.

By now the men in William Penn's London office were deep in research on the subject of *quo warrantos,* hoping to find some legal means to stave off the loss of the Pennsylvania charter. Penn also published a pamphlet called "The Excellent Privilege of Liberty and Property" to tell his people of their rights. In it he printed the text of Magna Carta, its two confirmations under Edward I, the text of his own charter and the text of his Frame of Government, with editorial comments on the background of each document. It was ably done, but Penn's real safety lay in the love that the King bore him. The two were faithful friends, and they remained so.

James II had need of friends. His reign had begun in violence, for the Protestant Duke of Monmouth, who was the late King's illegitimate son and very popular, had made a final attempt to seize the throne. The abortive revolution was savagely suppressed by the efficient Colonel Kirke and as savagely punished by Judge Jeffreys, who passed out death sentences with his usual anti-republican zeal.

Among those who died on the scaffold was Colonel Richard Rumbold, who had once been a lieutenant in Oliver Cromwell's regiment and who was still faithful to the old dreams. When Rumbold was executed in Edinburgh he gave a speech which showed how closely the fear of Catholicism and the fear of political tyranny were locked together in the minds of Englishmen. "I die this day in the defence of the ancient laws and liberties of these nations. . . . This is a deluded generation . . . and though popery and slavery be riding in upon them, do not perceive it. . . . I am sure there was no man born marked of God above another; for none comes into the world with a saddle on his back, neither any booted and spurred to ride him."

Englishmen supported the Monmouth rising for a variety of reasons. A friend of Penn's sympathized with it, for instance, because King James had unwisely proclaimed on his accession that he could use the customs revenues that had been voted for life to his brother but which had not yet been granted by Parliament to him—"our constitution to the utmost degree violated by King James taking the Customs before they were granted by the Parliament, for if a King of England can levy sixpence without the consent of our representatives, he may as justly and legally take all the rest."

Parliament granted the money willingly. The destruction of so many of the charters had altered the pattern of voting in the boroughs, and the conservatives who were now in power were only too willing to cooperate with James II. Unfortunately, the new King failed to cooperate with them. Secure in the conviction that he must redress the wrongs of the persecuted religious minority to which he belonged, he managed to antagonize the Protestant country gentlemen whose good will his brother Charles had cultivated so assiduously. As for the ill will of the rest of the country, he had that already.

Nevertheless, most Englishmen were content to wait quietly, for the King had no male heir. Next in line to the throne was his daughter by his first wife, and the Princess Mary was a Protestant. Moreover, she had married a Protestant, for her husband was William of Orange. The young Dutch prince was her first cousin, and he was keeping closely but carefully in touch with English politicians.

On the tenth of June, 1688, the whole situation suddenly changed. King James' second wife unexpectedly bore him a son, and the Roman Catholic ruler of England now had a male successor. In this same month, James committed a final act of ill-timed good intentions and told all the clergy in the Church of England to announce a policy of religious toleration from their pulpits. The Archbishop of Canterbury and six bishops refused, and James had them arrested as "trumpeters of sedition."

Their trial lasted one day only. On the 30th of June, all seven were acquitted. On the same day, seven peers of the realm set aside their deep political differences and sent a joint letter to the Prince of Orange to come and rescue them.

William of Orange was a remarkable man, a steady foe of the royal absolutism that Louis XIV of France represented and that James II of England so much admired. The United Provinces of the Netherlands agreed to the risky step of supplying him with an invasion fleet, and he landed in England the fifth of November, 1688.

King James might still have been able to save himself if he had made a stand, for he was the anointed ruler of England and William was a Dutch usurper. But the only decisive step the King had taken was in September, when he canceled the writs that had been sent out to call a November Parliament into session. He increased the size of the army but gave it no real support, and in December he composed a letter for the Earl of Feversham to read to the troops: "I do not expect you should expose yourselves by resisting a foreign army and poisoned nation."

Finally King James fled the country, announcing that he would be ready to return "when my subjects' eyes may be opened." William Penn risked imprisonment on a charge of high treason by keeping up a correspondence with him, but the average Englishman felt nothing but relief that this most unsuitable of monarchs had departed.

James left behind him no government at all. Parliament was not in session, since the writs had been destroyed, and only the King could authorize a new election.

The thing was managed with the aplomb of true Englishmen. The House of Lords, which was a permanent body, joined with all the past members of the House of Commons who were in town and with the chief London officials, and this group authorized William of Orange to send out writs for a new election. In these writs it was carefully specified that voting in the boroughs was to be "according to ancient usage," which meant that the surrender of the charters under the *quo warrantos* was to be considered void.

Parliament met in January of 1689, and was known as the Convention Parliament. By the end of the month, the House of Commons had hammered out a resolution which it sent to the House of Lords, stating that James II "having endeavored to subvert the constitution of the kingdom by breaking the original contract between the King and the people, and . . . having violated the fundamental laws, and having withdrawn himself out of the kingdom, has abdicated the government and that the throne is thereby vacant."

The House of Lords made a few changes in the wording, but its leader was Lord Halifax and there were no changes in the basic idea. Princess Mary arrived from Holland on the 12th of February, and the following day she and her husband received Lords and Commons at Whitehall. Lord Halifax read aloud the Declaration of Rights, outlining the terms under which Parliament was offering them the Crown, and William and Mary agreed to its restrictions.

England went its way with the calm of a country that had just achieved a constitutional miracle. It had exchanged a government which did not please the people for one that did, and the new monarch was so soundly and even excessively Protestant that he was heard to refer to the great traditional ritual of the coronation as "those silly old papist ceremonies."

In New England meanwhile, the colonists had been seeing Roman Catholics lurking under every bush. Governor Andros had shown special energy in pushing back the French and their Indian allies on the frontier, and since no good could be believed of Andros, the rumor hardened into accepted fact that he had sent the militia out under popish commanders as part of a plot to deliver up the whole of New England to Catholic France.

The details of what happened next will probably never be known. A supporter of Governor Andros claimed that the men of Boston had been plotting revolution for a long time. "This was not a sudden heat or violent passion of the rabble but a long-contrived piece of wickedness." One of those who took part in the revolution maintained, on the other hand, that it was the result of a sudden decision in April. "It was in the month of April that we had news . . . concerning a descent made upon England by the Prince of Orange for the rescue of the nation from popery and slavery. Then a strange disposition entered in the body of our people to assert our liberties."

It was clearly the news of William's accession that set the Boston mobs into action, but it seems equally clear that the gentlemen of Boston could not have taken control so promptly and smoothly if there had not been a great deal of preliminary preparation.

These gentlemen met on the 18th of April in the Council Room and drew up a written statement to make clear to all the world that they possessed the right of revolution. They began with the fact that they had been deprived of their Assembly and continued with a long list of what they felt to be the tyrannies of Governor Andros. Now that they had received word of "the noble undertaking of the Prince of Orange" to preserve the English nation "from the horrible brinks of popery and slavery," they were entitled to move in an orderly fashion to preserve Massachusetts Bay from the same fate. Appended to this *Declaration* was a formal letter calling upon Governor

Andros to surrender, and the astonished man, knowing as he said "no cause or occasion for the same," had no choice but to submit.

The gentlemen of Boston were now calling themselves the Council of Safety, and they represented every shade of political opinion, united as in England against a common threat. The head of the Council was the former Governor of Massachusetts Bay. "The Honorable Simon Bradstreet, Esq., was chosen by them for their President, who though he be well towards ninety years of age . . . retains a vigor and wisdom that would recommend a younger man to the government of a greater colony." Bradstreet had once been a moderate, pressing for compromise with England. He was now the head of a revolutionary Council of Safety and heading what in fact was an armed rebellion.

Like England, Massachusetts Bay found itself without a government. Writs of election could not be sent out by the Governor, since there was none. Therefore the Council decided on the first of May to ask each town to send delegates to a general meeting in Boston to discuss the problem, and sixty-six delegates from forty-four towns arrived as the representatives of the people. For this occasion all the normal restrictions on the franchise were lifted, and both "freemen and inhabitants" had been permitted to vote in the town meetings that chose the delegates and drafted their instructions.

There was a great deal of argument among the sixty-six delegates about what ought to be done. Finally it was decided to return to the charter until word had been received from King William, and Simon Bradstreet again took up his office as Governor of the colony.

A genius for propaganda was built into the New England temperament, and the Council of Safety sent copies of its *Declaration* to all the other colonies in the Dominion so that they too could rise up against the yoke that had been imposed upon them. When Andros sent in his report, he was obliged to admit that the whole structure had fallen apart. "By the encouragement and persuasion of those of the Massachusetts, the several other provinces and colonies in New England as far as New York have disunited themselves and set up their former separate charter or popular governments without charter."

The three New England colonies of Connecticut, Plymouth and Rhode Island all returned quietly to their former governments, but in New York there was tragic violence. There had been a deep political split in the New York Assembly before it ceased to exist, and the popular party, mostly Dutch, had found its champion in the German-born Jacob Leisler. Leisler tried to combine the revolt against the Dominion with an attack on the local oligarchy of property owners, and in the end he was executed. In Maryland there was violence also, for the Protestants had been growing increasingly restless under the domination of a Proprietor who was a Roman Catholic. The insurgents marched on the town of St. Mary's and overthrew the government there in a revolution which was very like Boston's on a smaller scale.

Driven by a variety of impulses, each colony affirmed its right to a separate existence and as much liberty as it had known in the past, and it was left to the new ruler of England to decide what to do with them all.

It seemed clear that it would not be desirable to keep the old forms of government, so untidy and potentially so seditious. As one report put it: "If New England be restored to the usurped privileges they had in 1660 and the old Proprietors of New Jersey, New York and other islands and places to what they pretend, it will so confound the present settlement in those parts and their dependence on England, that 'tis hard to say where the mischief will stop."

King William had appointed a new set of men to serve as his Lords of Trade, and their recommendations were the same as the earlier group that had served under the Stuarts. The Dominion had proved to be of great value in the defense of the long and vulnerable wilderness frontier that separated the English and French possessions, and since England had gone to war against Louis XIV as soon as William ascended the throne, this argument alone should have been decisive. Moreover, it was clearly going to be very difficult to work out any sort of uniform trade policy with a string of colonies sprawled out along the coast and all claiming the right to make their own laws—"they esteeming," as Andros put it, "no laws to be binding on them but what are made by themselves."

If King William had followed the dictates of safety and the advice of his Lords of Trade, he would have set up some form of centralized government in America. Since he was not a communicative man it is not known what brought him to a contrary decision, but it was probably his ancestry and the traditions of his house.

William was the great-grandson of that earlier Prince of Orange, William the Silent, who had led the United Provinces of the Netherlands in a revolt against their legal Catholic ruler, and who had helped them commit an act which conservatives called sedition. On a July day in 1581, the delegates of the Dutch people gathered at The Hague and issued a formal declaration of independence. The document stated that when a ruler oppresses his people, "seeking opportunities to infringe their ancient customs, exacting from them slavish compliance, then he is no longer a prince but a tyrant, and they may not only disallow his authority but legally proceed to the choice of another prince."

It was a reiteration of this same principle—that if the king broke the contract his people were free to revolt—that had brought the great-grandson of William the Silent to the throne of England. No one knew better than he that men with a long tradition of political freedom cannot safely be ruled against their wills. A Dominion could be imposed in the name of order but it could only be maintained by force of arms, and pressure would be answered by counterpressure. The reports from America had made it clear that the colonists understood only one kind of unanimity: unanimous opposition to arbitrary control.

The alternative was to work out with each colony some sort of mutually agreeable solution, and this was the course that William chose. As Increase Mather said approvingly, "We have a king now that will not act contrary to law."

Connecticut and Rhode Island received their old charters back again, for the Attorney General ruled that they had been taken illegally, and both colonies retained the right to elect their own Governors under the terms that had been established in the 1660's. New York was given a royal Governor, under a more normal arrangement, but he arrived with clear instructions to call a representative assembly.

It was much more difficult to reach an acceptable compromise with Massachusetts Bay, which also wanted its own charter back again. Given in 1629 to a long-dead trading company, it was wholly unsuited to contemporary conditions, but Increase Mather had been sent to England to try and negotiate its return while James II was still on the throne. Mather was still there during the Convention Parliament and managed to get it included in one of the bills, but while it passed the House of Commons it was defeated in the House of Lords. He and his colleagues clung, however, to their negotiations, behaving with such vigor and self-confidence that one of William's ministers was obliged to point out that it was not true that "the agents of New England were plenipotentiaries from another sovereign state."

Massachusetts did not get its old charter back again. But in 1691 it was given a new one, and in a single, majestic and interminable paragraph the colony was given nearly everything it had asked for except the right to select its own Governor. It was allowed to absorb the whole of Plymouth colony into its jurisdiction, and its claim to the province of Maine was confirmed. It was allowed to choose the twenty-eight Assistants who made up the Council, or upper house, and while it was forced to abandon a religious qualification in voting for members of the lower house, this was by now so unpopular a measure that it could not have been maintained much longer in any case.

Nearly all the English colonies, whether they were royal or proprietary, now had the same pattern of government—a Governor, an upper house and a lower house, all combining together to make the laws. Like the original arrangement at Jamestown it reflected the English system on a smaller scale, since the upper house or Council corresponded to the House of Lords, the lower house to the House of Commons and the Governor to the King.

The basic difference lay in the fact that the colonial assemblies had no control over their Governors whereas, since the Declaration of Rights, the English Parliament had a very real control over the King. For the whole of the seventeenth century, a battle had been fought between the Crown and the men of property in England over where the sovereignty lay. Even in the relatively quiet reign of James I, men like Sir Edwin Sandys had been talking about what they called English liberties. The conflict had exploded into open war under Charles I, subsided into an increasingly uneasy truce under Charles II, and then ended in an absolute triumph when James II went off into his uncomprehending exile. William and Mary ascended the throne under a written contract which made it impossible, ever again, for a ruler of England to impose his will on Parliament, and the event came to be known as the Glorious Revolution because it worked.

No one was more aware of the magnitude of this achievement than John Locke. He had been living in exile in Holland ever since his patron, the Earl of Shaftesbury, failed in a premature attempt at revolution, but he had remained closely connected with the forces in England that had been trying to deprive James of the throne. Locke's name was on a list of conspirators against the peace of the realm, and he had refused an offer from William Penn to intercede for him with the King.*

Locke was a foe of everything that King James believed, and in fact he had been working on a book that justified revolution against an unjust monarch. He had begun it in answer to an elaborate defense of the doctrine of the divine right of kings that had been written by Sir Robert Filmer. It was still unfinished when England deposed the last of the Stuart kings and Locke saw the argument of his book gloriously vindicated.

He returned to England on the 12th of February, 1689, in the same

---

*Penn habitually used his friendship with King James in an effort to encourage him to leniency, and even Increase Mather had to admit that he tried to be helpful. "To give Mr. Penn his due, he did in my hearing in the King's closet (when no one has been present besides the King, Penn and I) advise King James to be kind to his subjects in New England."

ship that brought Mary back to be Queen and by her invitation. He had with him only the first and last sections of his manuscript and decided to publish them as they were. He called the book *Two Treatises of Government* and issued it anonymously that same year.

In his preface Locke acknowledged the fragmentary nature of the work and explained why he had published it. He hoped that it would serve to establish the throne of "our great restorer, our present King William; to make good his title, in the consent of the people . . . and to justify to the world the people of England, whose love of their just and natural rights, with their resolution to preserve them, saved the nation when it was on the very brink of slavery and ruin."

The book was a great success. It summarized in lucid and vigorous prose the new ideas on government that men had been arguing about for the whole of that tormented century, and based the argument on reason and on antiquity. Locke was able to prove to his readers that the Glorious Revolution was not the political aberration it appeared to be to most Europeans. It was, on the contrary, a triumph of right and reason and based on first principles of government.

Sir Robert Filmer had maintained that monarchy was the most ancient form of government, since it had its roots in the institution of the father as the head of the family. Locke maintained otherwise. He said that when men had been in a state of nature they had followed an older and better law: "The state of Nature has a law of Nature to govern it . . . and Reason, which is that law, teaches all mankind . . . that being all equal and independent, no one ought to harm another in his life, health, liberty or possessions." It was upon this principle that Locke based his argument of government by consent. "Men being, as has been said, by Nature all free, equal and independent, no one can be put out of this estate, and subjected to the political power of another, without his own consent."

Said Locke: "That which begins and actually constitutes any political society is nothing but the consent of any number of freemen capable of a majority to unite and incorporate into such a society." He admitted that he could not support this view with any written records. "There are no instances to be found . . . of a company of men independent and equal one amongst another, that met together, and in this way began and set up a government." Nevertheless, since "government is everywhere antecedent to records," it seemed clear that this must have been the way it was in man's earliest days.

What Locke was really describing was the way primitive societies might have behaved if they had been composed entirely of Englishmen, and in fact that was exactly the way Englishmen had behaved in America. Each time they found themselves without an accredited government, in what Locke would have called a state of nature, they created one. They united into an incorporated society and signed a written pledge that they would operate by consent of the majority.

It was in this fashion that the Mayflower Compact had been created fourteen years before John Locke was born, and it was in this fashion that similar written agreements were worked out in Connecticut, New Haven, Providence, Rhode Island and New Hampshire. Locke was not describing government as it had once been. He was describing government as Englishmen wished it to be, and it was this determination that had culminated in England in the Glorious Revolution.

Locke defined government as the union of the people "for the mutual preservation of their lives, liberties and estates, which I call by the general name, property." He did not, however, make clear, in that lucid but somehow vague prose of his, what he meant by the people. He established to his satisfaction that the right of consent lay with them, but he did not say who they were. Nor did he need to, since the majority of his readers would automatically conclude that he meant the voters of England.

Those who did not possess the vote were considered by men like Locke as not quite belonging to the human race, and this tendency was increasing in England as the propertied classes grew richer and the laboring class more degraded. Locke, for instance, loved children, watched them constantly, and wrote brilliantly on the subject of their education. Yet when he became a member of the Board of Trade he worked out a plan to save English parishes the small sum that was paid out for the schooling and maintenance of pauper children until they were old enough to earn their living. Locke's horrible recommendation was that all such children be put to work at the age of three, being fed only bread, with a little gruel in the winter "if it be thought needful." Not only were the unpropertied classes unfit to have the vote, but it was beginning to be doubted that they were human beings at all.

Locke's readers no longer believed in the divine right of kings. They had come instead to believe in the divine right of property, and the more prosperous England became, the more this conviction hardened into a kind of Holy Writ. The forces of reform were not altogether silenced but they never gathered up enough energy to affect this complacent tyranny. What the reformers called the rights of man became in this context almost seditious, and it was not until the nineteenth century that Parliament made the first cautious change in the election law of the forty-shilling freeholder that had bound Englishmen since 1430.

The American colonies also grew steadily more prosperous, and in them the same conviction hardened in the same way. As a promoter for the colony of East Jersey put it, dominion must "follow property." It no longer seemed conceivable that a responsible man could suggest, as Colonel Rainsborough had once suggested, that "the poorest he that is" had a right to a share in the government.

The steady growth of this conviction was especially evident in Virginia, which had recovered promptly from the brief radicalism of Bacon's Rebellion. The first General Assembly that met after his death put the franchise back to what it had been at the beginning of the decade. Freemen remained disqualified, but the vote was given to householders as well as freeholders. Seven years later, in 1684, householders were disfranchised. Finally, an Act passed in 1699 not only reaffirmed the new rule but imposed a fine of five hundred pounds of tobacco on anyone who tried to vote in Virginia if he were not a freeholder.

South Carolina had begun with a liberal franchise; almost any white Protestant of the standard age of twenty-one was permitted to vote. The colony turned against its Proprietors in 1719 (one man quoting Locke on the right to revolt against tyranny) and by this time apprentices and seafaring men had been excluded from the vote. In 1745 a heavy limitation of the suffrage was attempted. As the preamble to the Act put it: "It may be of evil consequence to give a right to any person or persons to vote . . . who . . . are not possessed of a sufficient freehold and personal estate." Fourteen years later the franchise was widened again although the preamble was kept intact. It was now necessary for the voter to own a hundred acres of land or to have paid an annual tax of ten shillings. However, to be eligible to a seat in the lower house a man had to own five hundred acres of land and ten slaves, or property worth £1,000, and power tended to concentrate in the hands of the rich merchants who lived in the rapidly growing port city of Charleston. North Carolina came under the control of the Crown in 1729, a few years later than South Carolina. This area was very isolated, without a port and thinly populated. After some confusion the franchise there was finally limited to freeholders who owned at least fifty acres.

The very prosperous colony of New York had tried at first to maintain the traditional English standard of the forty-shilling freeholder, but it was soon decided that this was too liberal. "Men of no great figure, tailors and other mean conditions," were getting themselves elected, and in 1699 the forty-shilling freehold was changed to one worth forty pounds.

New Jersey became a Crown colony after the two parts were reunited at the beginning of the century, and the franchise requirements were set by an

Act for the Better Regulation of Elections which was passed in 1725. This specified that the voter must be a freeholder and worth fifty pounds. The New Hampshire election law of 1728 also specified that voters must possess real estate worth fifty pounds.

Rhode Island decided in 1724 that a voter must be a "freeholder of lands, tenements or hereditaments" worth a hundred pounds, or forty shillings a year. Since Rhode Island never succeeded in behaving quite like any other colony, the right to vote was made inheritable and extended also to the "eldest son of such a freeholder." Rhode Island held a corporation charter, and it was quite normal in English corporations for the eldest son of a freeman to be automatically eligible for membership.

Some of the colonies were willing to accept a money qualification as a substitute for land. The Massachusetts charter of 1691 specified that the voter was to have a freehold "to the value of forty shillings per annum at the least or other estate to the value of forty pounds" (or fifty pounds according to another copy of the same charter). Connecticut decided in 1702 to have the same arrangement, a forty-shilling freehold or forty pounds in personal estate. Pennsylvania required fifty acres of land or fifty pounds in personal estate. In Maryland it was fifty acres or forty pounds, and in Delaware the same.

The last of the thirteen colonies to come into existence was Georgia. Since it was originally set up on a semimilitary basis, it did not acquire a representative assembly until the middle of the eighteenth century. In 1752 it was taken over from its trustees by the Crown, and the voting requirement was the normal one of at least fifty acres of land.

The reason why land rather than money was usually made the basis of the franchise was expressed very clearly by one of the Proprietors of West Jersey. "Those persons are fittest to be trusted with choosing and being legislators who have a fixed, valuable and permanent interest in lands. . . . Money is an uncertain interest, and if it be admitted a qualification equal to land, an Assembly may be packed of strangers and beggars who will have little regard to the good of the country . . . and may oppress the landed man with heavy taxes." This was, of course, an exaggeration, since any colony which permitted a money qualification set the sum high enough to keep out undesirables; nevertheless, in America as in England, land stood for political power.

The restrictions on the franchise did not weigh very heavily on the average American, since land was not hard to obtain. Benjamin Franklin said proudly in 1772 that every New Englander was a freeholder, and while this was a patriotic exaggeration pardonable in a man who was traveling abroad, his remark had a good deal of truth in it. As a matter of fact,

Massachusetts had a more liberal franchise in 1772 than in the days of John Winthrop, when only Congregationalists were permitted to vote.

Moreover, the suffrage restrictions were weakened in America, as they were in England, by a marked tendency to ignore them. A man knew his neighbors, and anyone who could be trusted to make the proper decision at the polls was not going to be questioned too closely. Unless the election was hotly contested, many Americans did not bother to vote at all, especially in areas where the roads were bad or non-existent, and in hotly contested elections it was remarkable what an ingenious man could do and still stay within the letter of the law.

For instance, in a Virginia election in 1736, Charles Carter transformed his supporters into freeholders by giving them half-acre tracts of land "either on, or some few days before the day of the said election, in consideration for their voting for the said Charles Carter." The Virginia legislature therefore passed a law defining a freehold as a hundred acres of land, or twenty-five acres with a house on it, or a house and lot in town. Even this did not check the ingenuity of a determined voter, and in 1762 one Thomas Payne bought from one Mary Almond, for ten shillings, a little shed she had been using to keep milkpans in. He carried it off with a horse and cart and placed it "on his said lot, on purpose (as he acknowledged) to qualify himself to vote in that election." The Virginia House of Burgesses ruled that his vote was not valid and then hurriedly passed yet another law, this one stating that the house of the voter must be at least twelve feet square.

In spite of an occasional flurry of excitement when there was a closely fought contest, there is no evidence that the restrictive franchise was disliked in America. It had behind it the whole weight of English law and of local custom, and, above all, it guaranteed political stability. By now, most Americans were willing to agree that society could tolerate a certain amount of religious diversity and still survive, but no one had seriously suggested that it might also be possible to tolerate political diversity. Therefore the laws that linked the franchise to the possession of property were wholly acceptable, because they ensured that the voters would act and think alike.

The American colonies entered the eighteenth century in a very different mood from the one that had characterized the turbulent seventeenth. Political experimentation had ceased, and an orderly pattern had evolved of which control by men of property was a characteristic and integral part.

If there were any protests from the disfranchised, they were too faint to be heard. In fact, everything seemed remarkably calm in America on the subject of the vote, as calm as it had seemed in England until a revolutionary war had opened a path for the Levelers.

Part Two

You cannot plant an oak in a flowerpot.

—JAMES HARRINGTON

Chapter Eight

Early in the eighteenth century, William Penn wrote a letter to a friend in which he complained of the arrogance of American politicians:

> There is an excess of vanity that is apt to creep in upon the people in power in America, who, having got out of the crowd in which they were lost here . . . think nothing taller than themselves but the trees. . . . I have sometimes thought that if there was a law to oblige the people in power, in their respective colonies, to take turns in coming over for England, that they might lose themselves again amongst the crowds of so much more considerable people at the Custom-house, Exchange and Westminster Hall, they would exceedingly amend in their conduct at their return and be much more discreet and tractable and fit for government.

Penn was accurate in his description but wrong in his diagnosis. The Americans were, in fact, only behaving like Englishmen.

As the House of Stuart could testify, the men of the English House of Commons had never been "discreet and tractable and fit for government." They had, in fact, been so unruly and so arrogant that they had waged a battle against the supremacy of the Crown for the whole of the seventeenth century. Parliament ceased to behave in this manner after William and Mary ascended the throne, but only because it had won the argument.

167

In the American colonies, the behavior which Penn deplored was the result of this same struggle for sovereignty and was fought by the same kind of men. They were men of property who had learned to be skilled parliamentarians, and they never doubted that it was they, and not the colonial governors, who were entitled to rule. Respectfully, doggedly, persistently, they fought all up and down the coast for more power, and the reluctant temporary concession won from one governor was presented to the next as an unshakable tradition. They had in their armory every parliamentary device that the English House of Commons had worked out in the previous century, and they were well informed on the details of that long and successful struggle. An American assembly of 1762 found it quite natural to reinforce its argument by quoting the Parliament of 1604 on the subject of "the prerogative of princes."

The royal governors did their best to check this erosion of their authority, but their position was a difficult one. The last of the Stuart kings had tried to establish a single colonial policy, and this ill-advised attempt at efficiency under Governor Andros had nearly led to disaster. Since then, no real policy of any kind had come into existence. Each governor was given the same general instructions, which were neither flexible nor realistic, and when he tried to make them work the government at home gave him little assistance. The chief official body with which the harried governors corresponded was the Board of Trade, a semiprofessional group which King William had set up to replace the old Lords of Trade, and while the Board could draft reports and hear complaints it had no power to decide government policy. Since there was no single authority to direct the colonies, the various ministries—the Treasury, the War Office, the Admiralty and so on—divided the various problems among themselves as they came up. They were struggling with a colonial population which had been about three-quarters of a million in King William's day and which had grown to some two and a half million by the time King George III came to the throne.

The persistent, unremitting energy of the American assemblies varied in strength and efficiency from colony to colony. South Carolina, with its great port of Charleston and its rich merchants and planters who went to England for their legal training, was able to summon up much more political energy than the isolated colony of North Carolina. Yet it was the Governor of North Carolina who said in exasperation, "The Assembly think themselves entitled to all the privileges of a British House of Commons."

This running battle between the governors and the assemblies was fought everywhere except in Rhode Island and Connecticut, the two colonies whose charters gave them the right to elect their own governors. Pennsylvania, Delaware and Maryland were still owned by proprietors, but the governors sent out by the Penn and Calvert families faced the same pressures as the ones sent out by the Crown.

Some of the royal governors had been born in America, like Benning Wentworth of New Hampshire or William Bull of South Carolina, but this made no difference to the way the assemblies resisted them. Few men had more trouble with his assembly than Governor Bull, in spite of the fact that he was personally very popular. As for Governor Wentworth, he fought the legislature successfully in New Hampshire not only because he was a clever man and strongly entrenched in local politics, but also because he was a patient man and did not risk a battle with his assembly except at a time when the treasury was reasonably full. It was by withholding approval of money bills that the colonial legislatures won their greatest victories, and they never let out of their hands the powerful weapon that the English House of Commons had used so successfully against the Stuarts.

Decade after decade, the colonial governors struggled with the colonial assemblies as William Penn had struggled with his. One of them, echoing almost Penn's own language, said that the state of affairs he had discovered on his arrival was intolerable. The mechanism of government had become "unhinged, the political balance . . . entirely overturned, and all the weights that should trim and poise it . . . by different laws thrown into the scale of the people." Such a governor had one final weapon—he could dissolve the assembly. Yet this did him little good, since the next one to be elected invariably consisted of the same kind of men.

An embattled governor of Maryland went so far in his exasperation as to call the men of the Maryland house of delegates "levelers in their principles." This was not true at all. They were no more of that opinion than Cromwell and Ireton had been. They wished to extend their own political control upward, but they had no intention whatsoever of sharing it with those below. Nor was there any risk that this would ever happen, as long as the suffrage laws remained intact as a solid bulwark to protect power and property.

It was a situation that worked fairly well on the whole, because England and America shared a profound respect for constitutional government. What no one realized was that they were not interpreting it the same way. The English took it to mean respect for the British Parliament; the Americans took it to mean respect for the colonial assemblies.

This situation might have continued indefinitely if the home government had not suddenly decided to end its long policy of drift and set up a more orderly relationship with the colonies. The latest war with France had ended in 1763 with Great Britain a colossus, in possession of the vast territories in North America that had once belonged to France. The Empire was also in possession of a huge debt, much of it incurred in America, and the men of property in the House of Commons had no wish to submit to higher taxation in England if it could be avoided. When the Chancellor of the Exchequer suggested a Stamp Tax, they agreed with him warmly. It was to apply to all printed documents in the colonies, from newspapers to insurance policies, and could be expected to bring in about sixty thousand pounds a year.

Since this was the first direct tax that had ever been imposed upon the colonies, it was put off for a year and then debated with great care. Various objections were raised in the House of Commons, but only one man there, a London alderman, had the eccentricity to suggest that Parliament did not have the constitutional right to impose such a tax. The House of Commons gave its approval late in February, 1765, and the House of Lords early in March.

The Stamp Tax touched the colonists on the most sensitive nerve they possessed. From the beginning of their history it had seemed to them as absolute as Holy Writ that an Englishman could be taxed only by his own representatives. When Governor Winthrop tried to levy a tax on Watertown in the days when representative government had not yet come into existence in Massachusetts Bay, the Reverend George Phillips rallied his fellow townsmen with the warning "that it was not safe to pay moneys after that sort, for fear of bringing themselves and posterity into bondage." When Governor Andros tried to levy a similar tax in the days when representative government had been briefly destroyed in Massachusetts Bay, the Reverend John Wise reasserted the same principle, "that no taxes shall be levied on the subjects without consent of an assembly."

The principle had gone unquestioned ever since. A man could not be taxed without the consent of his own representatives, and to Americans that meant the colonial assemblies.

The first sign of trouble came from Virginia. The Governor there was the cultivated and popular Francis Fauquier, and he wrote the Board of Trade early in June that a new member of the House of Burgesses whose name was Patrick Henry had used "very indecent language" on the subject of the Stamp Tax. Governor Fauquier also enclosed four resolutions that had been passed by the House of Burgesses on the subject and laid stress on the fact that Henry had waited until the more stable older members had gone home so that he could carry the "young, hot and giddy members" with him in passing the resolutions.

Whether intentionally or not, Governor Fauquier was being very misleading. No rational member of the House of Burgesses, whether young or old, was going to stand idly by while the most precious power he possessed, the power of taxation, was taken away from him. It is true that Peyton Randolph, the aristocratic Speaker of the House, tried to defeat the resolutions, but only because he differed on the question of timing and tone. Randolph himself had drafted the protest to the King against the Stamp Tax which the House of Burgesses sent to England the year before.

A French traveler in Virginia heard Patrick Henry deliver the speech and went back to hear more. "I returned to the assembly today and heard very hot debates still about the stamp duties. . . . One of the resolves . . . was that any person that would offer to sustain that the Parliament of England had a right to impose or lay any tax or duties whatsoever on the American colonies, without the consent of the inhabitants thereof, would be looked upon as a traitor and deemed an enemy to his country." The Frenchman could not have known it, but the wording was an echo of the resolution passed in the tumultuous session of the House of Commons in 1629 by Sir John Eliot and his friends, when it was agreed that anyone who maintained the King's right to impose tonnage and poundage "shall . . . be reputed a betrayer of the liberties of England and an enemy to the same."

Americans took great pride in the fact that Parliament's long battle against Stuart tyranny had ended so triumphantly. Now they found history repeating itself with the roles reversed, since it was Parliament that was now playing the tyrant. An American tourist like Benjamin Rush of Philadelphia could stand in the meeting place of the House of Commons and feel all the emotions of a seventeenth-century Englishman. "This . . . is the place where the infernal scheme for enslaving America was first broached. Here the usurping Commons first endeavored to rob the King of his supremacy over the colonies. . . . O cursed haunt of venality, bribery and corruption!"

Such Americans believed that taxation without representation was the first step toward slavery, and a Massachusetts lawyer named John Adams was willing to risk his life rather than to submit. "A contest appeared to me to be opened to which I could foresee no end, and which would render my life a burden, and property, industry and everything insecure. There was no alternative left but to take the side which appeared to be just, to march intrepidly forward in the right path, to trust in Providence for the protection of truth and right, and to die with a good conscience and a decent grace if that trial should become indispensable."

It was difficult for the average Englishman to believe that the Americans could really be serious. "No man, above the degree of an idiot, would risk his life, property and all that he holds dear in this world . . . for the sake of shunning payment of a shilling or eighteenpence for a sheet of stamped paper." Such Englishmen had forgotten that John Hampden took exactly the same risk rather than pay twenty shillings in the ship-money case.

The next session of Parliament opened in an unhappy state of mind. Trade with America was at a standstill, and alarmed business interests in London had obtained the cooperation of a new ministry in launching a campaign for the repeal of the Stamp Act. Parliament could ignore news of rioting in America, as it had already ignored petitions from the colonial legislatures. But when similar petitions began to come in from the major manufacturing cities of England, this was the kind of language that Parliament understood.

The House of Commons discussed the matter long and carefully, turning itself into a Committee of the Whole so that all the members could talk freely. The debates started on the third of February, 1766, and lasted eight or ten hours each day. Finally, at two o'clock in the morning of February the 22nd, it was voted to repeal the Stamp Act. Nevertheless, the world's greatest empire could hardly admit defeat, nor could a legislative body which had overthrown two kings accept colonial limitations on its authority. Therefore, the House of Commons passed a Declaratory Act which affirmed the right of the British Parliament to do what it wished with the colonies in all cases whatsoever.

In the great manufacturing towns of England, like Bristol and Birmingham, bells were rung and bonfires lighted to celebrate the repeal of the Stamp Act, and in America there was similar rejoicing. In the sudden atmosphere of good feeling, it was easy for the colonists to convince themselves that the Declaratory Act did not mean what it said. Nevertheless, the radicals among them were now well organized and on the alert for any signs of incipient tyranny, so that Great Britain could hardly make a move without blowing up a storm somewhere. Americans had always been touchy about their rights; they now felt they had a firm constitutional basis for increased watchfulness and became even more difficult to govern.

The position of the British government was made still more complicated by the fact that it was fighting a somewhat similar battle at home. John Wilkes, that gamecock of a journalist, had published in 1763 an attack on the policies of King George III which had been officially branded "a false, scandalous and seditious libel." In its effort to punish Wilkes, the government found itself involved in a set of battles that involved the fundamental principles of *habeas corpus* and free speech. Wilkes went abroad for a time after his shocked and virtuous colleagues in the House of Commons had deprived him of his seat, but he was back again in 1768 and ran again for Parliament. The voters of Middlesex County returned him by a huge majority, and the House of Commons refused to admit him. Twice more the voters elected Wilkes and the Commons annulled the returns. The government imprisoned him, and there was a riot near his prison. Five or six of his supporters were killed—massacred by the upholders of law and order—and public fury rose to such a pitch that sixty thousand people in England signed petitions for his release.

Americans considered JohnWilkes a warrior for constitutional freedom and embraced his cause as their own. A London society that was trying to raise money to pay his debts sent circulars to the colonies, and there was an especially prompt and generous response from South Carolina. In December of 1769, its Commons House of Assembly voted to send the huge sum of fifteen hundred pounds in support of "the just and constitutional rights and liberties of the people of Great Britain and America."

It was characteristic of the South Carolina legislature that it did not ask the consent either of the Council or of Governor Bull. It merely voted, and by a top-heavy majority, to borrow the money from the treasury with the idea of paying it back in the next money bill, and Christopher Gadsden, the rich Charleston merchant who had introduced the bill, was made a member of the committee that was responsible for getting the money into the hands of Wilkes' supporters in England.

The shocked amazement of the Board of Trade when it was informed what the South Carolina legislators had done was equaled only by the shocked amazement of the legislators themselves that anyone should question their right to dispose of the money as they saw fit. They stated that any attempt to limit their authority in money matters was a "seditious doctrine," and for five years legislation came to a standstill in South Carolina while the men of the Commons House of Assembly fought for what seemed to them to be an absolute principle.

Apart from this constitutional battle in South Carolina and the brief spurt of violence that was called the Boston Massacre, the decade of the 1770's opened in a relatively peaceful manner. Even in prickly Boston most of the areas of controversy seemed to have disappeared in the general atmosphere of peace and prosperity, and continued warnings of small groups of political radicals had no effect on what one Virginian called the "insensibility" of the people. The mood was very like that of England in the 1630's, when the country was also prosperous and at peace and where a small political blunder was sufficient to light the fuse that set off the underground charge of dynamite.

The blunder that set off the English revolution was Archbishop Laud's well-intentioned effort to reform the liturgy in the Scottish churches, and the blunder that set off the American Revolution was equally well meant. In 1773, the stockholders of the East India Company, which was nearly bankrupt, met in their General Court and decided to petition Parliament for the right to dispose of a huge surplus of tea by selling it under special arrangements to the American colonies. The current ministry handled the bill skillfully and it passed Parliament almost unnoticed.

In the autumn seven ships set sail from England, and the duty on the tea they carried was to be paid in the four American ports of Boston, New York, Philadelphia and Charleston. Benjamin Rush of Philadelphia, reacting precisely as the embattled Presbyterians of Scotland had reacted to Archbishop Laud, saw the whole thing as a vicious conspiracy—"the machinations of the enemies of our country to enslave us by means of the East India Company." If the duty were paid on the tea, he and men like him were convinced that America would be "undone forever."

Six weeks before the ships were due in port, the Boston newspapers started a barrage of warning. When the three ships destined for Boston finally arrived, huge mass meetings were called in protest. People came from all the neighboring towns, and the climax occurred on the 16th of December. It was a day of cold and rain, and the meeting ended with the people trooping down to the waterfront. There they watched silently while three well-disciplined groups, disguised as Indians and armed with hatchets, boarded the three ships. With an otherwise scrupulous regard for property, they hacked the tea chests open and dumped their contents overboard.

The House of Commons heard the news in a state of shock, for the Boston tea had been worth about nine thousand pounds. Again there was a long debate; but this time there were few men who were willing to defend the American conduct and the Boston Port Bill passed both Houses by heavy majorities. The bill closed the harbor to shipping, and its intention was to strangle the city into submission. All that it actually achieved was to make Boston a martyr.

Two months later, on the 20th of May, 1774, an Act was passed to prevent the recurrence of such behavior in Massachusetts. It was optimistically entitled "An Act for the Better Regulating the Government of the Province," and it made various changes in the way Massachusetts was to be governed. Town meetings were prohibited, unless specially authorized, and juries were no longer to be elected. The right to select the members of the Council was given to the royal governor, since, as the Act pointed out, this was the custom in His Majesty's other colonies. What Parliament neglected to point out was the fact that the right to select the members of the Council had been given to the Massachusetts legislature by the royal charter of 1691, under King William, and that not even the Stuarts had tried to abrogate a Massachusetts charter without a *quo warranto*.

On the same day, an Act was also passed to govern the vast territories that Great Britain had won from France. Under the terms of the Quebec Act, the inhabitants were to keep their Roman Catholic religion, laws were to be made by a Council appointed by the Crown, and all taxation, unless purely local, was specifically reserved to be the right of the British Parliament. Moreover, the boundaries of this new form of government in North America were to extend south as far as the Ohio River, deep in territory that the American colonists looked upon as their own.

From the point of view of the English government, these Acts were a statesmanlike attempt to increase efficiency and to reduce the threat of disorder. To the Americans, they seemed even worse than the ones that had been imposed in the days of Governor Andros and his Dominion. They called them the Intolerable Acts and felt a trap closing on them.

Back in 1765, in the days of the Stamp Tax, the colonists had tried to decide on a uniform course of action and some of them had sent delegates to a Stamp Act Congress that met briefly in New York City. One of the delegates had been Christopher Gadsden of South Carolina, who was convinced that all the colonies must act in concert. "That province that endeavors to act separately will certainly gain nothing by it. There ought to be no New England men, no New Yorker, etc., known on the Continent, but all of us Americans." This was a hard doctrine for thirteen stubborn and very individualistic colonies to accept, and nothing less than the Intolerable Acts could have brought them together, nine years later, in another general congress. This time it was to meet in Philadelphia, the largest city in America and the most centrally located, and the date was set for the fifth of September, 1774.

The colonial governors could not be expected to sit complacently by while the colonial legislatures chose delegates to a continental congress and voted the money for their expenses. Yet such a congress would have no authority unless it was authorized by the people, and this meant working through the legislatures. How to do this, and yet avoid a direct confrontation with the governors, was a problem that each colony solved in its own way.

Rhode Island encountered no difficulty at all, since its charter permitted it to elect its own governor. Its delegates arrived in Philadelphia with an authorization from the General Assembly and a confirmation from the Governor of Rhode Island, "given under my hand and the seal of the said colony . . . in the year of our Lord 1774 and the 14th of the reign of his most Sacred Majesty, George the Third."

Massachusetts, on the other hand, not only had a royally appointed Governor but a very formidable one. He was Thomas Gage, Commander in Chief of all the British forces in North America, and he had been made Governor of Massachusetts in the spring because it clearly required a military man to enforce the Intolerable Acts. As the port of Boston was closed, Governor Gage called the Massachusetts legislature into session at Salem so that it could make plans to pay for the tea. Instead, the legislature set up a committee to make plans in secret for the coming Continental Congress.

When the committee made its report on June the 17th, the Massachusetts legislators listened behind locked doors and approved the plan by a vote of 129 to 12. One member, pretending to be ill, was allowed to leave and told the Governor what was happening. Gage at once sent the Secretary with a proclamation that the legislature was dissolved, a declaration which he was obliged to read on the other side of the door. It was a scene very like the one in the House of Commons on that March day in 1629, when the Gentleman Usher of the Black Rod read a similar proclamation on the other side of a locked door while Sir John Eliot and his friends took the first step toward revolution.

In South Carolina, the legislature used the excuse of hot weather to meet unusually early one August morning. Before Governor Bull realized what it was doing, the Commons House of Assembly had voted fifteen hundred pounds for a distinguished slate of delegates to the Continental Congress, a slate that included Christopher Gadsden. These men had been chosen the month before, when the legislature was in recess, by what was called "a general meeting of the inhabitants of this colony." The meeting was held in Charleston and attended by over a hundred men, elected by the people in the same way that the legislature had been elected. The difference was that the Governor had not called this meeting together, and therefore he could not dissolve it.

The colony of New Hampshire pushed this same process one step further. Its royal Governor dissolved the legislature in June. In July, its leaders gathered at a tavern and arranged for an assembly, elected by the people, to meet at Exeter, a river town a few miles south of the capital city of Portsmouth. Eighty-five delegates arrived at what was called a Provincial Congress and appointed two men to go to Philadelphia. No funds were available to pay the expenses of Major John Sullivan and his fellow delegate, since the legislature was not in session. Therefore each New Hampshire town taxed itself voluntarily and the money was handled by a treasurer in Exeter. As the Governor of New Hampshire said regretfully, "The spirit of enthusiasm which generally prevails through the colonies will create an obedience that reason or religion would fail to procure."

In the much more conservative colony of New York this spirit of enthusiasm did not prevail. The delegates from New York County arrived in Philadelphia with a document, undated and unsigned, which stated vaguely that they had been chosen "by duly certified polls taken by proper persons in seven wards." Nearly every other colony, however, sent a formal, signed statement with its delegation, sometimes from a committee but more usually from the kind of extralegal assemblies that had been set up in South Carolina and New Hampshire and which were called either Conventions or Provincial Congresses.

The most formal statement of legality came from the delegation that represented the three Delaware Counties. This stated that "the freeholders and freemen of the said counties" would normally have looked to their duly elected legislature for assistance in the redress of their grievances against Great Britain. This was not possible since the legislature had been adjourned until the end of September, and therefore their leaders had chosen "the next most proper method of answering the expectations and desires of our constituents and of contributing our aid to the general cause of America." They had authorized the freeholders and freemen to elect delegates to a Convention which in turn had chosen the delegation for the Congress in Philadelphia.

The one colony which did not succeed in sending a delegation was Georgia. It was handicapped by a relatively inexperienced legislature, a very popular Governor, and the fact that it was a long way from Philadelphia. There was a flurry of letters and resolutions, and a gathering which claimed to represent the people did manage to meet in August; but it lacked enough political power to be able to send delegates to what was called the First Continental Congress.

It was an act of optimism to call it continental, since the twelve delegations that met in Philadelphia on the fifth of September, 1774, represented a fringe of land on the eastern seaboard and only a fraction of the area that Great Britain now owned in America. It was the fraction, however, which England had founded, fiercely determined not to be deprived of its rightful English liberties, and however much the fifty-six delegates might disagree about everything else, they were united in their conviction that they spoke for America. As Silas Deane, one of the delegates from Connecticut, put it: "The sense of Connecticut is . . . that the Congress is the grandest and most important assembly ever held in America, and that the *all* of America is entrusted to it and depends upon it."

Peyton Randolph was the unanimous choice as President of the Congress. He was still Speaker of the House of Burgesses in Virginia and he had presided over the Convention that sent the Virginia delegation to Philadelphia. Randolph had received his legal education in England, and he was presiding in Philadelphia over an assemblage of gentlemen who shared his parliamentary skills. As John Rutledge of South Carolina pointed out, "Doubtless the usage of the House of Commons would be adopted in our debates . . . as every gentleman was acquainted with that usage."

John Adams was one of the delegates from beleaguered Massachusetts, and he sometimes felt that his colleagues were almost too accomplished. "There is so much wit, sense, learning, acuteness, subtlety, eloquence, etc. among fifty gentlemen, each of whom has been habituated to lead and guide in his own province, that an immensity of time is spent unnecessarily." Much of this oratory was practiced in the Committee of the Whole, where the delegates could engage in informal and lengthy discussions while they tested out among themselves how far they and their constituents were prepared to go.

The device of the Committee of the Whole was an extremely useful piece of parliamentary machinery and they used it frequently. It had been invented for them by a similar group of incipient revolutionaries in the days of King James I. Shortly after he came to the throne, James had decided that he could prevent debates in the House of Commons by forbidding the Speaker of the House to be present. The House, with brisk political ingenuity, promptly set up a special committee which included everyone there, elected a chairman for it and continued as before.

The debates that were conducted in Philadelphia by the Committee of the Whole have not survived. The Secretary of the Congress, Charles Thomson, was a political appointment and not as energetic and conscientious as some of his colleagues. He was being paid, in any case, to record in the minutes what Congress had decided upon and not the way it had been decided. John Adams arrived in Philadelphia hoping to keep a daily journal of the proceedings, but his good intentions evaporated under the strain and in the end he did not even find enough time to make entries in his diary. No delegate to this or to any of the subsequent Continental Congresses managed more than a few random jottings, and one of them mourned the loss to history. "All its councils, designs and discussions having been conducted by Congress with closed doors, and no member, as far as I know, having even made notes of them, these, which are the life and soul of history, must forever be unknown."

The delegates' most difficult problem was to stay united, and it was this that accounted for the slowness with which they moved. John Adams grew impatient of what he called the "nibbling and quibbling" as they argued every line of an address to King George, but it was this carefulness which held together men who were in fact deeply divided. Some of them, like Adams, were beginning to believe that peace with Great Britain was no longer possible, some were willing to accept peace at almost any price, but the majority were sure that an honorable reconciliation could be achieved—that goal "most ardently desired by all good men."

Inevitably they published a Declaration of Rights, "as Englishmen their ancestors in like cases have usually done," and they had no difficulty in agreeing to a list of rights that started with the fundamental one: "That they are entitled to life, liberty and property, and that they have never ceded to any sovereign power whatever a right to dispose of either without their consent."

The men of the First Continental Congress adjourned on the 26th of October, 1774, agreeing to meet again in Philadelphia on the tenth of the following May if there had been no redress of grievances by then. William Bradford and his son, who were the official printers for the Congress, brought out the Journal of its proceedings so that every American could read what had happened there. The design on the title page was of twelve outstretched arms, with Magna Carta at their base.

Before it adjourned, Congress told the colonies to choose delegates to the May meeting as soon as possible, and in the case of New Hampshire this responsibility rested with the Provincial Congress meeting at Exeter. Its chairman was the "Speaker in the late General Assembly," and by the end of the year it was sending out mandates as though it were the official government of the colony; for the royal Governor of New Hampshire had almost completely lost control.

His name was John Wentworth and he was a nephew of the great Benning Wentworth who had ruled New Hampshire so vigorously for a quarter of a century. John Wentworth was a delightful individual—aristocrat, Harvard graduate and thorough gentleman—and he had inherited all the political connections that made the family name synonymous with local government. He greatly loved the land that the Wentworths ruled, and in the days of the Stamp Act he had served as London agent of New Hampshire in an effort to get the tax repealed.

All through the autumn of 1774, Governor John Wentworth struggled to keep the peace against mob violence, and he might have succeeded if Great Britain had not made a well-meant effort to assist him. It decided to place an embargo on the shipment of arms and ammunition to the colonies, and all the colonial governors were so informed. The Governor of Rhode Island promptly told the Massachusetts radicals of the plan, and Paul Revere brought the news to Portsmouth, riding "express from the committee in Boston to another committee in this town."

The ammunition in New Hampshire was stored in a fort about five miles downriver which controlled the entrance to Portsmouth harbor, and Major John Sullivan, who had recently been serving as a delegate to the Continental Congress, took a force of four hundred men to go and capture it. The governor of the fort wrote piteously to John Wentworth: "I told them on their peril not to enter. They replied they would." They did, and made off triumphantly with a hundred barrels of gunpowder.

Next door to New Hampshire, another royal Governor was trying to do his best in an impossible situation. This was Thomas Gage, who had lived in America for years, and very happily. He and his charming wife had been very much at home in New York society, George Washington valued him as a friend, and he had even become a member of the American Philosophical Society. His popularity vanished, however, when he took the oath of office as Governor of Massachusetts and made it clear that he intended to enforce the Intolerable Acts.

When Governor Gage sent out the usual writs of election of the October General Court, he scheduled it to meet in Salem, now the official capital of the colony. Public fury was at such a height by October of 1774 that he canceled the writs, but ninety members of the General Court arrived nevertheless. When Governor Gage failed to put in an appearance, they said his behavior had been unconstitutional. They therefore turned themselves into a Provincial Congress and adjourned to reassemble at Concord.

Gage was convinced that the present British policy would end with armed rebellion in Massachusetts, and his only miscalculation was his belief that the rest of the colonies would not support New England. Early in September he had started fortifying Boston Neck, and he felt that if he were sent twenty thousand men he could guarantee victory. Gage knew that Parliament could not go on talking about supremacy unless it were prepared to prove it, and he wrote to an English official in December: "I hope you will be firm. . . . Affairs are at a crisis, and if you give way it is forever."

English public opinion was divided, as it had been over the Wilkes case. In London there was a great deal of sympathy for the American cause, and the city of London presented King George with a petition on behalf of the colonies and in opposition to the ministry's policy of coercion. The petition was presented by the Lord Mayor of London, who that year was John Wilkes himself.

King George was a constitutional monarch, and his highly unfavorable opinion of the American colonies could not have been translated into action unless Parliament agreed with him. But Parliament was composed mostly of conservative men of property and agreed with him warmly. The current policy of the ministry had the support of large majorities in both Houses, and early in February, 1775, Massachusetts was officially declared to be in a state of rebellion.

This meant that Governor Gage was free to use the troops which he had been holding with such scrupulous correctness in Boston, and in April he was directly authorized to take the offensive. The Provincial Congress planned to hold its April meeting in Concord, and Gage waited until it adjourned. Then he sent his soldiers to Concord to capture some ammunition that had been stored there, and again Paul Revere rode in warning. The battles of Lexington and Concord were fought on the 19th of April, 1775, and the Revolutionary War had begun.

Each side maintained that the other had fired the first shot, but there was no question which side made the first move in the propaganda battle that followed. The Provincial Congress, which had planned to meet again in May, changed its plans and met at once. On a Sunday afternoon it formed a committee to prepare a report which would be a "true and authentic account of this inhuman proceeding." Then it sent the report by special packet ship to England, with instructions to circulate it in every town there. As a result, the English newspapers were printing a vivid account of the brutality of Gage's soldiers and the heroic self-defense of the American farmers nearly two weeks before Gage's more colorless official report was available. The New Englanders had been masters from the first of the art of propaganda, but here they really surpassed themselves.

The Massachusetts Provincial Congress made it very clear to Englishmen why it had turned to them for support. "It is the united efforts of both Englands that must save either. But . . . whatever the price our brethren in the one may be pleased to put on their constitutional liberties, we . . . assure you that the inhabitants of the other . . . are inflexibly resolved to sell theirs only at the price of their lives."

The Revolutionary War had many causes—social, economic and even religious—but to the men who fought it the central issue seemed clear. They fought against tyranny, as the men of the English revolution had fought more than a century before, and, like them, they could not bring themselves to admit that they had taken up arms against their lawful king. Therefore they fought only against his wicked advisers in protection of their liberties, and once His Sacred Majesty realized this fact, all would be well again.

An American army chaplain called it "the unhappy civil war," and it was literally so. "Neighbor was against neighbor, father against the son." There was no special economic or social pattern in the way Americans made up their minds which side to be on, any more than there had been in England. Some of the richest noblemen in England took up arms against Charles I, and some of the richest merchants in America took up arms against George III. A man like Christopher Gadsden was unaffected by the Intolerable Acts and had every reason to want close trade relations with Great Britain. He had just finished building in Charleston the largest wharf in the colonies and it was intended for the transoceanic shipping trade. Yet when Gadsden arrived in Philadelphia as a delegate to the First Continental Congress, he was "for taking up his firelock and marching direct to Boston."

Americans of this kind called themselves "Whigs" and they called their fellow Americans who disagreed with them "Tories." This had no relation to the current use of the word in England, where the great landowners of the Whig party were almost as conservative as their Tory opponents. It belonged more truly to the first political use of the two words back in the days when the Earl of Shaftesbury had tried to stage a rebellion against Charles II. Shaftesbury's followers were called Whigs by the opposition, and it was said of them that their "language is Overturn, overturn." They in turn nicknamed their opponents Tories and accused them of being so blindly monarchial that they believed that kings were "dropped down from Heaven with crowns on their heads, and that all their subjects were born with saddles on their backs." The two words had long since ceased to mean anything so extreme in England, but in America the revolutions of the seventeenth century were being fought over again and with the same slogans.

Very few effective pamphlets or newspapers came to the defense of the American Tories once the war had begun, and the energy of the powerful American press was concentrated almost entirely on the same side. It was a side, however, that represented various levels of opinion—radical, moderate and conservative—all expressing themselves vigorously in print and telling each other what ought to be done.

The basic responsibility for this decision rested with the Continental Congress, which reassembled in Philadelphia as planned on the tenth of May, 1775. This time it did not meet in Carpenters' Hall but in the State

House, and it was evident that the shots fired at Lexington and Concord had made the people more radical in their choice of delegates. Massachusetts had sent John Hancock to give support to John and Samuel Adams, cousins and fellow revolutionaries. Hancock and Samuel Adams were the only two men in Massachusetts whom the British had proclaimed they would never pardon, and when the President of the Congress, Peyton Randolph, was called back to Virginia, Hancock was elected to succeed him. The story goes that Benjamin Harrison of Virginia, who loved a joke, placed him bodily in the chair. "We will show Mother Britain how little we care for her, by making a Massachusetts man our president, whom she has excluded from pardon by a public proclamation."

Hancock had hoped, rather unrealistically, that he would be elected Commander in Chief of the army, but that responsibility went to a member of the Virginia delegation, George Washington, in the middle of June. The New Hampshire delegates voted for Washington with the rest, and by that time New Hampshire soldiers were already in the field. The Battle of Bunker Hill was fought on the 17th of June, 1775, two days after Washington's appointment, and two of the regiments there were made up of New Hampshire men.

In New Hampshire itself, Governor John Wentworth was still clinging to some semblance of order. The Provincial Congress at Exeter had all the records and was running the colony, but the Assembly was still officially in existence at Portsmouth. Wentworth adjourned it until September, expecting to open the session in person, but by July he had completely lost control. He and his family were forced to take refuge in the fort below Portsmouth, which was protected by the guns of the British warships in the harbor.

Wentworth tried not to feel bitterness. "I will not complain, because it would be a poignant censure on a people I love and forgive. For truly I can say, with the poet in his *Lear,* 'I am a man more sinned against than sinning.'" The warship left the harbor in August, and Wentworth and his family were obliged to leave with it. Half an hour later, the fort was wrecked by a New Hampshire mob.*

What the Provincial Congress at Exeter called, somewhat euphemistically, "the sudden and abrupt departure of His Excellency, John Wentworth, Esq., our late Governor," left the colony without any authorized govern-

---

* John Wentworth was the great-grandson of Thomas Wentworth, Earl of Strafford, who had been beheaded by Parliament in 1641, eight years before King Charles. The Wentworth family in both England and America had good reason to feel that from time to time the English race went a little mad.

ment. New Hampshire had never had a charter, and in October the Provincial Congress instructed its delegates to the Continental Congress to use their "utmost endeavors" to persuade Congress to tell them what to do.

John Adams had been waiting for this. Almost alone among the Congress delegates in Philadelphia, he had been urgently aware that the American colonies could not fight a revolution without at the same time assuming some form of self-government. As he said, "This subject . . . lay with great weight upon my mind as the most difficult and dangerous business that we had to do."

Its difficulty and danger lay in its grave threat to the unity of Congress. Thirteen colonies were represented now, since an official delegation from Georgia had at last arrived, but the fabric of unity was very frail and could not endure any sudden weight upon it. Not only would self-government be a difficult thing in itself—a leap in the dark—but it would cut the tie that bound each colony to the Mother Country and make a final reconciliation almost impossible.

John Adams did not want reconciliation. He was sure that the old relationship with Great Britain would never return and the sooner the fact was recognized, the better. Therefore he was sure that the Continental Congress "ought to recommend to the people of all the states to institute governments for themselves, under their own authority, and that without loss of time."

When the New Hampshire delegation made its request for guidance in October of 1775, John Adams saw his opportunity and seized it vigorously. He delivered a long speech on the subject, with nine subheadings, and Congress created a committee to take the matter under consideration. The Committee on the New Hampshire Instructions was obliged to report back that it could not come to an agreement, and a debate in full Congress followed. Since the Secretary took no notes, there is no record of what was said, but the New Hampshire delegation was deeply impressed. It reported back to the Provincial Congress at Exeter that the tone of the debate had been "truly Ciceronial; the eminent speakers did honor to themselves and the continent."

The final resolution, which passed on the third of November, was very cautiously worded. Congress authorized the men of New Hampshire to "establish such a form of government as in their judgment will best produce the happiness of the people and most effectually secure peace and good order in the province, during the continuance of the present dispute between Great Britain and the colonies." John Adams had tried hard to strengthen the wording. "By this time I mortally hated the words 'province,' 'colonies' and

'Mother Country' and strove to get them out of the report. The last was indeed left out, but the other two were retained. . . . Nevertheless, I thought this resolution a triumph and a most important point gained." It was indeed a triumph, and a very characteristic achievement on the part of a country which had been training itself in self-government ever since its founding.

Thus the honor fell to little New Hampshire to be the first of the future United States of America to create a constitution. The Provincial Congress at Exeter put it together in a week and finished it on the fifth of January, 1776.

The constitution was a rudimentary affair, since it was designed only "to continue during the present unhappy and unnatural contest with Great Britain." The lower house, to be elected directly by the people, was to be called the House of Representatives or the Assembly. It in turn would choose twelve reputable men from among its members to serve as an upper house or Council. Each house would choose its own presiding officer, but there would be no executive to take the office that Governor John Wentworth had vacated. The provincial Congress then voted to accept the constitution it had just made, turned itself into a House of Representatives, and was thus able to face the future with a written form of government securely in its possession.

The New Hampshire constitution made no mention of voting qualifications, because there was no need. This subject had been argued out already, when the previous Provincial Congress met in November.

New Hampshire had been operating under an election law, passed in 1728, which specified that voters must possess £50 worth of real estate. This was an eminently satisfactory arrangement to the men in the area around Portsmouth, where the harbor shipping and the lumber industry had concentrated so much wealth. It was less satisfactory to the men on the western frontier who had come upriver from Connecticut, or those in the southern part of the colony who had come over the border from Massachusetts. Their interests had never been adequately represented in the legislature that met in Portsmouth but the situation changed after the Provincial Congresses began to meet in Exeter. When the delegates to the fourth Provincial Congress gathered together in the autumn of 1775, half of them came from the inland counties.

The Wentworths had been in control of New Hampshire for most of the century, and the fall of that great ruling house was like the uprooting of a massive tree. In the loosened soil new growths began to spring up, and one of these showed itself early in November: the Provincial Congress decided to cut the £50 requirement for the franchise down to £20.

This was a very great concession, but it was not considered sufficient.

No record of the debates has survived but, ten days later, on the 14th of November, 1775, the Provincial Congress of New Hampshire decided to let anyone vote if he paid taxes.

John Sullivan wrote reassuringly, "No danger can arise to a state from giving the people a free and full voice in their own government." If by the people he meant the taxpayers, he would have found few Americans to agree with him. For it was an astonishing thing that New Hampshire had done, the first sign that the crust which had formed in America on the subject of the franchise could crack under the pressure of war.

Chapter Nine

The next colony to try its hand at writing a constitution was South Carolina. Its delegates also asked the Continental Congress for the right to set up some form of self-government, and Congress gave permission on the fourth of November, 1775, a day after the authorization to New Hampshire.

The political situation in South Carolina was entirely different, for here there had been no overturnings. The great port of Charleston remained the center of political power, and the gentlemen who lived there kept the authority firmly in their own possession. For they were themselves the revolutionists and they rode on the crest of a rising wave.

The British authorities had removed the unfortunate Governor Bull, since he obviously had no control of the situation. They sent out instead that courteous and accomplished gentleman Lord William Campbell, arming him with a whole new set of instructions. These turned out to be useless since Campbell arrived in Charleston on June 17, 1775, the same day as the Battle of Bunker Hill. The following month, the Commons House of Assembly informed the new Governor blandly that since its right to assemble rested upon his authorization, the people of South Carolina had elected a provincial congress instead, or, as they put it, had "wisely appointed another representative body." In September, Campbell fled on a British warship, as Governor Wentworth of New Hampshire had done, and both colonies asked the Continental Congress for the right to set up their own governments.

The South Carolina legislators managed to strike the same note of righteous legality mingled with outrage that they had maintained earlier over the Wilkes affair: "Lord William Campbell, late Governor, on the fifteenth day of September last, dissolved the general assembly of this colony and no other hath been since called, although by law the sitting and holding of general assemblies cannot be intermitted above six months." Campbell had also "carried off the great seal and the royal instructions," and in the opinion of William Henry Drayton, the President of the South Carolina Provincial Congress, this clear parallel to the behavior of James II of England gave them "a clear right to effect another revolution." There was a time when Drayton had called Christopher Gadsden a "traitor or madman" for the violence of his revolutionary opinions, but by 1776 they were brothers in the same cause.

Gadsden came back to Charleston in February of 1776, leaving his post in the Continental Congress so that he could join the committee of prominent men who had been assigned the task of writing a constitution for the colony. Their draft was ready early in March, and the Provincial Congress resolved itself into a Committee of the Whole to debate it.

The question of the franchise aroused very little interest. It was decided to leave almost intact the current election law, which required the ownership of fifty acres of land or a town lot or its equivalent in taxes. Eleven words were added for clarification, but there were no other alterations. The legislators themselves were required to be large holders of property, so that there was no danger of any sudden shift of power in South Carolina.

South Carolina decided to have a chief executive, but the motion to name him Governor was defeated. Possibly this was because the title had unpleasant connotations, and he was styled President instead. (Two years later, however, when a second constitution was written for South Carolina, the President was renamed the Governor and the upper house was named the Senate.) As soon as the constitution had been approved, the Provincial Congress disbanded itself, as the similar body in New Hampshire had done. It then reassembled the same afternoon, now the General Assembly and the legal government of South Carolina.

Two months later, on the tenth of May, 1776, John Adams and his fellow radicals in the Continental Congress finally achieved their goal. A resolution was passed which gave all the colonies the right to self-government instead of doling the privilege out piecemeal. "Resolved, that it be recommended to the respective assemblies and conventions of the United

Colonies, where no government sufficient to the exigencies of their affairs have been hitherto established, to adopt such government as shall, in the opinion of the representatives of the people, best conduce to the happiness and safety of their constituents in particular and America in general."

John Adams was jubilant, as he had every right to be. He hailed the resolution as "an epocha, a decisive event," and wrote to a friend of his early in June: "We are in the very midst of a revolution, the most complete, unexpected and remarkable of any in the history of nations. . . . Every colony must be induced to institute a perfect government."

One of the first to respond was New Jersey. It too was being governed by a Provincial Congress, which imprisoned the royal Governor in June. He was Sir William Franklin, son of Benjamin Franklin, and his foe in the war that had divided so many American families. Even so, the Provincial Congress did not go to extremes and it was careful to emphasize that the constitution would be void if New Jersey should come again "under the protection and government of the crown of Britain."

This Provincial Congress was the fourth to be held in New Jersey, but the first that had not been elected solely by freeholders. Up to this point, New Jersey had been operating under an Act for the Better Regulation of Elections passed in 1725. It required the voter to possess a £50 freehold, and once the war began this requirement began to seem unjust and restrictive. As a resident of New Jersey put it in September of 1775: "Many true friends of their country, who are obliged to pay taxes, are excluded from the privilege of a vote in the choice of those by whom they are taxed, or even called out to sacrifice their lives." This was the same argument that had been advanced at Putney during the English revolution. Men who fought and paid taxes had a right to share in the government, or, to put the argument in the language of the current revolutionary slogan, there should be no taxation without representation.

This newspaper letter went on to suggest that petitions be sent to the Provincial Congress on the subject. The towns in the eastern part of New Jersey responded with such vigor that they could not be ignored, and the third Provincial Congress debated the subject for four days in February, 1776. It could not bring itself to a complete liberalization of the franchise, but it did decide to abandon the freeholder requirement. When the next Provincial Congress set itself to write a constitution, the new voting arrangement duly became Article Four: "All inhabitants of this colony, of full age, who are worth fifty pounds proclamation money, clear estate in the same . . . shall be entitled to vote for representatives in Council and Assembly."

New Jersey completed its constitution on the second of July, 1776, and three days earlier, on the 29th of June, the men of Virginia had finished theirs. The tone of their document was entirely different. New Jersey had termed itself, cautiously and accurately, a colony. Virginia considered itself to be already a free commonwealth, and the magnificent Virginia constitution announced this fact with eloquence and energy to the whole world.

The representative body that wrote the constitution did not call itself a Provincial Congress but a Convention. A year earlier it had been meeting in the church of the little village of Richmond and referring respectfully in the minutes to "our worthy Governor, Lord Dunmore." Now it was meeting in its rightful home, the House of Burgesses in Williamsburg, and Lord Dunmore had become in its eyes a roving outlaw.

Peyton Randolph had served as presiding officer of the Convention when it met at Richmond, and he had instructed his colleagues to proceed "with that prudence, dignity and order which had distinguished their conduct on all former occasions." His sudden death in Philadelphia ended the long career of that most conservative of radicals—a true Virginia gentleman—and when the Convention met in Williamsburg in May of 1776 it was presided over by another conservative, Edmund Pendleton.

The creation of a constitution for Virginia was the climax of all those generations of legislators who had met in Jamestown in the seventeenth century and at Williamsburg in the eighteenth, and who were now prepared to create a written government for all future generations. It was to be no temporary affair, as the constitution of South Carolina had been. It was, in the proud words of Richard Henry Lee, to be "a permanent system of liberty."

Lee was serving in the Continental Congress as head of the Virginia delegation, but he left Philadelphia on the 13th of June so that he could be in Williamsburg to assist in the final days of shaping what he called that "mighty work." Carter Braxton was also serving in Congress, having taken the place of Peyton Randolph when that honored man died, and he offered his advice to his fellow Virginians in the shape of a published address.

Braxton was a radical as far as relations with Great Britain were concerned, but he was a conservative in regard to the internal affairs of Virginia. He warned the delegates to the Convention not to permit anything in the proposed constitution that would extend political power downward, since "a disinterested attachment to the public good . . . never characterized the mass of the people in any state." It was Braxton's opinion that the best way to protect Virginia from the masses was to have the members of the upper house chosen by indirect election and serving for life.

Edmund Pendleton, the presiding officer of the Convention, also wanted the Senate to serve as a shield against the people. He too wished the Virginia Senators to hold office for life, "unless impeached, and to have been chosen out of the people of great property." Yet Pendleton did not bring up this suggestion at the Convention, since he knew it would be ignored. It "seemed so disagreeable to the temper of the times I never mentioned it."

The temper of the Virginia Convention was not in the direction of aristocracy, but it was not in the contrary direction either. Its guiding star was that apostle of the middle way, John Locke. The men of the Convention were the political heirs of the Englishmen who achieved the Glorious Revolution, and the words of the man who set himself to justify that Revolution were part of the whole fabric of their thinking.

It was Locke who had supplied the basis for the rejection of the Stamp Tax. He had written: "If anyone shall claim a power to lay and levy taxes on the people, by his own authority and without such consent of the people, he thereby invades the fundamental law of property and subverts the end of government." It was Locke who assured them that revolution was justified if their governors tried to exert power in an arbitrary way, for "by this breach of trust they forfeit the power the people had put into their hands for quite contrary ends." Therefore the people had the right, in Locke's words, "to resume their original liberty, and by the establishment of a new legislative (such as they shall think fit) provide for their safety and security."

The men of the Virginia Convention did not set themselves to the writing of a constitution until they had first created a Bill of Rights. Its chief architect was George Mason, and he was responsible for the clarity and eloquence of its sixteen sections; but the principles it set forth had been in the process of building for centuries, and it was John Locke who supplied the words. Section One of the Bill of Rights summarized the fundamentals of government as Locke had already stated them, in Mason's clear summary:

> That all men are by nature equally free and independent, and have certain inherent rights, of which, when they enter into a state of society, they cannot, by any compact, deprive or divest their posterity; namely, the enjoyment of life and liberty, with the means of acquiring and possessing property, and pursuing and obtaining happiness and safety.

Section Two continued with the same magnificent rhetoric derived from the same source:

> That all power is vested in, and consequently derived from, the people; that magistrates are their trustees and servants, and at all times amenable to them.

Locke was writing a philosophical essay and not trying to create a working constitution, and he was not obliged to explain what he meant by the "people." The Virginia Bill of Rights necessarily had to be more specific, and it addressed itself to this point in Section Six, which declared that "all men having sufficient evidence of permanent common interest with and attachment to the community have the right of suffrage."

This was the principle upon which Colonel Ireton had based the whole of his argument during the debate at Putney. A voter had to be possessed of what Ireton called "a local, a permanent interest," and it was in defense of this doctrine that Ireton and Cromwell had clung so tenaciously to the forty-shilling freehold. They hoped and believed that when the revolution was over the landed gentry would be securely in control, safe from any threat of royal power against their domination and equally safe from any threat to their political authority from below.

The gentlemen of Virginia remained of the same opinion as their English counterparts. The constitution was adopted seventeen days after the Bill of Rights was approved, and the single sentence on the franchise made it clear that the discussion of political equality in the Bill of Rights had been rhetoric only. "The right of suffrage in the election of members for both houses shall remain as exercised at present."

The Virginia Convention conducted its debates on the constitution under the device of the Committee of the Whole, so that every man could be heard, and Edmund Pendleton, the presiding officer, said later that the whole constitution had been "disputed inch by inch." Nevertheless, another member noted that there had been no difference of opinion on the subject of a freeholder franchise. "It was not recollected," said Edmund Randolph austerely, "that a hint was uttered in contravention of this principle. There can be no doubt that, if it had been, it would have perished under discussion." George Mason had been hoping to liberalize the franchise slightly by permitting householders and the holders of certain kinds of non-freehold leases to vote, but even Mason had no thought of letting landless men take part in anything so sacred as the government of Virginia.

No other colony was quite able to match this calm achievement on the part of the Virginia legislators, stopping the clock of history so firmly and with such dignity at precisely the point they deemed desirable. Ireton and Cromwell had not been able to achieve this, bedeviled as they were by that triumvirate of radical journalists, Lilburne, Walwyn and Overton, and some of the leaders of the American Revolution found it equally difficult. They were faced by only one such journalist, but his name was Thomas Paine.

Paine was a newcomer to the colonies, and when he arrived from

England in November of 1774 he had seemed a mild enough individual. He had been interested in America ever since he had encountered, as a schoolboy, a natural history of Virginia, and when Benjamin Franklin met him in London he liked him enough to give him a letter of introduction. Paine arrived in Philadelphia intending to teach geography to young ladies and gentlemen, but since he was obviously a competent journalist he was offered the editorship of a new magazine, *The Pennsylvania Magazine or American Monthly Museum*.

The magazine was well named, since it was a museum-like clutter of whatever interested Paine's roving mind. There was a great deal of information about machinery, which happened to be Paine's special field. There were cultural extracts, historical items, and reports of births, marriages and deaths in prominent families at home and abroad. ("The lady of His Excellency Governor Wentworth of a son at Portsmouth in New Hampshire.") There was advice on the building of frame houses, a piece of ornamental prose on the subject of Cupid and Hymen, and in January of 1776 a poem describing the feelings of a dying Negro whose mind, "naturally brave and elevated," had become deranged through the death of his wife.

There was also in this January issue, placed opposite an explanation of how to distill fresh water from salt, the text of a speech that George III had delivered to Parliament late in October. In it the King stated that he had acted up to now with moderation, "still hoping that my people in America would have discerned the traitorous views of their leaders." This was now no longer possible. "Those who have long too successfully labored to inflame my people in America . . . now openly avow their revolt, hostility and rebellion." No course was open but "to put a speedy end to these disorders" by the full armed might of Great Britain, until such time as "the unhappy and deluded multitude against whom this force will be directed shall become sensible of their error."

The people of Philadelphia were able to read King George's speech on the tenth of January, 1776, and on this same day a pamphlet went on sale that Paine had written and entitled *Common Sense*. He had planned the timing deliberately, and it was a source of pride to him that "both of them made their appearance in this city on the same day."

Paine was one of the many Englishmen to whom liberty was the breath of life, and as soon as he arrived in America he had identified himself passionately with the colonial cause. He met Benjamin Rush in a bookstore run by the magazine's publisher, and the distinguished physician suggested that Paine might like to write a pamphlet on the question. As Rush remembered it, Paine "readily assented to the proposal, and from time to time he called at my house and read to me every chapter of the proposed pamphlet as he composed it." It was Rush who suggested the title *Common Sense.*

Paine had thought of serial publication and then changed his mind, for he had produced a very inflammatory piece of work. It did not advocate merely a continuation of the struggle, a point on which most Americans were in full agreement. It advocated independence, which was so radical a stand in January of 1776 that very few Americans were open advocates of it.

James Allen, a rich Philadelphia lawyer, held the opinion that seemed to be the intelligent one at the moment. Allen believed that Americans were fighting for "a great and glorious cause. . . . If we fall, liberty no longer continues an inhabitant of this globe." But Allen did not believe that this could possibly justify trying to destroy the framework that bound Great Britain and her colonies together, and he branded a declaration of independence as "totally foreign to the original plan of resistance."

Thomas Paine thought otherwise, and *Common Sense* exploded like a match touched to dynamite. It sold more than a hundred thousand copies in its first three months, and total sales were five times that amount. Christopher Gadsden was waving a copy in February when he arrived in Charleston to help write the South Carolina constitution, and a minister in Connecticut read the whole of it from his pulpit instead of delivering a sermon.

It was not only because Paine advocated an instant separation from Great Britain that the colonists read him with such excitement. It was the way he did it. Paine wrote as though the world had been new-made that January, and as though the Americans need be bound by nothing whatever in all of past history. As he put it in that cool, lively, practical style of his: "A long habit of not thinking a thing wrong gives it a superficial appearance of being right." In Paine's opinion all the accumulation of history, all the centuries-old trappings of privilege, were so much nonsense, and his brisk contempt for antiquity even included that object of veneration the British constitution. Nor did he see any reason to reverence the anointed ruler of England, for, as he said blandly, "There is something exceedingly ridiculous in the composition of monarchy."

Paine pointed out to his delighted American hosts that they now constituted one-eighth of the inhabited globe, and that they were quite free to ignore the past for the tyranny it was and to start over again. Anything short of a declaration of independence would clearly be mere patchwork, and he ended the pamphlet by assuring his readers that the step would not really be so painful after all: "These proceedings may at first appear strange and difficult, but, like all other steps which we have already passed over, will in a little time become familiar and agreeable; and until an independence is declared, the continent will feel itself like a man who continues putting off some unpleasant business from day to day, yet knows it must be done, hates to set about it, wishes it over, and is continually haunted with the thoughts of its necessity."

To most Americans the pamphlet came as an explosive relief. Paine had demolished the whole of the middle ground upon which they had been trying with increasing difficulty to stand, and the idea of independence began to seem not only possible but quite natural. *Common Sense* crystallized what many people had been thinking and feeling but could not have expressed so clearly, and emotionally it marked the turning point in the American Revolution.

Since Paine was a true revolutionary, he was able to be a consistent one, and the point of view of the gentlemen of Virginia in relation to the suffrage was totally foreign to his way of thinking. Nineteen years later he published in Paris a pamphlet called *Dissertation on First Principles of Government,* and in it he attacked the idea of tying property to the vote with the same vigor with which he had attacked the idea of tying the American colonies to England. He did it, moreover, by the same application of common sense:

> It is dangerous and impolitic, sometimes ridiculous and always unjust, to make property the criterion of the right of voting. . . . When a brood-mare shall fortunately produce a foal or a mule, that by being worth the sum in question shall convey to its owner the right of voting or by its death take it from him, in whom does the origin of such a right exist? Is it in the man, or in the mule?

It was Paine's conviction that "the right of voting for representatives is the primary right by which other rights are protected. To take away this right is to reduce a man to a state of slavery, for slavery consists in being subject to the will of another, and he that has not a vote in the election of representatives is in this case." Paine respected political stability, but he was sure that a limitation on the franchise was not the way to achieve it: "In a political view of the case, the strength and permanent security of government is in proportion to the number of people interested in supporting it. The true policy, therefore, is to interest the whole by an equality of rights, for the danger arises from exclusions. It is possible to exclude men from the right of voting, but it is impossible to exclude them from the right of rebelling against that exclusion."

No man could have agreed less with this point of view than another great revolutionary, John Adams. Adams, like his colleagues in Virginia, was a conservative when it came to the question of voting and he believed that Paine's theories could lead only to chaos.

A member of the Massachusetts legislature named James Sullivan decided in May of 1776 that the time had come to liberalize the suffrage in Massachusetts, since the Continental Congress had now given all the colonies the right to create their own governments. Overworked as he was, Adams took the time to write Sullivan a long, careful letter to explain how dangerous it would be to increase the number of voters. "It is certain, in theory, that the only moral foundation of government is the consent of the people. But to what an extent shall we carry this principle?"

John Adams was a disciple of James Harrington, and he believed so ardently in the principles laid down in *Oceana* that it was almost his political Bible: "Harrington has shown that power always follows property. This I believe to be as infallible a maxim in politics, as that action and reaction are equal is in mechanics." Harrington had taught that the best way to achieve a stable government was to divide property among as many people as possible, and it was a source of pride to Adams that the colony of Massachusetts, with its numerous small landholdings, had followed this principle, however unconsciously, from its beginnings.

It seemed to Adams that nothing could be more unwise than to upset so excellent a system by tinkering with the franchise, and he closed his letter to Sullivan with a graphic description of what would occur if even a small liberalization were permitted: "Depend upon it, sir, it is dangerous to open so fruitful a source of controversy and altercation as would be opened by attempting to alter the qualifications of voters; there will be no end of it. New claims will arise; women will demand a vote; lads from twelve to twenty-one will think their rights not enough attended to; and every man who has not a farthing will demand an equal voice with any other in all acts of state." The ultimate result would be "to confound and destroy all distinctions, and prostrate all ranks to one common level," a situation which seemed quite as shocking to John Adams as it would have to John Winthrop himself.

Adams called Thomas Paine a "disastrous meteor" and considered him to be one of the most dangerous influences to which America had ever been subjected. Yet the two men were allies in May of 1776 since they both wanted the same thing. They wanted the Continental Congress to declare independence from Great Britain, and they therefore wanted to break the power of the Pennsylvania General Assembly, since it refused to instruct its delegates to agree to so radical a step.

The position of the vast majority of the men in the Assembly resembled that of James Allen, who was one of its newly elected members; independence was "totally foreign to the original plan of resistance." The instructions to its Congress delegates in November, confirmed the following April, were to "utterly reject any propositions . . . that may . . . lead to a separation from our Mother Country."

Paine had made a frontal attack on these Pennsylvania instructions when he wrote *Common Sense:* "A set of instructions for the delegates were put together . . . and after being approved by a *few,* a *very few* without doors, were carried into the House and there passed *in behalf of the whole colony.*" His furious italics informed the world of what every Pennsylvanian knew already, that the colony was governed by a small, relatively conservative political élite which had permitted itself to become increasingly isolated from the will of the people.

In the rich, busy, noisy city of Philadelphia, with its lively population and its many newspapers, the Pennsylvania Assembly held its meetings in an island of entrenched privilege. Originally made up of Quakers, and still consisting largely of propertied men in or near the city, it ruled as though by divine right. The Assembly had won a conclusive victory over William Penn at the beginning of the century when it achieved its Charter of Privileges, and since then its rise to power had continued unchecked. There was no upper house to hamper it, and the series of governors sent out by the Penn family had never been able to exert any effective political control.

Nor could the people. There was no legal way for the majority of the inhabitants of Philadelphia to express political dissent, since every city voter had to possess £50 worth of personal estate. It was easier to vote in the country, where the requirement was fifty acres of land, but there was no danger of loss of control in this direction either. The three counties of Bucks, Chester and Philadelphia, which made up the rich and conservative eastern section of the colony, had the right to elect twenty-four delegates to the Assembly. This left twelve delegates to be elected by all the other counties in Pennsylvania put together, and therefore, as Paine had said, the government was under the control of a very few men.

William Penn had made a policy of attracting to his colony as many nationalities as possible, and by now the Quakers were completely outnumbered. "By great importations from Ireland . . . the Presbyterians exceed the Quakers. And the Germans are without doubt more than either." The Germans made up about a third of Pennsylvania's population by 1776 and were not politically-minded, but the same could not be said for the Presbyterians from Ireland, the people whom later generations called Scotch-

Irish. They had been moving from Scotland to northeastern Ireland all through the seventeenth century, since the English authorities were changing the nature of Roman-Catholic Ulster by settling it with Protestants. At the beginning of the eighteenth century, these Presbyterian settlers found a new and restrictive set of British rules not to their liking, and they began emigrating from Ireland to America. They were especially attracted to Pennsylvania, and in 1719 alone twelve shiploads arrived. They pushed out to the frontier, and in political matters were considered as tumultuous as Oliver Cromwell himself. "They still have Oliverian spirit in them, and if ever a revolution is attempted to set up themselves independent of their Mother Country, it will arise from this prevailing Presbyterian faction."

By May of 1776, these Scotch-Irish were fiercely ready for independence from Great Britain. So were the voteless and vigorous artisans of Philadelphia. Within the Continental Congress, many of the delegates from the other twelve colonies had also grown increasingly radical. But meeting in the same building as the Congress was the Pennsylvania Assembly, refusing adamantly to change the instructions of its delegates. Under the circumstances, a man like John Adams became automatically the ally of the Pennsylvania radicals who wanted to destroy the Assembly.

The power to do this was put into their hands. When Congress approved on the tenth of May the resolution to let all the colonies form their own governments, it made Adams chairman of a committee to write a preamble. His text, which was much longer than that of the resolution, stated that all such governments must be formed "under the authority of the people," and everyone knew that this was aimed directly at the Pennsylvania Assembly. When the text of the preamble came up for debate in Congress, James Wilson fought hard to prevent its passage. He was the most brilliant jurist in Pennsylvania and he expressed the basic position of the moderates: "Before we are prepared to build a new house, why should we pull down the old one?"

Even before the preamble was approved (by a very narrow margin) the men of the Assembly knew what a battle they faced. The text of the Congress resolution was read aloud by William Bradford in his popular coffee-house, and men like James Allen and his friends remained silent. "We stared at each other. My feelings of indignation were strong, but it was necessary to be mute." Allen resolved to oppose the radicals "vehemently in the Assembly, for if they prevail there, all may bid adieu to our old happy constitution and peace."

The strategy of the radicals, however, was to bypass the Assembly. On the 20th of May, which was the day it came back into session in the State

House, the radicals called a public meeting in State House Yard. In spite of the rain there was an attendance of nearly four thousand people, listening to the text of the resolution that Congress had passed and the long preamble that John Adams had written.

Then the people in State House Yard passed a series of resolutions of their own. One of them denounced the instructions that the Assembly had given its delegates to the Continental Congress. Another said that the Assembly should not remain in existence because it lacked the authority of the people as specified in the preamble. Only one man there, a grocer, voted against this resolution, and the vote was unanimous in favor of calling a constitutional convention to write a new form of government for Pennsylvania.

The revolutionary county committees assumed the responsibility for working out the rules under which this convention would operate. Over a hundred delegates from these committees met in Carpenters' Hall on the 18th of June and worked for a week on the arrangements for the convention that would meet in Philadelphia in July. They were very thorough. As one of the delegates put it, "We are resolved to clear every part of the old rubbish out of the way and begin upon a clean foundation."

One of the questions which this June conference had to decide was under what rules the people should vote for delegates to the constitutional convention. It was decided that anyone who served in the militia and paid taxes should be permitted to vote. It was also decided, however, that no one could be permitted to vote unless he was in favor of independence from Great Britain, and that he must be prepared to take an oath to this effect before he could be permitted to cast his vote for a delegate to the constitutional convention.

Moderates like James Wilson, trying desperately to play for time, were forced to fight on two fronts. They were trying to prevent the Continental Congress from passing resolution in favor of independence, and they were trying to prevent the destruction of the Pennsylvania Assembly. They failed in both and with this failure lost their political influence for the time being.

As a result, the constitution that was written in Philadelphia in July was the work of men who had had almost no political experience. They had not been permitted to serve in the Assembly, and when they gathered together in the middle of the month they saw no reason why they should not pull the old government up by the roots and start over again.

John Adams considered the resulting constitution "the worst that has been established in America," and he was convinced that Thomas Paine must have had a hand in writing it. But Paine was in the army by then, serving as unpaid secretary to a local brigadier general, and there is no reason to doubt his statement that he did not see the text of the Pennsylvania constitution until it was published.

The one great name the radicals could count on for support was that of Benjamin Franklin, elderly, distinguished and with an international reputation. When he retired from a successful career as a Philadelphia businessman and entered politics, he was elected to the Assembly and became one of its leading members. As one of his enemies had pointed out with reluctant admiration during an especially bitter political brawl, Franklin was "perfectly acquainted with every zig zag machination" of the savage art of getting and keeping political control. Joseph Galloway had been his lieutenant in the Assembly, and by 1776 Galloway had hardened into a symbol of everything that was repressive and resistant to change. Franklin himself had grown as a tree grows. Just turned seventy, and the most honored man in America, he was quite willing to be a revolutionist not only against Great Britain but in domestic affairs also.*

Franklin did not fear a constitution which would give more power to ordinary men, and he was quite willing to lend the prestige of his great name to the constitutional convention. It opened in the State House on the 15th of July, and he was unanimously chosen to be the presiding officer.

By the end of September, the Pennsylvania constitution was finished. Its creators had taken over the text of the Virginia Bill of Rights almost intact, but not the Virginia plan of government. The Pennsylvania radicals did not wish to bring back the office of governor and they set up an executive council instead. Nor would they tolerate the existence of an upper house. All power was to be vested in the Assembly, as it had been before, but this time they were going to make sure that it really represented the people.

The franchise requirements were altered in what was the most radical move of all. The constitution gave any man the right to vote if he had lived in Pennsylvania for a year, was twenty-one years old and had paid taxes. Sons of freeholders were permitted to vote even if they had no taxable property, and ultimately a test oath was required so that no man could vote unless he was willing to swear that he approved of the new constitution.

---

* Franklin reversed the normal pattern of the average human being and became increasingly radical as he grew older. The glorious youthfulness of his old age is not reflected in his autobiography, which covers only the first fifty years of his life and makes no mention of his career in politics. When Franklin read the manuscript over, he remarked that it would be of "general use to young readers exemplifying strongly the effects of *prudent* and *imprudent conduct* in the commencement of a life of business." In the latter part of Franklin's wonderful life, prudence was not his outstanding political characteristic.

Benjamin Rush had been one of the group in Carpenters' Hall who set up the convention machinery in June, and he had wanted a new government for Pennsylvania as ardently as he wanted independence from Great Britain. Yet when the document was completed, he began to grow uneasy; it seemed to him that the new government was "rather too much upon the democratical order." By the following May he was openly alarmed—"It has substituted a mob government to one of the happiest governments in the world"—and he ended as its implacable foe. "They call it a democracy—a mobocracy in my opinion would be more proper. All our laws breathe the spirit of town meetings and porter shops." As for one of Rush's friends, the new government helped to kill him. "His hatred to the new constitution of Pennsylvania and his anticipation of its evils were such as to bring on a political hypochondriasis, which it was said put an end to his life."

No one seemed to be willing to encourage in Pennsylvania the spirit of compromise that was normally so central to American politics. The supporters of the constitution were as rigid as their opponents and set up the Test Oath in an effort to disfranchise everyone who disagreed with them. For years the two sides raged at each other, creating so poisoned an atmosphere that Rush remarked it was better to be a soldier than a politician, since "in battle men kill without hating each other."

Franklin was serving his country abroad during this period, but he was unperturbed by the shift of power that had put the Assembly into the hands of the Presbyterians. "It is a fact that the Irish emigrants and their children are now in possession of the government of Pennsylvania by their majority in the Assembly . . . and I remember well the first ship that brought any of them over." He returned to Philadelphia in 1785, to what he thought would be an old age of quiet retirement, and was immediately asked to serve on the executive council as the one man to whom both sides were still speaking.

Franklin accepted the office on the understanding that he would try to heal the breach. John Jay wrote him from New York that "unless you do it, I do not know who can," and the Marquis de Lafayette made the same point in a letter from Paris.

By an almost unanimous vote, Franklin was elected president of the council and in his first message to the Assembly he suggested that the time had come to alter the Test Oath. Franklin did not criticize the law—he never criticized anything openly if he could avoid it—but he indicated that it would be "now expedient" to revise it. The following year he was reelected unanimously and his suggestion was taken. After the fourth of March, 1786, no one could be disfranchised in Pennsylvania for refusing to approve of the constitution.

Franklin's deft public manner misled many people into thinking that he had no fundamental convictions of his own. As Alexander Graydon put it: "His demeanor to both parties was so truly oily and accommodating, that it always remained doubtful to which he really belonged. . . . I have been told by a gentleman who acted with him as vice president, that he . . . even declined the trouble of thinking. As to the constitution . . . it did not appear . . . that he had ever read it."

Graydon was wholly mistaken. Franklin had not only read the Pennsylvania constitution but he believed ardently in the principle upon which it was based. In 1789 the decision was made to call a new constitutional convention to revise it, and the *Federal Gazette,* which was a conservative newspaper, suggested some improvements. Franklin was by now a very old man (he died the following April) but this did not prevent him from writing a long and vigorous reply to the *Gazette*'s November suggestions.

The *Gazette* recommended that Pennsylvania get itself an upper house and that only very rich men be elected to it. Franklin inquired sharply why it was "supposed that wisdom is the necessary concomitant of riches," and then launched into an attack on the basic principle of property voting: "The combinations of civil society are not like those of a set of merchants, who club their property . . . and may therefore have some right to vote . . . according to their respective contributions; but the important ends of civil society, and the personal securities of life and liberty there, remain the same in every member of the society, and the poorest continues to have an equal claim to them with the most opulent." Therefore, said Franklin firmly, he remained opposed to any system which gave "the rich a predominancy in government."

The new constitutional convention met in Philadelphia on the 25th of November, 1789, and it was clear that both sides had at last learned the wisdom of Franklin's gift for compromise. Men like James Wilson, who had opposed the old constitution so vigorously, said nothing whatever in open criticism of it, and both sides met each other halfway. Pennsylvania's constitution was brought in line with the procedures that were working well in the other states, and from that time forward the state had a single executive and a two-house legislature; but the franchise was left unchanged, except that the residence requirement was changed to two years and the state or county tax had to have been assessed "at least six months before the election."

Thus the great state of Pennsylvania retained the same taxpayer suffrage that had seemed suitable in little rural New Hampshire. This was not at all the result that John Adams had hoped for when he helped make it possible, in 1776, for Pennsylvania to write its first constitution. But at least Adams could comfort himself with the reflection that a taxpayer was a man of property and that even the radicals had not brought into being his nightmare vision of a voter without a farthing.

Chapter Ten

In April of 1776, the independence of the thirteen colonies still seemed very far away, in spite of the hard work of the radicals in the Continental Congress and the increasingly rigid position taken by Great Britain. Carter Braxton, who had been a delegate since December, wrote his uncle in Virginia on the 14th of April, "I am convinced the assertion of independence is far off. If it was to be now asserted, the continent would be torn in pieces by intestine wars and convulsions," since the colonies disagreed with each other about so many things. "And yet," Braxton ended his letter incredulously, "without any adjustments of those disputes and a variety of other matters, some are for lugging us into independence."

These advocates of independence included most of Braxton's fellow Virginians. It was the following month that the Virginia Convention met at Williamsburg, and before the delegates started the task of writing a constitution they passed a unanimous resolution "that the delegates appointed to represent this colony in General Congress be instructed to propose to that respectable body to declare the United Colonies free and independent states."

The resolution was presented to Congress by Richard Henry Lee, chief of the Virginia delegation, and debate on the subject started on the seventh of June. After three days it was clear that there were not enough votes in favor of so radical a step, and the subject was postponed for three weeks.

Congress did, however, appoint a five-man committee to draft the text of a Declaration of Independence so that it would be available when needed.

Lee was the normal choice for committee chairman, since he had introduced the resolution. But by this time the Virginia Convention had finished the Bill of Rights and was ready to turn its attention to the constitution. Lee wanted, as he said, to be present during "the formation of our new government," and he left Philadelphia on the 13th of June to take part in what seemed to the men of Virginia the most important act of the century.

Since the five-man committee to write the Declaration of Independence necessarily had to include a Virginian, John Adams campaigned hard for a younger member of that delegation whose name was Thomas Jefferson. "Though a silent member in Congress, he was so prompt, frank, explicit and decisive upon committees and in conversation . . . that he soon seized upon my heart, and upon this occasion I gave him my vote and did all in my power to procure the votes of others." Adams was so successful that Jefferson received the highest number of votes and automatically became chairman.

Adams was of course elected to the committee and so was Roger Sherman, whom he praised as being "a solid, sensible man." Franklin was chosen to represent Pennsylvania, and the fifth member, Robert R. Livingston, also came from the middle colonies. Livingston was a wealthy New Yorker who had attended the Stamp Act Congress the previous decade and served on the committee that had drafted its address to the King. New York was represented by a highly conservative delegation at the Continental Congress, and Livingston was the only one of its members who was in favor of independence.

Jefferson was the least experienced member of what was a very distinguished committee, and he owed what reputation he had to a single pamphlet he had written. Back in 1774, he had drafted instructions for the delegation sent by Virginia to the First Continental Congress, and when it was decided that they were too radical to be used, some of his friends had them printed. Since then the views of the delegates to the Continental Congress had been moving steadily toward Jefferson's position and he was made very welcome when he himself finally arrived in Philadelphia as a delegate.

Like so many of the men there, Jefferson had trained to be a lawyer. He studied under George Wythe, that well-loved Virginian of "dove-like simplicity and gentleness of manner" who was also a delegate to the Continental Congress. Jefferson was still a young law student on that electric day back in 1765 when Patrick Henry made his attack on the Stamp Tax. Henry's oratory seemed impressive enough to the French traveler, who was not emotionally involved. To young Thomas Jefferson, Henry spoke " as Homer wrote."

Jefferson was twenty-two years old when he stood at the door of the lobby of the House of Burgesses and listened to the debates over the Stamp Tax. Like all Virginians, he took the greatest pride in the House, and in his case it was in part a possessive pride. His father and grandfather had both served in it, and the Speaker of the House, the great Peyton Randolph, was his first cousin once removed. Jefferson's mother was a Randolph and that made him a part of the interlocking network of family relationships which bound the House of Burgesses together in much the same way that a network of family connections in England bound together the great landed families who dominated the House of Commons.

The procedures of the House of Burgesses, in their pride and dignity, were directly derived from English practice. The ceremony with which the royal governor opened the session in Williamsburg resembled as closely as possible the pageantry with which the ruler of England opened Parliament at Westminster. Within the House, the Burgesses ranged themselves like their counterparts in the House of Commons, parallel to the side walls. Before them on the dais was the robed Speaker, with the mace that was the symbol of his office, and before him sat the clerks, robed also.

When Jefferson was twenty-three he went on a trip through some of the other colonies, and the young Virginian was much amused by the countrified way that the government was conducted in neighboring Maryland. The legislators met in Annapolis in an old courthouse "which, judging from its form and appearance, was built in the year one." The Speaker was an unimpressive little old man, the clerk did not know how to read aloud properly, and the legislators gabbled among themselves. They voted informally and did not even know the correct way to address the Speaker.

Three years later, in 1769, Jefferson himself was elected to the Virginia House of Burgesses. He entered the most civilized political club in America, firmly united on its four main points of privilege, power, tradition and solidarity, and the voters of Albemarle County had every reason to suppose that he would remain faithful to the traditions and standards of his class.

He did not. Jefferson became a radical, and one of the most consistent in America. His fellow Virginians were radicals because they believed that British policies threatened their way of life, and they expected to go back to the old way of doing things after the war was over. Jefferson wanted a new way, since he thought that the old way put too much power into the hands of a favored few. Like Benjamin Franklin, he wanted a form of government that was really based upon the consent of the governed, and he never ceased to be faithful to this dream.

At first, Jefferson's political career seemed normal enough. He was at once put on a committee—the first of the enormous number on which he served during the course of his long and useful life. The function of this one was to draft an address of welcome to the new royal Governor, Baron de Botetourt. He was a member of the famous Berkeley family and had arrived in Virginia late the previous year.

The Governor arrived duly in his magnificent state carriage, but the ornamental address of welcome was not the one Jefferson had written. His fellow committee members had altered the text, and Jefferson could still remember, half a century later, how much his feelings had been hurt. "Being a younger man as well as a young member, it made on me an impression porportioned to the sensibility of that time of life." Jefferson never rid himself of this particular form of sensibility. He was a careful writer, and once he had the sentences to his liking he did not wish to see them changed.

Not long after the new Governor's arrival, Richard Henry Lee had written to a friend with typical Virginia assurance: "His Lordship's good sense, affability and politeness give general pleasure, but how far his political opinions may agree with those of Virginia remains yet to be known."

As soon as the session opened it became clear that they did not agree, and eight days later Governor Botetourt dissolved the legislature. It had been planning a series of resolutions which he found offensive, and he naturally assumed they could not be passed if the House of Burgesses was not in session. In this he was mistaken. Jefferson and his fellow legislators moved down the street to the Raleigh Tavern. There they reassembled, elected the Speaker of the House, Peyton Randolph, as their presiding officer, and passed the offending resolutions.

The meeting was held in the large public room which was called the Apollo, and which was the only nonpolitical place in Williamsburg large enough for such a gathering. All up and down the coast, revolutionary groups were meeting in taverns, but the Virginians characteristically had a very handsome room for their meeting. With its great marble fireplace, it was normally used for large social gatherings, and earlier in the decade Jefferson had been "dancing with Belinda in the Apollo."

The dissident legislators had the full support of their home counties, and all of them were returned to office in the next election, as Jefferson said proudly, except "the very few who had declined assent to our proceedings." During the next five years there was relative political calm. Then the news came, in 1774, that Boston was to be punished for the Tea Party by the closing of the port, to go into effect the first of June. Jefferson and his friends "rummaged over" the collection of documents that John Rushworth, the seventeenth-century English lawyer and shorthand expert, had gathered together to record an earlier revolution. They found in it the device of proclaiming a day of fasting and prayer to arouse public attention and decided to do the same.

Virginia had a new Governor by now, but Lord Dunmore behaved in the same fashion in 1774 as Lord Botetourt had behaved in 1769. "The Governor dissolved us, as usual. We retired to the Apollo, as before." The plan was to gather at the House of Burgesses on the morning of the first of June and from there form a stately procession to the church, carrying with them the mace that was the symbol of their legislative authority. Jefferson reported with great pride on the result. "The effect of the day, through the whole colony, was like a shock of electricity, arousing every man and placing him erect and solidly on his center."

The Virginia Convention met in August, and Jefferson was a delegate from Albemarle County. He never reached Richmond, where a meeting had been planned in the church, because he became ill on the road. He sent instead a set of resolutions he had drafted for the use of the delegates who were to be sent to the First Continental Congress. It was in the form of an address to King George, listing American grievances, and was much too extreme for most of the delegates at the Virginia Convention. They "stopped at the half-way house" of admitting that Parliament possessed every kind of authority over the colonies except the authority to tax; Jefferson maintained that one hundred and sixty thousand English voters had no right to make laws for four million Americans and that the colonies owed their loyalty only to the King.

Jefferson's friends had the manuscript published without his knowledge and gave it the title *A Summary View of the Rights of British America*. It was widely read in both England and the colonies, and when Jefferson himself went as a delegate to Philadelphia the following year, his reputation as a writer had preceded him. John Adams considered the *Summary View* "a very handsome public paper," and it was one of his reasons for pressing so strongly in 1776 to get Jefferson on the five-man committee that was assigned to write the Declaration of Independence.

John Adams seems to have been the first man to notice that Jefferson's radicalism was not confined to his political views. Commenting on Jefferson's habitual silence during Congress debates, Adams remarked: "The most of a speech he ever made in my hearing was a gross insult on religion, in one or two sentences, for which I gave him immediately the reprehension which he richly merited." Jefferson had intended no insult to religion. He was not anti-Christian. But he was the foe of organized, accepted dogma in society, whether in religion or in anything else, and when he spoke of freedom he was not thinking only of freedom from Great Britain.

Like every other Virginian in May of 1776, Jefferson was deeply interested in the constitution that was being created at Williamsburg, and he suggested wistfully in the middle of the month that perhaps the Virginia Convention would be willing "to recall for a short time" all its Congress delegates so that everyone could be there to help. "It is a work of the most interesting nature and such as every individual would wish to have his voice in. In truth it is the whole object of the present controversy; for should a bad government be instituted for us in future it had been as well to have accepted at first the bad one offered to us from beyond the water without the risk and expense of contest."

Since Jefferson was not permitted to leave Philadelphia, he wrote his suggestions out and sent them down to Williamsburg. Edmund Pendleton, the presiding officer, wrote Jefferson that he had received the manuscript "on the day on which the Committee of the Whole had reported to the House the plan they had agreed to . . . so long in hand, so disputed inch by inch, and the subject of so much altercation and debate, that they . . . could not . . . have been induced to open the instrument again."

Under no circumstances, however, would the Virginia Convention have given serious consideration to Jefferson's wish that the franchise should be widened. He made several drafts of this section, but the general idea was that anyone who had a small piece of property in town or twenty-five acres in the country, or who paid a municipal tax, should be entitled to vote.

In August, Jefferson tried to explain to Pendleton by letter what his basic idea had been: "I was for extending the right of suffrage (or in other words the rights of a citizen) to all who had a permanent intention of living in the country. Take what circumstances you please as evidence of this, either the having resided a certain time, or having a family, or having property, any or all of them."

Jefferson wrote this letter so pressed for time that he was sitting "at a committee table while the committee is collecting," and he and Pendleton were both so extreme in their views that neither one had had a hearing at the Virginia Convention. Yet in their August correspondence on the constitution they never forgot the scrupulous courtesy of Virginia gentlemen. Nor did Jefferson forget that he was the younger man. "You have lived longer than I have and perhaps may have formed a different judgment on better grounds;

but my observations do not enable me to say I think integrity the character-istic of wealth. In general I believe the decisions of the people, in a body, will be more honest and more disinterested than those of wealthy men."*

Jefferson did not like the constitution of which most Virginians were so proud. He thought it gave a disproportionate power to the eastern counties, and that it should have been offered to the voters for ratification. When there was some talk in the following decade of calling a convention to amend it, he wrote out a new set of suggestions in connection with the franchise. He was now willing to let a man vote if he had been "enrolled in the militia."

Jefferson made the same point in a book he had written, *Notes on the State of Virginia,* which he published in 1785. He began by apologizing for the constitution of 1776: "This constitution was formed when we were new and inexperienced in the science of government." He then made a list of its chief defects and this was Number One:

> The majority of the men in the state who pay and fight for its support are unrepresented in the legislature, the roll of freeholders entitled to vote not including generally the half of those on the roll of the militia or of the tax-gatherers.

It has since been decided that Jefferson may have underestimated the number of freeholders in Virginia in the 1780's. What he was objecting to, however, was not the numerical situation, which of course shifted from decade to decade, but the injustice inherent in the basic situation.

Jefferson was never able to reconcile himself to a franchise which under-lined so firmly the doctrine of political inequality. Almost alone among his fellow Virginians, he believed that their Bill of Rights spoke the truth when it said, "All men are by nature equally free and independent." He could not consent to the contrary doctrine that some men were born to be in sub-jection.

In this he was very like Thomas Paine, who became a good friend of his. But whereas Paine would have been quite willing to pull down the whole edifice of government and start over again on the basis of pure reason, Jefferson had less the spirit of a brilliant housewrecker and more that of a gardener. He knew that there would always be differences of sunlight and space and growing weather, but he was sure that this made no difference to

---

* Jefferson was too polite to mention a scandal in Virginia which took place in the previous decade and supported this point of view. John Robinson, who had been Treasurer of the colony, died in 1766, and an auditor found that an enormous amount of public money was missing. Robinson had calmly given it out to members of his class who were in need of funds.

the nature of the seed, and his solution was always to ensure more sun and space, not less.

It seemed to Jefferson that if property was used as the basis for political privilege it became a form of tyranny, and when he took his place in June of 1776 as chairman of the committee to write the Declaration of Independence he did not bring with him the set of political preconceptions that would have been normal for his class and time.

It was not easy for a man as self-assertive as John Adams to serve under a younger and less experienced man in connection with a subject upon which he himself had labored so long. He had, however, a selective memory, and half a century later he re-created the events in his memory the way they should have been instead of the way they actually were. It seemed to John Adams then that the five-man committee met a few times, drafted some minutes and then "appointed Mr. Jefferson and me to draw them up in form and clothe them in a proper dress." He could even recollect the precise words which the two of them used when they discussed who should do the actual writing. Adams: "You can write ten times better than I can." Jefferson: "Well, if you are decided, I will do as well as I can."

Jefferson's memory was not perfect either but he had taken notes at the time and felt justified in correcting this version. "The committee of five met; no such thing as a subcommittee was proposed, but they unanimously pressed on myself alone to undertake the draft. I consented; I drew it; but before I reported it to the committee, I communicated it *separately* to Dr. Franklin and Mr. Adams, requesting their corrections, because they were the two members of whose judgments and amendments I wished most to have the benefit. . . . I then wrote a fair copy, reported it to the committee, and from them, unaltered, to Congress. This personal communication and consultation with Mr. Adams he had misremembered into the actings of a subcommittee."

Three years after the committee met originally, Adams had had a different recollection. "The committee consisted of Mr. Jefferson, Mr. Franklin, Mr. Harrison, Mr. R. and myself, and we appointed Jefferson a subcommittee to draw it up." Adams was very sleepy when he made this particular note in 1779, and he forgot that it was Roger Sherman and not Benjamin Harrison who was the fifth man on the committee. Nevertheless, this earlier version supports Jefferson's contention that he was the whole of the subcommittee, and confirms the impression that the resulting paper was the work of a single mind.

Jefferson had left his Chestnut Street lodging late in May, before the heat of a Philadelphia summer set in, and had taken rooms with a young

German who had built a new brick house on the outskirts of town. Jefferson rented the whole of the second floor, with its bedroom on one side of the stairs and its parlor on the other. The rooms were furnished, but he brought with him a portable writing desk of his own design which his previous landlord had made for him, and it was on this that he wrote and rewrote his draft of the Declaration of Independence.

There was a very practical reason why such a Declaration had to be made. As Richard Henry Lee had pointed out in April, "No state in Europe will either treat or trade with us so long as we consider ourselves subjects of Great Britain," and the function of the Declaration was to make the act of separation seem legitimate.

There were two precedents for the document. The first was the declaration of independence which had been issued by the United Provinces of the Netherlands—sometimes known as "the United States"—in the days of William the Silent, Prince of Orange. The second was the Declaration of Rights under whose terms a later Prince of Orange had been permitted to displace James II and ascend the throne of England. Both these events marked the overthrow of an accredited governor but neither made any fundamental alteration in the form of government. It was Jefferson's task to make a much more radical revolution seem not only legitimate but understandable.

Jefferson had a clear idea what his responsibility was as the writer of the Declaration of Independence: "Not to find out new principles, or new arguments never before thought of, not merely to say things which had never been said before; but to place before mankind the common sense of the subject, in terms so plain and firm as to command their assent, and to justify ourselves in the independent stand we are compelled to take. Neither aiming at originality of principle or sentiment, nor yet copied from any particular and previous writing, it was intended to be an expression of the American mind, and to give to that expression the proper tone and spirit called for by the occasion. All its authority rests, then, on the harmonizing sentiments of the day, whether expressed in conversation, in letters, printed essays, or in the elementary books of public right, as Aristotle, Cicero, Locke, Sidney, etc." Jefferson saw himself as an inheritor only, drawing upon the vast body of writings that were the general possession of mankind, and it was as an inheritor that he wrote:

> We hold these truths to be self evident: that all men are created equal; that they are endowed by their Creator with certain inherent and inalienable rights; that among these are life, liberty and the pursuit of happiness.

The choice of words was a familiar one. It was derived from John Locke, and the Virginians had already used it in their Bill of Rights. But Jefferson made a curious omission which Locke would never have permitted himself. It was an omission which the Virginians had not made either: "All men are by nature equally free and independent, and have certain inherent rights . . . namely, the enjoyment of life and liberty, with the means of acquiring and possessing property, and pursuing and obtaining happiness and safety."

A few months later in this same year of 1776, Pennsylvania wrote its very radical constitution and echoed the same point in its own Bill of Rights: "All men are born equally free and independent, and have certain natural, inherent and inalienable rights, amongst which are the enjoying and defending life and liberty, acquiring, possessing and protecting property, and pursuing and obtaining happiness and safety." A year later, Vermont also wrote a radical constitution, and the same point reappears: "All men are born equally free and independent, and have certain natural, inherent and inalienable rights, amongst which are the enjoying and defending life and liberty, acquiring, possessing and protecting property, and pursuing and obtaining happiness and safety."

In the following decade, Vermont wrote a second constitution. The wording of this passage was altered slightly but there was no change in the meaning: "All men are born equally free and independent, and have certain natural, inherent and inalienable rights; amongst which are the enjoying and defending life and liberty, acquiring, possessing and protecting property and pursuing and obtaining happiness and safety."

It was only Jefferson, writing the document that was to cast the longest shadow of them all, who left out the word *property*.*

The major part of the Declaration of Independence consisted of a list of the reasons why the American colonies considered themselves justified in throwing off the yoke of Great Britain. Locke had maintained that when there had been "a long train of abuses, prevarications and artifices," all tending toward tyranny, the people had the right to declare themselves free of a government which had not fulfilled its part of the compact; and Jefferson therefore supplied in his turn a list of the "long train of abuses and usurpations" committed by King George the Third.

---

* An earlier draft of this passage is extant, so it is clear this was no afterthought on Jefferson's part. The earlier draft reads: "We hold these truths to be sacred and undeniable; that all men are created equal and independent, that from that equal creation they derive rights inherent and inalienable, among which are the preservation of life and liberty and the pursuit of happiness."

The time had passed when Americans tried earnestly to picture the King as a benevolent monarch whose wishes had been consistently thwarted by a perfidious Parliament. In recent months, and especially since the publication of *Common Sense,* King George had become more and more the focus of American fury, as Charles I had finally become in the eyes of men like Cromwell. It was a vigorous list that Jefferson made, as unjust as John Pym's Remonstrance, and as effective.

When Jefferson had the whole of the Declaration to his satisfaction, he incorporated the minor changes suggested by other members of the committee and then delivered it on Friday, the 28th of June, to Charles Thomson, Secretary of Congress. On this same Friday the Maryland Convention voted to abandon its previous opposition to independence and instructed its delegates to vote for the resolution that Richard Henry Lee had presented in May.

The following Monday, which was the first of July, the Continental Congress turned itself into a Committee of the Whole to debate Lee's resolution. After it adjourned for the day, a series of frantic struggles behind the scenes continued, and the next day the radicals finally achieved a majority. Congress took the huge and irrevocable step of separation from Great Britain. "Resolved, that these United Colonies are, and of right ought to be, free and independent states."

Congress next turned its attention to the text of the Declaration of Independence, and Jefferson found the delegates much more critical than his fellow committee members had been. John Adams took the responsibility of trying to get it through intact, fighting for it, as Jefferson said gratefully, with zeal and ability. Jefferson himself sat silent while Franklin, who was next to him, tried to cheer him up with a story about a hatter who had planned to have eight words on his sign after his name and, upon the advice of a series of friends, removed them all.

The long, eloquent opening of the Declaration of Independence survived almost intact. Its rhythms were familiar, and in any case they had no practical application. But many other parts were objectionable to the delegates for various reasons, and especially unpopular was the section on Negroes and slavery.

Of all forms of tyranny, Jefferson hated slavery the most. His first act as a legislator had been to attempt to mitigate it in Virginia, and in spite of a great deal of evidence to the contrary he remained convinced that the majority of his fellow Virginians agreed with him. In *A Summary View* this was one of the few things he blamed on King George rather than on Parliament: "The abolition of domestic slavery is the great object of desire in those colonies where it was unhappily introduced in their infant state. But previous to the enfranchisement of the slaves we have, it is necessary to exclude all further importations from Africa; yet our repeated attempts to effect this by prohibitions, and by imposing duties which might amount to a prohibition, have been hitherto defeated by His Majesty's negative."

Two years later, when he wrote the Declaration of Independence, Jefferson again attacked the King's use of his veto power in connection with slavery and now with even more energy: "He has waged cruel war against human nature itself, violating its most sacred rights of life and liberty in the persons of a distant people who never offended him, captivating and carrying them into slavery in another hemisphere or to incur miserable death in their transportation hither. . . . Determined to keep open a market where men should be bought and sold, he has prostituted his negative for suppressing every legislative attempt to prohibit or to restrain this execrable commerce."

Congress was only too happy to blame King George for every sin in the calendar, but it could not bring itself to believe that Negro slavery was a sin. To many of the delegates it seemed to be not only a legitimate business practice but also one which was fundamental to the economy. Georgia, for instance, had sent no delegates to the first meeting of the Congress and its good will was important to the success of the subsequent ones. Georgia had an economy based almost exclusively on indigo and rice, both of which needed slaves for their cultivation. The planters of South Carolina had also grown rich on indigo and rice, and their tobacco plantations were worked by slaves. So were those of Virginia. As for New England, although it was now making tentative efforts to denounce the slave traffic, part of its prosperity had been based on the three-way traffic of molasses, rum and African slaves. As Jefferson said, "Their people had very few slaves themselves, yet they had been pretty considerable carriers of them to others."

It might be true, as Congress had just agreed, that in an abstract, theoretical sense all men were created equal. Yet, from the business point of view, it seemed equally clear to many of the delegates that some men were merchandise only.

The whole section on slavery was finally struck out, and various other alterations were made—most of them in the interests of brevity and simplicity. On the fourth of July the altered text was finally approved by a vote of twelve to nothing, New York abstaining.

It was two days earlier that the fact of independence had come into existence, and John Adams wrote triumphantly to his wife: "The second day of July, 1776, will be the most memorable epocha in the history of America. . . . It ought to be solemnized with pomp and parade, with shows, games, bells, bonfires and illuminations, from one end of the continent to the other, from this time forward, forevermore." Instead, with a surer instinct, it was not the day of the act but the day of the word that was celebrated, and it was the fourth of July that bore out John Adams' prophecy.

In 1826, on the fiftieth anniversary of the acceptance of the text of the Declaration of Independence, the city of Washington, D.C., planned an especially elaborate celebration. Jefferson was still alive, and the mayor of Washington asked him if he could attend. The letter arrived at Monticello in June, and Jefferson answered it on the 24th of the month, only eight days before he died.

To answer it at all must have been difficult, yet it was a Jefferson wholly unchanged by old age who wrote back to describe what the Declaration of Independence meant to him:

> May it be to the world what I believe it will be (to some parts sooner, to others later, but finally to all), the signal of arousing men to burst the chains under which monkish ignorance and superstition had persuaded them to bind themselves, and to assume the blessings and security of self-government. . . . All eyes are opened, or opening, to the rights of man. The general spread of the light of science had already laid open to every view the palpable truth, that the mass of mankind has not been born with saddles on their backs, nor a favored few booted and spurred, ready to ride them legitimately by the grace of God.

The image of the arrogant horsemen was not his. It came from the speech that Colonel Rumbold delivered on the scaffold before he was executed for his part in the Monmouth rising. It had been quoted in several of the books in Jefferson's library, but Jefferson carried the words of the stubborn old warrior far beyond anything that Rumbold had intended.

This kind of an expansion of the original intention often took place in the American imagination, and the Liberty Bell is an example. Back in the days when the Pennsylvania Assembly decided to celebrate the fiftieth anniversary of its political triumph over William Penn, it commemorated the occasion by having a bell cast in London and inscribed with a verse from the Book of Leviticus: "Proclaim liberty throughout all the land unto all the inhabitants thereof." Like the other bells in Philadelphia, it was rung when the Declaration of Independence had its official reading in State House Yard, and when the British occupied the city it was smuggled out into the country for safety. In time, all America joined in calling it the Liberty Bell and it was no longer remembered that its original purpose had been to celebrate a local victory over William Penn.

The Declaration of Independence did not owe its birth to an especially lofty impulse. Some such document was a necessity if America was to get a loan from France, and the Continental Congress had not intended it to be a manifesto for human equality. Yet by a glorious accident, the writing of it was given to one of the few real radicals in Congress, and in the end the result was as Jefferson foretold. In the long years of struggle that followed in America, in the attempt to set up a government which, in the words of the Declaration, really did derive its just powers from the consent of the governed, the words of that eloquent opening stood as allies, growing in power the more often they were invoked.

Jefferson had not been correct when he called his version "an expression of the American mind." But it was, as it turned out, an expression of its heart.

Chapter Eleven

The Declaration of Independence was signed on the fourth of July, in the usual way, by John Hancock as President of the Congress and Charles Thomson as Secretary. Orders were sent out "that it be proclaimed in each of the United States," and it was of course widely reprinted. *The Philadelphia Magazine,* for instance, ran the text in its July issue, along with the new state constitutions of New Jersey and Virginia.

Later on in the month Congress decided that it had treated the document too casually. It was decided that a copy engrossed on parchment should be placed on Hancock's desk the second of August and signed that day by all the delegates present in the State House—later to be named Independence Hall.*

The men who signed the document that day in August were not in every case the same men who had voted on the fourth of July. Benjamin Rush, for instance, was a new member. He was awed by the presence of so many illustrious colleagues and doubly awed by the occasion itself, for they were committing themselves, soberly and formally, to an act of treason.

---

* A decade later, tourists in Philadelphia were being told that the Declaration of Independence had been signed in Carpenters' Hall but in fact only the First Continental Congress had met there.

Rush remembered very well the "awful silence which pervaded the house when we were called up, one after another, to the table of the President of Congress to subscribe what was believed by many at that time to be our own death warrants." It was a silence broken only by a joke from the irrepressible Benjamin Harrison, who remarked that since he was fat he would at least hang quickly. Later on in the year, other delegates arrived and the Secretary gave them the document to sign. Robert R. Livingston never did sign it, although he was a member of the committee that wrote it. Livingston went back to New York and was kept so busy there that he did not reappear in Philadelphia.

Just under John Hancock's large, trim signature in the center of the page were those of the Maryland delegation, and one of them, Charles Carroll, was also a newcomer. He had been elected to Congress in the middle of July in recognition of his services in persuading the Maryland Convention to vote for independence, and he had been calling himself Charles Carroll of Carrollton ever since his father settled on him, as the only son, the vast Carrollton estates.

Charles Carroll of Carrollton had not meant to enter politics, but he began using his new signature the previous decade in the vigorous letters he wrote to denounce the Stamp Tax. He opposed it on the principle that no property would be safe if "a set of men at so great a distance, so little acquainted with our circumstances and not immediately affected" were given the power to levy taxes, and it could fairly be said that Carroll became a revolutionary in defense of property. He never doubted its sanctity or its power, and unlike Thomas Jefferson who signed below in the same column, he was sure that government should remain in the hands of the rich and the wellborn. In his eyes, the separation from Great Britain was not supposed to be followed by any shift in the basis of political power at home.

The people of Maryland were not all in agreement with this point of view. When elections were held for the Convention that was to meet in Annapolis in August to write the Maryland constitution, it was clear that there was some unrest about the voting requirements. Each voter was supposed to possess fifty acres of land or forty pounds, but some of the Maryland counties believed that the old rules were no longer applicable. St. George's County decided that "every taxable bearing arms, being an inhabitant of the county, had an undoubted right to vote for representatives at this time of public calamity," and when the local election judges decreed otherwise it got itself new judges. In Frederick County, the voting for Convention delegates was done equally illegally "by a majority of voters, resident of the district, who had armed in the defense of the country." When the Convention met in

August both these elections were declared void, since the fact that a man was fit to fight for his country did not mean he was fit to vote.

Charles Carroll of Carrollton was a delegate to the Convention from Anne Arundel County, and even here there were disturbances. An officer in the militia went so far as to say that if his men were not permitted to vote they could not be expected to fight. The ferment continued after the Convention opened, and Carroll was shocked to be presented with a suggested plan of government, "democratical in the extreme," which had been circulated among his constituents and carried a large number of signatures. Carroll resigned rather than submit to such a plan, but in any case his work was done. He served on the committee of seven which drafted the Maryland constitution and its accompanying Bill of Rights.

Unlike the Virginia Convention, the Maryland Convention was deeply concerned with the question of suffrage reform. A resolution was presented which gave all taxpayers the vote, and it was defeated by a narrow margin. Yet in the end the conservatives triumphed. In the constitution, the franchise was set at a fifty-acre freehold or at personal property worth thirty pounds in current money. This slight reduction of ten pounds meant very little, since none of the voters had the power to elect members of the upper house.

The Senate was made the impregnable stronghold of the very rich. Its fifteen members were to be selected every five years by an electoral college, and no man could be considered for office unless he possessed property worth a thousand pounds. A member of the first group of Maryland Senators remarked with some understatement: "The Senate does not appear to me to be a child of the people at large." He went on to point out that although the whole membership of the two houses consisted of eighty-nine men, eight would have it in their power "to counteract eighty-one. Will they submit?" It seemed probable that they would not, considering the general state of mind of the people of Maryland, but for the moment the political theories of men like Charles Carroll of Carrollton had triumphed.

East of Maryland, the little state of Delaware also decided to have two houses in its legislature. It had come out from under the shadow of Pennsylvania at the beginning of the eighteenth century, when William Penn gave it a separate government, but it had never had any real identity. It was known as the Counties of New Castle, Kent and Sussex, but now it was able to assume a proud new title as the state of Delaware. Its constitution was written quickly during three weeks in August and September of 1776, and there were no changes in the franchise.

The state of Georgia took much longer. It ordered an election as soon as the text of the Declaration of Independence arrived, but the delegates who gathered in Savannah in October did not finish the constitution until the following February. Pennsylvania's radical constitution had made a deep impression on the Georgia delegates, who decided to have a legislature of only one house. The voting requirements also showed the influence of Pennsylvania radicalism: "All male white inhabitants of the age of twenty-one years, and possessed in his own right of ten pounds value, and liable to pay tax in this state, or being of any mechanic trade . . . shall have a right to vote." The reaction of the Georgia conservatives was similar to that of their counterparts in Pennsylvania, and a Savannah merchant said passionately that the constitution, being "very democratical," had put the "power into such hands as must ruin the country, if not timely prevented."

In these battles between the radicals and the conservatives, one side or the other usually won a clear victory. In North Carolina, however, there was a seesaw battle for control that made it difficult to write any constitution at all.

North Carolina was isolated by its hills and lack of roads and made tempestuous by the quarrels among its settlers. The men along the frontier were in many cases Tories, but the men who held political power were ardent supporters of the Revolution. In May of 1775 they forced the royal Governor to leave, and in April of the following year, the North Carolina Provincial Congress, which was meeting at Halifax, told its delegation in the Continental Congress to vote for independence.

This was a month before Congress had nerved itself to pass the resolution giving each colony the right of self-government. Nevertheless, the men of Halifax behaved as though it had, and it was in April that they appointed a committee to draft a constitution.

They all agreed that North Carolina should be an independent state, but no one could decide what kind of a state it ought to be. The unhappy committee met every evening, conscientiously listening to arguments from both sides. On the question of the suffrage, predictably, the radicals wanted reform and the conservatives were determined to oppose them.

The committee referred the whole problem back to the Provincial Congress, which could not come to any conclusion either. It was finally decided that the next Congress, meeting in November, should operate as a constitutional convention, and instructions were sent out that "the good people of this now independent state of North Carolina pay the greatest attention to the election," which was set for the 15th of October.

The election was a lively one, but care was taken to see that it was also honest. A complaint of physical coercion in Orange County was referred to the Committee of Privileges and Elections, which decided that "the tumult and disorderly behavior was occasioned by people over-anxious to get into the courthouse to vote." The Provincial Congress, however, refused to accept the report of its committee, and the five delegates to the Congress from Orange County were obliged to give up their seats while a new election was held there. The precaution was justified, since only one of these five delegates kept his seat in the new election.

The chief function of this Provincial Congress was to write a constitution, and by this time there were several state constitutions that could serve as models. When North Carolina's representative in the Continental Congress sent the texts down, he expressed the hope that the delegates would not follow the example of Pennsylvania and have a one-house legislature—that "many-headed monster" so beloved by political radicals.

The men of the fifth Provincial Congress meeting at Halifax were as divided as the men who had been elected to the previous one. The conservatives wanted "to preserve the right of property" while their opponents "evinced a desire to reduce the whole political system to the lowest radicalism and wildest democracy." Both sides, however, were at last willing to compromise. They elected a moderate as their presiding officer, and in the end the constitution was moderate also.

This willingness to compromise showed especially in the section on the franchise, which set up two qualifications for voters. In the case of the Senate, a voter had to have a fifty-acre freehold. But in the case of the lower house, which was not the stronghold of property, the arrangement was as liberal as it was in Pennsylvania: "All freemen of the age of twenty-one years, who . . . shall have paid public taxes shall be entitled to vote for members of the House of Commons."

The men who wrote the constitution for New York State encountered a different set of difficulties, compounded by the fact that so much of New York was enemy country. By the end of June in 1776, the harbor was full of more than a hundred British warships and a large number of the inhabitants were delighted to have them there.

The war had added one more source of confusion to New York politics, which had always been chaotic. Because of the almost feudal system of land tenure which had been inherited from the old Dutch days, political control was largely a matter of pull and counter-pull among the leading families and their revolving satellites. A complex and fluid situation became still more complicated when the politicians also had to align themselves as Whigs and

Tories, and only Whigs could do anything so traitorous as to write a constitution. As John Jay's son put it feelingly, "To institute . . . a permanent government . . . was . . . a work not to be accomplished without difficulty and danger."

In the end, the New York constitution was chiefly the work of John Jay and his two fellow aristocrats Robert R. Livingston and Gouverneur Morris. All of them had graduated from King's College and they were rich men and close friends. They were also experienced politicians, and since they were supporters of the Revolution they were able to avoid the loss of power that had been the fate of moderates like James Wilson of Pennsylvania. As Livingston put it: "Wilson will remember that I long ago advised that they should yield to the torrent if they hoped to direct its course."

A New Yorker like John Jay had no patience with the current radicalism in Pennsylvania, since, as he said, "the mass of men are neither wise nor good." He was convinced that the men of property ought to rule the country, or, as his son put it, it was "a favorite maxim with Mr. Jay that those who own the country ought to govern it." Jay was acutely aware that unless men like himself supplied the necessary leadership, the power in New York State would fall into the hands of inexperienced radicals as it had in Pennsylvania.

His good friend Livingston arrived back from the Continental Congress in time to be a delegate to the fourth New York Provincial Congress, which voted its approval of the Declaration of Independence on July the ninth. The following day this Provincial Congress turned itself into a Convention and took up the very difficult task of trying to run a revolutionary government in a state which still had a royal governor and which was the headquarters for the British army.

On the first of August, Gouverneur Morris moved that the Convention set up a committee to draft a constitution. The thirteen who were chosen to work on it were conservatives, moderates and radicals in their views on government, united only in their determination to resist domination by Great Britain. The three strongest members on the committee were Jay, Morris and Livingston, but especially Jay.

It would have been difficult enough to draft a successful constitution under the best of circumstances, but the men of the New York Convention had to do it on the run. "The Convention frequently found it necessary, in consequence of the inroads of the enemy, abruptly to adjourn and again to assemble in another place. Thus at different times they met at Harlaem, Kingsbridge, Philips's Manor, Fishkill, White Plains, Poughkeepsie and

Kingston." It was at Kingston, in a room over the local jail, that those imperturbable men were meeting early in March of 1777 when the text of a constitution was at last ready for their consideration.

It was understandable that the committee had failed to meet any of its earlier deadlines. It was remarkable that it had managed to produce any sort of a draft at all. Yet, under Jay's guidance, it came up with a very vigorous document which won John Adams' wholehearted approval because it was the first to balance adequately the different departments of government. It was Jay's special achievement that he was able to stake out a practical middle course in spite of pressures from both sides, while at the same time keeping the current balance of political power intact. He and his friends might be obliged to conduct their meetings over a jail in radical Ulster County, but they kept the machinery of government firmly in their experienced hands.

Formal debates on the text of the proposed constitution began in March, 1777, in the midst of the Convention's normal and onerous work of running a revolutionary government. The discussion continued until past the middle of April, Sundays included, for the text had to be read paragraph by paragraph, debated, rewritten, voted upon, reread and voted upon again.

On Sunday, the sixth of April, there was a second reading of the paragraph on the franchise. The subject was complicated by the fact that New York, having patterned itself on the English system, had both county and borough voting. County voting was limited to freeholders whose land was worth forty pounds or brought an annual rental of forty shillings. Borough voting, which applied to Albany and New York City, was open to anyone who was free of the corporation. In New York City the entry fee was five pounds. In Albany it was three pounds, twelve shillings for a merchant or thirty-six shillings for an artisan.

The Convention decided that from now on the voter must possess "a freehold of the value of twenty pounds within the said county or have rented a tenement therein of the yearly value of forty shillings." Most of the delegates would have liked to disfranchise the city artisans entirely, but John Jay, who was from New York County, managed to push through an amendment which permitted them to keep their right to vote if they had been freemen of New York City or Albany on or before the 14th of October, 1775. All this applied only to the lower house; a voter for Governor, Lieutenant Governor or a member of the Senate had to possess a freehold worth a hundred pounds.

Like the Virginians, the men who served in the New York Convention had stopped the clock, and they did it to the accompaniment of a good deal of debate. Two Sundays later they were still arguing over the text of the various paragraphs, although they were acutely aware that the constitution was long overdue. On the afternoon of the second Sunday, they abruptly pulled themselves together. The text of the constitution, with all its additions and erasures, was read straight through. "The general question being put thereon, it was agreed to by every member present," with only one voice raised in dissent. This belonged to Colonel Peter R. Livingston, who still felt the constitution was too radical. Then, with what must have been an enormous sense of relief, the Convention authorized one of its secretaries to have the text printed in Fishkill and "to give gratuities to the printer and his workmen, at his discretion, to obtain dispatch."

The New York constitution incorporated into its text the whole of the Declaration of Independence; and the next constitution, that of Vermont, also had something to say on the subject of independence. It stated vigorously that it was "absolutely necessary, for the welfare and safety of the inhabitants of this state, that it should be . . . independent." It was not, however, independence from Great Britain to which Vermont was referring. It was independence from New York.

Vermont was not one of the original thirteen states. In fact, it was still not a state at all but a wedge of land quarreled over by its neighbors. Massachusetts and New Hampshire had at last given up their claims but New York refused to do the same, and the men of Vermont were infuriated by the bland effrontery of the makers of the New York constitution, talking about the sins of King George and refusing to recognize their own.

The makers of the Vermont constitution not only rectified this omission but at one point found an almost perfect parallel. In Jefferson's original version of the Declaration of Independence, he had listed as one of the sins of "our British brethren" that they had permitted "their chief magistrate to send over not only soldiers of our common blood, but Scotch and foreign mercenaries to invade and destroy us." The constitution of Vermont made the same accusation against the people of New York: "They have hired foreign troops, emigrants from Scotland, at two different times, and armed them, to drive us out of possession"—an act as heinous in the eyes of Vermonters as the unwise decision to hire Hessian troops had been in the eyes of the rest of America.

New York finally abandoned its claims in 1790, and Vermont was able to enter the Union. But in 1777 Vermont considered itself already a state, and its delegates gathered at Windsor for six days in July to write a constitution.

The Vermont constitution was modeled on the radical one in Pennsylvania, with a single legislature instead of the cautious balance of two houses that nearly every other state had approved. As for the franchise, Vermont went even farther than Pennsylvania had done and authorized complete manhood suffrage. Any adult male who had lived a year in Vermont and who was "of a quiet and peaceable behavior" would be permitted to vote if he had taken a public oath to support the public good as established by the constitution. Unlike the arrangement in Pennsylvania, he did not need to be a taxpayer.

This was not the violent break with tradition that it seemed to be, since it was apparently assumed that every adult male Vermonter would possess some kind of property. As the constitution phrased it: "Every freeman, to preserve his independence (if without a sufficient estate) ought to have some profession, calling, trade or farm whereby he may honestly subsist." In a rural economy like Vermont's, it was not difficult to preserve the definition of a freeman as Harrington had given it more than a century ago in *Oceana:* "Freemen are such as have wherewithal to live of themselves; and servants, such as have not." Harrington had not hesitated to give the vote to this first class of men, and Vermont was merely doing the same.

By this time nearly every state in the Union had created on paper the new frame of government under which it intended to live. Two obvious exceptions were Rhode Island and Connecticut, both of whom already had charters that gave them the right of self-government. Their devotion to these two precious documents can be illustrated by the story Benjamin Rush told of Connecticut's Roger Sherman. "Patrick Henry asked him in 1774 why the people of Connecticut were more zealous in the cause of liberty than the people of other states. He answered, 'Because we have more to lose than any of them.' 'What is that?' said Mr. Henry. 'Our beloved charter,' replied Mr. Sherman."

Both of these were corporation charters, with corporation voting. This was the principle that Benjamin Franklin had attacked so briskly in his extreme old age when he pointed out that civil society was not a group of merchants. Connecticut, however, was a conservative state and perfectly content with the old arrangement. It seemed quite satisfactory that the charter which had been given the people in 1662 was still governing them in 1777.

The winter of 1777–1778 was the one in which the American army was stationed at Valley Forge, and a war that had never gone very well was now going very badly. Yet in a time which could so easily have been one of confusion and fear, ten American states had written out their forms of government. It was an achievement which could only be matched in that earlier span of American history, from 1638 to 1640, when eight groups of New Englanders created and signed compacts of self-government.

The second was the far greater achievement. The little New England papers were all the products of like-minded groups. The constitutions of 1776 and 1777 were born of contrary forces and had to strike a balance, sometimes with the greatest difficulty, between the conservatives who wanted the people to have very little share in the government and the radicals who wanted them to have a great deal.

It was here that the revolutionists of eighteenth-century America had so great an advantage over their counterparts in seventeenth-century England. The radicals at Putney designed their constitution for the whole of the kingdom, but even if they had succeeded in getting it adopted by the army, there would still have remained the impossible task of enforcing it in every county in England. In America, where there were so many units of government, one state could write a radical constitution, and the state next door could write a conservative one. A whole series of political experiments could be set in motion simultaneously and each state could watch the others to see how they were working out in practice.

It was John Adams, more than any other man, who had started all this writing of constitutions, and he regarded the activities of the various Provincial Congresses and Conventions with the fond anxiety of a mother hen. It was his ardent hope that every state would have a legislature of two houses to supply the necessary internal balance, and he was horrified when Pennsylvania decided otherwise. Adams said he half expected its people to beg King George "to take them again under his protection" rather than to live under such a constitution.

Pennsylvania had had a one-house legislature since the beginning of the eighteenth century, a point which Adams conveniently ignored. According to current political theory, a single house was supposed to be more responsive to the will of the people and it therefore had the support of the radicals. Moreover it had specifically, in 1776, the support of Thomas Paine.

When Pain wrote *Common Sense,* he added to his call for independence a few "straggling" thoughts on the kind of governments that should be instituted by the states afterward. One of these was a legislature of one house only. John Adams was willing to concede that Paine's suggestion rose from "simple ignorance and a mere desire to please the democratic party in Philadelphia," but he "dreaded the effect so popular a pamphlet might have among the people and determined to do all in my power to counteract the effect of it." Adams had been jotting down his own thoughts on the subject, and the pamphlet he published to counteract Paine was entitled *Thoughts on Government, Applicable to the Present State of the American Colonies.*

Adams rejoiced that the people had been given the opportunity "to form and establish the wisest and happiest government that human wisdom can contrive," and he offered his fellow Americans an ideal system based on the best Harringtonian principles. He gave a list of six reasons why no people could ever be free or happy with a legislature of one house only, since it would destroy the principle of checks and balances. One of the most important of all balances was to maintain the political power of property, and it was in the upper house that property had its stronghold.

Adams had definite views on the franchise but he did not mention them in *Thoughts on Government.* He said only that it was better to make changes "in times of greater tranquility than the present. . . . At present it will be safest to proceed in all established modes to which the people have been familiarized by habit."

This was precisely the point of view of the Virginians, and when Richard Henry Lee wrote Patrick Henry in April of 1776 he was fortunate in being able to send a copy. "The enclosed pamphlet on government is the production of our friend John Adams. . . . It proves the business of framing government not to be so difficult a thing as most people imagine." Patrick Henry, who was a member of the committee that drafted the Virginia constitution, wrote Adams to say that he was in full agreement with him. "The sentiments are precisely the same I have long since taken up." As soon as the new constitution was approved, Henry himself was elected Governor. He took the oath of office on the fifth of July, 1776, and moved into the Governor's palace in Williamsburg, where he wore a scarlet cloak and was called His Excellency.

John Adams was also approached by the Congress delegates from North Carolina, anxious to bring home every piece of advice they could on the subject of government, and it may have been partly because of the steady demand for his opinion that Adams put it down in printed form. New Jersey also made use of it, and by the time New York was ready to write its constitution the little book had become a classic on government. Robert R. Livingston wrote a friend in October of 1776 that he was "sick of politics and power . . . nor would in my present humor give one scene of Shakespeare for a thousand Harringtons, Lockes, Sidneys and Adams to boot." Nevertheless Livingston and the other men on his committee must have possessed very well-thumbed copies of *Thoughts on Government* since they followed its advice so closely. As for Adams, he returned the compliment by pronouncing New York's to be the best constitution that had yet been adopted. It had failed to take his advice on one point and had permitted direct election of the Governor by the people instead of through the legislature, but this was not a great risk since each man that voted for Governor had to have a £100 freehold.

Curiously enough, the one state which had not solved the problem of creating a new government was John Adams' own state of Massachusetts, and when New York finished its constitution in the spring of 1777, Massachusetts was still hopelessly far from any solution of the problem.

This was all the more unjust since Massachusetts had been the first colony to turn for advice to the Continental Congress. Back in 1775, three days after the battles of Lexington and Concord, its Provincial Congress met at Watertown and found itself faced with the problem of running a war without any legal authority. Some of the delegates wanted to go back to the original charter of 1629, which gave the colony the right of self-government, but such a defiance of the charter of 1691 would have run the risk of losing the sympathy of the other colonies.

The Continental Congress received two urgent messages from Massachusetts, requesting its advice, and it finally took refuge in a masterly piece of legalism. Let Massachusetts go back to the charter of 1691, which Governor Gage had violated, and rule without any royal official "until a governor of His Majesty's appointment will consent to govern the colony according to its charter."

This involved new elections, and they came at a time of special trouble. Dr. Joseph Warren, the greatly loved President of the Provincial Congress and the colony's most honored leader, was killed on the 17th of June in the retreat from Breed's Hill to Bunker Hill; yet even this disaster could not prevent the men of Massachusetts from behaving in a correctly constitutional manner. Each town in the Massachusetts jurisdiction was instructed to elect delegates to "a great and general court or assembly" to be held in Watertown in July. The Provincial Congress dissolved itself, the newly elected General Court took over the reins of government, and Massachusetts was once more operating under the charter of 1691 except that the executive functions were now being exercised by the Council instead of by a royal governor.

The following May all the colonies were given the right of self-government, and under the benign eye of John Adams new constitutions began to shoot up like green trees. Only Massachusetts held back. The delegates to the General Court found it impossible to come to any sort of agreement and it was easier to keep the old charter with a few minor alterations.

The town of Pittsfield, in western Massachusetts, sent the General Court an eloquent protest against so slack an arrangement. Even if judicial procedures were reformed "and multitudes of other things be done to still the people—all is to us nothing while the foundation is unfixed, the cornerstone of government unlaid." Not only did the town of Pittsfield want a constitution but it wanted it to be ratified by the people. The theory that the General Court could write a constitution and then "impose it upon the people . . . appears to us to be the rankest kind of Toryism, the self-same monster we are now fighting against."

Five months later, the eastern town of Concord carried the same point one step further. It insisted that the General Court was "by no means a body proper to form and establish a constitution," even if the people did ratify it afterward, and that a convention should be called for that purpose alone.

The Council, which operated as the upper house of the legislature, disliked this suggestion extremely. The radicals in Massachusetts wanted a one-house legislature, like the one in Pennsylvania, and the Council could see itself being voted out of existence.

Others were opposed to the idea because a constitutional convention would bring into the open other sources of controversy between the radicals and the conservatives and make it difficult to prosecute the war. James Sullivan, for instance, wrote the Speaker of the House in March of 1777: "I am very uneasy since I heard that you were upon a plan of a new constitution. I dread the controversy about the qualifications of electors." When Sullivan wrote John Adams the year before he had been in favor of suffrage reform, but by now he had come around to Adams' view that it was better not to rock the boat on that particular subject. Whichever way the matter might be decided, whether "in favor of the men of estate, or to give all an equal vote, one party or the other will be disaffected."

After months of argument and delay, the General Court finally worked out a draft of a proposed constitution and sent it to the towns for their approval. The franchise was based on the compromise that other states had found useful: a taxpayer qualification for the lower house and a property qualification of sixty pounds for Governor, Lieutenant-Governor and Senate.

The constitution pleased no one; some of the towns considered it too radical and others not radical enough. The most determined opposition came from rich Essex County, which feared that it would give too much political power to the counties in western Massachusetts, and twelve towns of Essex County sent delegates to a convention to consider the matter. These gentlemen debated the proposed constitution and finally decided that "the framing of a constitution . . . should be postponed till the public affairs are in a more peaceable and settled condition." They also decided that they ought to ascertain "the true principles of government, applicable to the territory of the

Massachusetts Bay," and set up a committee for this purpose. The committee report was the work of a brilliant young Newburyport lawyer named Theophilus Parsons, and it was such an eloquent statement of the conservative position that the Essex Convention had it printed in a pamphlet of some sixty pages and made sure that it was given wide circulation.

John Adams must have been delighted by the *Essex Result* when he read it, for it was very persuasive in its recommendation of a strong executive and a government of checks and balances. Theophilus Parsons had a very clear sense of the importance of property and he felt that the Senate should be apportioned on the basis of wealth rather than of population; the richer the county, the more Senators it should be permitted to send to the legislature. (In this way, the western counties would never be able to gain control.) Sixty pounds seemed a reasonable requirement for anyone who was to be permitted to vote for a Senator, but Parsons did not think it was necessary to hedge the voting for Governor in the same way. "For as the executive power hath no control over property . . . the consent of the property-holders need not be considered as necessary." Therefore, the *Essex Result* considered it safe to permit a taxpayer franchise in voting for the chief executive.

The unlucky constitution that the General Court had proposed was overwhelmingly rejected by the towns of Massachusetts, and for a time the legislature abandoned its efforts to write a constitution. This set the western counties to talking ominously of secession, and at last the General Court gave in. It authorized the calling of a constitutional convention, which was to meet in Cambridge on the first of September, 1779.

It was decided to let every free adult male vote for delegates to the convention, a concession permitted only once before in the history of Massachusetts. This had been back in Simon Bradstreet's day, when the colony was trying to put together a temporary government after it had disposed of Governor Andros. The reason in both cases was the same—an effort to get as much unity as possible by permitting everyone to be heard.

When the town of Braintree conducted its election, it was able to avail itself of a stroke of good fortune. John Adams had arrived back from Europe the week before and was more than willing to serve in the constitutional convention. Never was a man better qualified to write a constitution, single-handed if necessary. As the *Essex Result* had put it prophetically: "The man who alone undertakes to form a constitution ought to be an unimpassioned being, one enlightened mind . . . perfectly acquainted with all the alienable and inalienable rights of mankind." John Adams could hardly be called unimpassioned, but all the rest was true of his well-stored and learned mind.

On the fourth of September, the convention appointed a committee of thirty to write the constitution, and the committee promptly appointed a subcommittee of three. This consisted of James Bowdoin, who was president of the convention, and the two Adamses. Bowdoin ostensibly chaired the committee, but he and Samuel Adams wisely left the writing of the draft to the illustrious third member, and the convention went into adjournment until October to await the result.

It was a glorious opportunity for John Adams to bring together all his theories on government and he approached his task reverently. He put in the text a formal acknowledgment of the "goodness of the great Legislator of the universe in affording us, in the course of His Providence, an opportunity, deliberately and peaceably, without fraud, violence or surprise, of entering into an original, explicit and solemn compact with each other."

It was also an opportunity to curb what he called elsewhere "those democratical principles which have since done so much mischief in this country." He was not even willing to open the Bill of Rights in what by now was the classical manner and he wrote instead, "All men are born equally free and independent," since he did not think they were all born equal. His colleagues changed it back to the more familiar rhythm that had now become standard in any Bill of Rights. "All men are born free and equal, and have certain natural, essential and inalienable rights; among which may be reckoned the right of enjoying and defending their lives and liberties; that of acquiring, possessing and protecting property; in fine, that of seeking and obtaining their safety and happiness."

Nevertheless, while men might be equal in theory they soon ceased to be so in practice, and the constitution which was approved by the thirty-man committee and submitted to the convention was based on the principle that property was power. This was made so clear that one of the convention delegates suggested that the word *Massachusetts* be struck out and "that the word *Oceana* be substituted in its stead." The motion did not pass, but the ghost of James Harrington must have been delighted.

The constitution created by John Adams contained in it everything he had been advocating for the other states and which had been followed most closely, so far, by New York. It was a government of checks and balances, with a strong executive. It had the legislature of two houses which Adams considered the foundation of all good government, with the Senate representing property and the House of Representatives the people. Adams approved of the device Theophilus Parsons had suggested, and he apportioned the Senators among the various counties according to the amount of money each paid into the state treasury. He also agreed with Parsons that the voters who elected the Senate should possess sixty pounds' worth of property.

Adams did not agree with Parsons, however, that taxpayer suffrage would be permissible in voting for Governor and for members of the House of Representatives. As he had told James Sullivan back in 1776, he saw great risks in any kind of suffrage reform, and in his draft of the constitution every voter in Massachusetts had to be worth sixty pounds.

This did not seem unjust to the rest of the committee. The charter already had a requirement of forty pounds sterling, and the new requirement was not in sterling. This meant that there would be only a slight rise of somewhere between twelve and seventeen percent. Since property was very widely distributed in Massachusetts, most adult males were already able to vote, and those who could not had no doubt grown accustomed to the situation.

When the constitutional convention reconvened at the end of October, it began with a discussion of the Bill of Rights and found itself involved in a long and bitter argument over the one section for which Adams was not responsible. This was an attempt to impose Congregationalism as a tax-supported and therefore a state religion. Adams attended the sessions as long as he could but he had to leave for Europe in the middle of November. Thereafter, news of what the convention was doing came to him only by boat.

It was not until January that the actual frame of government came up for discussion. It was hoped that attendance would be better then, since all the autumn activities, especially those of the county courts, would be over. To encourage the arrival of more delegates, the convention also voted to insert a notice in the newspapers, pointing out that the constitution was "designed for the benefit of the remotest ages of this commonwealth," and that the "collective wisdom" that was needed could only be achieved by "general and constant attendance."

In January, the worst winter in living memory descended upon Massachusetts. Only sixty delegates, instead of what should have been nearly three hundred, were present when the much-postponed meeting finally took place in Boston. This handful agreed upon a complicated system of ratifying the constitution: each town was to vote separately on each clause, and a two-thirds vote would be considered approval.

Since only a few more delegates seemed to be arriving, the convention finally turned to the frame of government, and the article on the franchise was discussed on a Thursday morning late in February, with only sixty-four delegates present. Formerly, each voter in Massachusetts had been obliged to possess real estate worth two pounds a year in income, or personal property worth forty pounds. Under the proposed article, he would be obliged to possess real estate worth three pounds a year or personal property worth sixty pounds. Thirty-seven of those present voted in favor of the increase, twenty-seven voted against it; and so it passed.

The text of the proposed constitution was printed, and eighteen hundred copies were sent to the selectmen of all the towns in the Massachusetts jurisdiction. This included Maine, and the process would necessarily be slow. The convention agreed to meet again in June to tabulate the results and announce to the state whether or not it had at last achieved a constitution.

No selectman waited for the text with more ardor than Joseph Hawley, of the town of Northampton in western Massachusetts. In the previous October he had written to his old friend Samuel Adams expressing his joy that the men of Massachusetts were "free and at full liberty to make ourselves free to all generations." The two men had worked together in the days when Massachusetts was moving toward armed rebellion, and Hawley had made a great name for himself by his brilliant oratory, his legal knowledge, his profound sense of honor, and his conviction that America had no choice but to fight, even though Great Britain was the greatest military power in the world. "We must put to sea; Providence will bring us into port."

Hawley served for ten years in the Massachusetts legislature, and when Joseph Warren was elected President of the third Provincial Congress, Hawley was elected Vice President. But Warren died at Breed's Hill, and the following year Hawley was forced into retirement by a mental disorder.

It was his dream that the constitution would bring greater freedom to the people of Massachusetts. He had not thought that the plan would be to take some of their liberty away, and he was appalled when he read the article on the new suffrage requirement.

The town of Northampton held four meetings on the subject of the constitution; the last of the four began at nine in the morning and did not break up until sundown. The final result was a report of twenty-three pages, which arrived in Boston just two days before the deadline and which seems to have been written by Hawley himself. The bulk of the report was an attack on the franchise requirement.

A Boston town meeting had stated, back in the days of the Stamp Act: "If taxes are laid upon us in any shape without our having a legal representative where they are laid, are we not reduced from the character of free subjects to the miserable status of tributary slaves?" Now, sixteen years later, the state of Massachusetts was proposing to treat some of its inhabitants "precisely as Britain intended and resolved to treat all the men of America, that is to say, to bind us in all cases whatsoever, without a single vote for the legislature who were to bind and legislate for us."

Hawley himself had the right to vote, and so did most of the men in the town of Northampton. What they were fighting for, as Colonel Rainsborough had fought at Putney, was the right of all men to have representation. No one knew if anyone in America would keep that right for long, since the war was going badly, but Hawley spoke for the future. "Shall we who hold property, when God shall have fully secured it to us, be content to see our brethren, who have done their full share in procuring that security, shall we be content and satisfied, we say, to see these our deserving brethren on election days . . . ashamed to show their heads in the meetings of freemen, because, by the constitution of the land, they are doomed intruders if they should appear at such meetings? The thought is abhorrent to justice and too afflictive to good minds to be endured."

Hawley reinforced the point with a letter of his own, addressed to the convention delegates reconvening in Boston to count the votes. He said that a small committee could do this. What the convention as a whole ought to be doing was to discuss the various points that had been raised in the town meetings. "The hands of the people without doors laid the foundation of this revolution; their hands ought also to finish it."

In Hawley's eyes, as in Jefferson's, the revolution was not merely against Great Britain but against everything that was unjust or repressive. By a difficult and bloody path Massachusetts had earned the right to govern itself, and the constitution was the "main issue and fruit to be reaped and enjoyed from the vast expense, infinite sufferings and torrents of precious blood, of the more than five years' war, undertaken and patiently sustained, that we might be happy in the secure fruition of rights and liberty in this land."

Hawley admitted that there had always been a heavy limitation of the suffrage in Massachusetts, as there still was in Rhode Island and Connecticut, and he covered this point also in his letter: "You may perhaps reply that such persons as are in effect excluded from voting in the said elections have been wont to be excluded from voting in elections in this and the neighboring governments. Pray, gentlemen, consider, did this or any of the neighboring governments enjoy constitutions that were built on a bill of rights?" The first article of the Massachusetts Bill of Rights said that all men were born free and equal, the fifth said that all power was derived from the people, and it was on "the first and fifth articles aforesaid," that Joseph Hawley, lawyer and patriot, took his stand.

Hawley sent this letter to a Boston newspaper, the *Independent Gazette,* but it was never printed. This time there was no well-organized opposition to the constitution such as there had been in the days of the *Essex Result,* and the eloquent but scattered protests from some of the towns, in opposition to the franchise requirement, carried no weight with the delegates when the convention reconvened in Boston. They even managed to ignore the more numerous and very vigorous protests against the idea of tax support for Congregationalism, which certainly had not passed by a two-thirds majority. The need for a constitution was very great, and they announced that it had been ratified.

John Adams received the news with pride and thankfulness. Back in 1776, when Virginia was preparing to write its constitution, he had written to his friend Patrick Henry: "The decree is gone forth, and it cannot be recalled, that a more equal liberty than has prevailed in other parts of the earth must be established in America." Now his own beloved Massachusetts had finally acquired a constitution, the last of them and the best, and Adams said exultantly: "No government was ever so perfectly made upon the principle of the people's right and equality."

John Adams and Joseph Hawley were both lawyers, and they had worked together ardently for the cause in which they both believed. Both of them saw the Massachusetts constitution as the climax of the Revolution. But to John Adams it was the fulfillment of all their hopes, while to Joseph Hawley it was, in part at least, a betrayal.

Chapter Twelve

When Richard Henry Lee rose in the Continental Congress on the seventh of June, 1776, to propose independence from Great Britain, he proposed at the same time that the colonies set about the formation of a national government. "The eyes of Europe are fixed upon us. . . . If we are not this day wanting in our duty, the names of the American legislators of 1776 will be placed by posterity" beside the names of earlier founders of government "whose memory has been, and ever will be, dear to virtuous men and good citizens."

As soon as independence was approved on the fourth of July, Congress appointed a committee of three to design a seal for the new government, choosing Jefferson, Adams and Franklin. Jefferson served on eleven committees with Franklin, but this was not one of their more successful collaborations. Jefferson felt that the seal should include Hengist and Horsa, those "Saxon chiefs . . . whose political principles and form of government we have assumed." Franklin suggested Moses and the Red Sea, while Adams inclined toward the classical figure of Hercules flanked by those two opposites, Virtue and Sloth. Their final recommendation was not accepted by Congress, and the design for the seal was not decided upon until six years later.

There was no hurry, since the form of government had not been agreed upon either. The thirteen-man committee which had been assigned the task of working out articles of confederation brought in its report on the 12th of July, 1776, after a series of bitter battles, and as soon as the text was discussed in Congress the battle started all over again.

The root of the difficulty was the problem of how to apportion political power among the thirteen states in the confederation. The smaller states pressed for the retention of the present arrangement in Congress—one state, one vote—while the larger states naturally felt that this was unjust and that they should have more voting power. As Jefferson said, the smaller states were "under apprehensions that they would be swallowed up by the larger ones. We were long engaged in the discussion; it produced great heats, much ill humor and intemperate declarations from some members." In the end, the smaller states won the victory, and Article Five stated that "each state shall have one vote."

By the middle of November, 1777, the Articles of Confederation were ready to be sent to the state legislatures for ratification, accompanied by an apologetic letter in which Congress explained how great the difficulties had been. The thirteen state legislatures immediately encountered difficulties of their own. In some cases, they were slowed down by the mechanics of the thing. New Hampshire, for instance, had to have two hundred and fifty copies printed for distribution, so that the Articles could be debated in each town and instructions sent with their delegates to the state legislature. Some legislatures agreed quickly and some very reluctantly. The last to hold out was Maryland, because of a dispute over western lands, and it was not until 1781 that Maryland finally gave in.

The Articles of Confederation were finally ratified on the first of March, 1781, and the Continental Congress assumed its new title: the United States in Congress Assembled. There was otherwise not very much change. The same president continued in office; the same delegates sent by the state legislatures continued to wrestle with the same problems. The chief difference was the slackening of the wartime fervor that had held the delegates together in the face of a common enemy. It was in October of this same year of 1781 that Cornwallis surrendered at Yorktown and the end of the long war came in sight.

Under the circumstances, it had been an achievement to get a central government that worked at all. Cromwell had attempted the same thing in England and had struggled unsuccessfully for years to find some sort of representative government to replace the framework that the revolution in England had destroyed. The Americans ended their own revolution against the Crown with thirteen political frameworks which were all working fairly well. The problem which they had not solved, and had no useful precedent for solving, was how to get the thirteen to work together harmoniously and effectively.

No state was willing to concede to any other the sovereignty which they had denied to Great Britain, and thirteen sovereignties made an unwieldy package. There was no real central authority; there was no taxing power; there was no way to amend any of the Articles except by the unanimous agreement of thirteen states, which was impossible. Yet the Congress of the United States lurched along with a kind of dogged patience, heroically attempting to surmount its handicaps and in a measure succeeding.

James Madison, who served as a delegate from Virginia, said that they kept the vessel afloat "by standing constantly at the pump, not by stopping the leaks which have endangered her." Many other members were equally conscious of these leaks, and from the beginning of the decade there had been suggestions that a meeting ought to be called to discuss the subject. Nothing came of them, and by the summer of 1786 Congress was still debating possible amendments to the Articles of Confederation.

During this same summer of 1786, a storm blew up in Massachusetts on the subject of government. No state had a constitution more admired by experts or more disliked by the people themselves. Only four months after the constitution was ratified one of the towns had tried to get it annulled, and during the past six years discontent had been increasing. The Senate was especially disliked as both useless and repressive; John Adams had designed it carefully to represent the propertied interests, and the people of western Massachusetts felt it was incapable of understanding their financial problems.

This was especially true of returned soldiers, who found themselves struggling under heavy taxes imposed by a Senate they had not wanted in the first place. As a contemporary remarked sympathetically, such people "could not realize that they had shed their blood in the field to be worn out with burdensome taxes at home or . . . to secure to their creditors a right to drag them into courts and prisons." Yet the Senate had its problems too. "With such high-wrought notions of freedom in the people, it was difficult for the legislators . . . to govern without appearing to tyrannize."

The Massachusetts legislature adjourned on the eighth of June, 1786, without making any effort to improve the situation, and the people took matters into their own hands. Fifty towns in the western part of the state sent delegates to a revolutionary meeting called the Hampshire Convention, declaring soberly and from the depths of their hearts: "This meeting is constitutional." They compiled a list of their grievances, and the first one was "the existence of the Senate." It was not easy to forget that a recent revolution had been won by force of arms, and since the former soldiers could see no other way out, they picked up their guns again. One of their leaders was Daniel Shays, promoted for gallantry at the Battle of Bunker Hill and with so distinguished a war record that Lafayette himself had presented him with a sword. He now turned revolutionist, along with many others like him, and Massachusetts was engulfed in what was called Shays' Rebellion.

Jefferson, who was serving as minister to France, was not alarmed when he heard the news. He wrote Mrs. John Adams, whose husband was serving as minister in London, that he liked to see Americans "awake and alert. . . . The good sense of the people will soon lead them back, if they have erred in a moment of surprise." Abigail Adams, who shared her husband's political views, wrote back firmly: "Ignorant, restless desperadoes, without conscience or principles, have led a deluded multitude to follow their standard, under pretense of grievances which have no existence but in their imagination." This was exactly what King George had said when men like her husband had led an earlier rebellion against accredited authority, and she and the King both used the same phrase—the "deluded multitude."

When the revolt was finally put down the following February, all but four of the rebels were pardoned, and eventually the Massachusetts legislature even pardoned Daniel Shays himself. It had thought briefly of punishing the more hardened offenders by taking away their right to vote, but times had changed since John Winthrop used this weapon so successfully and the whole idea petered out.

Nevertheless, Americans had endured some six months of watching the collapse of law and order in Massachusetts, and one of the most profoundly shocked was Daniel Shays' former Commander in Chief, George Washington. A patriot who had served brilliantly under Washington's command was now defying the very government he had fought to bring into existence. "What, gracious God, is man, that there should be such inconsistency and perfidiousness in his conduct? It is but the other day that we were shedding our blood to obtain the constitutions under which we now live, constitutions of our own choice and making; and now we are unsheathing the sword to overturn them. The thing is so unaccountable that I hardly know how to realize it, or to persuade myself that I am not under the illusion of a dream."

Washington felt that the Massachusetts authorities had shown great weakness in not suppressing the revolt instantly and that law and order were now threatened everywhere. "When this spirit first dawned, probably it might easily have been checked; but it is scarcely within the reach of human ken, at this moment, to say when, where or how it will end. There are combustibles in every state, which a spark might set fire to."

It seemed to Washington that the root of the whole difficulty was the flabbiness of the Articles of Confederation. As he had written his friend John Jay in August, just before the rebellion broke out in Massachusetts: "I do not conceive we can exist long as a nation without having lodged somewhere a power which will pervade the whole Union in as energetic a manner as the authority of the state governments extends over the several states." In December he was still writing passionately to his friends from Mount Vernon that only a strong central government could save the country from the "awful crisis" which was facing it.

It had been planned to hold a meeting in Philadelphia the following May, to discuss possible changes in the Articles of Confederation, but Washington refused to serve as a delegate from Virginia. He thought that "the darling sovereignties of the states" would never surrender themselves to a central national authority, and that things would have to be much worse before they could become better. "I believe that the political machine will yet be much tumbled and tossed, and possibly be wrecked altogether, before such a system . . . will be adopted."

It was clear to Washington's fellow Virginians, and especially to James Madison, that the proposed convention in Philadelphia could not succeed without him. Washington was the savior of his country, the one symbol of unity it possessed, and the pressure on him to leave his retirement grew increasingly urgent. All through the spring of 1787, Washington went on refusing. It was not until the 27th of April, less than three weeks before the opening date, that Washington wrote Henry Knox that he had given in and was leaving for Philadelphia the following Monday.

Congress had authorized the convention in February, and with quite a good grace. It had even managed to scrape together enough money out of an almost empty treasury to pay for the services of a secretary, a doorkeeper and a messenger. When it turned out that the convention had not amended the old form of government but created a new one instead, Congress paid the clerks who engrossed the document as well as a bill of thirty-six dollars for the stationery. The total cost of the Constitution of the United States thus came to $1165.90, making it perhaps the best bargain in history.

Congress had been meeting in New York City for the past two years, in a handsome room on the second floor of the City Hall. But Philadelphia was the logical city for a constitutional convention, and the State House was the logical place. It was this hospitable building that had sheltered the Continental Congress, and it was here that the Declaration of Independence had been signed.

The delegates were supposed to have their first meeting in the State House on Monday, the 14th of May, but by then only two delegations had arrived. The first, from Virginia, included George Washington, who had come early. The other, from Pennsylvania, included the almost equally honored Benjamin Franklin. In Franklin's case it was merely a matter of changing his hat when he entered the State House on Monday, since he was serving as president of the executive council of Pennsylvania, which met in the same building.

Franklin was over eighty, and well aware that he was a very old man to be serving on such a difficult assignment. "I seem to have intruded myself into the company of posterity, when I ought to have been abed and asleep." Yet the long strain seemed to agree with him, and one of the delegates from Georgia, who jotted down his impressions of his colleagues, wrote in admiration that Franklin had "an activity of mind equal to a youth of twenty-five years of age."

Each day, the Virginia and Pennsylvania delegations met and waited, and on Thursday Washington was able to record in his diary that the South Carolina delegation had arrived. Little by little the other delegations drifted in, and on the 25th of May it was at last possible to open proceedings with a quorum of seven states. By that time only one New England delegate had arrived—Rufus King of Newburyport—and he wrote in some embarrassment to a friend in Connecticut: "I am mortified that I alone am from New England. . . . Pray hurry on your delegates." Connecticut cooperated, but the rest of New England was less obliging. The New Hampshire delegation did not arrive until July, since the legislature had not voted money for expenses. As for Rhode Island, it remained true to its traditional inability to cooperate and never sent any delegation at all.

On the opening day, the delegates experienced one moment of complete agreement: they unanimously elected Washington president. He was not always the presiding officer, since whenever the convention formed itself into a Committee of the Whole it had its own chairman; but his dignity, his dedication and his very high reputation had a great deal to do with making the Constitutional Convention a success.

Back in 1774, when John Adams had learned that he was to serve as a delegate to the First Continental Congress, he came home from a long walk to write in his diary: "We have not men fit for the times. We are deficient in genius, in education, in travel, in fortune—in everything. I feel unutterable anxiety." Now, thirteen years later, the men of America could meet in Philadelphia in the proud knowledge that they had indeed been fit for the times. They had fought and won a war. They had set up a series of governments for themselves and another for the United States. And if the latter needed to be totally remade, they were prepared to do that too.

Nearly every delegate there had had a great deal of practical political experience. Most of them had worked on the formation of the state constitutions, or had served in the state legislatures, or in Congress. Behind them stretched a long history of government which, if it did not extend quite to Hengist and Horsa, was nevertheless part of the air they breathed.

They were acutely conscious of the weight of their current responsibility. George Mason, who had been the chief architect of the Virginia constitution, was a member of the Virginia delegation, and he wrote his son on the first of June: "I never before felt myself in such a situation and declare I would not, upon pecuniary motives, serve in this convention for a thousand pounds per day. The revolt from Great Britain and the formations of our new governments at that time were nothing compared to the great business now before us. . . . The influence which the establishment now proposed may have upon the happiness or misery of millions yet unborn is an object of such magnitude as absorbs, and in a manner suspends, the operations of the human understanding."

The delegates were also acutely aware that they were trying to do something that had never been attempted before. All Europe was watching with intense interest the outcome of an effort to create a republican government which could operate successfully over thirteen state governments. To most Europeans, the word *republican* was a synonym for chaos, and monarchy was the safest form. It was up to the infant United States to prove not only that representative government could work but that it could work on a national level. James Madison, with his usual clarity of mind, stated the difficult goal they had set for themselves—"the double object of blending a proper stability and energy in the government with the essential characters of the republican form, and of tracing a proper line of demarcation between the national and state authorities."

The delegates were well aware of the historic nature of the event, and most of them arrived with the intention of taking notes. This was all the more necessary since the secretary who had been hired for the Convention, William Jackson, was not a very energetic individual. Like Charles Thomson, who was still serving as secretary of Congress, he saw no reason to record any of the debates.

Some of the delegates strove valiantly to take notes on the speeches, but their good intentions crumbled as the meetings dragged on behind closed doors through the whole of that long, hot summer. Only James Madison held to his resolve to get the whole thing down on paper, and he said afterward that the strain had nearly killed him. The notes he took were not published until after his death, but in 1815 Jefferson was able to tell Adams that the record existed: "The whole of everything said and done there was taken down by Mr. Madison, with a labor and exactness beyond comprehension."

When William Pierce of Georgia wrote his character sketches of the delegates, he said of Madison that he was "a gentleman of great modesty, with a remarkable sweet temper," who always seemed to be "the best informed man of any point in debate." Most of them were well educated on the subject of government, but Madison was more learned than any. "In a very able and ingenious speech," he was able to make a survey of "all the beauties and defects of ancient republics" and to compare "their situation with ours wherever it appeared to bear any analogy."

The only American who could have rivaled Madison in this kind of scholarship was John Adams. He was currently serving as minister at the Court of St. James's, but he was in Philadelphia in spirit, since he was represented in the bookstores by a stout little volume which he had finished writing in his Grosvenor Square residence on the first of January. Adams had not known that a convention was being planned, but his book was published in time to be available to the delegates.

It was called *A Defense of the Constitutions of the United States of America* but it was chiefly a defense of the Massachusetts one. After Adams arrived in Europe, "every western wind brought us news of town and county meetings in Massachusetts . . . condemning my constitution." It was chiefly the Senate that these meetings condemned, and Adams had encountered the same point of view in liberal political circles in France. Men like Condorcet and Turgot were hoping to set up a legislature of one house only in France, in imitation of the one their beloved Franklin had established in Pennsylvania, and Adams developed what was almost a monomania on the subject. So that he might wash his hands "of the blood that was about to be shed in France, Europe and America," he wrote his *Defense*. There he pointed out in a cloud of learned references and with special support from James Harrington that there must be a balance of power, a representation of the rights of property and a separation of the legislature into two houses.

Benjamin Rush noted on the second of June that "Mr. Adams' book has diffused such excellent principles among us that there is little doubt of our adopting a vigorous and compounded federal legislature." This was, in fact, one of the few subjects on which there was prompt agreement. The Pennsylvania delegation voted for a single house, apparently out of courtesy to Franklin, but all the other delegations wanted a two-house legislature.

This was what they already possessed in their own state governments, with the single exception of Georgia; and by 1790 Georgia, like Pennsylvania, had altered its constitution to correspond to the rest. The delegates knew by practical experience that the existence of an upper and lower house made it possible to accommodate the two great sources of political energy, with property represented in the Senate and the people in the House of Representatives.

The delegates also knew, and were able to share the knowledge with their colleagues, that some of the devices which had been written into the state constitutions had not been successful. General C. C. Pinckney, for instance, was one of the delegates from South Carolina. He said that the arrangement on money bills had been "a source of pernicious disputes between the two branches. The constitution is now evaded by informal schedules of amendments handed from the senate to the other house." John Langdon of New Hampshire was able to report that the system which was used there for electing the chief executive had not worked either. "In New Hampshire the mode of separate votes by the two houses was productive of great difficulties."

At one point during the debates, Madison mourned the fact that there was "so little direct experience to guide us." The subject under discussion at the time was the number of years a Senator should be permitted to serve before he was obliged to face reelection, and Madison went on to say, "The constitution of Maryland was the only one that bore any analogy to this part of the plan." The analogy was in fact very close, and Madison's lament only served to emphasize the extraordinary amount of tested, practical experience that was available to the delegates at the Constitutional Convention.

All the state constitutions, hammered out so patiently and the result of so many compromises, were in print. They had been published by order of Congress in 1781, and the hardworking delegates referred to them constantly. In a sense, these documents were the true founding fathers of the federal Constitution. The great leap of the imagination on the part of the delegates lay in the fact that they were willing to use the smaller patterns as a model for the greater one, and to attempt on a continental scale the kind of republican government which, according to nearly all political theorists, could be made to succeed only in a relatively small geographical area.

All the delegates liked to decorate their speeches with classical examples and recent European authorities. To be able to state, "The great Montesquieu says," was to give weight to any argument. But they followed such experts only when the experts agreed with them and not otherwise. They followed in the main their own political experience, expanding it by listening carefully to each other and remembering always that they had to produce a government which would work.

An exception to this point of view was Alexander Hamilton, the brilliant young lawyer who was serving in the New York delegation. Hamilton had worked vigorously to bring the Constitutional Convention into existence, and he hated the Articles of Confederation because of their slackness and inefficiency. He wanted a strong central government where there would be no room for waste or weakness, and he believed that the time had come when this might be achieved. "The people are gradually ripening in their opinions of government—they begin to be tired of an excess of democracy."

On the 18th of June, Hamilton rose to speak, having been "hitherto silent on the business before the Convention," and delivered a long, careful speech on what would be an ideal government for the United States. He pointed out that the "vast and expensive apparatus" of thirteen state governments was undesirable, and so was the current and to his mind excessive emphasis on representative government. "The people . . . seldom judge or determine right."

Hamilton suggested instead a chief executive and a Senate which would be completely separated from the will of the people. Let the Senators "hold their places for life, or at least during good behavior. Let the executive also be for life." Some "gentlemen . . . suppose seven years a sufficient period to give the Senate an adequate firmness, from not duly considering the amazing violence and turbulence of the democratic spirit."

Since the people would still be able to express their will through the state legislatures, if not in the national government, Hamilton had a plan for the states also. He suggested that "the governor or president of each state shall be appointed by the general government," and that this national government should also be permitted to exercise a veto power over anything which a state legislature had approved. Hamilton said he was reluctant "to shock the public opinion by proposing such a measure. On the other hand, he saw no other necessity for declining it."

The delegates listened to Hamilton's long speech, and some of them expressed their admiration of it. Then they went back to the realities of political life. They took up once again the burden of trying to write a constitution that would be acceptable to the real world of 1787.

It was a struggle they nearly lost, and the rock upon which the Convention almost foundered was the question of how to divide political power among the thirteen states. This was the problem that had been argued with such bitterness during the previous decade when the Articles of Confederation had been written, and on that occasion the victory had gone to the smaller states. The larger states had no intention of letting this happen again, and the more the argument raged, the more embittered both sides became.

The delegates argued the matter for three weeks, in an atmosphere of increasing fear and suspicion, and by the end of June there was a stalemate. "Great zeal and pertinacity had been shown on both sides, and an equal division of votes on the question had been reiterated and prolonged, till it had become not only distressing but seriously alarming. It was during that period of gloom that Dr. Franklin made the proposition for a religious service."

Franklin remembered very well a set of earlier meetings in that same room. "In the beginning of the contest with Great Britain . . . we had daily prayer in this room for the Divine protection. . . . Do we imagine we no longer need His assistance?" Since the Convention was "groping as it were in the dark to find political truth," it would do well to turn to a power outside its own strength. Otherwise, "we shall succeed in this political building no better than the builders of Babel. . . . And, what is worse, mankind may hereafter . . . despair of establishing governments by human wisdom, and leave it to chance, war and conquest."

Franklin's suggestion was turned down. Hamilton and several others felt that such a move would look like panic. It was also pointed out, which was no less than the truth, that there was no money to pay for a minister.

Two days later, on the 30th of June, Franklin tried to get through a compromise motion. "When a broad table is to be made, and the edges of the planks do not fit, the artist takes a little from both and makes a good joint." By now, the air was so thick with fury that one delegate hinted his state might secede from the Union. This was Gunning Bedford of Delaware, very well aware that the state of Virginia had sixteen times the population of his own. "Will you crush the smaller states . . . ? Sooner than be ruined, there are foreign powers who will take us by the hand."

The following Monday, the Convention took another vote and again there was a tie. The impasse was complete, and apparently unbreakable. Elbridge Gerry of Marblehead, who was not usually an eloquent man, implored his fellow delegates to consider the situation as a whole: "Something must be done, or we shall disappoint not only America but the whole world. . . . We must make concessions on both sides. Without these the constitutions of the several states would never have been formed."

General Pinckney had moved that a committee which would represent all the states should be set up "to devise and report some compromise," and this idea at least was approved. The committee met over the fourth of July, which could not have been a day of rejoicing for anyone there, and as soon as it turned in its report the fighting started all over again. Hamilton had returned to New York by now, and Washington wrote him on the tenth: "I *almost* despair of seeing a favorable issue to the proceedings of our Convention and do therefore repent having had any agency in the business. . . . I am sorry you went away. I wish you were back."

By this time, the delegates were no longer meeting in their downstairs room in the State House, since the state Supreme Court was in session. A New England minister who was visiting Philadelphia in the middle of July caught a glimpse of the Court in session—the judges robed in scarlet and the lawyers in black—and he mentioned that the room upstairs was "now occupied by the Continental Convention." He made it his business to meet as many of the Convention delegates as possible, and he particularly enjoyed having tea with Franklin under a mulberry tree in the great man's garden. "Everything about him seems to diffuse an unrestrained freedom and happiness . . . an uncommon vivacity which seems as natural and involuntary as his breathing." Franklin, at any rate, was not in the mood of near despair that was burdening Washington.

Franklin was a very experienced politician and so were most of the delegates. When they met again the following Monday, it was against a background not only of heated public debate but of a great deal of private maneuvering—a step-by-step meeting of minds so that it would be possible to reach a reasonable conclusion. The basis of the final compromise was simple and ingenious: an equal vote for each state in the upper house and representation by population in the lower. After that, an enormous amount of hard work remained to be done, but there was no further threat of disaster. In August, Washington was able to write Henry Knox that a general framework of government was at last taking shape. "I am fully persuaded it is the best that can be obtained at the present moment, under such diversity of ideas as prevail."

Diversity of ideas was inevitable, and some of them cut across state lines. A classic area of conflict, and one which had been argued passionately during the making of each of the state constitutions, existed between those who wanted the people to have more power and those who wanted them to have less. The problem inevitably came up during the Constitutional Convention and consisted chiefly of attempts to check the democratic tendencies of the lower house by giving additional power to a propertied and aristocratic Senate.

It was the custom—dating back at least as far as the days of Charles the First—to call the lower house a "democracy" since it was directly responsible to the people. It was in this sense that Edmund Randolph used the word when he rose on the 29th of May, the first real working day of the Convention, to propose a plan of government that had been drafted by the Virginia delegation. He began by pointing out that the states had erred in giving too much power to the lower house:

> Our chief danger arises from the democratic parts of our constitutions. It is a maxim which I hold incontrovertible, that the powers of government exercised by the people swallows up the other branches. None of the constitutions have provided sufficient checks against the democracy. The feeble Senate of Virginia is a phantom. Maryland has a more powerful Senate, but . . . it is not powerful enough. The check established by the constitution of New York and Massachusetts is yet a stronger barrier against democracy, but they all seem insufficient.

Randolph was asked to expand on this point later, and obliged. "He observed that the general object was to provide a cure for the evils under which the U.S. labored; that in tracing these evils to their origin every man had found it in the turbulence and follies of democracy; that some check therefore was to be sought for . . . and that a good Senate seemed most likely to answer the purpose."

Edmund Randolph was currently the Governor of Virginia, and in cordial agreement with him was John Rutledge, late Governor of South Carolina. Rutledge had resigned from office when the second state constitution was written in South Carolina, because he would not accept its new provision that the Senate was to be elected directly by the people. He agreed, however, to serve as a delegate to the Constitutional Convention in the following decade, and there he tried to ensure that both houses should be elected indirectly so as to protect them from the dangers of turbulence and folly. So beautiful in the eyes of such men was the dream of an upper house totally divorced from the popular will that one of the delegates from Delaware said wistfully that the Senate of the United States ought to undergo "such a refining process as will assimilate it as near as may be to the House of Lords in England."

This delegate from Delaware was John Dickinson. Back in the days when he had been a power in Pennsylvania politics, he had worked with the other moderates to slow down the passage of the Declaration of Independence and to block the creation of the radical Pennsylvania constitution. He had been chairman of the committee which had the difficult task of drafting the Articles of Confederation, and since then he had retired to his estate near Dover. He was elderly and unwell, but he had come out of retirement to help bring a new government to America.

During those difficult days in Pennsylvania in 1776, Dickinson's close friend and ally had been James Wilson, and Wilson was also present at the Constitutional Convention, serving in the Pennsylvania delegation. It would have been reasonable to expect that Wilson also would support the conservative cause, but he did not. He emerged in the Convention as an almost reckless champion of the rights of the people.

Wilson fought with consistency and vigor for the idea of direct elections. He was sure that the United States Senate should be elected by the people instead of through the state legislatures, and he even had a theory that the chief executive of the nation should be elected in the same way. "Mr. Wilson said he was almost unwilling to declare the mode which he wished to take place, being apprehensive that it might appear chimerical. . . . He would say, however, at least in theory, that he was for an election by the people."

George Mason of Virginia respected the good sense of the people as much as anyone, but he knew that this idea was nonsense. "A government which is to last ought at least to be practicable. Would this be the case if the proposed election should be left to the people at large? He conceived it would be as unnatural to refer the choice of a proper character for chief magistrate to the people as it would to refer a trial of colors to a blind man."

A great deal of discussion went into the best way to choose a President, and the final solution was admittedly clumsy. Each state legislature was to supervise the appointment of as many electors as its size entitled it to, and each elector was to cast his vote for two men. The man with the highest number of total votes would be President, and the man with the next highest Vice President. This device turned out to be unworkable and was changed in 1804, although the principle of indirect election through an electoral college still persisted.

As for the Senate, this institution also was to be protected from the people, and the two Senators from each state were to be chosen by their respective legislatures. This idea lasted until 1913, when it was amended out of the Constitution. In the end, Wilson's reckless faith in the people turned out to be more prophetic than the judicious caution of the majority of his colleagues.

It was extremely difficult for the men of 1787 to peer into the future and try to imagine what the United States would be like, so that they could frame a government that might be expected to endure under very different conditions. Young Charles Pinckney thought that there would be no extremes of wealth and poverty in the future nation. Therefore it would be unnecessary to erect a shield in the Constitution to protect men of property, "because in a new country, possessing immense tracts of uncultivated lands, where every temptation is offered to emigration and where industry must be rewarded with competency, there will be few poor and few dependent."

James Madison took a different point of view. He was sure that the United States would become a great industrial nation and that the delegates must face realistically the future problem of the industrial poor. Madison's solution was the one that England depended on—the simple and time-honored device of exclusion: "In England, at this day, if the elections were open to all classes of people, the property of the landed proprietors would be insecure. . . . Our government ought to secure the permanent interests of the country against innovation. Landholders ought to have a share in the government."

What Madison wanted was some provision in the Constitution "to protect the minority of the opulent against the majority" so that there would be no risk that the opulent might be "overbalanced in future elections." Since an increase of population would inevitably "increase the proportion of those who will labor under the hardships of life," any gesture toward political equality would mean future disaster. "Symptoms of a leveling spirit . . . have sufficiently appeared . . . to give notice of the future danger."

Nevertheless, Madison believed ardently in a republican form of government, and he argued vigorously for direct elections in the lower house. So did his fellow Virginian, George Mason, who defined the House of Representatives as "the grand depository of the democratic principle of the government. It was, so to speak, to be our House of Commons." Many of the New England delegates were strongly opposed to direct elections in the House, especially Roger Sherman, who was now mayor of New Haven. "Mr. Sherman opposed the election by the people, insisting that it ought to be done by the state legislatures. The people, he said, immediately should have as little to do as may be about the government. They . . . are constantly liable to be misled." However, most of the delegates knew that this was a risk that would have to be taken, and they agreed to direct elections by the people in the House of Representatives.

The question then arose, what people? The members of the House of Commons were elected by corporations and forty-shilling freeholders and were therefore protected from any leveling impulses. But in America, the states had all set up different requirements for voting, and it was not clear which of these requirements should be used on the national level.

The problem was left to the Committee of Detail, which met late in July to pull together the various ideas that had so far been discussed and to set them down on paper in an orderly manner. When the question of the franchise came up in this Committee, it was talked over with great care and the final conclusion was that each state should retain its own system in voting for its representatives. James Wilson, who was a member of the Committee of Detail, said later: "This part of the report was well considered by the Committee, and he did not think it could be changed for the better. . . . It would be very hard and disagreeable for the same persons, at the same time, to vote for representatives in the state legislature and to be excluded from a vote for those in the national legislature."

James Wilson knew how it felt to be the victim of arbitrary exclusion. He was born in Scotland and had arrived in America in his early twenties. When he went briefly to live in Maryland, "he found himself, from defect of residence, under certain legal incapacities which never ceased to produce chagrin, though he assuredly did not desire and would not have accepted the offices to which they related. To be appointed to a place may be a matter of indifference. To be incapable of being appointed is a circumstance grating and mortifying."

James Wilson, through experience, knew a truth that Joseph Hawley knew through the power of his imagination. Wilson called this kind of exclusion "one of the most galling chains which the human mind could experience" and throughout the whole of the Constitutional Convention he fought "against abridging the rights of election in any shape." Most of the time he had not been successful, but at least he could keep the Committee of Detail from abridging them still further.

The Committee report was ready for debate on Monday, the sixth of August. Each delegate was given a printed copy of the twenty-three articles that had been decided upon in committee, with wide margins to leave room for making notes.

Full debate started the following morning, and since Section One concerned itself with the House of Representatives, the first subject to be discussed was that of the franchise. The Committee of Detail had suggested that "The qualifications of the electors shall be the same . . . as those of the electors in the several states, of the most numerous branch of their own legislature," that is to say, of the lower house. A member of the Pennsylvania delegation at once moved that the whole of this sentence be struck out.

The delegate from Pennsylvania was Gouverneur Morris, a brilliant and aristocratic New Yorker who was making his home in Philadelphia because he had failed in a battle with the Governor of New York on the subject of the state's policy with Vermont. Morris moved that a different sentence be "substituted which would restrain the right of suffrage to freeholders." Another member of the Pennsylvania delegation, Thomas Fitzsimons, promptly seconded the motion.

Oliver Ellsworth of Connecticut disagreed. He said that "the right of suffrage was a tender point, and strongly guarded by most of the state constitutions. The people will not readily subscribe to the national constitution, if it should subject them to be disfranchised." Pierce Butler of South Carolina supported Judge Ellsworth: "There is no right of which the people are more jealous than that of suffrage."

Then John Dickinson rose to his feet to tell these two speakers that they were mistaken. "Mr. Dickinson had a very different idea of the tendency of vesting the right of suffrage in the freeholders of the country. He considered them as the best guardians of liberty; and the restriction of the right to them as a necessary defense against the dangerous influence of those multitudes, without property and without principle, with which our country, like all others, will in time abound. As to the unpopularity of the innovation, it was in his opinion chimerical. The great mass of our citizens is composed at this time of freeholders and will be pleased with it."

Gouverneur Morris backed Dickinson vigorously. "The time is not distant when this country will abound with mechanics and manufacturers who will receive their bread from their employers," and such people could never be trusted. He also agreed with Dickinson that such a decision would be popular. "Nine-tenths of the people are at present freeholders and these will certainly be pleased with it."

James Madison took the same side, for he was haunted by a vision of the industrial poor. "In future times a great majority of the people will not only be without landed but any other sort of property. . . . The rights of property and the public liberty will not be secure in their hands." Therefore it was clear that the freeholders "would be the safest depositories of republican liberty."

What the delegates were trying to achieve was to keep the country republican, which was a sufficiently radical idea in 1787, without the risk of having it collapse into that generally feared condition, democracy. It was their responsibility to produce a durable form of government—"a system which we wish to last for ages"—and most of them were convinced that the road to safety lay in some form of exclusion.

Benjamin Franklin thought otherwise. When he looked into the future he did not see a faceless mob. He saw people, the same kind of people who had fought and won a Revolution. "Dr. Franklin . . . observed that in time of war a country owed much to the lower class of citizens. . . . If denied the right of suffrage it would debase their spirit and detach them from the interest of the country." Franklin considered it of the utmost importance "that we should not depress the virtue and public spirit of our common people, of which they displayed a great deal during the war, and which contributed principally to the favorable issue of it." Nor did he like the excuse that had been offered in England when the freeholder requirement first came into existence. He "quoted as arbitrary the British statute setting forth the danger of tumultuous meetings, and under the pretext narrowing the right of suffrage to persons having freeholds."

The debate ended when the delegates agreed, by a large majority, to accept the wording of the report of the Committee of Detail on the franchise. If the Convention had been held ten years earlier, the vote might very well have gone in the contrary direction and the freeholder principle would have been embedded in the Constitution. But the vigorous debates during the writing of the state constitutions had broken the old pattern and it was no longer possible to return to it.

Nathaniel Gorham, who was one of the delegates from Massachusetts, was characteristic of the kind of practical political experience that these men were able to draw on. Gorham served in the Massachusetts General Court, in its Provincial Congress, and in both houses of its subsequent legislature, including three terms as Speaker. He served on the committee that drafted the Massachusetts constitution and had just ended a term as presiding officer of the Congress of the United States. Gorham said that "he had never seen any inconveniency from allowing such as were not freeholders to vote." He pointed out that "the elections in Philadelphia, New York and Boston, where the merchants and mechanics vote, are at least as good as those made by freeholders only." Moreover, such a restriction of the franchise would not work. "The people have long been accustomed to this right in various parts of America and will never allow it to be abridged."

Whenever a political compromise of this kind was written into the Constitution, the hearts of some of the delegates sank. As the work went on through that hot August the list of compromises increased, and in the end the Constitution became a document that some of the delegates could not in conscience support.

Chief of these was George Mason. Few men could have brought to Philadelphia more ardor, more dedication or more wisdom. Yet on the last day of August, Mason announced that "he would sooner chop off his right hand than put it to the Constitution as it now stands." Two weeks later, still following the truest light of which he was capable, he refused to sign it. So did Governor Randolph of the same delegation.

Benjamin Franklin had much more reason than the two Virginians to dislike the finished Constitution. It rejected most of the principles he had supported during the making of the Pennsylvania constitution of 1776 and corresponded much more closely to the kind of government John Adams approved. The day after Mason refused to sign, Franklin asked the members of the Pennsylvania delegation to come and confer with him. "It was reported that he did it to acquaint them of his disapprobation of certain points, and the impossibility of agreeing to them."

The rumor was incorrect. Franklin had in fact called the delegation together "to allay every possible scruple and make their votes unanimous."

He intended to make a speech on the subject the following morning, but since he was too feeble to stand up, his friend James Wilson read it for him. It could very well have been written by a young man of twenty-five, one who was lively, witty and infinitely optimistic, except that it clearly had behind it half a century of experience.

Being Franklin, he naturally illustrated the point of the speech with one of his many stories. This one was about the French lady who said meditatively to her sister: "I don't know how it happens, sister, but I meet with nobody but myself that's always in the right." Franklin did not think that anyone should be too sure of being right, and his speech incorporated the essence of American political experience:

Mr. President,

I confess that there are several parts of this constitution which I do not at present approve, but am not sure I shall never approve of them. For, having lived long, I have experienced many instances of being obliged . . . to change opinions . . . which I once thought right but found to be otherwise. . . .

When you assemble a number of men to have the advantage of their joint wisdom, you inevitably assemble with those men all their prejudices, their passions, their errors of opinion, their local interests, and their selfish views. . . . It therefore astonished me, sir, to find this system approaching so near to perfection as it does, and I think it will astonish our enemies. . . .

I cannot help expressing a wish that every member of the Convention who may still have objections to it would, with me, on this occasion, doubt a little of his own infallibility—and to make manifest our unanimity, put his name to this instrument.

255

Nearly everyone followed Franklin's lead. "Mr. Gouverneur Morris said that he too had objections, but considering the present plan as the best that was to be attained, he should take it with all its faults." Alexander Hamilton also urged signing. "No man's ideas were more remote from the plan than his own were known to be," but the alternative would be anarchy. In the end only three delegates refused to sign—Mason and Randolph of Virginia and Elbridge Gerry of Massachusetts.

While the ceremony of signing was going on, Franklin looked toward the President's chair, on the back of which was a sun, and said to the delegates nearest him, "Now at length I have the happiness to know that it is a rising and not a setting sun." The President himself had equal reason to be content. There was a final dinner at the City Tavern, and then, as Washington noted in his diary, he retired "to meditate on the momentous work which had been executed."

In general it was a cautious piece of work, with all the safeguards that the political wisdom of the time dictated, but at one important point the delegates had thrown caution to the winds: they decided to offer the Constitution to the people for ratification. This had not been done in the case of any of the earlier state constitutions, not even the radical one in Pennsylvania. The first time such a device had been tried was in Massachusetts, and the price was two attempts, several years of confusion, and vociferous dissatisfaction afterward. When New Hampshire wrote its second constitution, it followed the lead of Massachusetts and presented the document to the people for ratification; here the results were equally trying. The first draft was rejected. A second was submitted to the town meetings and encountered so many objections that it had to be rewritten, and it was not until 1784 that the new constitution was finally accepted and could be put into operation.

A safer way to get approval for the federal Constitution would have been to submit it to the state legislatures, but for once the delegates were not interested in safety. As Rufus King of Massachusetts pointed out, a public referendum was the only way "of obviating all disputes and doubts concerning the legitimacy of the new constitution." It was decided that the ratification should be done through special "assemblies to be chosen by the people," and, if nine of these state assemblies approved, the Constitution would go into operation as the new government of the United States.

Elbridge Gerry fought hard against so risky an arrangement. "Great confusion, he was confident, would result from a recurrence to the people. They would never agree on anything." So bitter would the arguments be that the result might even be civil war, and "in Massachusetts particularly he saw the danger of this calamitous event. In that state there are two parties, one devoted to democracy, the worst he thought of all political evils, the other as violent in the opposite extreme. From the collision of these in opposing and resisting the Constitution, confusion was greatly to be feared."

For a time it almost seemed that Elbridge Gerry might be right. The deep political differences that existed in all the states had been glossed over during the Constitutional Convention by "the mutual deference and concession which the peculiarity of our political situation rendered indispensable." They reappeared in full force when the delegates elected by the people gathered in the ratifying conventions. One side was sure that popular liberty would be crushed by a strong central government; the other side was sure that only a strong central government could save the nation from chaos. The assemblies rocked with charges and countercharges, but no one descended to blows in spite of Gerry's prediction. The collision was a mental one, and in some of the states the level of debate was extremely high.

By July of the following year, it was still not certain that enough states could be found to ratify the Constitution, and the battle raged with special fury in pivotal New York. There was even some talk that, if the Constitution was rejected there, "The city of New York, with Staten and Long Islands, will separate themselves from the state and join the Union."

Hamilton had thrown the whole of his brilliant, ardent nature into the fight to get New York to ratify, and he found strong allies in John Jay and James Madison. They collaborated with him in writing a series of newspaper letters to explain and justify the proposed new government, and these were collected in book form as *The Federalist*. When the battle ended in victory, these papers had played a large part in achieving it.

Madison wrote the section in *The Federalist* which explained the workings of the House of Representatives, and he found it unnecessary to spend much time on the franchise since the arrangement was so easy to justify: "To have reduced the different qualifications in the different states to one uniform rule would probably have been as dissatisfactory to some of the states as it would have been difficult to the Convention."

If Madison's own views had prevailed there would have been, of course, a freeholder franchise. He held very strong convictions on this subject, and a few years earlier he had one of his rare differences of opinion with Jefferson on the subject. In 1783, these two close friends were working together on possible reform of the Virginia constitution, and Jefferson particularly wanted to reform the franchise. He wanted it changed so that a man could vote if he had served in the militia or had lived a year in the state, and Madison wrote Jefferson a careful letter to explain why he was wrong.

Madison said Jefferson had failed to realize, in making such a recommendation, what would happen when the poor, with their contempt for property rights, began to multiply in Virginia. "The time to guard against this danger is . . . when the bulk of the people have a sufficient interest in possession or in prospect to be attached to the rights of property." Madison raised this same point again at the Constitutional Convention, and it was to accommodate this view, as well as all the others, that the compromise on the franchise was written into the Constitution.

Madison had taken careful notes of all the debates, and he did not intend to release them in his lifetime. But he knew that they would be published eventually, as a matter of public record, and he wanted the record to be an exact one. When he was a much older man he went over all the material with great care, and when he came to one of his own speeches, he paused. This was the speech on the seventh of August, in which he had defended the freeholder franchise, and he now added a footnote for posterity. "These observations in the speech of J.M. . . . do not convey the speaker's more full and matured view of the subject, which is subjoined. He felt too much at the time the example of Virginia."

Madison was still incapable of carrying the principle of political equality to its logical conclusion, but he had at last become convinced that the Virginia system was not a legitimate basis for a republican government: "Confining the right of suffrage to freeholders . . . violates the vital principle of free government, that those who are to be bound by laws ought to have a voice in making them."

Madison fought hard for the freeholder principle at the Convention, and he was defeated by the necessity for compromise, which was the dominant note in the writing of this Constitution as it had been in the writing of most of the constitutions that had preceded it. The result was a framework of government that was not only orderly but flexible. It gave all Americans, as it had given Madison, room in which to grow and to change their minds.

Chapter Thirteen

On a mild April day in 1789, George Washington took the oath of office as President of the United States. The first gentleman of Virginia was dressed in a suit of brown Connecticut broadcloth, manufactured in a Hartford factory which had opened only the year before. The ceremony took place at City Hall, which was still the seat of government, and Washington stood on a balcony overlooking Wall Street while the oath was administered by the Chancellor of the State of New York.

The Chancellor was Robert R. Livingston. Thirteen years earlier he had served on the committee that wrote the Declaration of Independence, and the country had come a long way since then. As Washington himself said the year before: "We may, with a kind of grateful and pious exaltation, trace the finger of Providence through those dark and mysterious events" which had culminated in a new government.

It was a moment of great national pride, and the streets and rooftops were filled with awed and excited spectators. Washington was loved and trusted by everyone, and he brought to the office not only his personal nobility and profound sense of duty but also the wholehearted devotion of the entire nation. Under his guidance, the people of the United States would be able to move forward in perfect unity, all conflicts ended.

It was a hopeful moment, and it lasted very briefly.

259

Benjamin Franklin, that experienced politician, had remarked the year before that a new government could not be set in motion as though it were a game of chess "played by a skillful hand, without a fault. The players of our game are so many, their ideas so different, their prejudices so strong and so various, and their particular interests, independent of the general, seeming so opposite, that not a move can be made that is not contested."

The debates during the Constitutional Convention had made it clear that there were two points of view on government in the United States, and it had been hoped that the new structure would accommodate them both. The House of Representatives, which was elected directly by the people, was to be, as George Mason put it, "the grand depository of the democratic principle of the government," while the President and the Senators, being elected indirectly, would represent a more sheltered and therefore a more sober point of view.

The House of Representatives was well aware of its special responsibility as the guardian of the interests of the people, and it might even be called touchy on the subject. Early in May the question came up how the new chief of state ought to be addressed, and the Senate decided that Washington's title should be: "His Highness the President of the United States of America and Protector of the Rights of the Same." This was a perfectly suitable decision; even the chief executive of a little rural state like New Hampshire was officially styled, by order of its constitution, "His Excellency." But the House of Representatives refused to elevate the President of the United States to any kind of titular dignity, and it was finally decided to give him no title whatsoever.

The year after Washington was inaugurated, the national government moved to Philadelphia and the two Houses of Congress took up borrowed residence in the county courthouse that had just been built next to the State House, home of so many earlier political battles. The Senate was given the second floor and assembled there in dignified isolation behind closed doors. The House of Representatives met downstairs, and in a very different atmosphere. There was a large gallery to accommodate spectators, and a special place was reserved next to the Speaker for the reporters who took the debates down in shorthand. The members of the House faced reelection every second year, and it was important to let their constituents know exactly what they were doing.

The conservatives were a minority in the House, and one of the most brilliant members of this minority was a Massachusetts lawyer named Fisher Ames. When he first took his seat he had not expected to encounter any real difficulties, and he was amused rather than otherwise to note that some of his fellow members were "more solicitous to establish . . . some high-sounding principle of republicanism than to protect property, cement the union, and perpetuate liberty." He soon found to his dismay that most of his colleagues in the House of Representatives expected the "high-sounding principle" to be taken seriously, and that this was especially true of James Madison. Ames had admired Madison when they both began to work together in the House of Representatives: "I think him a good man and an able man, but he had rather too much theory." By 1793 the House had split into two warring factions, and Ames, who was still in the minority, said bitterly, "Madison is become a desperate party leader."

The chief reason for the battles that had erupted in the House was that the Constitution gave it the right to originate all money bills. It could hardly have done otherwise, since this was the privilege that the House of Commons had won long ago in England and which each of the colonial lower houses had achieved in its turn. This meant that the House of Representatives would have to work closely with the Secretary of the Treasury, and the majority could not. For the Secretary of the Treasury was Alexander Hamilton.

Hamilton was in many ways very like John Winthrop. He resembled him in his gift for public service, his legal skill and his intellectual powers. He resembled him also in a conviction that the government should never be entrusted to the clumsy hands of the many but reserved to the skilled and propertied few. Winthrop had said to Hooker, when they argued over who should govern: "The best part is always the least, and of that best part the wiser is always the lesser." Hamilton had said the same thing at the Constitutional Convention: "All communities divide themselves into the few and the many. The first are the rich and well born, the other the mass of the people. The voice of the people has been said to be the voice of God; and however generally this maxim has been quoted and believed, it is not true in fact. The people . . . seldom judge or determine right."

Unlike Franklin, Hamilton really believed that the new government could be run with complete efficiency—"played by a skillful hand, without a fault." He also felt that in many cases the hand should be his own, since "most of the important measures of every government are connected with the Treasury." He was especially anxious to create a fiscal policy which would make rich and wellborn Americans interested in supporting the young government, and he counted it one of the strengths of the Constitution that it had "the good will of most men of property in the several states who wish a government of the Union able to protect them against domestic violence and the depredations which the democratic spirit is apt to make on property."

This was not at all the point of view that was entertained by the majority of men in the House of Representatives, and they opposed Hamilton's fiscal theory with one of their own: "A love and veneration of equality is the vital principle of free governments. It dies when the general wealth is thrown into a few hands."

Hamilton had no difficulty getting the majority of the Senate to agree with him. But the majority of the House became more and more openly his enemy, and James Madison was its leader.

Up to now, Madison and Hamilton had been allies. They had worked together to bring a constitutional convention into existence, and both of them had attended the Annapolis Convention which was the forerunner of the meeting in Philadelphia. After the Constitution had been written, they worked together to get it ratified, and they collaborated so smoothly on *The Federalist* that it is not easy to detect from internal evidence which one of them is the speaker. Yet as soon as the new government went into operation, Madison and Hamilton found themselves on the opposite sides of what seemed to them both a matter of principle.

It was, at any rate, a difference in emphasis. As Madison had already pointed out, the makers of the Constitution had tried to create a government which would combine "a proper stability and energy . . . with the essential characteristic of a republican form." Hamilton, as Secretary of the Treasury, set himself to the creation of stability and energy, while Madison, as leader of the House of Representatives, found himself increasingly concerned with the question of maintaining the republican form.

It had never occurred to Hamilton that he and Madison would become enemies. As he said in 1792: "When I accepted the office I now hold, it was under a full persuasion that from similarity of thinking, conspiring with personal good will, I should have the firm support of Mr. Madison in the general course of my administration." Hamilton had not expected to get the support of Thomas Jefferson, who was Secretary of State in Washington's Cabinet, but he found it hard to believe that Madison would side against him. "It was not till the last session that I became unequivocally convinced of the following truth—that Mr. Madison, cooperating with Mr. Jefferson, is at the head of a faction decidedly hostile to me and my administration and actuated by views, in my judgment, subversive to the principles of good government and dangerous to the union, peace and happiness of the country."

Jefferson, by this time, was convinced in his turn that Hamilton was trying to subvert "step by step the principles of the Constitution." He wrote Washington in 1792 that Hamilton's "system flowed from principles adverse to liberty and was calculated to undermine and demolish the republic."

What had happened was that two parties had come into existence in the United States, an event so unexpected and in theory so undesirable that no one liked to admit it had happened. Although the makers of the Constitution had tried earnestly to prepare for all eventualities, the formation of political parties had never occurred to them. It was for this reason they had decided that the man with the highest number of votes in the electoral college would be President and the man with the second highest, Vice President, the two working together as political leaders of a united country. To the eighteenth-century mind, the word "party" was still a synonym for "faction" and a dreaded sign of schism and irresponsibility.

In time, it became possible to realize that the two-party system was a source of political stability in America, but in 1792 it seemed to be a clear sign that the country was falling apart. Each side was therefore convinced that the other was trying to subvert the Constitution and they had even acquired rival newspapers, hurling insults at each other with the experienced vigor born of generations of local political wrangling.

It was at about this time that the two parties gave themselves names. Hamilton's side called themselves the Federalists, hoping to suggest that they were the only Americans who wanted a strong federal government. This was hardly fair to the opposition since its leader, Madison, had fought hard for one. The party he headed was sometimes called the Madisonians, but it preferred to call itself the Republicans. This was hardly fair either, since it implied that the Federalists did not want a republican form of government.

Both sides wanted a republic, and both sides wanted the new government to be strong and successful. Where they differed, and with increasing bitterness, was on the best way to bring this about. Each time a question of government policy arose, opinion split in two, and by 1794 Senator Taylor could say, "The existence of two parties in Congress is apparent. The fact is disclosed almost upon every important question."

To President Washington, that symbol of national unity, no development could have been more alarming. He had been hoping to retire at the end of his term of office, and when he prepared his Farewell Address with Madison's help in May of 1792 he stressed his dream of harmony for America. "We are *all* the children of the same country. . . . The only strife among us ought to be who should be foremost in . . . giving every possible support . . . to the Union." He had been doing his best to mediate between

Jefferson and Hamilton at Cabinet meetings, but the difference of opinion between the Secretary of State and the Secretary of the Treasury was so fundamental that Jefferson finally offered his resignation, and Washington accepted it.

The political atmosphere had again become as heated as it was during that June of 1787 when Washington had feared, as he wrote Hamilton, that the Constitutional Convention would fail. In those days the quarrel had been between the large states and the smaller ones. Now it was a more ancient quarrel, and one which predated the formation of the states. The Revolution had released it, it had made its appearance in each of the battles over the state constitutions, and now it had moved to a national arena.

Nine years before the Constitution was written, Christopher Gadsden noted that there was "a disease amongst us far more dangerous than anything that can arise from a whole herd of contemptible, exportable Tories." Gadsden expected the Constitution to cure this disease, since it would serve as a bulwark against popular "tumult, instability and inefficiency." It had not cured it. Instead, what Fisher Ames called "the factious, leveling spirit" had taken root in the House of Representatives.

The difference of opinion between the Federalists and the Republicans would have been violent enough if it could have been confined to domestic issues. But Hamilton's fiscal policy was based in part on closer ties with Great Britain, and this brought up the highly controversial question of how the United States ought to conduct itself toward Britain's enemy, France.

During the Revolution, France had been America's indispensable ally. When the British army surrendered at Yorktown, nearly nine thousand French soldiers were under Washington's command and fifteen thousand Frenchmen were in the fleet that supplied the naval blockade. Under the circumstances it seemed wholly suitable that when the old Congress met in New York, in its handsome room on the second floor of City Hall, there should be a full-length portrait of General Washington on one wall and, on another, life-sized portraits of King Louis XVI and his Queen, Marie Antoinette, "drawn by the King's own portrait painter and presented by His Majesty to Congress."

The King had sent soldiers and money to America out of self-interest, as a continuation of the war that France had been waging with Great Britain for most of the century. But individual Frenchmen like the Marquis de Lafayette came to America because they were political liberals and wanted to take part in a warfare against royal tyranny.

The French had been leaders throughout the eighteenth century in a brilliant extension of the political theories that England had been discussing during the seventeenth. There had been an increasing emphasis on political equality and on the rights of man, but it remained discussion only. When Rousseau wrote in 1762, "Man was born free, and everywhere he is in chains," there was an emotional response but no way to translate it into political action. France had held its last representative assembly in 1614.

The American Revolution seemed to move all this discussion into the realm of political reality. The Declaration of Independence stated that the rights of man and the principles of equality were at the basis of the American action, and European reformers believed that the Revolution was based on a much more theoretical set of abstract propositions than it actually was.

The subsequent American achievements in the field of self-government were followed closely in Europe, and five different editions of the state constitutions were published in France between 1776 and 1786. In 1787, when the Americans created a Constitution for the whole of the United States, the Marquis de Condorcet himself translated it into French.

Three months after Washington was inaugurated as the first President of the United States, the people of Paris stormed the Bastille. Lafayette sent the key of that great state prison to President Washington, and with it an accompanying letter: "It is beyond doubt that the principles of the United States opened the gates of the Bastille, and consequently it is in America that the key to the Bastille must find its rightful place." The storming of the Bastille on July 14, 1789, set in motion a series of events that seemed to be fulfilling the dreams of men like Lafayette, and two years later the French were able to set themselves to the task of writing a constitution. As the French Assembly wrote to the American Congress in January of 1791: "Twenty-six millions of men, breaking their chains and seriously occupied in giving themselves a durable constitution, are not unworthy the esteem of a generous people who have preceded them in that noble career."

When Louis XVI informed Congress that he had accepted the new French Constitution, the two Houses sent characteristic replies. The Senate contented itself with sending best wishes for "the freedom and prosperity of the French nation, and the happiness and glory of the monarch presiding over it." The House of Representatives, after a brisk debate, decided to say nothing about the glory of monarchs. Instead, it expressed the wish that "the wisdom and magnanimity displayed in the formation and acceptance of the constitution" would bring about "the most perfect attainment of its object, the permanent happiness of so great a people." The vote was 35 to 16, with Madison voting in favor of this wording and Fisher Ames, predictably, against it.

In spite of all the good wishes for the durability of the French constitution, it lasted only a year. Louis XVI was either unwilling or unable to conduct himself as a constitutional monarch, and in August of 1792 the French Assembly ordered elections for a new legislature, to be called the National Convention. The men of this Convention met in September, abolished the monarchy and set up a republic instead, proclaiming September 22 to be the first day of Year One of a new calendar.

They acted in the ardent conviction that a new and better age had dawned for the whole world, and invited men who had fought against tyranny in their own countries to become honorary members of the French republic. Washington, Hamilton and Madison all received invitations, but only Madison accepted.

America felt at first that this birth of a sister republic was a glorious sequel to its own struggle against royal tyranny, and when France was invaded by alarmed European powers many Americans celebrated the new republic's military victories as excitedly as if they had been their own. In January of 1793, nearly every state in the Union was having pageants and feasts and celebrations, and the people of Massachusetts had an especially glorious time. The Boston festivities culminated in a banquet in Faneuil Hall, with Samuel Adams presiding and French and American flags fraternally displayed. Plymouth had a parade and a ball, preceded by a sermon whose text came from the Book of Daniel: "He removeth kings."

The King of France was indeed removed, for it was in this same month of January that the French Convention voted, by a narrow majority, to execute him. Louis XVI went to the scaffold like Charles I, the victim of the same political rigidity that the Stuart king had shown, and the same wave of incredulous horror went over the conservatives. It was now the turn of the English court to go into mourning, and of France to be looked upon as a "hell of demons and parricides."

The following month, France declared war on Great Britain. The United States remained officially neutral, but unofficially the two parties took sides passionately. The Federalists were for law and order and Great Britain; the Republicans were for liberty and equality and France, and one more source of bitterness was added to an overcharged situation.

On the eighth of April, 1793, the first envoy from the new French republic landed in Charleston on his way to Philadelphia. The young man's name was Edmond Genêt, and he found himself surrounded by waves of popular enthusiasm which he did his best to encourage. Some prominent lawyers and businessmen in Pennsylvania took advantage of the excitement which his arrival generated to set up a political club which would act as a brake on Hamilton's policies. They first thought of calling themselves the

Sons of Liberty, but Genêt suggested that the organization be named the Democratic Society of Pennsylvania.

Alexander J. Dallas, the distinguished state attorney, was one of the founders of the Society and chairman of the committee that wrote its constitution. David Rittenhouse was elected president, and a statement of purpose was issued on the 17th of July. In addition, a circular letter was sent out to encourage the formation of similar clubs elsewhere: "Should the glorious efforts of France be eventually defeated . . . this country, the only remaining depository of liberty, will not long be permitted to enjoy in peace . . . the happiness of a republican government." In fact, there already seemed to be signs that "the spirit of freedom and equality" in America was being eroded by "the pride of wealth and the arrogance of power," and it was clear that a very close watch would have to be kept on the government.

Citizen Genêt was obliged to ask for political asylum in America, for the Terror ruled France, and he did not dare to return. The French Revolution was eating its own young, and the American Federalists pointed out that this was the inevitable result of trying to proclaim political equality. As a Charleston lawyer put it in 1794, "inequality of condition" was inevitable in Nature, and "it would be rather presumptuous to attempt to establish civil society upon principles repugnant to her laws." The Federalists intended no such presumption, and they looked upon the Democratic Clubs as a highly dangerous development.

Under various local titles, these Clubs had sprung up all over the country by 1794. They were linked by a network of correspondence similar to the one used during the Revolution, and with it they could coordinate the frequent and vigorous public statements with which they criticized the administration. The Newark Republican Society, which was founded that spring, was characteristic of most of them. A dry-goods merchant and some of the officers in the local militia were its leaders, and its constitution stated that the purpose of the organization was the "general dissemination of political knowledge."

A conservative gentleman of Massachusetts had noted, the previous December, that a similar development was taking place in Boston. "Some grumbletonians amongst us . . . are about to form a Democratic Club which I think they call the Massachusetts Constitutional Society. I . . . suppose they consider themselves as the guardians of the Rights of Man and overseers of the President, Congress and . . . heads of the principal departments of state." That was exactly what the Boston organization did consider itself, and it was to the American Revolution it turned in support of its position. "Till this period the art of government had been but the study and benefit of the few, to the exclusion and the depression of the many." Now it belonged to the many, in this dawn of the equal rights of man. Or, as a lady of Virginia put it in describing the Democratic Society in the newly formed state of Kentucky, it was a "hellish school of rebellion and opposition to all regular and well-balanced authority."

The Democratic Clubs were especially active in denouncing an excise tax that the government had placed on whiskey. Every previous effort to impose an excise tax had run into difficulties, and Hamilton himself said in *The Federalist* that "the genius of the people will ill brook the inquisitive and peremptory spirit of excise laws." Nevertheless, as Secretary of the Treasury, he had imposed the excise tax on whiskey, and there had been continual trouble. The settlers on the other side of the Allegheny Mountains felt that the tax pressed on them unjustly, and, in 1794, the four counties of western Pennsylvania flared into armed revolt.

The farmers of western Pennsylvania managed to convince themselves that they were patriots protesting a second Stamp Tax. Liberty poles sprouted, a committee of public safety was formed, and a flag, each of whose stripes represented one of the rebellious counties, flew over a meeting which gathered in August of 1794 on the west bank of the Monongahela River. Since there were over two hundred delegates to this meeting and no building was large enough to house them, they gathered in an open field and sat on the grass or on fallen trees. Nevertheless, they conducted themselves in a parliamentary manner, with a chairman to preside over them and a secretary to record the minutes.

The secretary was Albert Gallatin. He was a Swiss aristocrat, born in Geneva, and his grandmother had obtained for him a colonel's commission in the army of her friend, the Landgrave of Hesse. Gallatin refused to serve with the Hessians in a war against America and liberty, and when she gave him an indignant cuff on the ear he ran away. He reached New England in time to support the Revolution with cash contributions and "on several occasions acted as a volunteer." Then he settled down in western Pennsylvania and became one of its most influential politicians. He served three years in the state legislature, and then Pennsylvania elected him to the Senate. There he made it clear that he was an open foe of Hamilton's policies, and the Senate, by a close vote, got rid of him on a technicality.*

---

* The Senate's position was that Gallatin at the time of his election "had not been nine years a citizen . . . as is required by the Constitution." Gallatin's position was that the British laws concerning aliens had been done away with in the Revolution and that "every man who took an active part in the American Revolution was a citizen according to the great laws of reason and of nature."

Gallatin hated the whiskey tax. On the other hand, he disapproved strongly of armed rebellion and agreed to serve as a delegate to the meeting on the Monongahela because he hoped that men like himself could control the militant extremists. He said that it was not the duty of good citizens to stand aloof but to "be useful either in restoring tranquillity or in preventing the repetition of outrages. . . . I do not claim any greater share of political or physical courage than other men, but I did not hesitate to attend the meeting."

President Washington sent out peace commissioners, and Gallatin was a member of the committee that went to talk with them. On his return, he told his embattled fellow Americans that they deceived themselves if they thought their revolt bore any resemblance to that of the patriots of the Revolution, since in their case the law they were opposing by force had been passed by the representatives of the people. The vote was taken by secret ballot and the extremists lost.

It was arranged with the peace commissioners that all the voters in the four rebellious counties were to appear at their local polling places to sign declarations of loyalty. But, for a variety of reasons, not enough of them put in an appearance to supply the needed reassurance, and, on the 24th of September, Washington set into motion the huge citizens' army that had been waiting to quell the rebellion. The governors of four states supplied him with men, there were volunteers from some of the others, and nearly thirteen thousand troops marched over the mountains and into western Pennsylvania.

The Democratic Clubs warmly approved the President's action. As the Baltimore Republican Club put it: "The conduct of the President . . . in calling forth the militia to suppress so dangerous a spirit . . . was wise, prudent and constitutional." The Club's own members shouldered their muskets to march into the field, and the same thing was true of the various Democratic Clubs of Pennsylvania. It was said that so many of them were serving in the army that they could have called a meeting and had a quorum.

Hamilton went with the army and took over the supervision of the campaign. He arrested hundreds of men, for, as he said, "without rigor everywhere . . . the next storm will be infinitely worse than the present one." In the end, all the prisoners had to be released for lack of evidence against them. Only two men were convicted of treason in the Whiskey Rebellion, and President Washington pardoned them both.

What Washington could not forgive were the Democratic Clubs, which for months had been attacking both the whiskey tax and the general conduct of his administration. Toward the end of August he had written the

Governor of Virginia: "I consider this insurrection as the first *formidable* fruit of the Democratic Societies; brought forth I believe too prematurely for their own views, which may contribute to the annihilation of them. . . . I early gave it as my opinion to the confidential characters around me, that if these Societies were not counteracted (not by prosecution, the ready way to make them grow stronger) or did not fall into disesteem from the knowledge of their origin and the views with which they had been instituted by their father, Genêt . . . they would shake the government to its foundation." In October, when Washington was preparing the speech he planned to deliver to Congress on the Whiskey Rebellion, he wrote privately to his new Secretary of State: "My mind is so perfectly convinced that if these self-created societies cannot be discountenanced that they will destroy the government of this country, that I have asked myself . . . where would be the impropriety of glancing at them in my speech."

The President delivered his report to Congress on the 19th of November and in it he asked his fellow Americans to consider if the insurrection had not been "fomented by combinations of men who, careless of consequences . . . have disseminated, from an ignorance or perversion of facts, suspicions, jealousies and accusations of the whole government." The Senate, sending him a warm letter of thanks, added its own thoughts on this particular subject: "Our anxiety, arising from the licentious and open resistance to the laws in the western counties of Pennsylvania, has been increased by the proceedings of certain self-created societies . . . proceedings, in our apprehension, founded in political error, calculated if not intended to disorganize our government."

The House of Representatives found itself in a difficult position. Many of its own members were supporters of the Democratic Clubs, and the wisest course was to ignore the whole subject. James Madison chaired the committee that drafted the reply of the House to the President, and no mention was made in it of self-created societies.

As soon as the committee presented its draft to the House for its approval, a Federalist rose to move an insertion. This was Thomas Fitz-simons, who, when he served in the Pennsylvania delegation to the Constitutional Convention, had attempted to limit the franchise to freeholders. In the recent elections, he had lost his seat in the House of Representatives to a member of the Democratic Society of Pennsylvania, and he had even more reason than the average Federalist to dislike the Democratic Clubs. He conceded that they were "not strictly unlawful, yet not less fatal to good order and true liberty," and he wished the House to insert the following sentence: "We cannot withhold our reprobation of the self-created societies which have risen up in some parts of the Union, misrepresenting the conduct of the government and disturbing the operation of the laws, and which, by deceiving and inflaming the ignorant and the weak, may naturally be supposed to have stimulated and urged the insurrection."

It was not difficult to maintain that a vote in favor of this resolution was a vote in favor of law and order. At the moment, a hundred and fifty men were in prison, charged with high treason for their part in the Whiskey Rebellion, and it seemed to be a time of real danger. The President himself, in the letter of gratitude he had just sent the Senate, had spoken gravely of "our enemies from within and from without."

Nevertheless, there was a contrary point of view to be considered before the House joined the President and the Senate in a condemnation of the Democratic Clubs. For, as the Newark Republican Society had said: "Any attempts to prevent enquiry into the conduct of government is as dangerous to civil liberty as to raise in arms against its constitutional operations."

An extraordinary debate followed. The men in the House of Representatives were all patriots, all ardently desiring the safety, strength and happiness of their country, yet not even the delegates from Maryland could agree among themselves where that safety lay. Both sides called upon the Constitution, drew examples from all kinds of political experience, and each day grew more angry.

On Wednesday, the 26th of November, Fisher Ames addressed the House in one of the strongest speeches of his career. He was younger than Madison, he was a much more effective orator, and he had never been more desperately in earnest. As his son said of him later, "Mr. Ames apprehended that our government had been sliding down from a true republic towards the abyss of democracy," and the lawyer from Massachusetts was well aware that the debate was a crucial one.

In Ames' own state, a century before, there had been a formal effort to suppress heresy as the result of the Hutchinson controversy. The synod had denounced eighty-two heresies in the same confident way that the Senate of the United States had just denounced what it called "political error," and on this earlier occasion the political leaders of Massachusetts Bay had created what seemed to them a fair definition of sedition. "Sedition doth properly signify a going aside to make a party. . . . When the minds of the people being assembled are kindled or made fierce upon some sudden occasion, so as they fall to take part one against another, this is sedition." To Fisher Ames this was still an adequate definition. The old question had again arisen: "What will you do with men dissenting?" and the same answer still seemed to be the correct one: You will silence them.

Ames was convinced that a threat had been posed to the peace of the nation through permitting the government to be criticized. "Let us ask a moment's pause to reflect what would have been the fate of America, if these parricide clubs had really proceeded in poisoning the public mind as completely as they attempted to do." Fortunately they had failed, and all that the House was being asked to do was to behave as the Senate had done. "The question is simply, will you support your chief magistrate? . . . Will you ever suffer this House, the country, or even one seditious man in it, to question for an instant whether your approbation and cooperation will be less prompt and cordial than his efforts to support the laws?" Both the President and the Senate had denounced the self-created societies, and could the House put itself in the dangerous position of seeming to protect the Clubs? "Besides the unspeakable dishonor of this patronage, is it not rekindling the firebrands of sedition? Is it not unchaining the demon of anarchy?"

The following day, James Madison rose to reply to Fisher Ames. Back in 1784, Madison had joined with some influential fellow Virginians in creating a kind of literary society to protect America from "the innovations of ambition and the designs of faction." They had pledged themselves to write papers on every aspect of government, "being convinced that the surest mode to secure republican systems of government from lapsing into tyranny is by giving free and frequent information to the mass of people." Ten years later, Madison found himself faced with the choice either of risking "faction" or of suppressing political criticism, and he chose the former. As he stated in the speech in which he answered Fisher Ames: "Opinions are not the objects of legislation." In a free society, every man had a right to his own opinion and an equal right to express it. "If we advert to the nature of republican government, we shall find that the censorial power is in the people over the government, and not in the government over the people."

In the end Madison was victorious. The address which the House sent to Washington made no mention of self-created societies. But the basic question had not been resolved, and it returned to haunt the nation in the next administration.

To understand the function of dissent in government would have been to admit, from a practical point of view, the existence of parties, and President Washington could not do this. High-minded eighteenth-century gentleman that he was, he clung to his vision of a united nation in which everyone should be in agreement. It seemed to him that the increasingly vociferous criticism of his administration was a blow at government itself and that the divisive course the Republicans were pursuing might well end in the destruction of the nation.

In the summer of 1796, Washington applied himself once more to the writing of his Farewell Address. This time he did not turn to Madison for assistance, but to Hamilton. Since the President wanted early newspaper publication, he even asked Hamilton what editor should be given the manuscript and how the matter should be handled. "Will it be proper to accompany it with a note to him? . . . Let me ask you to sketch such a note as you may judge applicable to the occasion."

Hamilton wrote out the first draft of the Farewell Address, and Washington, when he went over it, found it necessary to make very few changes. The Address as a whole was an eloquent appeal for unity, and when he made slight alterations it was usually to strengthen the original point. Hamilton, for instance, wrote in the first draft, "Let me . . . caution you in the most solemn manner against the baneful effects of party spirit." Washington chose a stronger verb and changed it to: "Let me . . . warn you in the most solemn manner against the baneful effects of the spirit of party."

In certain types of government this spirit might have its uses, but not in a representative government like the United States: "There is an opinion that parties in free countries are useful checks upon the administration of the government and serve to keep alive the spirit of liberty. This, within certain limits, is probably true, and in governments of a monarchial cast patriotism may look with indulgence, if not with favor, upon the spirit of party. But in those of the popular character, in governments purely elective, it is a spirit not to be encouraged."

Washington's successor as President was John Adams, who agreed with this warmly. Adams considered the Democratic Clubs "very criminal," and he felt that Washington's administration had suffered unjustly from their criticism—"the President doing what is right, and clubs and mobs resolving it to be all wrong."

When Adams was a young man, some of his Massachusetts neighbors had been full of revolutionary theories. The register of deeds and one of the local merchants had both been "great sticklers for equality as well as deism; and all the nonsense of these last twenty years were as familiar to them as they were to Condorcet or Brissot." Another of these early neighbors, an attorney, "carried his doctrine of equality to a greater extremity, or at least as great, as any of the wild men of the French Revolution." Adams was well aware that the cry for political equality was not exclusively French, but this made him all the more anxious to protect America from the blood and anarchy that would be the inevitable result of such mistaken notions. As he noted in a letter he wrote in 1790: "Too many Frenchmen, after the example of too many Americans, pant for equality of persons and property. The impracticability of this God Almighty has decreed."

Adams overestimated the French devotion to equality. In the constitution which the French created in 1791, the franchise was heavily restricted; taxpayers could vote only in local elections, and in national ones they had to be considerable holders of property. The constitution created in 1793, the glorious Year One of the French republic, did indeed have universal male suffrage, but it never went into operation. The constitution reposed unused in its ark of cedarwood while a committee of twelve men ruled France during the Terror. When the French Convention reassembled in 1795, still another constitution was created. This one entrusted the executive power to a Directory of five men, and it restricted the franchise so heavily that the vote was confined, for all practical purposes, to about thirty thousand men of property.

Since the Directory was essentially the product of a counter-revolution, men who had been exiled from France during its years of upheaval were able to return. One of these was Talleyrand, who had become an admirer of Alexander Hamilton during the period he spent in America. Talleyrand was not, however, an admirer of Americans in general, and when he became Minister of Foreign Affairs in the new French government he treated the American envoys with open contempt. President Adams made the correspondence public in 1796, identifying Talleyrand's three agents only as X, Y and Z, and a furious anti-French spirit swept over the United States. War with France now seemed to be inevitable, and the Federalist party the country's only savior.

The more extreme Federalists never doubted that a swarm of French agents, aided and abetted by a misguided and possibly traitorous Republican party, was trying to soften up the country for invasion. In May of 1798, a Boston minister was able to announce solemnly from his pulpit that the same sinister international organization that had caused the French revolution had now invaded America. He knew this to be true for he had read a book called *Proofs of a Conspiracy*.

Robert Goodloe Harper of South Carolina made somewhat the same charge in the House of Representatives, where the Federalists now had a majority. Harper had once been a political radical himself and in fact had served as vice president in the Charleston Democratic Club. However, by 1798, he had become a dedicated Federalist, and now that Fisher Ames had retired he was the chief spokesman for the conservative cause in the House.

James Madison had also retired from the House of Representatives, and his place as leader of the opposition had been taken by Albert Gallatin. When Gallatin answered Harper's charge of disloyalty, he tried to put the whole subject in perspective by pointing out that it was possible for men to disagree politically without accusing each other of sedition. "Never shall I erect myself into a high priest of the constitution, assuming the keys of political salvation and damning without mercy whomsoever differs with me in opinion. But what tone is assumed, in respect to us, by some gentlemen on this floor?" To be a Republican was not necessarily to be a traitor and a fool, as the Federalists seemed to believe. "If you think us deprived of common integrity, you might at least allow us some share of common sense."

Gallatin underestimated the real passion which animated the more extreme Federalists in their crusade to save the country from disaster. It was only two months after this speech in the House that a bill was introduced into the Senate to outlaw dissent by defining it as treason.

The bill was introduced by James Lloyd of Maryland. Lloyd had won his seat by only one vote but acted with the assurance of a man who felt he had the whole state behind him. He had always held a rather simplified view of government and when he ran for office on an earlier occasion he had announced: "Behold, in the opposition to me, an attempt to subvert the laws of our country." The bill to combat sedition which he offered his colleagues in the Senate in June of 1798 included the death penalty, since for all practical purposes, in his opinion, the United States was already at war with France.

The Senate modified the Sedition Bill and sent it to the House, where it was the responsibility of Robert Goodloe Harper to steer it through. His chief antagonist in the debate was Albert Gallatin and they took up the warfare where Fisher Ames and James Madison had left it four years earlier.

Gallatin was not a good orator, partly because of his heavy foreign accent, but his speeches were successful because they were so clear and orderly in their presentation. He considered the Sedition Bill "subversive of the principles of the Constitution" and said why. Its basic assumption was "that whoever dislikes the measures of Administration and of a temporary majority in Congress, and shall . . . express his disapprobation and his want of confidence in the men now in power, is seditious, is an enemy, not of Administration but of the Constitution, and is liable to punishment."

Gallatin might have the better of the argument but Harper had the votes. The Sedition Bill passed the House and President Adams signed it into law on the 14th of July. Its basic purpose was to silence the editors of Republican newspapers, and it provided that anyone who "shall write, print, utter or publish . . . any false, scandalous and malicious writing or writings against the government of the United States, or either House of the Congress . . . or the President . . . to bring them . . . into contempt or disrepute" should be heavily fined or imprisoned.

In the early days of the founding of America, the Virginia Company had tried to impose law and order in Jamestown by punishing anyone who uttered "unseemly and unfitting speeches" against those in authority. This was one of the mistakes that ultimately forced a change in the government, since the decree was wholly contrary to the nature of the men the Virginia Company was trying to govern. The Federalists made the same mistake. Through the untiring efforts of the current Secretary of State, Timothy Pickering, they managed to try and to imprison a great many Republican editors, but the ones that remained were only roused to new vigor. As Fisher Ames wrote sympathetically to Pickering, they were "as unconquerable as the weeds."

Years later, when John Adams and Thomas Jefferson finally became friends again, Jefferson mentioned the "terrorism" of this time. Adams wrote back indignantly: "You never felt the terrorism of Shays' Rebellion in Massachusetts . . . the terrorism of Gallatin's insurrection in Pennsylvania . . . the terrorism excited by Genêt in 1793 when ten thousand people in the streets of Philadelphia, day after day, threatened to drag Washington out of his house and effect a revolution in the government." To Adams the Sedition Act was a legitimate attempt to maintain law and order in a time of increasing political unrest. To Jefferson it was a "reign of witches."

Since Jefferson had received the second highest number of votes in the electoral college, he was Vice President of the United States and therefore the presiding officer of the Senate. He was also, as the result of a development which the makers of the Constitution had not foreseen, the leader of the opposition party in America. To the young he had become a symbol of freedom of speech, and in 1799, when a college student wrote him on the subject, Jefferson replied with his usual vigor: "To preserve the freedom of the human mind . . . and freedom of the press, every spirit should be ready to devote itself to martyrdom; for as long as we may think as we will, and speak as we think, the condition of man will proceed in improvement."

When Jefferson was Secretary of State, he had written Washington: "No government ought to be without censors; and where the press is free, no one ever will. . . . Nature has given to men no other means of sifting out the truth either in religion, law or politics." He had always been an enemy of tyranny, in whatever field, and to him tyranny of the mind seemed more insupportable than any other.

The Sedition Act was a war measure, justified as Pitt had justified similar acts of repression in England, but the war between France and the United States never took place. President Adams suddenly decided not to placate the extremists in his own party, and in 1799 he opened peace negotiations. He was rightly proud of what he had done, and he later said he would like only one achievement recorded on his tombstone, that he "took upon himself the responsibility of the peace with France."

The more extreme members of the Federalist party were horrified, and one Congressman threatened to resign. "I have sacrificed as much as most men . . . to support this government and root out democracy and French principles. . . . I can and will resign if all must be given up to France."

In the next presidential campaign, the Federalist party found itself deprived of the war issue, saddled with the unpopular Alien and Sedition Acts, and split by internal wrangling. Moreover it faced a terrible foe, since Jefferson was the chief Republican candidate for the presidency. It was well known that he was not only a fanatic who would usher in the worst excesses of the French Revolution in a rage for political equality but that he was also a foe to religion who would destroy Christianity in America.

Like many prominent men of the eighteenth century, Jefferson was a deist—a foe not to religion but to dogmatism in religion. But in so savagely fought an election insults were freely hurled on both sides, and the charge of atheism was more persistently pressed against Jefferson than any other. As a writer for the *Newark Gazette* put it, with great dignity and three exclamation points: "At the present solemn and momentous epoch, the only question to be asked by every American, laying his hand on his heart, is, 'Shall I continue in allegiance to God and a religious President, or impiously declare for Jefferson and no God!!!' "

The deity whose dominion was threatened in this election was not the God of the churches. It was the god of property, the divine right of the rich and wellborn to rule America. It was certainly an exaggeration when a Maryland Federalist stated that "all the wealth and respectability" were on the Federalist side, but it was nevertheless true that two different theories of government were involved. It was a "contest between discordant Democracy and scientific Federalism," and it took real faith to believe that anything so untidy and so irrational as the rule of the people might be safer and more effective than the orderly theories of the Federalists.

An election which was already confused and bitter was made still more complicated by the unrealistic election procedure that had been written into the Constitution. Two Republicans tied for first place, and when the election was thrown into the House of Representatives there was a deadlock there also. Finally, on the 17th of February, 1801, and on the thirty-sixth ballot, Jefferson was elected President.

He chose for his Cabinet men like himself; Madison became his Secretary of State and Gallatin his Secretary of the Treasury. The inauguration was held the fourth of March at the new seat of government in Washington, D.C., and John Adams could not bring himself to be present. He left the capital very early that morning, and his friend Christopher Gadsden wrote him sympathetically the following week: "Long have I been led to think our planet a mere bedlam, and the uncommonly extravagant ravings of our own times, especially for a few years past . . . have greatly increased and confirmed that opinion. . . . Where is the spot in which are not many thousands of these mad lunatics?"

Back in 1776, Adams and Gadsden and Jefferson had all been brothers-in-arms, united in a war against the tyranny of Great Britain. Jefferson, however, had been fighting more than one kind of tyranny and he therefore continued to be a revolutionist after the other two had ceased.

In his Inaugural Address, Jefferson called the government of the United States "the strongest government on earth." Because it rested on diversity and not on forcible conformity, and because its strength was the strength of free men, no limits whatever need be put on the right of freedom of speech. "If there be any among us who wish to dissolve this union, or to change its republican form, let them stand undisturbed, as monuments of the safety with which error of opinion may be tolerated when reason is left free to combat it."

It had seemed to the men of the early seventeenth century that it would be dangerous to permit religious diversity. It still seemed to most men that it would be dangerous to permit political diversity. Yet Jefferson said it was not, and he looked upon his election as a triumph over the rigidity of the past. "The revolution of 1800 . . . was as real a revolution in the principles of our government as that of 1776 was in its form; not effected indeed by the sword, as that, but by the rational and peaceable instrument of reform, the suffrage of the people."

Chapter Fourteen

On a July day in 1795, Thomas Paine stood facing his fellow delegates of the French Convention. He had written out a speech which was an attack on the latest French constitution, and he stood listening while one of the secretaries translated it into French.

Six years earlier, also on a day in July, the Bastille had been stormed and the French Revolution had begun. When Lafayette sent the key of the Bastille to Washington, it was through Paine he transmitted it, for Paine hoped as ardently for the success of the French struggle against royal tyranny as for the American one. When France became a republic and offered honorary citizenship to a select list of foreigners, Paine accepted at once, for he was one of these "who had distinguished themselves in defending, explaining and propagating the principles of liberty."

Paine was elected a delegate to the Convention of 1792 and, like his friend the Marquis de Condorcet, he voted against the execution of the King. He was one of the moderates who served on a nine-man committee to write the constitution for the new French republic early in 1793, and Condorcet was its chairman.

Back in 1776, the New York Convention had taken up the multiple burden of trying to create a constitution, govern a state, suppress counter-revolutionaries and fight a war, and it had succeeded remarkably well on all four counts. The French Convention faced these same problems but on a titanic scale. The country was invaded by the alarmed powers of Europe, wrenched apart by internal conflicts and lacking any kind of tested political framework that could serve as a guide.

Condorcet was ready with the constitution on the 15th of April, 1793, a week after Citizen Genêt arrived in America as the representative of the new republic. The document was already a political unreality, for moderates like himself had lost control of the French Convention. In the end, the government was in the grip of a committee of twelve whose power was even more absolute and more centralized than that of the Sun King whose efficiency the Stuarts had so much admired. The committee of twelve also was efficient, but its symbol was the guillotine.

When the Terror was over, Condorcet was dead and the old dreams had died with him. When Paine was released from a French prison and took his place once more in the Convention, he found that his colleagues were quite content to write a new constitution which made no pretension to the kind of idealism that had been written into the earlier one. Its Declaration of Rights still spoke eloquently of political equality, but only two political forces were recognized in the franchise—property and the army. Voting was restricted to taxpayers and then subjected to such a complicated system of indirect voting that the actual franchise was in the hands of some thirty thousand well-to-do men. Soldiers were permitted to vote; but the right was inherent in their profession, not in them, and could not be passed down to their sons.

Paine believed that the right to vote was the root of freedom, and when he wrote his *Dissertation on First Principles* in this same year of 1795 it was with the single purpose of denouncing a limited franchise and of reviving what had once been the French dream: "If you subvert the basis of the revolution, if you dispense with principles and substitute expedients, you will extinguish that enthusiasm and energy which have hitherto been the life and soul of the revolution."

Paine's speech before the Convention in July had the same purpose. He implored his fellow delegates to set up a committee to compare the proposed constitution with the eloquent statements in the Declaration of Rights, so that the two documents would be consistent. No one rose to support what he had said.

Until the end of the decade, France was ruled under this constitution by a five-man Directory and a legislature of two houses; then a coup d'état made it clear that the army was its real ruler. The revolution against Charles the First in England ended with Cromwell; the one in France ended with Napoleon.

The American Federalists were sure that the same thing would happen under a Republican president. When the head of the College of New Jersey, Samuel S. Smith, read the text of Jefferson's first message to Congress, he prophesied darkly that the United States would soon be "torn asunder or, like France, sink under the power of one despot who will come to save us from the more dreadful will of a million. Good men will be obliged to retire from public affairs; blockheads and villains will soon hold the rein and the scourge over us."

Meanwhile the movement toward political equality continued peacefully in America. It had, in fact, been continuing throughout the whole of the 1790's and its ally was the federal Constitution.

When the makers of the Constitution discussed the problem of admitting new states into the Union, they had found themselves faced with a delicate situation. If the western states were permitted to multiply unchecked, they would soon be in a position to challenge the political power of the original thirteen. Or, as Gouverneur Morris expressed it candidly, "If the western people get the power into their hands, they will ruin the Atlantic interests."

A motion was made at the Constitutional Convention "to limit the number of new states to be admitted to the Union in such a manner that they should never be able to outnumber the Atlantic States." Some of the delegates must have been greatly tempted to vote for a device that promised safety; nevertheless, they refrained. The motion was not accepted, and each new state that entered the Union was free to come in on its own terms.

It took no prophet to foresee that these new states would move in the direction of manhood suffrage; the men of the frontier usually did. Albert Gallatin had been a delegate from Fayette County when Pennsylvania wrote its second constitution in 1790, and he tried hard to get the taxpayer requirement changed to full manhood suffrage. He failed, since the western delegates were outnumbered by the men from eastern Pennsylvania, but it was natural to have tried. A year later, Vermont was at last admitted to the Union, freed from the fetters that had bound it to New York. It had long since written its own constitution and had come out for full manhood suffrage.

The first new states to enter the Union were Kentucky and Tennessee, both from the other side of the mountains. Kentucky was the western part of Virginia, and it became a state in 1792 in time to cast all its votes for Jefferson in the next presidential election. Tennessee was the western part of North Carolina and it entered the Union four years later.

If Virginia had been able to impose its own voting pattern on Kentucky, the new state would of course have had freeholder suffrage. Once, long ago, Virginia had itself been a frontier community, and in those days all its white males had the vote. Now it was rich and old and conservative, clinging to a freeholder franchise as its shield against change. Nevertheless, the Constitution made it impossible for Virginia to impose its will on the new state to the west.

Kentucky County had had freeholder suffrage; as the state of Kentucky, it leaped into complete manhood suffrage: "All free male citizens of the age of twenty-one years, having resided in the state two years, or the county in which they offer to vote one year next before the election, shall enjoy the rights of an elector." When the men of Tennessee gathered together in a constitutional convention in 1796, they made voting even easier: "Every freeman . . . being an inhabitant of any one county in the state six months immediately preceding the day of election, shall be entitled to vote."

It was a source of great strength to the young United States that the framers of the Constitution had been willing to run such risks and permit such flexibility. It was a source of equal strength that the people of the original thirteen states were willing to take risks also.

The shining example of this point of view at the turn of the century was Maryland. Maryland was nearly as old as Virginia and possessed almost exactly the same history of a franchise that had steadily narrowed. The state constitution put the power firmly in the hands of the propertied class, and Maryland was especially admired for its Senate. The Senators were not voted directly into office, so that they were free from any pressure that might be exerted by the people, and they had to be possessed of "wisdom, experience and virtue" and property worth a thousand pounds. The members of the lower house, the House of Delegates, were elected directly by the people, but each voter had to have either a fifty-acre freehold or personal property worth thirty pounds.

This was the constitution that Charles Carroll of Carrollton had helped to write, and he had hoped it would shelter Maryland from the winds of change. But all the rich men were not like Charles Carroll. There was Michael Taney, for instance, a landed gentleman of Calvert County who kept his pack of foxhounds, voted Federalist in the national elections, and in general behaved like any other Maryland aristocrat. Nevertheless, on the fifth of December, 1797, Michael Taney introduced into the Maryland House of Delegates a bill calling for complete manhood suffrage.

No one knows what Taney's reasons may have been. His son, the future Chief Justice, was himself a member of the House of Delegates two years later, and he made this point: "My family and friends generally were Federalists, and so was I. But at the time of which I am speaking, it was not thought expedient, or right in principle, to carry these party divisions and conflicts into the concerns of the state."

Michael Taney was not alone in his point of view, since three Federalists put up a similar bill in 1799. An outraged Maryland commentator remarked, "I am astonished at the popular delusion and madness that possesses men of property, when I see them assent to a change in our constitution and give men without any property the vote." Another pointed out, however, that there was a precedent for this kind of behavior, since "some of the wealthiest lords of England are the greatest supporters of the people's liberties."

Each of these franchise bills passed the House of Delegates and was defeated in the Senate. Public opinion was on the side of suffrage reform, especially in the great port of Baltimore; but public opinion could not reach the Senate, meeting in Annapolis and safely sheltered from any pressure by the voters.

In 1800, one of the new faces in the House of Delegates was that of Edward Lloyd, who had just come of age. He was the owner of a vast estate since the death of his father four years earlier, and he became at once a leader of the reform party in the House. His bill was delivered out of committee on the 24th of November and passed by the large majority of 57 to 11. It gave the suffrage to all white males, and an attempt to water it down was overwhelmingly defeated.

Maryland was not a frontier state. It had existed as a political unit since 1635, and it possessed one of the most conservative of the state constitutions. To see it putting out green leaves in this fashion was very unsettling to the men of experience, wisdom, virtue and a thousand pounds who made up the Senate.

By this time the Senators were well aware that some kind of compromise would have to be offered and they suggested a taxpayer qualification. This, they said, would serve to maintain "the wise principle laid down in our bill of rights . . . that every man having property in, a common interest with, and an attachment to the community ought to have a right of suffrage." This precise echo of the political philosophy of Colonel Ireton was still the normal one in America, but Edward Lloyd and his associates were fighting for a different principle. The answer the House returned to the Senate was worthy of Colonel Rainsborough himself: "When we reflect that liberty is the common and natural right of all men, we cannot agree to sanction that doctrine which makes property the measure of it."

The Senate hastened to reply: "We do not consider natural liberty and the right of suffrage as the same thing. . . . Admitting all men to be equally free by nature, it does not follow that in all circumstances they should equally participate in the affairs of government." With an obvious reference to Baltimore, the third largest city in America and vociferous in its demands for suffrage reform, the Senate added: "We extend our views to future times, when an immense increase of population may and will take place in our country, and when a considerable portion of that population will probably be . . . destitute of property and without sufficient virtue and knowledge to resist . . . ambitious men, desirous of raising themselves to power, even on the ruins of public liberty and happiness."

The House, which by now had a Republican majority, hit upon a new device. In December of 1801 it threatened to call a constitutional convention, so that the rules by which the Senate was elected could be legally changed. Anything was better than that, and when a new suffrage bill was introduced in 1802 the Senate agreed to it unanimously.

The 195th session of the Maryland legislature closed on January 11, 1803, and both Houses gathered to watch the Governor sign the engrossed bills and affix the seal of Maryland. The bills were the usual miscellany, from a restraint of geese in Dorchester County to a plan for a new road in Anne Arundel County which would start at the Widow Robinson's gate and intersect with another near the Methodist meeting house. Number 20 was "an act to confirm an act, entitled, An act to alter such parts of the constitution and form of government as relate to voters and qualifications of voters," and when the Governor signed it, history had been made. Maryland became the first of the original thirteen states to divorce the franchise from the ownership of property. Since the wording was somewhat vague, a further Act was passed in 1810 to make it clear that the same principle applied to national elections, and at that time it was incorporated into the constitution as an amendment "that every free white male of this state, above twenty-one years of age" and a qualified resident, "shall have a right of suffrage."

In neighboring Virginia, an intrepid legislator introduced a similar bill in 1802 and it was promptly defeated. The following year a gentleman of Virginia rejoiced that his beloved state had been spared the horrors that would certainly make their appearance in Maryland. "Such has been the folly and weakness of the people of Maryland . . . that their very wheelbarrow men may be carried to vote. . . . Great God! is it possible that a state can exist long under such a government? We have to bless ourselves in Virginia that the right of suffrage has saved us in some degree from the calamity of democracy, alias mobocracy."

The fact that a man who pushed a wheelbarrow in Baltimore had the same voting rights as Charles Carroll of Carrollton was accepted with perfect equanimity by the people of Maryland. The threatened mobocracy failed to develop, and by so much the hands of reformers in other states were strengthened.

Another aristocrat among the reformers was Charles Pinckney of South Carolina. He belonged to the wealthy and privileged group that was centered in Charleston, and he served as a delegate to the Constitutional Convention along with his distinguished cousin, General C. C. Pinckney. Then he horrified his friends and relatives by becoming a Republican and worked hard to get Jefferson elected.

Pinckney was so popular with the voters that he was repeatedly elected Governor of South Carolina, and after an interlude as Jefferson's minister to Spain, he was back again in Charleston in 1806. He ran again and successfully for the governorship, with emphasis on suffrage reform. The constitution of 1790 had given the vote to any white man over twenty-one who had a fifty-acre freehold, a town lot, or who "paid a tax the preceding year of three shillings sterling towards the support of this government." In 1810 the reformers won the battle for an enlarged franchise, and an amendment to the constitution gave the vote to all white males except soldiers and paupers.

It was a considerable achievement but there was no basic shift in political power. Members of both houses still had to be large property holders. Moreover, election districts were divided in such a way that the small, rich, conservative parishes of the tidewater region had a top-heavy representation, and as long as this continued to be true, South Carolina would be ruled on the basis of wealth rather than of population.

During the course of this battle for reform, a writer for a Charleston newspaper made effective use of the arguments of Abraham Bishop. Bishop was trying to alter the suffrage in Connecticut, and if a state like Connecticut was considering reform it should be possible anywhere.

Politically speaking, Connecticut was still living in the seventeenth century, and if Theophilus Eaton had returned to New Haven he would have found remarkably few changes since the days when he ruled as a judge in Israel. Church and state were still operating in a repressive alliance, and most of the Connecticut clergy joined gladly with the men of property in resistance to change.

Their great ally was the charter that Charles II had given the colony in 1662. It placed all political power in the hands of the General Assembly, which could make and unmake laws in whatever fashion it pleased. The upper house, which was still being called the Council, consisted of the

Governor, the Lieutenant Governor and twelve Assistants. They met in secret session, with a veto power over the lower house, and its members usually remained in office unless they went into federal politics or died.

The membership of the lower house was almost equally stable, and one Connecticut legislator had been elected by his constituents fifty-six times. Back in 1776, the qualifications for a Connecticut voter were "maturity in years, quiet and peaceable behavior, a civil conversation, and forty shillings freehold, or forty pounds personal estate in the list of rateable estates." A quarter of a century later, the only change was that this had been put into American money—seven dollars a year in rentals or a hundred and thirty-four dollars in personal estate.

The average voter in Connecticut was a man who had a stake in the status quo and a profound respect for property. No state was more devoted to the Federalist party, and while a few Connecticut Federalists were willing to consider suffrage reform, the vast majority wished things to remain exactly as they were, with the conservative men of property ruling a land that had no wish for change.

The presidential election of 1800 shook Connecticut like an earthquake, and a horrified young minister wrote in his diary: "I do not believe that the Most High will permit a howling atheist to sit at the head of this nation." Jefferson's supporters mounted a real political campaign in Connecticut, and this in itself was an unprecedented event. A candidate for the Republican party toured the eastern counties of the state openly soliciting votes, and this was considered a clear example of the depths to which revolutionary dema-gogues could sink. There had never before been any electioneering in Connecticut.

The leader of this campaign was Abraham Bishop. He was the son of a highly respected deacon of New Haven and should normally have taken up law or entered the ministry after he graduated from Yale. Instead, he went on a tour of Europe in 1787, and what he saw and heard in France stirred him profoundly. He returned to New Haven to live in the old family residence on the corner of Elm Street, but he found it impossible to settle down mentally; he composed what was meant to be a Phi Beta Kappa address and it ended up as a revolutionary pamphlet. Its target was the alliance of church and state which held Connecticut so tightly in the grip of the past, and as a result Abraham Bishop emerged as one of the political leaders among the local Republicans. He helped organize political rallies, and served as principal speaker and pamphleteer for the party in Connecticut.

One of Bishop's classmates at Yale was Noah Webster, and the great lexicographer had also been a political radical in his younger days. He came by this legitimately, for the first of his family had come to Connecticut as a follower of the Reverend Thomas Hooker and after Hooker died had been expelled for dissent. Noah Webster continued to be a radical in his views on education and on language, but he tightened into an extreme conservative in politics. When he glanced over his own writings of twenty years earlier he noted in the margin, "charming dreams" and "We grow wiser with age."

After the election of 1800, Webster wrote one of his friends to report the result in New Haven: "We have defeated the Jacobins in this town; in others the victory is upon their side." It was customary to call the Republicans Jacobins, so as to connect them with the more sinister manifestations of the French Revolution in its rage for political equality. The Republicans in Connecticut were trying to extend the franchise to men who had paid taxes or served in the militia, and Noah Webster knew well how dangerous this would be. "The principles of corruption are spreading fast in Connecticut."

In 1802, the Connecticut Republicans were able to muster fifty-eight votes in the lower house in favor of extending the franchise. They were easily defeated by one hundred and eighteen Federalists. Noah Webster was one of these, and he delivered a vigorous speech to his fellow legislators on the disaster that would befall Connecticut if property were to be divorced from the vote. The "principle of admitting everybody to the right of suffrage prostrates the wealth of individuals to the rapaciousness of a merciless gang who have nothing to lose and will delight in plundering their neighbors. . . . We should be careful not to open the avenues which may lead to our destruction."

Noah Webster believed that education could be the light and savior of mankind, but, unlike Jefferson, he did not connect this idea with the question of the franchise, and he was quite sure that political equality would bring chaos. Like Captain Bargrave, worrying about the same situation in long-ago Virginia, he proposed a hierarchy of voting procedure. Under Noah Webster's suggested formula, each taxpayer in Connecticut would be permitted to cast one vote; those who had a higher rating on the tax lists could cast two votes, and very rich men and clergymen could cast three.

The suffrage debates in Connecticut continued, and were watched with intense interest by Thomas Paine, who was living a few miles over the border in the neighboring state of New York. Paine had arrived back from Europe in 1802 and President Jefferson welcomed his old friend warmly. Or, as a Federalist newspaper put it: "Our pious President thought it expedient to dispatch a frigate for the accommodation of this loathsome reptile." In 1804, Paine settled on a farm in New Rochelle which the state of New York gave him in grateful recognition of his services during the American Revolution.

Paine still felt the "passion of patriotism" for America that had been his when he wrote the first of his *Crisis* papers in 1776, and he longed to see the country accept the principle of political equality. He not only followed the suffrage debates eagerly in the Connecticut papers, but he also contributed two articles of his own to a newspaper in Hartford. Both of them called for a constitutional convention in Connecticut to bring an end to the ancient fetters of government by charter.*

The device of a constitutional convention was the only way to dig the conservatives out of their entrenched position in Connecticut, since as long as the General Assembly was permitted by the charter to rule unchecked it could pass whatever laws it pleased. Even the judges were under its control; in 1802 the Supreme Court of Connecticut had sentenced a man for sedition because he was an advocate of manhood suffrage. As one of the reformers said truly, "Property, sacred property, is regarded as all in all by our Federal politicians."

In 1808, the Connecticut *Courant* was able to point out proudly to its readers that the state was still standing firm: "While the billows of democracy have beat upon us, while state after state has fallen . . . Connecticut alone has maintained her station." However, it was becoming increasingly difficult to maintain it, now that the reformers were basing their whole strategy on persuading the voters that Connecticut needed a constitution.

Finally, in 1816, all the minority groups closed ranks and ran a coalition ticket which gave them control, at last, of the General Assembly. The Assembly authorized the calling of a constitutional convention, and on the fourth of July, 1818, the freemen of the various towns gathered to elect their delegates.

The convention worked for three weeks in August and September and then presented the document to the people for ratification. The vote of approval was a narrow one; but it was approval nevertheless, and Connecticut at last shook off the bonds of its antiquated charter government. The constitution gave the franchise to every white male over twenty-one who had

---

* In 1806, Paine found himself the astonished victim in New York of what he was trying to destroy in Connecticut, when the election inspectors in New Rochelle refused to let him vote on the ground that he was not an American citizen. Paine claimed citizenship on the same grounds that Gallatin had done, and pointed out that he had taken the oath of allegiance from John Hancock himself. He decided that all the New Rochelle election inspectors must have been Tories during the Revolution, since he could not bring himself to admit that while every American patriot fought for liberty in 1776, relatively few of them fought also for equality.

served in the militia or paid taxes, with the characteristic Connecticut reservation that he must have "a good moral character."

It was a huge concession for so cautious a state to bring itself to a taxpayer qualification, although by now this was becoming a standard practice. When Ohio entered the Union in 1803, it admitted to the franchise any white male who had paid a state or county tax, and several of the eastern states by the turn of the century had rewritten their constitutions to include this compromise. It was what a gentleman in New Jersey called "the criterion of taxability," and he only wished that his own state would adopt it too.

The New Jersey gentleman was named William Griffith, and in 1799 he issued a lively book called *Eumenes* on the suffrage situation in his state. It was unavoidably lively, for New Jersey had put itself in a position worthy of a comic opera on the subject of the vote.

When New Jersey wrote its constitution in June of 1776, before the Declaration of Independence had been signed, it decided that "all inhabitants of this colony, of full age, who are worth fifty pounds proclamation money . . . shall be entitled to vote." To remove any doubts about the voter's eligibility, it was decided the following year that he should make the declaration: "I verily believe I am twenty-one years of age and worth fifty pounds lawful money."

As William Griffith pointed out in *Eumenes,* this device had given rise to "the most preposterous notions of mental evasion." One voter who took the oath was asked how he could do such a thing when he possessed much less property than the law required. The voter responded placidly that he had done rightly, for he had sworn that he himself was worth fifty pounds and "he valued himself at a great deal more than that." The result, said Griffith, was that the vote in New Jersey was being thrown away on "every vagabond in the country." In his own county he knew of two hundred laborers who were not paying taxes but who were voting nevertheless.

An even worse situation than this had arisen, since the New Jersey constitution had neglected to say anything about the sex of the voters and had merely spoken of "inhabitants." A married woman could not claim to be worth fifty pounds since whatever she possessed belonged to her husband, but there was nothing to prevent widows and spinsters from voting if they had enough property. In fact, an eccentric member of the legislature, a Quaker from the western part of the state, had even argued that it was their right.

William Griffith, like any normal man of the period, knew that women were unfit to vote, but his real objection lay elsewhere: "The great practical mischief . . . resulting from their admission, under our present form of government, is that the towns and populous villages gain an unfair advantage over the country, by the greater facility they enjoy over the latter, in drawing out their women to the election." Griffith estimated glumly that there were at least ten thousand widows and spinsters in the state, and no one seemed to be quite sure what the constitution had intended. In general, women voters were "admitted or rejected, just as it may suit the views of the persons in direction."

This woolly-mindedness on the part of New Jersey election officials finally led to open madness. There was an argument in 1806 between Newark and Elizabeth over the location of a new courthouse for Essex County, and to decide which town should have it, a special election was held. In the excitement of the moment, even married women rushed out to vote and so did girls under twenty-one. If a single vote did not seem to be sufficient they voted a second time, and years later the people of Newark could point with pride to two ladies who had been in their 'teens in 1806 and who had "voted six times each." To complete the absurdity, men and boys began dressing up as women to cast yet another vote themselves, and in the end the election had to be declared void.

This was not the first time there had been a turnout of more than a hundred percent in Essex County, and by 1806 there were already plans under consideration to amend the election laws. None of the legislators was inclined to blame the women, since everyone had behaved alike, but an eloquent speech recommended that the vote be given to white men only and the bill passed both houses by large majorities. The requirement of fifty pounds was reduced to the "taxability" that Griffith had advocated, and New Jersey joined the increasing number of states with a taxpayer requirement.

Six years later, Louisiana entered the Union, also with a taxpayer requirement. Unlike the other new states, however, Louisiana was a long-established community, and the original European residents, who were French, had no wish to be outvoted by a flood of new arrivals. It was decided that no one could vote unless his name was on the tax list, and it was so difficult to get on the tax list that in New Orleans only one man in five had the franchise.*

Louisiana became a state in 1812, and for a time the War of 1812 brought western expansion to a halt. Then the depression that followed sent

* During an especially vigorous presidential campaign in the middle of the century, a single tax collector in Louisiana issued fifteen hundred false tax receipts so as to qualify would-be voters. Dishonest election practices sprouted anywhere in the United States where there was a lively campaign issue.

a wave of settlers across the mountains, and the next four states entered the Union at the rate of one a year. Indiana, Illinois and Alabama gave the vote to all white males; only Mississippi stipulated that they must have paid taxes or served in the militia.

The next state to enter the Union was Missouri, and this was the first one to lie completely west of the Mississippi River. From Maine to Missouri was a distance of nearly fifteen hundred miles, and it was clear that the political theorists had been mistaken when they insisted that representative government could not be made to work over such vast distances. Missouri wrote its constitution in the summer of 1820 and gave the franchise to "every free white male citizen" who had reached the age of twenty-one and was a qualified resident.

The previous year Maine shook itself loose from its long domination by Massachusetts, and its state constitution was written at Portland in December of 1819. As long as it was a part of Massachusetts, Maine had been obliged to conform to the heavy property qualification for voting that John Adams had written into the Massachusetts constitution. Under its new constitution, Maine gave the vote to all males "excepting paupers, persons under guardianship, and Indians not taxed."

The state of Massachusetts had been aware for some time that it would have to reconsider its own constitution, and the departure of Maine provided a fitting occasion. Any attempt to alter John Adams' masterwork was a solemn undertaking, and the towns vied with each other in sending their best men, who gathered in the State House in Boston on the 15th of November, 1820.

One of the delegates was John Adams himself. He had retired from public life after Jefferson defeated him for the presidency, and he was now an old man in his eighties. But he accepted the invitation with real pride and pleasure, and moved into Boston temporarily to be near the State House. He refused to preside over the convention because of his age and infirmities, and was given a place of honor at the presiding officer's right hand. Adams informed his fellow delegates that the Boston Athenaeum had offered them the use of its library collections, and then the great state of Massachusetts settled down to consider what changes should be made in its constitution.

A small group of conservatives wanted as few changes as possible, and the leader of this group was a delegate from Salem, the very distinguished Joseph Story. He was an Associate Justice of the Supreme Court of the United States, and in his younger days he had been a supporter of Jefferson. Like many men, however, he had altered as he grew older, and now Story was using his great eloquence to support the conservative cause.

291

His greatest ally was the brilliant young Boston lawyer Daniel Webster, who, as Story said, "gained a noble reputation" for his work in this convention. Webster told his colleagues to read Harrington and he himself was convinced that power and property could not be severed in a republic: "In the absence of military force, political power naturally and necessarily goes into the hands which hold the property."

Neither Webster nor Story spoke for the majority of the delegates. They owed their success in the convention to the fact that they were superbly organized, or, as Justice Story preferred to put it, to the fact that they were "a minority in number but with a vast preponderance of talent and virtue and principle."

The question of the franchise came up in December, and one of the first to speak in favor of reform was the Reverend Edmund Foster. He was a delegate from Littleton, a farming community near the New Hampshire border, and he spoke as a practical man. All Massachusetts voters were supposed to have a freehold of £60 or one bringing in an annual income of £3, which meant $200 or $10 in current money, and Foster said this occasioned a great deal of trouble at every election. "Have you the tools of any trade? Yes. What else? A pair of steers my father gave me. And if this was not enough, then, he said, a note, which is never intended to be paid, makes up the balance." As a result, nothing "was so ardently desired as an alteration in this part of the constitution. Men who have no property are put in the situation of the slaves of Virginia; they ought to be saved from the degrading feelings."

Forty years earlier, Joseph Hawley had said the same thing. His appeal had roused no response among the delegates, but now a great many were on his side. Elihu Slocum of Dartmouth said "he recollected that in 1775 the saying was current, that taxation and representation should go hand in hand. Take this text and apply it to the men who are excluded by this qualification from the rights of voting. Who are they? The laboring parts of society. How long have they been fettered? Forty years. Who achieved our independence? This class of men." He added tartly that "if a man was a Newton or a Locke, if he is poor, he may stand by and see his liberties voted away." The Reverend Joseph Richardson of Hingham went even farther afield to find an example: "The present constitution would have excluded our Saviour from this privilege."

The conservatives, for their part, evoked the specter that had haunted so many debates on the subject of the suffrage. There was an increasing emphasis on manufacturing in the state of Massachusetts, and this would mean a future rabble of the industrial poor. Justice Story cited the example of the English town of Manchester "where there are five or ten thousand wealthy persons, and ninety or one hundred thousand of artisans reduced to a state of vice and poverty and wretchedness which leave them exposed to the most dangerous political excitements." His own beloved commonwealth was a long way, at the moment, from this kind of imbalance, but the future must be considered and so must basic principles.

Warren Dutton, a prominent conservative from Boston, made it clear what these principles were. The vote was not a right. "It was in the nature of a privilege, and as such it was connected with many virtues which conduced to the good order of society." Clearly it would be unjust "that men without a dollar should in any way determine the rights of property." Moreover, as the number of voters increased, men who could not be trusted to vote wisely would give political power to some favorite of the moment. "In that case, the form of a republican constitution might remain, but its life and spirit would have fled. The government would be essentially a democracy, and between that and a despotism there would be but one step."

The question of the franchise was presented to the Committee of the Whole, which voted to abolish all property requirements. Fisher Ames had once remarked, "I dislike the Committee of the Whole," and he had good reason. So large a group of men was difficult to manipulate and almost impossible to control. It was difficult for the Massachusetts conservatives to dominate the convention in open discussion, but in the end they managed to get the decision of the Committee of the Whole reversed, and a taxpayer requirement was voted instead.

Daniel Webster had said that it was "the part of political wisdom to found government on property." He also knew that it was the part of political wisdom to admit that times were changing, and it was satisfactory to him that the concession was made and the principle preserved. As Webster said, he would be "content with the smallest tax. There was a great difference between this and universal suffrage."

John Adams was too old and frail to take part in the debates, but he could not resist one last public statement on the subject he loved so well—the theory of government. In the course of it he included a discussion of the importance of linking property to the vote and surged into a vivid and inaccurate account of how disreputable the supporters of universal suffrage had been:

> The French revolution furnished an experiment, perfect and complete in all its stages and branches, of the utility and excellence of universal suffrage. . . . The government got into the hands of peasants and stage-

players, and from them descended to Jacobins, and from them to the sans-culottes. . . . And thus it has happened in all ages and countries in the world, where such principles have been adopted and a similar course pursued. All writers agree that there are twenty persons in Great Britain who have no property for one that has. If the radicals should succeed in obtaining universal suffrage, they will overturn the whole kingdom and turn those who have property out of their houses. . . . Our ancestors have made a pecuniary qualification necessary . . . for electors, and all the wise men of the world have agreed in the same thing.

The old man paid for his excursion to Boston by having to spend nearly two months in bed, but there is no question that he had enjoyed himself. As he wrote a friend: "In the course of forty years I have been called twice to assist in the formation of a constitution for this state. This kind of architecture, I find, is an art or mystery very difficult to learn and still harder to practice."

The friend to whom he wrote was the son of Benjamin Rush, who had died in 1813. The elder Rush had remained intimate with both Adams and Jefferson, and their long estrangement was a grief to him. The year before his death, the two men began corresponding again, and Adams was the first to write. In his delighted reply, Jefferson went back to the days when they had worked together to create a nation: "A letter from you calls up recollections very dear to my mind. It carries me back to the times when, beset with difficulties and dangers, we were fellow laborers in the same cause, struggling for what is most valuable to man, his right of self-government."

Adams would not have called it a right. To him, it was a privilege, possessed only by men of property. In 1776, most Americans agreed with him, but by now most Americans were beginning to agree with Jefferson.

Jefferson went on to say in his letter that nothing had ever been achieved in America without difficulties, and so far these had all been surmounted. "So we have gone on, and so we shall go on, puzzled and prospering beyond example in the history of man."

Puzzled and prospering, the United States entered the third decade of the nineteenth century, still struggling with the difficult art of self-government but growing more and more convinced that it was possible to found it upon political equality. Only two of the larger states in the Union had failed to make any kind of compromise—New York and Virginia—and New York was the next to capitulate

Chapter Fifteen

Conservative New Yorkers had been watching with alarm the suffrage activities in New England, and in 1817 an Albany newspaper expressed the hope that the morals of Connecticut would not vanish in a "whirlpool of democratic liberty and Jacobin frenzy." Not only had both Connecticut and Massachusetts changed their suffrage laws but New Yorkers could also read in their newspapers about mass meetings held in England to demand suffrage reform. Chancellor James Kent, most prominent and respected of all New York jurists, knew exactly what would happen if universal suffrage were permitted there: "The radicals in England, with the force of that mighty engine, would at once sweep away the property, the laws and the liberties of that island like a deluge."

In the eyes of such men the state of New York was deeply fortunate, protected as it was by the constitution that John Jay had created in 1777. The city of New York had by now grown so huge that it had one-tenth of the population of the whole state; but its workmen remained safely disfranchised, while those who were not city dwellers were kept under control by the freehold qualification.

The constitution was designed to protect a political fabric unlike that of any other state; a dynasty like that of the Van Rensselaers could not be found anywhere else in America. Its founder was an Amsterdam jeweler back in the early days of Dutch rule who had succeeded in settling a very large area by the application of intelligent farming methods which he exercised by remote control from Holland. Under the patroon system, he owned one and three-quarter million acres of land—a huge, almost feudal area where the tenants voted as the lord of the manor wished.

The current head of the family, General Stephen Van Rensselaer, was a well-loved man; but the patroon was a political anachronism in the nineteenth century, and the kind of power that Jay's constitution was trying to protect was no longer a political reality. The original New York counties along the Hudson River no longer held the balance of power. The western part of the state was filling up with settlers, while to the south there was New York City, a restless young giant which was already being called the future London of America. It was no longer possible to live comfortably in the narrow structure that John Jay had built, and the politicians knew it.

Chief among these politicians was Martin Van Buren. He had come to Albany as a state senator, and within ten years he was in control of the Republican party in New York. As a practical man, Van Buren was not willing to commit himself to complete manhood suffrage, although his Albany paper had come out in favor of it, but he knew that some changes would have to be made.

Van Buren's chief political opponent was Governor DeWitt Clinton, with his formidable personal following, and the Governor also had some stake in suffrage reform. Most people, in fact, were willing to consider a certain amount of change rather than to permit reform pressure to build up to dangerous heights. As Rufus King, who was now living in New York, sensibly remarked, it was "the duty of every government to concur in and approve measures which they could not if they would hinder—in this way things are stopped from going to extremes."

It was decided to hold a constitutional convention, to meet at Albany the end of August, 1821. Rufus King and Martin Van Buren were both delegates. So were Chancellor Kent and General Stephen Van Rensselaer, those two pillars of resistance to change. So were a great many ardent young radicals, eager to seize the opportunity to bring New York up to date.

Van Buren's faction, tightly disciplined and organized, was in control from the first, and as far as the suffrage was concerned its aim was to reach a reasonable compromise. The chairman of the committee assigned to make a recommendation on the suffrage was Nathan Sanford, recently retired as a United States Senator and in every way a practical politician, as he showed in his report. "To me, and the majority of the committee, it appeared the only reasonable scheme that those who are to be affected by the acts of the government should be . . . entitled to vote for those who administer it." This did not mean, of course, that the principle should be applied literally. It meant that the committee recommended that the franchise be enlarged to include anyone who paid taxes, served in the militia, or worked on the roads.

Chancellor Kent had a seat in the right aisle, and he rose to deride the "notion that every man that works a day on the road, or serves an idle hour in the militia" was fit to take part in the noble act of self-government. He spoke of his pride in the present constitution, "formed by those illustrious sages and patriots who adorned the Revolution." He spoke of the incorruptible virtue of the present voters, those "free and independent lords of the soil, worth at least $250 in freehold estate." He spoke of the dangers that lay in store for the state if the committee report were to be accepted. "By the report before us, we propose to annihilate, at one stroke, all those property distinctions and to bow before the idol of universal suffrage. . . . I greatly fear that our posterity will have reason to deplore in sackcloth and ashes the delusion of the day."

A young lawyer from Rensselaer County answered him. His name was David Buel and he was no orator, but he was very clear that times had changed. "When our constitution was framed, the domain of the state was in the hands of a few. The proprietors of the great manors were almost the only men of great influence." But by now the theory upon which freeholder voting was based had clearly become antiquated. "Our community is an association of persons—of human beings—not a partnership founded on property." Nor could Buel see any reason why future voters should be expected to degenerate into an ignorant rabble. "The provision already made for the establishment of common schools will, in a very few years, extend the benefit of education to all our citizens. The universal diffusion of information will forever distinguish our population from that of Europe."

General Stephen Van Rensselaer, who was sitting in the right aisle three seats away from Chancellor Kent, found it impossible to understand such a point of view: "There is in every community a portion of idle, profligate and abandoned men; and it is unjust and impolitic that this description of people should have it in their power to control the government and the property of the industrious, the virtuous, and moral part of the community." Particularly the General feared the "vast mass of combustible material in the city of New York," which could only be kept under control by keeping it voiceless.

In full agreement was another distinguished gentleman in the right aisle, Chief Justice Spencer. He spoke eloquently of the freeholder franchise as that great shield "which the wisdom of the sages and patriots of the Revolution have erected for our protection," but when he proposed an amendment to weaken Sanford's recommendation it was voted down 100 to 19.

The conservatives in the New York convention were not well organized, and neither were the radicals. The majority of the delegates were under the control of Martin Van Buren, who was one of the political geniuses of the nineteenth century, and under his leadership the convention voted for substantially the same arrangement that the suffrage committee had originally suggested. It gave the vote to taxpayers, members of the militia, and those who worked on the roads.

The compromise turned out to be unworkable. Some New Yorkers, for instance, were volunteer firemen, exempted from service in the militia, and they found that this exemption deprived them of the franchise. Another group, those who worked on the roads, found that their right to vote depended on the overseer of highways, who drew up the list of names and could exclude whatever men he wished. When DeWitt Clinton ran successfully for reelection as Governor, he made further suffrage reform a part of his platform, and when he addressed his new legislature in January of 1825, he made it very clear where he stood: "Without the rights of suffrage, liberty cannot exist. It is a vital principle of representative government."

An amendment to the constitution removed the cumbersome compromise which had been put together at the convention. It gave the vote to every white male over twenty-one who had lived in the state one year and his own county six months, and the amendment was ratified so easily in 1825 that hardly a voice was raised in protest. Four years earlier, Chancellor Kent had warned solemnly, "We stand . . . on the very edge of the precipice." Now that they had finally nerved themselves to jump over it, they found that there was no great problem in the change of terrain. The principle of universal suffrage, which, as Chancellor Kent had noted with such regret, was running a triumphant course from Maine to Louisiana, now included his own state and no one seemed to be any the worse for it.

New York also made a change in the election law that controlled the voting for the President of the United States. It decided to permit the people of the state to vote directly for the members of the electoral college instead of having this done by the state legislature. It no longer seemed as necessary as it once had to shield the President from the direct will of the people, and when the polls opened for elections in the autumn of 1828, only two states— South Carolina and Delaware—still clung to the idea that the electors should be chosen by the state legislatures.

The Federalists had for some time failed to exert any influence in national politics, but two points of view still existed in America on the subject of government. One branch of the Republican party called itself the National Republicans, and in the election of 1828 it supported the incumbent President, John Quincy Adams. The other branch called itself the Democratic Republicans and offered as its presidential candidate a great military hero, General Andrew Jackson of Tennessee.

Jackson's party was quite willing to be known by another name, the Democrats, for a word that had once been feared and despised had now come to seem, to a great many Americans, a title of honor. It seemed so to Jackson himself, who believed ardently in the right of the people to participate in their own government, and he terrified the men of the opposition party, who foresaw chaos if he were elected President.

The election of 1828 was almost as savage and opinionated as the election of 1800 had been, and there was the same bitterness after it was over. Like his father before him, John Quincy Adams refused to attend the inauguration of his successful rival, and the conservatives waited for the country to fall apart.

In the eyes of a man like John Randolph of Roanoke, the election of Jackson was an unrelieved calamity. "The country is ruined past redemption." What he meant was that the country was changing. It had in fact been changing steadily ever since the signing of the Declaration of Independence, an event which occurred three years after Randolph was born, and it was a tribute to the political skill of succeeding generations that the alterations, which were so fundamental, had come about so gently.

One of the signers of the Declaration of Independence was still alive in 1828. This was Charles Carroll of Carrollton, now over ninety, and in the year of Jackson's election Carroll celebrated the fourth of July by laying the foundation stone for the Baltimore and Ohio Railroad, the first passenger railroad in the United States. The vast spread of public transportation was one of the many forces that were helping to break up old ideas and accelerate the changes that the conservatives found so undesirable.

During Jackson's second administration, a brilliant Frenchman named Alexis de Tocqueville was traveling in the United States, ostensibly to study prison conditions but actually to investigate the workings of American self-government. His *Democracy in America* was a masterpiece of acute observation, but de Tocqueville did not always cast his net wide enough when he asked his questions. "General Jackson, whom the Americans have twice elected to be the head of their government, is a man of violent temper and very moderate talents; nothing in his whole career ever proved him qualified to govern a free people and indeed the majority of the enlightened classes of the Union has always opposed him." These members of the enlightened classes also told de Tocqueville a great deal about the dangers of letting city workmen have the vote, and he put that down too: "I look·upon the size of certain American cities, and especially on the nature of their population, as a real danger which threatens the future security of the democratic republics of the New World; and I venture to predict they will perish from this circumstance, unless the government succeeds in creating an armed force which, while it remains under the control of the majority of the nation, will be independent of the town population and able to repress its excesses."

Thomas Jefferson, who died two years before Jackson was elected President, had also feared the heavy concentration of people in the cities, but Jefferson had put his faith in education. In his view, it was ignorance, with its resultant tyranny, that could be the one real threat to the future security of the United States, and ignorance was curable.

Jefferson had never ceased to dislike the constrictions that his fellow Virginians had written into the state constitution. The freeholder franchise, to which they clung so devotedly, seemed to him a form of political tyranny, but he could never persuade the Virginia legislators to agree to his views. Nine years after the constitution was written they reduced the freehold requirement from a hundred acres of land to fifty, but farther than this they refused to go.

By 1790 they were receiving petitions to liberalize the franchise, and these increased in volume after the state of Maryland set so brilliant an example to reformers at the turn of the century. The War of 1812 intensified the pressure, since it made clear how unjust the restrictions were. In Loudoun County, for instance, there were twelve hundred men on the militia rolls but only two hundred had enough property to be able to vote. There was equal unrest in the cities of Virginia, where workmen and tenants and leaseholders, all disfranchised, grew increasingly resentful of a system that kept political domination in the hands of the few. Even more resentful were the rapidly growing counties on the other side of the mountains, almost impotent in a legislature which gave the bulk of the representation to the eastern counties.

In 1816 a mass meeting was held at Staunton, and delegates from thirty-eight Virginia counties met to demand a constitutional convention. Jefferson wrote one of its leaders in support of the idea, and he listed seven changes that ought to be made in the constitution. The first was the granting of "general suffrage," for, as Jefferson said truly, "I am not among those who fear the people."

Eight years later another group of delegates gathered in Staunton, and again Jefferson sent a letter attacking the constitution, this time authorizing newspaper publication: "The basis of our constitution is in opposition to the principle of equal political rights, refusing to all but freeholders any participation in the natural right of self-government." Jefferson's recommendation was the usual one that men who served in the militia or who paid taxes should be entitled to vote, and this was a sufficiently limited dream. Yet when he died the following year it was as far away as ever. Fifty petitions for reform were received by the Virginia legislature in 1826, and it ignored them all.

In 1829, the same year in which Jackson was inaugurated President of the United States, the commonwealth of Virginia at last gave in. A constitutional convention was authorized to meet in the capital city of Richmond on the fifth of October, 1829.

Governor Giles made it clear that they had gathered to discuss a venerated object. He said that the Declaration of Independence was "of incomparably less importance to mankind" than the Virginia constitution, and that the people of Virginia consented to celebrate the fourth of July instead of the twenty-ninth of June only because of their "noble, generous self-denial. . . . The Declaration of Independence is a mere act of diplomacy . . . whereas the Virginia Constitution is a written social document, the first ever entered into by man, and forms the most instructive model . . . for the whole human race."

Governor Giles was one of the delegates to the constitutional convention, and he joined a glittering array of Virginia notables. Two of his fellow delegates, James Madison and James Monroe, had each served two terms as President of the United States. A future President, John Tyler, was there, and so was Judge Upshur whom Tyler made his Secretary of State. John Marshall was there, now in his twenty-eighth year as Chief Justice of the United States Supreme Court, The Speaker of the United States House of Representatives was there, and so was an array of governors, judges, senators and prominent men. Crowds of visitors of both sexes jammed the hall to hear the debates, which were superbly recorded in their entirety by Arthur Stansbury, a brilliant and experienced reporter.

Some of the older men who were present in Richmond on the opening day of the convention said that the scene reminded them of the Constitutional Convention itself, and one of those who said so was James Madison. He was now nearly eighty and he entered the Hall of Burgesses like a figure from another age, his hair powdered and diamond buckles at the knee. He had never been a reformer in the sense that Jefferson was, but he wanted ardently whatever would be best for Virginia.

Madison and Chief Justice Marshall ceremoniously conducted James

Monroe to the antique walnut chair which he would use as presiding officer. Monroe was too old and feeble for so difficult an assignment; his chief qualification was the fact that he was by temperament a peacemaker. His term of office as President had been called the Era of Good Feelings and he hoped that the same atmosphere would prevail at Richmond. As he pointed out, concessions were going to be necessary on both sides.

Where the franchise was concerned, Monroe was relatively conservative. When he was serving as a member of the Virginia legislature in 1811, he had opposed a bill to modify the suffrage requirements; he said that he had seen "democracy run wild in France" and he was not going to let the same thing happen in Virginia. By 1829, however, Monroe had reached the point where he was willing to extend the suffrage, so long as the right to vote remained in the hands of "those who have a common interest in the country and may act as free and independent citizens."

Monroe expressed the hope that all the delegates would conduct themselves with courtesy. Tempers rose, and this hope turned out to be vain. The delegates did, however, express themselves with learning, eloquence, passion and at great length. As one of their number said with some truth, "The Old Dominion has long been celebrated for producing great orators."

The most courteous single statement on the subject of the franchise came not from the delegates but from the men of the city that was their host. On the 13th of October, the convention was presented with a document called *The Memorial of the Non-Freeholders of the City of Richmond*. Since the writers of the document did not possess land they could not vote, and to them this was slavery. "They alone deserve to be called free . . . who participate in the formation of their political institutions and in the control of those who make and administer the laws." It was bad enough to be deprived of the right to vote, but it was still worse to be given the excuse that they were unfit to exercise such a right. "Your memorialists feel the difficulty of undertaking calmly to repel charges and insinuations involving in infamy themselves and so large a portion of their fellow citizens. To be deprived of their rightful equality, and to hear as an apology that they are too ignorant and vicious to enjoy it, is no ordinary trial of patience."

The writers of the *Memorial* made the same point that Thomas Paine had made at the French Convention—that the constitution and the declaration of rights did not match each other. The Virginia Bill of Rights stated proudly, "All men are by nature equally free and independent," and the men of Richmond wanted the statement at last made a reality in the constitution.

As one of the western delegates pointed out, this statement on human equality predated 1776: "This is a position much older than these United

302

States, and flowed from a gentleman to whom, more than any other, these American states are indebted for all their civil and religious liberties . . . the legitimate father of the first article of the Bill of Rights . . . the author of the Essay upon the Human Understanding."

It had perhaps been a mistake to bring John Locke into the discussion, as Benjamin Watkins Leigh, one of the most eloquent of the orators on the conservative side, was quick to point out. "Locke has had a singular fate. His *Essay on Government* was written to maintain the throne of William and Mary . . . yet from his book have been deduced the wildest democracy and demented French Jacobinism. He exploded the right divine of kings—he showed that all government is of human institution; yet he is supposed to have established the divine right of democracy."

Mr. Leigh had to be corrected in his turn when he tried to use an illustration from the past. "It appeared, he said, that Bacon, a rebel, was the first who adopted the notion of universal suffrage in this country, and that he had it from the soldiers of Cromwell's army." It fell to John R. Cooke of Frederick County to correct Leigh by pointing out that the suffrage had been narrowed in Virginia at precisely the time when Cromwell was ruling in England. "This limitation of the right of suffrage was . . . set forth as one of the grievances by which the popular insurrection of 1676 was justified."

It was natural for an eastern conservative like Leigh to think of Bacon as a traitor, while a western reformer like Cooke considered him a patriot whose insurrection was justified. Cooke himself had been a leader in the struggle for reform since 1816, and he was beginning to think that another insurrection might be justified. "I tell you, sir, for I know it, that so sure as God is in heaven, the separation of this assembly without redressing, in some measure at least, the grievances of the non-freeholders, will be the signal for resistance, passive *at first,* to the constituted authorities."

John Randolph of Roanoke was one of the delegates to the convention and he also thought that there might be danger of armed conflict in Virginia. But in his opinion what would cause civil war was any attempt to reduce the political power of the freeholders. He had come to the convention with bitter reluctance and had made it clear from the first that he hated everything about it. When he was placed on one of the planning committees, he sat staring at the wall, his eyes focused on the eastern section of a map of Virginia, and contributed nothing but his contempt to the discussion. On the floor of the convention he contributed oratory, turning all his forces in a battle against oncoming democracy. "I am too old a man to remove; my associations, my habits and my property nail me to the Commonwealth. But were I a young man I would, in case this monstrous tyranny shall be imposed on us, do what a few years ago I should have thought parricidal. I would withdraw from your jurisdiction. I would not live under King Numbers."

It was not very clear where Randolph thought he might go for refuge, since nearly every state in the Union was now living under King Numbers. Moreover, they all seemed to be quite comfortable, and no signs of monstrous tyranny had developed. In fact, Richard Henderson of Loudoun County was able to point out that Virginia itself could supply an example of the success of non-freeholder voting. Unlike Richmond, Norfolk was classified as a borough, and "pot-boilers and mechanics" therefore had the franchise. "We have been taught to believe that the multitude in cities was more depraved and more liable to political delusion" than the freeholder, but in fact the record of the Norfolk delegates to the legislature had been excellent.

The question of suffrage reform was intertwined with the equally bitter subject of adequate representation in the legislature for the western counties, and both of them threatened the same thing—loss of power by the men of property in the eastern counties. Benjamin Watkins Leigh came from Chesterfield County, and he was perhaps the frankest, as he was certainly the most eloquent, in defense of this power. "No government can be just, or wise, or safe for Virginia, which shall place the property of the East in the power and at the disposal of the West. Whenever they shall take away the little earnings of my labor, or any part of them, whenever they shall seize the bread I earn for my children for their own local purposes—against my consent and the consent of all those who represent my interests—and I shall be bound to submit to such exaction, without means of redress, I shall be obliged to them, sincerely obliged to them, to take away my life too; I shall not desire to survive an hour."

In the end, after three months of debate, neither side got what it wanted. The conservatives were not able to preserve unchanged the sacred document "reared up for us, by our godlike forefathers, in the midst of imminent peril," but neither were the reformers able to bring into existence the new Virginia of which they dreamed. In the case of the franchise, an attempt to bring in a taxpayer suffrage was defeated 57 to 37. One slight concession was made, given with bitter reluctance; freeholder voting was expanded to include leaseholders and householders if they paid taxes.

This concession was so complicated that the franchise section of the new constitution read like a lawyer's brief. One sentence consisted of the following: "In case of two or more tenants in common, joint tenants, or parceners in possession, reversion or remainder, having interest in land the value whereof shall be insufficient to entitle them all to vote, they shall together have as many votes as the value of the land shall entitle them to; and the legislature shall by law provide the mode in which their vote or votes shall in such case be given."

This sort of thing might sound absurd to an outsider, but it did not seem so to a Virginian. It might be complicated; it might even be unworkable. But it maintained the basic principle that political power must remain in the hands of the men who owned the land, and it kept as a reality the ancient English principle of the forty-shilling freeholder.

Yet even the men of Virginia could not blind themselves to the fact that they were living in a changing world. Their constitutional convention ended in January of 1830, and two years later England abandoned the law of the forty-shilling freeholder which it had lived under since the Middle Ages. The great Reform Bill passed by the House of Commons took the first step toward widening the base of political power in England. It was a very cautious step. It expanded the suffrage to include certain kinds of copyholders, leaseholders and tenants-at-will, and the artisans of England were still disfranchised. But the idea that the government belonged to the people, not to the holders of property, had achieved its first small victory in England, and other victories followed.

In the United States, the presidential election of 1840 showed how completely the issue had been decided. The word "democracy" had by now become wholly respectable, and every American politician took advantage of the new state of affairs. The slogans and the campaign songs and the vast amount of noisy excitement were the surface manifestations of a phenomenon that would have been impossible at the turn of the century. Two and a half million people voted in this election—double the vote in the presidential election of 1832.

In the 1840 election, the question of the franchise was introduced only when it would be a useful stick with which to beat one's opponent. Martin Van Buren found it difficult to live down the fact that he had not supported universal suffrage in the New York constitutional convention of 1821, while William Henry Harrison had to face the charge that he had opposed a taxpaying qualification for Indiana when he had served there as territorial Governor in 1807. The vast majority of Americans had decided that the vote belonged to the people, and the word "democracy," which had once been a term of contempt, was now used everywhere and with increasing pride.

One exception remained. Aloof, rigid and unchanged in a changing world, the state of Rhode Island stood alone, still dedicated to the principle that had once seemed reasonable to them all.

Chapter Sixteen

Rhode Island had received its charter from Charles the Second, and now, nearly two centuries later, it clung to it still. The politicians praised it because it came to them from the hands of their beloved founder, Roger Williams, but they valued it because it kept the political power in the hands of the men of property.

The charter of Rhode Island, like the one which Connecticut had finally repudiated, put all the power into the hands of the General Assembly. No one could vote for a member of the Assembly except a freeholder or the eldest son of a freeholder, and in 1798 the value of the freehold had been set at $134.

The requirement that every voter must own a freehold had not been unreasonable in the eighteenth century. Rhode Island was a small state, but land was still available. The change took place early in the nineteenth century, when capital began to be invested in industry instead of in shipping. There was an increasing concentration of industrial workers in the area around Providence, and a rising tide of immigration after 1830, and this meant that only a minority of adult males could be owners of land. A coalition of voters in the farming townships to the south and west held the balance of power in the General Assembly, and as long as the vote remained restricted to landowners nothing could be changed.

In 1811, when there was an effort made in the legislature to expand the franchise, a Newport newspaper spoke disapprovingly of "the evil and wickedness of the bill." It was defeated, and so were all later attempts. In 1829 the General Assembly, having received a petition from citizens to amend the suffrage, chose Benjamin Hazard as chairman of the committee to bring in a report. Hazard was a lawyer from Newport, and he was so pleased with the contemptuous tone of the report that it was one of the few papers he ever signed.

From the time of its founding, and in spite of Roger Williams, Rhode Island had believed that power and property went together and that both could be divorced from responsibility. It was characteristic of the state that it used child workers after the practice had been discontinued in the rest of America, and that, even in 1831, three-fourths of the children working in American cotton mills were in Rhode Island. The status quo was eminently satisfactory to the men who held political power, and the charter was their protection.

The man who tried to destroy this tyranny was himself a member of the dominant middle class. Like Thomas Rainsborough, that earlier champion of the people, he did not come from the kind of background that might be expected to produce a radical.

His name was Thomas Dorr and he was the son of a wealthy Providence manufacturer and merchant. He went to Exeter and Harvard and then received his legal training under that most militant of New York conservatives, Chancellor Kent. When Dorr settled down in Providence, he was a model citizen—president of the local school board and a valued member of the Rhode Island Historical Society. He was also a man who hated injustice.

When Dorr entered the General Assembly, he was a moderate on the suffrage issue. He hoped for some sort of taxpayer compromise, of the kind that had been worked out in Connecticut, and in 1834 he helped form the Constitutional Party. Efforts to replace the charter of Rhode Island had been going on since 1792, but so far none of them had been successful.

It was the absolute rigidity of his opponents that drove Thomas Dorr to extremes. As his chief political foe, James Fenner, said in reluctant admiration, "Whatever Mr. Dorr does, he does from principle." Among those principles were justice and liberty, as they had been for Roger Williams, and Dorr did not consider them to be a matter of embalmed history. He believed they had a practical application in contemporary Rhode Island. Since this point of view ran counter to that of most of his fellow legislators, Dorr found himself forced into an increasingly radical position. In 1840 he became the head of the newly formed Rhode Island Suffrage Association, which advocated complete white male suffrage.

Dorr's supporters were the voteless men, the kind who "did military duty and worked the fire engines." Their strategy was to bypass the authorities and go direct to the people, and within six months the Association had chapters in nearly every township in Rhode Island. Their headquarters were in Providence, and on the 17th of April, 1841, they gathered there in what they called People's Day. Some three thousand men marched in a suffrage procession, carrying banners, and wearing badges that proclaimed, "I am an American citizen."

During the summer, the Suffrage Association made plans for a constitutional convention, one to which all white males over twenty-one could send delegates. What was called the People's Convention met in October of 1841 and wrote a constitution for Rhode Island. It was based on the principle that "all free governments are . . . established for the greatest good of the whole number," and it gave the vote to all white males over twenty-one, except paupers. In December this constitution was ratified by the same voters who had sent delegates, and in the eyes of Thomas Dorr and his supporters it was now the legal government of Rhode Island.

The General Assembly branded this constitution illegal, as it certainly was. The Assembly had authorized a constitutional convention of its own, but the freeholders had failed to ratify the document that was offered them. As a result, two elections were held in Rhode Island in April, 1842. Samuel Ward King was elected Governor under the provisions of the charter, by vote of the freeholders, and Thomas Dorr was elected Governor under the People's Constitution, by vote of the men this constitution had enfranchised.

Early in May both Governors prepared to deliver inaugural addresses to their respective legislatures, Dorr in Providence and King at Newport. The affair had its comic aspects but not to Thomas Dorr, and in his eloquent address on the third of May he traced the long battle conducted by the disfranchised and the final victory over a landed oligarchy. He then adjourned his legislature for two months while he went to Washington, D.C., to try to enlist President Tyler on his side.

Tyler had already promised his support to the charter government if there should be any disorders, and Dorr got his chief support from New York politicians who were trying to make capital out of the situation. As for the rest of the country, it watched in open fascination.

On the 16th of May, Dorr was back in Providence and welcomed by about three thousand people. Some of them were armed, and Dorr set up his headquarters in a neat frame house with very unmilitary-looking shutters.

His supporters marched up College Street and captured two brass cannons from the Arsenal, and Governor King called out the militia. King also sent a steamboat to get reinforcements, and local journalists let themselves go in picturing the terrors that threatened Rhode Island. "A Cataline, talented, reckless, *mad,* was attempting to subvert the liberties of the state, and was threatening with the torch and the dagger all who dared to oppose him." It was rumored that Dorr intended to attack the Arsenal, and "on that awful night, but few of the citizens of Providence retired to rest; or, if they did, retired not for slumber but, with watchful eyes and aching hearts, to await in the most painful suspense the dread spectacle of our fair city wrapt in flames and her streets deluged with blood."

Dorr did in fact attack the Arsenal that night. There was a dense fog, he had almost no ammunition for his two cannons, and his unnerved followers could not get the powder to ignite. It proved to be impossible to capture the heavily guarded stone building, and after this failure nearly all his followers deserted him except about fifty men who helped him drag the cannons back to his headquarters. At eight the following morning, Governor King's reinforcements were pouring into the city and Dorr learned that all the legislators in his own government had resigned.

Dorr himself did not seem to feel that anything had changed. His government was still the rightful one, since it had been authorized by the vote of the people, and he was still its rightful head. He tried to make a stand near a village, and Governor King called out fifteen hundred armed men. In Military Order Number 54, King reported that the "fort of the insurgents" had been stormed and the dread insurrection crushed. In fact, the hill was already deserted, so that the victory was not a difficult one. The government of Rhode Island, by now almost hysterical, trumpeted about in a state of high excitement, searching homes, making arrests, and treating prisoners with some violence. A reward of one thousand dollars was offered for Dorr's capture, but no one informed against him. When he returned to Rhode Island in October of 1843, it was of his own free will.

During his trial for treason, Dorr was permitted to speak in his own defense. "What I did I had a right to do, having been duly elected Governor of this state under a rightfully adopted and valid republican state constitution, which I took an oath to support." The attack on the Arsenal had been in obedience to this oath. "It was of great importance that the arms of the state should be recovered from the opposing government, which had rightfully ceased to exist."

Dorr based his long and eloquent defense on the conviction that a moral principle was involved which no legal action could destroy. "There are . . .

honest convictions which cannot be forced out of a man by any human process." He reminded his listeners that Galileo had been forced to recant by the Inquisition, but that this did not alter the fact that the earth continued to revolve around the sun. "The servants of a righteous cause may fail or fall in the defense of it. . . . But all the truth that it contains is indestructible."

Dorr was found guilty of treason and sentenced to life imprisonment at hard labor. There was an immediate outcry, and in the next election the successful candidate for governor ran on the promise that he would release Thomas Dorr.

The government of Rhode Island ran no risk in releasing him. He was a defeated man, and so was the cause for which he had fought so gallantly and so clumsily. Back in November of 1842, a constitutional convention had at last managed to produce a constitution which the voters were willing to ratify, and the document set up two kinds of citizenship in Rhode Island. Native-born white males no longer needed to be freeholders; they could vote if they had paid a dollar tax or served in the militia. Foreign-born white males still had to be freeholders and possessed of $134 worth of land.

In April of 1843, Dorr's chief political foe, James Fenner, ran for election in what was called the Law and Order Party, and one of his supporters stated the issue clearly: "The great question whether the political power of the state is to pass out of the hands of the middle classes is about to be decided. If it does not, peace and harmony will be restored. If it does, the forms of free government will remain but its salutary spirit will depart forever." Fenner won the election.

The constitution of Rhode Island went into effect in May and a ceremony was held in Newport in honor of the occasion. The men of the legislature and other dignitaries walked in a solemn procession to the church, where they heard a speech by William G. Goddard extolling the new frame of government. He said that an unrestricted suffrage would have endangered "the rights of property and the principles of liberty," and in support of this position he quoted approvingly from the famous speech that Chancellor Kent had delivered at the New York constitutional convention of 1821. Goddard added a tribute to the men who had defeated Dorr. In their "noble bosoms was formed the stern resolve to maintain, at whatever cost of treasure and of blood, the supremacy of the laws. . . . Not for a single moment could the men of Rhode Island brook the thought of surrendering this inheritance of freedom, derived from heroic sires, to be trampled in the dust by lawless feet."

The exclusion of immigrants from political rights remained in the constitution until 1886, when an amendment gave the vote to naturalized residents if they had served in the Civil War. Two years later, and forty-six years after the Dorr War, Rhode Island passed another amendment and this one disposed of the freeholder requirement altogether.

Thomas Dorr died, broken in health, in 1851, and he could be dismissed as a foolish revolutionary who did not have the wit to compromise when he could. But his example gave new impetus to reformers in other states. In Ohio, for instance, Samuel Medary was deeply impressed by the Dorr War. He headed a battle for a new state constitution, and when it was written in 1851, the taxpayer qualification disappeared and all white males could vote in Ohio. A friend of Medary's, David S. Reid, made the same attempt in North Carolina, which was still clinging to a freeholder requirement in voters for the upper house. Reid ran for Governor in 1848, in a reform movement that was directly influenced by the Dorr War, and lost by a narrow margin. Eleven years later, North Carolina accepted taxpayer suffrage.

The Dorr War made an especially deep impression on neighboring Connecticut, and final reform came easily in 1845, both parties claiming credit for a suffrage bill that eliminated all property requirements. As the Hartford *Times* put it, the bill had been "long desired and long postponed; but it passed, at length, with very little opposition and no excitement." In fact, the vote in the upper house was unanimous.

Other states behaved in the same manner and at about the same time. New Jersey abandoned its property qualification in 1844, and Louisiana in 1845. Virginia surrendered in the Reform Convention of 1850–51 and gave the suffrage to all white males, coming full circle back to the voting pattern that had existed in the first years at Jamestown.

Massachusetts submitted more slowly to the final divorce between property and the vote. In 1853 a constitutional convention was called to revise the suffrage, and a mass meeting was held at Faneuil Hall. The convention decided to abolish property qualifications in voting for state officials, but the people failed to approve the reform. The vote, however, was a close one, and the state of Massachusetts eventually took her place with the others.

There were delaying actions elsewhere, and attempts to find refuge in local arrangements, but the basic fact remained: the principle which linked property to the vote was by now almost completely discredited in the United States.

The jubilant victors called the result "universal suffrage," but it was not. It was suffrage for white males only. The majority of adult Americans were still disfranchised.

One form of exclusion had been largely eliminated by the middle of the nineteenth century, but the principle of exclusion remained. Its application varied from state to state and from time to time, rendering voteless Jews, Indians, Chinese, or whatever other group might be looked upon at the moment as a source of potential danger. But the most conspicuous victims of political exclusion, and the ones over whom the longest and bitterest battles were waged, were women and Negroes.

In the early days, when the vote rested on property qualifications, a free Negro who had the necessary requirements voted like any other man, and if this right was taken away there were protests. Early in the eighteenth century, the Board of Trade in London wrote the Governor of Virginia to ask why Negro freeholders had been disfranchised, since, as the Board's legal counsel put it: "I cannot see why one freeman should be used worse than another merely on account of his complexion." Governor Gooch, whose popularity rested on the fact that he usually agreed with the Virginia legislature, wrote back to defend its action. He said that enslaved Negroes had been conspiring against the local government, and while it was true there was no proof that free Negroes had joined the conspiracy, they had nevertheless been behaving "with insolence." The Virginia legislature had deprived them of the right to vote in order "to fix a perpetual brand" on them and thus make it possible to "preserve a decent distinction between them and their betters." In closing, Governor Gooch offered that immemorial excuse for injustice: "After all, the number of free Negroes and mulattos entitled to the privilege of voting at elections is so inconsiderable, that 'tis scarce worth while to take any notice of them in this particular."

Some of the reformers who worked the hardest to get the vote for white male Americans worked with equal ardor to make sure that the privilege was not shared by American Negroes. A particularly painful example of this was the New York constitutional convention of 1821. In some of the key wards in Brooklyn and New York City, Negro voters had opposed Martin Van Buren, and his organization was in control at the convention. It was therefore possible to pass a suffrage law which removed the freeholder qualification for white voters but left it clamped on Negro ones. A conservative who was trying to defend the freeholder requirement as the "anchor which had for forty years held us together" was able to point out with some glee that the reformers were quite willing to clutch this same anchor when it suited them: "Although property, either real or personal, was no correct test of qualification in the case of a white man, it was a very good one in that of a black one."

Suffrage reform in the southern states succeeded partly because it served to unite white men in a common cause. A delegate to the Virginia constitutional convention of 1829 sounded the first note of what was going to become a rising chorus when he said that the South would soon face a time "of peril and of danger. Is it not wise now, to call together at least every free white human being and unite them in the same common interest and government?" Henry A. Wise led a successful fight for white male suffrage in Virginia in the middle of the century, openly advocating what was known as the southern way of life, which, being translated, meant the absolute exclusion of the Negro from the right to vote.

The same thing happened in the North and with even less excuse. Connecticut abandoned its charter government in 1818 and opened its constitution by stating: "All political power is inherent in the people, and all free governments are founded on their authority." It then disfranchised all the Negroes in the state, under the apparent assumption that they were not people.

Pennsylvania did the same in its constitutional convention of 1837–38, and the propertied Negroes of Philadelphia implored their fellow citizens not to ratify this section of the new constitution. They asked them not to separate "what our fathers bled to unite, to wit, taxation and representation." The appeal was rejected. Pennsylvania, like New Jersey, joined the increasing number of northern states which restricted the ballot to white men only.

The last state to enter the Union without discriminating against Negroes in its constitution was Maine. Maine happened to have very few Negroes; what it was concerned about was its Indian population. Therefore its constitution of 1819 discriminated against Indians and would not permit them to vote unless they were payers of taxes.

After 1819, each new state that entered the Union wrote a constitution whose Declaration of Rights spoke ringingly of freedom and equality, and each constitution had a suffrage requirement that excluded Negroes. The idea became so familiar that "free, white and twenty-one" passed into the language as a litany, and when the Civil War broke out only five states in the Union were giving the Negro the vote. These were the New England states of Maine, New Hampshire, Vermont, Rhode Island and Massachusetts, and about six percent of the Negroes in the North lived within their borders. New York still permitted Negroes to vote if they were freeholders, and nowhere else in the United States could they vote at all.

After the blood and suffering of the Civil War had ended with victory for the North, an amendment to the Constitution in 1870 stated that a citizen's right to vote could not be abridged because of race, color, or previous condition of servitude. What defeated the law in practice was a phenomenon that de Tocqueville had remarked upon when he visited the United States earlier in the century. Although propertied Negroes in Pennsylvania still legally possessed the right to vote, it was not always permitted in practice, and de Tocqueville inquired about it: "Be so good as to explain to me how it happens that in a state founded by Quakers, and celebrated for its toleration, free blacks are not allowed to exercise civil rights. They pay taxes; is it not fair that they should vote?" The answer he got was a simple one: "In this country, the law is sometimes unable to maintain its authority without the support of the majority."

In the South, the majority knew exactly what it wanted; Mississippi and Virginia took the lead in working out a series of devices which would make it impossible for the amendment to the Constitution to have any effect. This was so successful that nearly all struggle ceased. A history of suffrage published in 1918 was able to state: "Public attention has ceased to focus upon the Negro cause; it is looked upon as lost."

In 1962, churches were being burned because they were being used to register Negro voters, but there was no longer a background of tacit national approval. President Kennedy was asked about the burnings at a press conference, and the vast majority of the nation agreed with him when he replied: "The right to vote is very basic. If we're going to neglect that right, then all of our talk about freedom is hollow." It was no longer believable that safety lay in exclusion; the cause which had been called "lost" was furiously alive and on the road to victory.

The denial of the vote to women was not based on a theory of safety. It was not based upon any theory at all. However an American male might feel on the subject of the franchise—however conservative, moderate or radical he might be on the question of voting by race or creed or nationality or property —he joined with his fellow males in one simple, emotional conviction: It was not possible to permit women to vote. An occasional eccentric might say there was no reason for this exclusion, but that only proved how eccentric he was.

It was in the colony of Maryland that a woman made the first attempt in American history to get the vote. Her name was Margaret Brent, and Governor Calvert thought so highly of her intelligence that he named her sole executrix of his will. In 1648 she asked the General Assembly to give her the right to vote, and the Assembly, for once unanimous, turned her down. In 1797, when a Maryland legislator wanted to show his contempt for a bill that advocated white manhood suffrage, he bitterly offered an amendment which would also give the vote to "women and children."

In all the states, women as voters were held in the same category as children and idiots, except for the brief period of absentmindedness in New Jersey which was soon rectified by its legislature. It was a satisfactory arrangement because it served, in Governor Gooch's memorable phrase, to preserve a decent distinction between them and their betters.

The wife of John Adams was his equal in wit, strength and intelligence, and everyone knew it. One of his friends called her "your Portia." Shortly before the Declaration of Independence was written, husband and wife had a brief exchange on the subject of political equality, and Abigail Adams said that she saw no reason why women should consider themselves bound by "laws in which we have no voice or representation." John Adams naturally supposed that she was joking; but if she was not, there was nothing she could do to change the situation.

In the middle of the nineteenth century, women of this kind banded together and held a convention in New York. They stated that women as well as men possessed certain fundamental rights, and that one of these was the right to vote. The crusade that followed was considered so absurd that "responsible statesmen and thinking men were slow to come to the point of considering it necessary to give the matter any serious attention." They were content to leave the matter to mockery and mobs, and it was not until after the Civil War that "men of the best type," now seriously alarmed, went out "in the field against the suffragists."

By the end of the nineteenth century, the women had finally settled for the heartbreakingly slow strategy of trying to fight the matter through, step by step, in each of the state legislatures. Their first great victory came in 1889 when Wyoming wrote its constitution. For the first time, a Declaration of Rights was written which was not immediately contradicted in the body of the document.

The Declaration of Rights in the Wyoming constitution stated: "All power is inherent in the people, and all free governments are founded on their authority. . . . Since equality in the enjoyment of natural and civil rights is only made sure through political equality, the laws of this state affecting the political rights and privileges of its citizens shall be without distinction of race, color, sex, or any circumstance or condition whatsoever, other than individual incompetency or unworthiness duly ascertained by a court of competent jurisdiction." Article Six of the constitution made the principle specific: "The rights of citizens of the State of Wyoming to vote and hold office shall not be denied or abridged on account of sex."

The history of the United States in the twentieth century has been that of a slow and sometimes very painful retreat from the illusion that a nation can proclaim political equality in principle and deny it in practice. It was

315

America's torment and its glory that its birth happened to coincide, thanks to Thomas Jefferson, with an extraordinary statement of principle. However reluctantly it might bring itself to obey that principle, it knew in the end that it had no other choice.

Back in the days of the New York constitutional convention of 1821, a delegate from Saratoga County, Colonel Samuel Young, stated firmly that "metaphysical refinements and abstract speculations are of little use in framing a constitution." He proved this by pointing out that if such things were followed to their ultimate and completely absurd conclusion, it would end with Negro women having the right to vote. This was, in fact, exactly what happened. A century and a half later, in the schools and barbershops and other polling places in the state of New York, such voters stand in line with the rest; and the descendants of Colonel Young, if there are any, stand unperturbed among them.

It is the mark of the excellence of an idea that the battle to establish it becomes in time forgotten. America moved very slowly on the subject of political equality for white men; the battle was not finally won until two hundred and fifty years after America was founded. Yet an idea which was once inconceivable and then controversial became in time so commonplace that the long warfare to establish it has been almost completely forgotten. The warfares that followed it will in time also be forgotten; and then America will truly have come of age and fulfilled the promise of its birth.

Identification of Quotations

Note to reader: This book does not have a bibliography. Material has been consulted in so many fields that it would be impractical to print so long a list. However, the following pages may be considered a partial bibliography, since, in general, the books and articles to which I have been the most indebted are also the ones from which I have taken quotations.

Chapter One

5   "Bay of Chesapeake . . ." Richard Hakluyt, *The Principal Navigations, Voiages, Traffiques and Discoveries of the English Nation,* 3 vols. (London, 1598–1600), Vol. III, p. 282.

5   "the virtuous . . ." David Beers Quinn, *The Roanoke Voyages, 1584–1590,* 2 vols. (London: The Hakluyt Society, 1955), Vol. II, p. 507.

5   "the name of the place . . ." Hakluyt, *Principal Navigations, Voiages . . . ,* Vol. III, p. 292.

5   "I greatly joyed . . ." Same, Vol. III, p. 293.

5   "my books . . ." Same.

5   "who had watched . . ." Same.

5   "to weigh anchor . . ." Same.

6   "full power . . ." *The Genesis of the United States,* edited by Alexander Brown, 2 vols. (Boston, 1890), Vol. I, p. 77.

7   "bring the infidels . . ." *The Federal and State Constitutions, Colonial Charters, and Other Organic Laws of the States, Territories, and Colonies Now or Heretofore Forming the United States of America,* edited by Francis

Newton Thorpe, 7 vols. (Washington: Government Printing Office, 1909), Vol. VII, p. 3784.

7   "as though he had been . . ." George Percy, "Observations," in Samuel Purchas, *Hakluytes Posthumus, or Purchas His Pilgrimes,* 20 vols. (Glasgow: Glasgow University Press, 1904–1907), Vol. XVIII, p. 411.

7   "The way to prosper . . ." *Genesis of the United States,* Brown (ed.), Vol. I, p. 85.

7   "upon any just cause" Same, Vol. I, p. 67.

7   "You must take . . ." Same, Vol. I, p. 84.

8   "Have great care . . ." Same, Vol. I, p. 83.

8   "the goodliest cornfields . . ." Percy, "Observations," in Purchas, *Hakluytes Posthumus* (Glasgow), Vol. XVIII, p. 411.

8   "They take . . ." Same, Vol. XVIII, p. 415.

8   "I well remember . . ." John Smith, *Advertisements for the Unexperienced Planters of New-England, or Any Where* (London, 1631), p. 32.

9   "childish factions . . ." *Sir Ferdinando Gorges and His Province of Maine,* edited by James Phinney Baxter, 3 vols. (Boston: Prince Society Publications, 1890), Vol. III, p. 158.

9   "dividing themselves . . ." Same, Vol. III, p. 161.

9   "a very excellent . . ." Same, Vol. III, p. 165.

9   "solemn meeting" Richard Hakluyt, *Virginia Richly Valued* (London, 1609), from The Epistle Dedicatorie.

10   "a most worthy . . ." Terence H. O'Brien, "The London Livery Companies and the Virginia Company," *Virginia Magazine of History and Biography* (April 1960), p. 140.

10   "an enterprise . . ." *Genesis of the United States,* Brown (ed.), Vol. II, p. 555.

10   "It is not convenient . . ." *Federal and State Constitutions,* Thorpe (ed.), Vol. VII, p. 3796.

11   "careful and understanding . . ." Same.

11   "one body . . ." Same, Vol. VII, p. 3803.

11   "They would never . . ." *Records of the Virginia Company of London,* edited by Susan Myra Kingsbury, 4 vols. (Washington: Government Printing Office, 1906–1935), Vol. II, p. 359.

11   "time and experience . . ." *Federal and State Constitutions,* Thorpe (ed.), Vol. VII, p. 3803.

11   "full power . . ." Same, Vol. VII, p. 3805.

12   "There is an equality . . ." *Commons Debates, 1621,* edited by Wallace Notestein, Frances Helen Relf, and Hartley Simpson, 7 vols. (New Haven: Yale University Press, 1935), Vol. VII, p. 641.

12   "a government . . ." *Records of the Virginia Company,* Kingsbury (ed.), Vol. III, p. 517.

12   "not powerful enough . . ." William Strachey, "A True Repertory . . . ," in Purchas, *Hakluytes Posthumus* (Glasgow), Vol. XIX, p. 46.

12   "utter unseemly . . ." William Strachey, *For the Colony in Virginea Britannia, Lawes Divine, Morall and Martiall* (London, 1612), p. 6.

12   "first ragged . . ." William Strachey, *The Historie of Travaile into Virginia Britannia,* ed by R. H. Major (London: The Hakluyt Society, 1849), p. 85.

13   "now much . . ." Ralph Hamor, *A True Discourse of the Present State of Virginia,* 1615 (Richmond: Virginia State Library, 1957), p. 27.

13   "great joy" *Records of the Virginia Company,* Kingsbury (ed.), Vol. I, p. 257.

14   "the solitary . . ." Same, Vol. III, p. 222.
14   "our infant . . ." Same, Vol. III, p. 219.
14   "to be ready . . ." Same, Vol. III, p. 155.
14   "submit himself . . ." Same, Vol. III, p. 157.
15   "long harangues" Same, Vol. III, p. 158.
15   "did expect . . ." Same.
15   "the great charter . . ." Same, Vol. III, p. 161.
15   "hoping . . ." Same, Vol. III, p. 177.
16   "very great . . ." *Select Documents of English Constitutional History,* edited by George Burton Adams and H. Morse Stephens (New York: The Macmillan Company, 1924), p. 190.
16   "a voice equivalent . . ." Same.
16   "manslaughters . . ." Same.
17   "It is fully agreed . . ." *Records of the Virginia Company,* Kingsbury (ed.), Vol. III, p. 176.
17 fn. "I, Dame Dorothy . . ." J. E. Neale, *The Elizabethan House of Commons* (New Haven: Yale University Press, 1950), p. 183.
18   "beaver hat . . ." Same, Vol. III, p. 221.
18   "cow-keeper . . ." Same.
18   "their skill . . ." Same, Vol. I, p. 251.
18   "Upon some dispute . . ." Same.
18   "governed by . . ." Same, Vol. IV, p. 223.
18   "and it is a shame . . ." Same.
18   "profuse . . ." Same.
19   "The mouth . . ." Same, Vol. IV, p. 416.
19   "them we call . . . dividing . . ." Same.
19   "suppress popular liberty" Same, Vol. IV, p. 417.
19   "We may . . ." Same, Vol. IV, p. 419.
19   "the uniting of Virginia . . ." Same, Vol. IV, p. 420.
20   "the true and ancient . . ." *Commons Debates, 1621,* Notestein, Relf, and Simpson (eds.), Vol. V, p. 412.
20   "I am a stranger . . ." George Unwin, *Industrial Organization in the Sixteenth and Seventeenth Centuries* (Oxford: Clarendon Press, 1904), p. 181.
20   "Natural Right . . ." *English Economic History, Select Documents,* edited by A. E. Bland, P. A. Brown, and R. H. Tawney (London: G. Bell and Sons, Ltd., 1914), pp. 443–44.
20   "make laws . . ." *Constitutional Documents of the Reign of James I,* edited by J. R. Tanner (Cambridge: Cambridge University Press, 1930), p. 268.
20   "and with reciprocal . . ." *Journals of the House of Commons, 1547–1628* (reprinted by order of The House of Commons, 1803), p. 493.
21   "pronounced . . ." *The Letters of John Chamberlain,* edited by Norman Egbert McClure, 2 vols. (Philadelphia: American Philosophical Society, 1939), Vol. I, p. 533.
21   "a perpetual . . ." William Robert Scott, *The Constitution and Finance of English, Scottish and Irish Joint-Stock Companies to 1720,* 2 vols. (Cambridge: Cambridge University Press, 1910–1912), Vol. II, p. 268.
21   "principal man . . ." Chamberlain, *Letters,* McClure (ed.) Vol. II, p. 305.
21   "a great breach . . ." *Records of the Virginia Company,* Kingsbury (ed.), Vol. I, p. 357.
22   "to infringe . . ." Same, Vol. II, p. 28.
22   "His Majesty . . ." Same, Vol. II, p. 35.
22   "We conceive . . ." Same, Vol. III, p. 683.

22   "bless them . . ." *The Sermons of John Donne,* edited by George R. Potter and Evelyn M. Simpson, 10 vols. (Berkeley and Los Angeles: University of California Press, 1953–1962), Vol. IV, p. 282.

22   "They allege . . ." *Records of the Virginia Company,* Kingsbury (ed.), Vol. II, p. 358.

22   "some show . . ." Same, Vol. II, p. 359.

22   "purses . . ." Same.

23   "if in the regulating . . ." See page 11.

23   "cry out . . ." *Records of the Virginia Company,* Kingsbury (ed.), Vol. II, p. 359.

23   "by reducing . . ." Same, Vol. II, p. 469.

23   "all the rest . . ." Same, Vol. II, p. 475.

23   "the highest pitch . . ." Same, Vol. IV, p. 476.

23 *fn.*   "the liberty . . ." Same, Vol. IV, p. 523.

24   "tyranny" *Journals of the House of Burgesses of Virginia, 1619–1776,* edited by H. R. McIlwaine, 13 vols. (Richmond: The Colonial Press, 1905–1915), Vol. I, p. 43.

24   "ruled by . . ." Ebenezer Hazard, *Historical Collections,* 2 vols. (Philadelphia, 1792–1794), Vol. I, p. 203.

24   "our former . . ." *Journals of the House of Burgesses of Virginia,* McIlwaine (ed.), Vol. I, p. 45.

25   "The Council . . ." *Federal and State Constitutions,* Thorpe (ed.), Vol. III, p. 1829.

25   "All men by nature . . ." *A Briefe Relation of the Discovery and Plantation of New England* (London, 1622), p. E.

25   "The general laws . . ." Same.

25   "their deputies . . ." Same, p. E$_2$.

25   "voices equal . . ." Same.

25   "counsel, assent and approbation . . ." *Federal and State Constitutions,* Thorpe (ed.), Vol. I, p. 71.

25   "with the counsel . . ." Hazard, *Historical Collections,* Vol. I, p. 163.

25   "thirty burgesses . . ." "A Description of the Province of New Albion . . . 1638," *Tracts and Other Papers Relating Principally to the Origin, Settlement, and Progress of the Colonies in North America,* edited by Peter Force, 4 vols. (Washington, 1836–1846), Vol. II, p. 30.

25   "and without . . ." Same.

26   "My house . . ." William Hand Browne, *George Calvert and Cecilius Calvert* (New York: Dodd, Mead and Company, 1890), p. 25.

26   "unity . . ." *Narratives of Early Maryland, 1633–1684,* edited by Clayton Colman Hall (New York: Charles Scribner's Sons, 1910), p. 16.

26   "They are generally . . ." Same, p. 44.

27   "with the advice . . ." *Federal and State Constitutions,* Thorpe (ed.), Vol. III, p. 1679.

27   "principalities . . ." "Sir Edmund Plowden's Advice to Cecilius Calvert, second Lord Baltimore, a letter of 1639," edited by Edward C. Carter II, *Maryland Historical Magazine* (June 1961), p. 122.

27   "true and absolute . . ." *Federal and State Constitutions,* Thorpe (ed.), Vol. III, p. 1679.

28   "The body of laws . . ." *Narratives of Early Maryland,* Hall (ed.), p. 156.

28   "demanded . . ." *Procedures and Acts of the General Assembly of Maryland, January 1637/8–September 1664* (Baltimore, 1883), Vol. I of *Archives of Maryland,* p. 12.

28   "privilege of parliament men . . ." Same.

28   "an ancient . . ." *Constitutional Documents of the Reign of James I,* Tanner (ed.), p. 305.

Chapter Two

29   "If the charter . . ." *Records of the Virginia Company,* Kingsbury (ed.), Vol. IV, pp. 194–95.

29   "those Brownists . . ." Same, Vol. IV, p. 194.

30   "popish . . ." William Bradford, *Of Plymouth Plantation, 1620–1647,* edited by Samuel Eliot Morison (New York: Alfred A. Knopf, Inc., 1952), p. 5.

30   "beginner . . ." "Governor Bradford's Dialogue" in *Chronicles of the Pilgrim Fathers,* edited by Alexander Young (Boston, 1844), p. 441.

30   "Far be it . . ." *The Notebook of John Penry, 1593,* edited by Albert Peel (London: Royal Historical Society Publications, 1944), p. 92.

30   "singular love . . ." Bradford, *Of Plymouth Plantation,* Morison (ed.), p. 32.

30   "Under God . . ." Same.

31   "whom I have found . . ." *Records of the Virginia Company,* Kingsbury (ed.), Vol. III, p. 72.

31   "a gold . . ." Bradford, *Of Plymouth Plantation,* Morison (ed.), p. 325.

32   "and with extreme . . ." *The Ferrar Papers,* edited by B. Blackstone (Cambridge: Cambridge University Press, 1938), p. 11.

32   "very rigidly . . ." "Governor Bradford's Dialogue," *Chronicles of the Pilgrim Fathers,* Young (ed.), p. 429.

33   "The people of the Family . . ." Thomas Fuller, *The Church History of Britain,* 6 vols. (Oxford: Oxford University Press, 1845), Vol. V, p. 329.

33   "The Lord's . . ." Bradford, *Of Plymouth Plantation,* Morison (ed.), p. 9.

33   "One neighbor . . ." James Howell, *Epistolae Ho-Elianae: Familiar Letters Domestic and Foreign* (London, 1754), p. 26.

33   "their plain . . ." Bradford, *Of Plymouth Plantation,* Morison (ed.), p. 16.

34   "contention" Same.

34   "the vile medley . . ." *Autobiography of Joseph Scaliger,* edited by George W. Robinson (Cambridge: Harvard University Press, 1927), p. 50.

34   "in peace and love . . ." Bradford, *Of Plymouth Plantation,* Morison (ed.), p. 18.

34   "the great licentiousness . . ." Same, p. 25.

35   "enjoy . . ." Edward Winslow, *Hypocrisie Vnmasked* (London, 1646), p. 89.

35   "Sir Thomas Smythe . . ." Bradford, *Of Plymouth Plantation,* Morison (ed.), p. 356.

35   "a religious . . ." Same, p. 34.

36   "They knew . . ." Same, p. 47.

36   "strangers" Same, p. 44.

36   "If ever we make . . ." Same, p. 56.

36   "have liberty . . ." *Records of the Virginia Company,* Kingsbury (ed.), Vol. I, p. 303.

36   "continual occasion . . ." *A Relation or Iournall of the Beginning and Proceedings of the English Plantation Setled at Plimoth in New England* [Mourt's Relation] (London, 1622), p. B3 verso.

36   "as men are careful . . ." Same, p. B4 recto.

37   "You are to become . . . which yourselves . . ." Same.

37   "in choosing . . ." Same.

37	"My daily . . ." Same, p. B₄ verso.
37	"to find some place . . ." Bradford, *Of Plymouth Plantation,* Morison (ed.), p. 60.
37	"give them . . ." *John Pory's Lost Description of Plymouth Colony,* edited by Champlin Burrage (Boston: Houghton Mifflin Company, 1918), pp. 35–36.
38	"that when they came . . ." Bradford, *Of Plymouth Plantation,* Morison (ed.), p. 75.
38	"In the name of God . . ." *Federal and State Constitutions,* Thorpe (ed.), Vol. III, p. 1841.
39	"Observing . . ." *A Relation or Iournall* [Mourt's Relation] (1622), pp. 2–3.
39	"joined themselves . . ." See page 33.
39	"It seems God . . ." John Smith, *Advertisements* (1631), p. 9.
39	"In these hard . . ." Bradford, *Of Plymouth Plantation,* Morison (ed.), pp. 76–77.
40	"in the best manner . . ." Same, p. 86.
40	"They hastened . . ." *Sir Ferdinando Gorges,* Baxter (ed.), Vol. II, p. 48.
40	"authority . . ." *A Relation or Iournall* [Mourt's Relation] (1622), p. A₃.
40	"A Relation or . . ." Same, title page.
40	"We have here . . ." Same, p. 70.
40 fn.	"have a fair . . ." *Records of the Virginia Company,* Kingsbury (ed.), Vol. I, p. 451.
41	"I know your weakness . . ." Bradford, *Of Plymouth Plantation,* Morison (ed.), p. 93.
41	"great combats . . ." Bradford, *Of Plymouth Plantation,* Morison (ed.), p. 373.
41	"They will be a strengthening . . ." Same, p. 129.
41	"They are too delicate . . ." Same, p. 144.
41	"vile and clamorous . . ." Edward Winslow, *Good Newes from New-England* (London, 1624), "To the Reader."
42	"towards the maintenance . . ." Bradford, *Of Plymouth Plantation,* Morison (ed.), p. 133.
42	"The more is . . ." Same, p. 142.
43	"the smallest number . . ." Same, p. 159.
43	"destitute of . . ." Same.
43	"not of the Separation" Same, p. 153.
43	"for they were willing . . ." Same.
43	"the Church of England . . ." Thomas Morton, "New English Canaan," 1632, *Tracts and other Papers,* Force (ed.), Vol. II, p. 81.
43	"a public meeting . . ." Bradford, *Of Plymouth Plantation,* Morison (ed.), p. 151.
43	"in church . . ." Same, p. 150.
43	"voices in all courts . . ." Same, p. 155.
43	"private meetings . . ." Same, p. 149.
43	"had a bastard . . ." Nathaniel Morton, *New-England's Memoriall,* 1669 (Scholars' Facsimiles and Reprints, 1937), p. 60.
44	"all and every . . ." Roland G. Usher, *The Pilgrims and Their History* (New York: The Macmillan Company, 1918), p. 152.
44	"all amongst them . . ." Bradford, *Of Plymouth Plantation,* Morison (ed.), pp. 186–87.
44	"for the better government . . ." *Federal and State Constitutions,* Thorpe (ed.), Vol. III, p. 1844.

44   "courts and elections" See page 43.

44   "neither do we . . ." "A Letter of William Bradford and Isaac Allerton, 1623," *The American Historical Review* (January 1903), p. 299.

44   "receiving or admitting . . ." *Federal and State Constitutions,* Thorpe (ed.), Vol. III, p. 1844.

44 *fn.*   "self-liking . . ." *The Black Book of Warwick,* edited by Thomas Kemp (Warwick, 1898), p. 369.

45   "admitted into . . ." *Records of the Colony of New Plymouth, in New England,* edited by Nathaniel B. Shurtleff:, 12 vols. (Boston, 1855–1861), Vol. I, p. 5.

45   "nipped . . . were incurable . . ." See page 34.

Chapter Three

46   "we have settled . . ." *A Briefe Relation of the Discovery and Plantation of New England* (London, 1622), p. D₃.

47   "the purses . . ." Frances Rose-Troup, *John White* (New York: G. P. Putnam's Sons, 1930), p. 395.

47   "being ill chosen . . ." *John White's Planters Plea,* 1630 (Rockport: The Sandy Bay Historical Society and Museum, 1930), p. 73.

47   "religious and well-affected . . ." William Dismore Chapple, "The Public Service of John Endecott in the Massachusetts Bay Colony," *Essex Institute Historical Collections* (October 1929), p. 405.

48   "much enlarged" *Records of the Governor and Company of the Massachusetts Bay in New England,* edited by Nathaniel B. Shurtleff, 5 vols. (Boston, 1853–1854), Vol. I, p. 383.

48   "a body politic . . ." Same, Vol. I, p. 386.

48   "It is well known . . ." Letter from John Winthrop to John Endecott, *Winthrop Papers,* 5 vols. (Boston: Massachusetts Historical Society, 1929–1947), Vol. III, p. 148.

49   "with great cost . . ." *Records of the . . . Massachusetts Bay,* Shurtleff (ed.), Vol. I, p. 387.

49   "four Great and General . . ." *Federal and State Constitutions,* Thorpe (ed.), Vol. III, p. 1853.

49   "body politic . . ." Same, Vol. III, p. 1852.

50   "the most wise . . ." *Records of the . . . Massachusetts Bay,* Shurtleff (ed.), Vol. I, p. 361.

50   "have the sole . . ." Same.

50   "an absolute . . ." Same.

50   "divers paper . . ." Same, Vol. I, p. 400.

50   "of the daily work . . ." Same, Vol. I, p. 401.

51   "great difference . . ." *John White's Planters Plea,* 1630, p. 62.

51   "Unless he will . . ." *Records of the . . . Massachusetts Bay,* Shurtleff (ed.), Vol. I, p. 390.

52   "that New England . . ." Cotton Mather, *Magnalia Christi Americana: or, the Ecclesiastical History of New England* (London, 1702), Book Three, p. 74.

52   "Those that love . . ." Francis Higginson, *New-Englands Plantation, with the Sea Journal and Other Writings* (Salem: The Essex Book and Print Club, 1908), p. 82.

52   "to be of one judgment . . ." *Records of the . . . Massachusetts Bay*, Shurtleff (ed.), Vol. I, p. 394.

52   "the outward form . . ." Sidney Perley, *The History of Salem, Massachusetts*, 3 vols. (Salem, 1924), Vol. I, p. 99.

52   "consulted with . . ." Cotton Mather, *Magnalia Christi Americana* (London, 1702), Book One, p. 18.

52   "a company . . ." Bradford, *Of Plymouth Plantation*, Morison (ed.), p. 224.

52   "tending to mutiny . . ." Chapple, "Public Service of John Endecott," *Essex Institute Historical Collections* (October 1929), p. 423.

53   "rash innovations . . ." *Records of the . . . Massachusetts Bay*, Shurtleff (ed.), Vol. I, p. 408.

53   "for the satisfying . . ." *The Stuart Constitution, 1630–1688; Documents and Commentary*, edited by J. P. Kenyon (Cambridge: Cambridge University Press, 1966), p. 155.

53   "What good . . ." *Commons Debates for 1629*, edited by Wallace Notestein and Frances Helen Relf (Minneapolis: University of Minnesota Press, 1921), p. 18.

54   "like sheep . . ." Same, p. 240.

54   "Popery . . ." Same, pp. 101–102.

54   "not being granted . . ." Same, p. 102.

54   "the malevolent . . ." John Rushworth, *Historical Collections of Private Passages of State*, 8 vols. (London, 1721), Vol. I, p. 661.

55   "sealed . . ." *Commons Debates for 1629*, Notestein and Relf (eds.) p. 20.

55   "When this plantation . . ." *Winthrop Papers*, Vol. IV, p. 173.

55   "very great esteem" *The Countesse of Lincolnes Nurserie* (Oxford, 1622) [in British Museum]. From the Dedication.

56   "Mr. White's call" *Winthrop Papers*, Vol. II, p. 103.

56   "Mr. Governor . . ." *Records of the . . . Massachusetts Bay*, Shurtleff (ed.), Vol. I, p. 49.

56   "persons of worth . . ." Same.

56   "provide a shelter . . ." *Winthrop Papers*, Vol. II, p. 91.

56   "I am still . . ." Same, Vol. II. p. 94.

56   "expecting . . ." Same, Vol. II, p. 103.

57   "Their main end . . ." Higginson, *New-Englands Plantation, with the Sea Journal and Other Writings* (Salem, 1908), p. 48.

57   "Plantations . . ." *Winthrop Papers*, Vol. II, p. 106.

57   "If he let pass . . ." Same, Vol. II, p. 148.

58   "Provided . . ." Vol. II, p. 152.

58   "a long debate" *Records of the . . . Massachusetts Bay*, Shurtleff (ed.), Vol. I, p. 51.

58   "As many of you . . ." Same.

59   "to a further trust . . ." *Winthrop Papers*, Vol. II, p. 161.

59   "Blessed be God . . ." Same, Vol. II, p. 168.

59   "I see . . ." Same, Vol. II, p. 177.

59   "It is a policy . . ." Same, Vol. I, p. 236.

59   "At a Court . . ." *Records of the . . . Massachusetts Bay*, Shurtleff (ed.), Vol. I, p. 70.

60   "I will appoint . . ." *II Samuel* 7:10 and John Cotton, *Gods Promise to His Plantation* (London, 1630), p. 1.

60   "to the rest . . ." *The Humble Request of His Majesties Loyall Subjects* (London, 1630), title page.

60   "ever acknowledging . . ." Same, p. 4.

60   "the joint asseveration . . ." *John White's Planters Plea* (1630), p. 59.

60   "dearly beloved . . ." *Winthrop Papers*, Vol. II, p. 50.

60   "by the fireside . . ." "Thomas Dudley's Letter to the Countess of Lincoln," *Tracts and Other Papers*, Force (ed.), Vol. II, p. 5 of letter.

60   "false and scandalous . . ." Same, p. 15.

61   "either in . . ." Same.

61   "denied baptism . . ." "John Cotton's Letter to Samuel Skelton," edited by David D. Hall, *William and Mary Quarterly* (July 1965), p. 480.

61   "I am afraid . . ." Same, p. 482.

61   "only as a sign . . ." *Winthrop's Journal*, "History of New England," *1630–1649*, edited by James Kendall Hosmer, 2 vols. (New York: Charles Scribner's Sons, 1908), Vol. I, p. 52.

61   "betwixt presbytery . . ." Fuller, *Church History of Britain* (Oxford, 1845), Vol. VI, p. 277.

61   "Both our practice . . ." *Winthrop Papers*, Vol. III, p. 139.

61   "clearer light . . ." Same, Vol. III, p. 172.

62   "to be poisoned . . ." *The Autobiography and Correspondence of Sir Simonds D'Ewes, Bart.*, edited by J. O. Halliwell, 2 vols. (London, 1845), Vol. II, p. 113.

62   "I could not . . ." Same, Vol. II, p. 112.

62   "About thirty . . ." *Winthrop Papers*, Vol. III, p. 200.

62   "holy society" Same, Vol. III, p. 321.

62   "costliness . . ." *Winthrop's Journal*, Hosmer (ed.), Vol. I, p. 279.

63   "divers of the elders' wives . . ." Same.

63   "not the multitude . . ." *John White's Planters Plea*, p. 63.

63   "of such as desire . . ." *Records of the . . . Massachusetts Bay*, Shurtleff (ed.), Vol. I, p. 79.

64   "For the establishing . . ." Same.

64   "For explanation . . ." Same, Vol. I, p. 87.

64   "unfit instruments" See page 57.

64   "the body of the commons . . ." *Records of the . . . Massachusetts Bay*, Shurtleff (ed.), Vol. I, p. 87.

65   "very strict . . ." Cotton Mather, *Magnalia Christi Americana* (London, 1702), Book Three, p. 197.

65   "that it was not safe . . ." *Winthrop's Journal*, Hosmer (ed.), Vol. I, p. 74.

65   "much debate" Same.

65   "The ground . . ." Same.

66   "their submission . . ." Same, Vol. I, p. 75.

66   "We should incur . . ." *Winthrop Papers*, Vol. IV, p. 388.

66   "grew into passion . . ." *Winthrop's Journal*, Hosmer (ed.), Vol. I, p. 78.

66   "He told them . . ." Same, Vol. I, p. 122.

66   "but not to make . . ." Same.

67   "None but the General Court . . ." *Records of the . . . Massachusetts Bay*, Shurtleff (ed.), Vol. I, pp. 117–18.

67   "All things . . ." *Winthrop's Journal*, Hosmer (ed.), Vol. I, p. 125.

67   "Being much divided . . ." Same, Vol. I, p. 71.

67   "In Boston . . ." Thomas Lechford, *New-Englands Advice to Old-England* (London, 1644), p. 14.

67 *fn.*   "Your overcoming . . ." Same, Vol. I, p. 114.

68   "When our teacher . . ." Thomas Hutchinson, *The History of the Province of Massachusetts Bay*, 2 Vols. (Boston, 1795), Vol. II, p. 440.

68   "an immediate revelation . . ." Same, Vol. II, p. 439.

68 *fn.*   "freemen at Marblehead . . ." *Records of the . . . Massachusetts Bay,* Shurtleff (ed.), Vol. II, p. 57.

69   "Sir Henry Vane . . ." James K. Hosmer, *The Life of Young Sir Henry Vane* (Boston: Houghton Mifflin and Company, 1888), p. 12.

69   "lead the rest . . ." Same.

69   "an obedient child . . ." *Winthrop's Journal,* Hosmer (ed.), Vol. I, p. 203.

69   "fierce speeches . . ." Same, Vol. I, p. 215.

69   "there was great . . ." Same.

69 *fn.*   "admitted . . ." *Records of the . . . Massachusetts Bay,* Shurtleff (ed.), Vol. I, p. 168.

69 *fn.*   "some blasphemous . . ." *Winthrop's Journal,* Hosmer (ed.), Vol. I, p. 232.

70   "were so divided . . ." Same, Vol. I, p. 257.

70   "committed her . . ." Same, Vol. I, p. 240.

70   "You have stept . . ." *Antinomianism in the Colony of Massachusetts Bay, 1636–1638,* edited by Charles Francis Adams (Boston: Prince Society Publications, 1894), p. 329.

70   "The ministers . . ." *Winthrop Papers,* Vol. IV, p. 493.

71   "very, very useful" Same, Vol. V, p. 30.

71   "went daily . . ." *Winthrop's Journal,* Hosmer (ed.), Vol. I, p. 115.

71   "at novelty . . ." "New-Englands Jonas Cast up at London," 1647, *Tracts and Other Papers,* Force (ed.), Vol. IV, p. 9.

71   "those who are . . ." Same, p. 8.

71   "liberties . . ." *Federal and State Constitutions,* Thorpe (ed.), Vol. III, p. 1857.

71   "too much unwarranted . . ." "New-Englands Jonas," *Tracts and Other Papers,* Force (ed.), Vol. IV, p. 11.

72   "Their deputies . . ." Thomas Hutchinson, *A Collection of Original Papers Relative to the History of the Colony of Massachusetts-Bay* (Boston, 1769), p. 202.

72   "Our deputies . . ." Same, p. 203.

72   "the very life . . ." *Winthrop's Journal,* Hosmer (ed.), Vol. II, p. 316.

72   "tending to sedition" Same, Vol. II, p. 297.

72   "If any man . . ." "New-Englands Jonas," *Tracts and Other Papers,* Force (ed.), Vol. IV, p. 17.

72   "Your father . . ." *Winthrop Papers,* Vol. V, pp. 140–41.

72   "Great laboring . . ." *Winthrop's Journal,* Hosmer (ed.), Vol. II, p. 323.

73   "Be tender . . ." *Winthrop Papers,* Vol. V, pp. 146–47.

Chapter Four

74   "Each ear . . ." Morton, *New-England's Memoriall,* 1669, p. 128.

75   "Sir, I see . . ." Cotton Mather, *Magnalia Christi Americana,* Book Three, p. 65.

75   "Indeed I was . . ." Same.

75   "service . . ." Hutchinson, *Collection of Original Papers Relative to . . . Massachusetts-Bay* (Boston, 1769), p. 56.

75   "After Mr. Hooker's . . ." William Hubbard, *A General History of New England from the Discovery to MDCLXXX* (Cambridge: Massachusetts Historical Society, 1815), p. 165.

75   "considering . . ." *Winthrop's Journal,* Hosmer (ed.), Vol. I, p. 133.

76   "Mr. Cotton . . ." Hubbard, *General History of New England,* p. 175.

76	"for their own . . . such houses . . ." Gilman C. Gates, *Saybrook at the Mouth of the Connecticut* (Connecticut, 1935), p. 14.
77	"Certain proposals . . ." Hutchinson, *History of . . . Massachusetts Bay* (1795), Vol. I, p. 433.
77	"two distinct . . ." Same.
77	"the Right Honorable . . ." Same, Vol. I, p. 434.
77	"by the consent . . ." Same.
77	"of leveling . . ." Edward Hyde, Earl of Clarendon, *The History of the Rebellion and Civil Wars in England,* edited by W. D. Macray, 6 vols. (Oxford: Clarendon Press, 1888), Vol. II, p. 547.
77	"a man . . ." *Two Speeches in Parliament of the Right Honorable William, Lord Viscount Say and Seale* (London, 1641), p. 9.
77	"the will . . ." Hutchinson, *History of . . . Massachusetts-Bay* (1795), Vol. I, p. 438.
77	"Nor need . . ." Same, Vol. I, p. 439.
77	"Democracy . . ." Same, Vol. I, p. 437.
77	"leading men . . ." Same, Vol. I, p. 439.
78	"this taxation . . ." D'Ewes, *Autobiography* (1845), Vol. II, p. 130.
78	"because each . . ." Rushworth, *Historical Collections* (1721), Vol. II, p. 505.
78	"Surely this argument . . ." Same, Vol. II, p. 585.
78 fn.	"No scutage . . ." *Select Documents of English Constitutional History,* Adams and Stephens (eds.), p. 44.
79	"women and . . ." *Winthrop's Journal,* Hosmer (ed.), Vol. I, p. 163.
79	"many houses . . ." "The Autobiography of Thomas Shepard," *Publications of the Colonial Society of Massachusetts* (Boston, 1932), Vol. XXVII, p. 384.
79	"full power . . ." R. V. Coleman, *The Old Patent of Connecticut* (Westport, 1936), p. 31.
79	"submit to . . ." p. 32.
79	"right and pretence . . ." Same.
79	"noble personages . . ." *Records of the . . . Massachusetts Bay,* Shurtleff (ed.), Vol. I, pp. 170–71.
80	"on the behalf" Same, Vol. I, p. 170.
80	"with the good liking . . ." Same, Vol. I, p. 171.
80	"the said inhabitants . . ." Same.
80	"holden at Newtown" *The Public Records of the Colony of Connecticut,* edited by J. Hammond Trumbull, 15 vols. (Hartford, 1850–1890), Vol. I, p. 1.
80	"His wife . . ." *Winthrop's Journal,* Hosmer (ed.), Vol. I, p. 181.
80	"like so many . . ." Coleman, *Old Patent of Connecticut,* p. 38.
80	"the time of our election" *Collections of the Connecticut Historical Society,* (Hartford, 1860–1924), Vol. I, p. 13.
81	"the magistrates . . ." Same, Vol. I, p. 1.
81	"two errors . . ." *Winthrop's Journal,* Hosmer (ed.), Vol. I, p. 289.
81	"I expostulated . . ." Same, Vol. I, p. 290.
81	"in matters . . ." *Collections of the Connecticut Historical Society,* Vol. I, p. 12.
81	"I must confess . . ." Same, Vol. I, p. 11.
81	"some rules . . ." R. V. Coleman, *A Note Concerning the Formulation of the Fundamental Orders Uniting the Three River Towns of Connecticut, 1639* (Westport, 1934), p. 7.
81	"join hearts . . ." Same.
81	"Take you . . ." *Deuteronomy* 1:13.

82   "The choice . . ." George Leon Walker, *Thomas Hooker* (New York: Dodd, Mead and Company, 1891), p. 125.

82   "To persuade . . ." Same.

82   "Forasmuch . . ." *Federal and State Constitutions,* Thorpe (ed.), Vol. I, p. 519.

82   "the supreme . . ." Same, Vol. I, p. 522.

82   "member . . ." Same, Vol. I, p. 520.

82   "a larger compass . . ." Hubbard, *General History of New England,* p. 309.

83   "been admitted . . ." *Federal and State Constitutions,* Thorpe (ed.), Vol. I, p. 520.

83   "It is ordered . . ." *Public Records of the Colony of Connecticut,* Trumbull (ed.), Vol. I, p. 8.

83   "by delaying . . ." Cotton Mather, *Magnalia Christi Americana,* Book Three, p. 66.

83   "in great peace . . ." Hubbard, *General History of New England,* p. 313.

84   "viewed . . ." *Winthrop's Journal,* Hosmer (ed.), Vol. I, p. 231.

85   "free to cast . . ." *Federal and State Constitutions,* Thorpe (ed.), Vol. I, p. 524.

85   "free burgesses . . ." Same, Vol. I, p. 525.

85   "the power of . . ." Same.

85   "that free planters . . ." Same.

85   "He came doubting . . ." Same.

85   "One from among . . ." *Deuteronomy* 17:15.

86   "where Master Davenport . . ." Lechford, *New-Englands Advice* (1644), p. 13.

86   "the drain or sink . . ." Jeremy Belknap, *The History of New-Hampshire,* 3 vols. (Philadelphia, 1784), Vol. I, p. 89.

86   "very tempestuous . . ." *Winthrop's Journal,* Hosmer (ed.), Vol. I, p. 57.

86   "Mr. Penry . . ." *The Complete Writings of Roger Williams,* 7 vols. (New York: Russell and Russell, Inc., 1963), Vol. I, pp. 380–81.

87   "Your dear father . . ." Same, Vol. VI, p. 239.

87   "I durst not . . ." Same, Vol. VI, p. 356.

87   "began to fall . . ." Bradford, *Of Plymouth Plantation,* Morison (ed.), p. 257.

87   "the religion . . ." *Winthrop Papers,* Vol. III, p. 148.

87   "I hope . . ." Bradford, *Of Plymouth Plantation,* Morison (ed.), p. 257.

87   "full of . . ." *Winthrop's Journal,* Hosmer (ed.), Vol. I, p. 162.

88   "broached . . ." *Records of the . . . Massachusetts Bay,* Shurtleff (ed.), Vol. I, p. 160.

88   "had drawn . . ." *Winthrop's Journal,* Hosmer (ed.), Vol. I, p. 168.

88   "which I feel . . ." Roger Williams, *Complete Writings,* Vol. VI, p. 335.

88   "I sometimes . . ." Same, Vol. VI, p. 99.

88   "The condition . . ." Same, Vol. VI, p. 4.

89   "We whose names are hereunder written . . ." Same, Vol. VI, p. 5.

89   "We whose names are hereunder, desirous . . ." *The Early Records of the Town of Providence* (Providence: Record Commissioners, 1892), Vol. I, p. 1.

89   "only in civil . . ." Same.

89   "persons . . ." Howard M. Chapin, *Documentary History of Rhode Island,* 2 vols. (Providence, 1919), Vol. I, p. 27.

89   "great questions . . ." John Cotton, *The Bloudy Tenent, Washed, and Made White in the Bloud of the Lambe* (London, 1647), title page.

90   "to turbulent . . ." Same.

90   "that body-killing . . ." Roger Williams, *Complete Writings,* Vol. I, p. 328.

90   "out of conscience . . ." *Winthrop's Journal,* Hosmer (ed.), Vol. I, p. 287.

90   "It was agreed . . ." *Early Records of the Town of Providence,* Vol. I, p. 4.

90   "discard him . . ." Roger Williams, *Complete Writings,* Vol. VI, p. 96.

90   "his poison" Same, Vol. VI, p. 142.

91   "were written . . ." Kenneth W. Porter, "Samuell Gorton, New England Firebrand," *The New England Quarterly* (September 1934), p. 443.

91   "We are come . . ." Chapin, *Documentary History of Rhode Island,* Vol. I, p. 172.

91   "that we are persecutors . . ." Edward Winslow, *Hypocrisie Vnmasked* (1646), pp. 60–61.

91   "Some few . . ." Roger Williams, *Complete Writings,* Vol. VI, p. 142.

91   "Whether . . ." Same, Vol. VI, p. 6.

92   "Lend us . . ." Edward Winslow, *Hypocrisie Vnmasked,* p. 58.

92   "no manner of . . ." Same, p. 56.

92   "It hath been told . . ." Roger Williams, *Complete Writings,* Vol. VI, pp. 263–64.

92   "the deep snow . . ." John Wheelwright, *Mercurius Americanus* (London, 1645), p. 24.

92   "Considering . . ." *Federal and State Constitutions,* Thorpe (ed.), Vol. IV, p. 2445.

93   "We were now . . ." John Clarke, *Ill Newes from New-England,* 1652, *Collections of the Massachusetts Historical Society,* series 4, no. 2 (Boston, 1854), p. 24.

93   "We whose names . . ." Samuel Greene Arnold, *History of the State of Rhode Island and Providence Plantations,* 3 vols. (New York, 1859), Vol. I, p. 124.

93   "a very honest . . ." *A Short Story of the Rise, Reign and Ruine of the Antinomians . . .* (London, 1644), p. 31.

93   "contrary minded" Hutchinson, *History of the Province of Massachusetts Bay* (1795), Vol. II, p. 447.

93   "I was not willing . . ." *Winthrop Papers,* Vol. IV, p. 246.

94   "perfect rule . . ." *Federal and State Constitutions,* Thorpe (ed.), Vol. I, p. 523.

94   "It is ordered . . ." Chapin, *Documentary History of Rhode Island,* Vol. II, p. 34.

94   "of Mrs. Hutchinson's . . ." *Winthrop's Journal,* Hosmer (ed.), Vol. I, p. 273.

95   "very tumultuous" Same, Vol. I, p. 299.

95   "It is agreed . . ." Arnold, *History of . . . Rhode Island,* Vol. I, p. 132.

95   "in his name" Same, Vol. I, p. 133.

96   "ordered, by the authority . . ." *Federal and State Constitutions,* Thorpe (ed.), Vol. VI, p. 3208.

96   "It is ordered and unanimously agreed . . ." Same, Vol. VI, p. 3207.

96   "A democracy . . ." *Winthrop Papers,* Vol. IV, p. 383.

96   "the island . . ." *A Short Story of . . . the Antinomians* (1644), near end of Preface.

96   "great strife . . ." Same.

96   "just asses" Edward Winslow, *Hypocrisie Vnmasked* (1646), p. 54.

96   "That inhabitants . . ." Chapin, *Documentary History of Rhode Island,* Vol. I, p. 265.

96 *fn.*   "gorbellied . . ." *Black Book of Warwick,* Kemp (ed.), p. 373.

97   "a free charter . . . full power . . . by the name . . ." *Federal and State Constitutions,* Thorpe (ed.), Vol. VI, p. 3210.

97   "Isle of Rhodes . . ." Irving Berdine Richman, *Rhode Island, Its Making and Meaning* (New York: G. P. Putnam's Sons, 1908), p. 242.

97   "in this bay . . ." Same, p. 242 fn.

97   "All men . . ." Same, p. 260.

97   "The form of government . . ." Same, p. 246.

Chapter Five

99   "without charge . . ." *Records of the Virginia Company,* Kingsbury (ed.), Vol. III, p. 608.

99   "receptacle . . ." Peter Heylyn, *Cyprianus Anglicus* (London, 1668), p. 369.

99   "ease and tranquility" Hubbard, *General History of New England,* p. 264.

99   "by imprisonment . . ." Same, p. 265.

99   "for the managing . . ." *Records of the . . . Massachusetts Bay,* Shurtleff (ed.), Vol. I, p. 125.

100   "It shall be lawful . . ." Same, Vol. I, p. 138.

100   "defend . . ." *Winthrop's Journal,* Hosmer (ed.), Vol. I, p. 145.

100   "If our patent . . ." Hubbard, *General History of New England,* p. 270.

100   "a great service . . ." *The Works of Archbishop Laud,* 7 vols. (Oxford, 1857), Vol. VI, p. 554.

100   "that stubborn kirk . . ." John Hacket, *Scrinia Reserata* (London, 1693), p. 64.

100   "pack of discontented . . ." John Gutch, *Collectanea Curiosa,* 2 vols. (Oxford: Clarendon Press, 1781), Vol. I, p. 238.

101   "they had now . . ." Clarendon, *History of the Rebellion* (Oxford, 1888), Vol. I, p. 222.

101   "be razed . . ." Rushworth, *Historical Collections* (1721), Vol. III, p. 217 of the Appendix.

101   "to the public good . . ." *Stuart Constitution,* Kenyon (ed.), p. 231.

101   "I have neither . . ." Rushworth, *Historical Collections* (1721), Vol. IV, p. 478.

101   "much altered . . ." *The Dictionary of National Biography,* 22 vols. (Oxford: Oxford University Press, 1921–1922), Vol. VIII, p. 1143.

102   "Little . . ." Bradford, *Of Plymouth Plantation,* Morison (ed.), pp. 351–52.

102   "so horrible" Peter Heylyn, *Cyprianus Anglicus* (1668) p. 499.

103   "establish church . . ." Thomas Edwards, *Gangraena* (London, 1646), Part Three, p. 218.

103   "all pulpits . . ." Clarendon, *History of the Rebellion* (1888), Vol. I, p. 269.

103   "under the new name . . ." "Governor Bradford's Dialogue," *Chronicles of the Pilgrim Fathers,* Young (ed.), p. 422.

103   "the bloody tenet . . ." Roger Williams, *Complete Writings,* Vol. III, p. 1.

103   "the grand design . . ." Edwards, *Gangraena,* Part One, p. 153.

103   "What will you do with men dissenting?" See page 73.

103   "The two things . . ." Edwards, *Gangraena,* Part Three, p. 140.

104   "headed . . ." Richard Baxter, *Reliquiae Baxterianae* (London, 1696), p. 57.

104   "The chiefest . . ." *The Letters, Speeches and Proclamations of King Charles I,* edited by Charles Petrie (London: Cassell and Company, Ltd., 1935), pp. 205–206.

104   "While the common . . ." *Winthrop Papers,* Vol. V, p. 206.

104   "the hobnails . . ." Joseph Frank, *The Levellers* (Cambridge: Harvard University Press, 1955), p. 132.

105   "A great part . . ." Baxter, *Reliquiae Baxterianae* (1696), p. 53.

105   "in their quarters . . ." Same, p. 53.

105   "the only and sole" H. N. Brailsford, *The Levellers and the English Revolution* (London: The Cresset Press, 1961), p. 117.

106   "A council . . ." C. H. Firth, *Cromwell's Army* (London: Methuen and Company, 1902), p. 57.

106   "who now in prudence . . ." *The Clarke Papers,* edited by C. H. Firth (London: The Camden Society, 1891), p. 214.

107   "Each county . . ." Frank, *The Levellers,* p. 123.

107   "The thing contrived . . ." Baxter, *Reliquiae Baxterianae* (1696), p. 61.

107 *fn.*   "the greatest . . ." Rushworth, *Historical Collections* (1721), Vol. IV, p. 762.

108   "a liberal . . ." *Puritanism and Liberty, Being the Army Debates (1647-9) from the Clarke Manuscripts with Supplementary Documents,* edited by A.S.P. Woodhouse (London: J. M. Dent & Sons, Ltd., 1938), p. 17.

108   "It is not enough . . ." *Puritanism and Liberty,* Woodhouse (ed.), p. 8.

108   "the spirits . . ." Same.

108   "he had the hardest . . ." Edward Peacock, "Notes on the Life of Thomas Rainborowe," *Archaeologia* (London, 1881), Vol. XLVI, p. 16.

108   "resolution . . ." Same.

109   "Let the difficulties . . ." *Puritanism and Liberty,* Woodhouse (ed.), p. 14.

109   "the people of England" Same, p. 443.

109   "the meaning is . . ." Same, p. 52.

109   "Really I think . . ." Same, p. 53.

109   "Give me leave . . ." Same.

109   "I think that no person . . ." Same, pp. 53-54.

110   "that is, the persons . . ." Same, p. 54.

110   "Neither by the law . . ." Same, p. 56.

110   "those who are . . ." Same.

110   "The foundation . . ." Same.

110   "permanent interest . . ." Same, p. 57.

110   "we are free . . ." Same, p. 58.

110   "By that same . . ." Same.

110   "I wish you would not . . ." Same, p. 59.

110   "must end in anarchy" Same.

110   "the interest of breathing" Same.

110   "I would fain know what we have fought for" Same, p. 61.

111   "which enslaves . . ." Same.

111   "I still say . . ." Same, p. 67.

111   "I would fain know what the soldier . . ." Same, p. 71.

111   "Perhaps there are . . ." Same, p. 73.

111   "I will agree . . ." Same, p. 77.

111   "Every person . . ." Same, p. 66.

111   "the army might . . ." Same, pp. 85-86.

112   "of settling . . ." F. Maseres, *Select Tracts Relating to the Civil Wars in England,* 2 vols. (London, 1815), Vol. I, pp. xliv-xlv.

112   "informed . . ." Same, Vol. I, p. xli.

112   "I . . . drew out . . ." Same.

112   "a leveling . . ." Gutch, *Collectanea Curiosa* (1781), Vol. I, p. 250.

112	"and monarchy . . ." C. V. Wedgwood, *A Coffin for King Charles* (New York: The Macmillan Company, 1964), p. 153.
112	"as a tyrant . . ." *Letters, Speeches and Proclamations of King Charles I,* Petrie (ed.), p. 258.
112	"This is my second . . ." Fuller, *Church History of Britain* (1845), Vol. VI, p. 425.
112	"not their having . . ." John A. R. Marriott, *The Crisis of English Liberty* (Oxford: Clarendon Press, 1930), p. 242.
113	"I can tell you . . ." Philip Warwick, *Memoires of the Reigne of King Charles I* (London, 1701), p. 177.
113	"This House . . ." *The Writings and Speeches of Oliver Cromwell,* edited by Wilbur Cortez Abbott, 4 vols. (Cambridge: Harvard University Press, 1937–1947), Vol. II, p. 646.
114	"a free Parliament" Same, Vol. III, p. 458.
115	"sent his wife . . ." *The Speeches and Prayers of Some of the Late King's Judges* (London, 1660), p. 1.
115	"I have many a time . . ." Same, p. 2.

Chapter Six

116	"see were erroneous . . ." Thomas Carte, *A Collection of Original Letters and Papers . . . Found Among the Duke of Ormonde's Papers,* 2 vols. (London, 1739), Vol. II, p. 319.
117	"residing at Leyden . . ." *Documents Relative to the Colonial History of the State of New-York,* edited by E. B. O'Callaghan, 15 vols. (Albany, 1853–1887), Vol. I, p. 22.
117	"to plant . . ." Same, Vol. I, p. 23.
117	"chambers of managers" *Federal and State Constitutions,* Thorpe (ed.), Vol. I, p. 61.
117	"The colonizing . . ." *Documents Relative to . . . New-York,* O'Callaghan (ed.), Vol. I, p. 39.
118	"unsuitable government" Same, Vol. I, p. 259.
118	"that those interested . . ." Same, Vol. I, p. 266.
118	"Each colony . . . Few taxes . . . The Governor . . ." Same.
118	"fairest soil . . ." Same, Vol. I, p. 359.
118 fn.	"chosen . . ." *Federal and State Constitutions,* Thorpe (ed.), Vol. I, p. 519.
119	"a dangerous . . ." *Winthrop Papers,* Vol. IV, p. 456.
119	"place called . . ." *A Short Story of the . . . Antinomians* (1644), near end of Preface.
119	"to erect . . ." *Laws and Ordinances of New Netherland, 1628–1674,* edited by E. B. O'Callaghan (Albany, 1868), p. 54.
119	"For we are . . ." *Documents Relative to . . . New-York,* O'Callaghan (ed.), Vol. II, p. 156.
120	"We humbly . . ." E. B. O'Callaghan, *History of New Netherland,* 2 vols. (New York: D. Appleton and Company, 1848), Vol. II, p. 245.
120	"Each would vote . . ." Same, Vol. II, p. 250.
120	"Is there . . ." Same, Vol. II, p. 247.
120	"We derive . . ." Same, Vol. II, p. 252.
120	"faction . . ." Same, Vol. II, p. 266.
120	"We, individuals . . ." *Documents Relative to . . . New-York,* O'Callaghan (ed.), Vol. II, p. 152.

120   "for the English . . ." Same, Vol. I, 269.

121   "to correct . . ." *Federal and State Constitutions,* Thorpe (ed.), Vol. III, p. 1638.

121   "desirous . . ." *The Glorious Revolution in America,* edited by Michael G. Hall, Lawrence H. Leder and Michael G. Kammen (Chapel Hill: University of North Carolina Press, 1964), p. 93.

121   "nothing being . . ." Same, p. 94.

122   "body corporate . . ." *Federal and State Constitutions,* Thorpe (ed.), Vol. I, p. 530.

122   "a body corporate . . ." Same, Vol. VI, p. 3213.

122   "lively experiment . . ." Thomas W. Bicknell, *Story of Dr. John Clarke* (Providence, 1915), p. 192.

122   "They crouched . . ." Viola Florence Barnes, *The Dominion of New England* (New Haven: Yale University Press, 1923), p. 5 fn.

123   "advice, assent . . ." *Federal and State Constitutions,* Thorpe (ed.), Vol. V, p. 2745.

123   "by the love . . ." Hazard, *Historical Collections* (1792), Vol. I, p. 165.

124   "this equal sap . . ." *The Oceana of James Harrington and His Other Works,* edited by John Toland (London, 1700), p. 204.

124   "Freemen are . . ." Same, p. 436.

124   "to set up . . ." Same, p. xx.

125   "that excellent . . ." Maurice Cranston, *John Locke, A Biography* (New York: Longmans, Green and Company, 1957), p. 120.

125   "the sacred . . ." *Federal and State Constitutions,* Thorpe (ed.), Vol. V, p. 2786.

125   "suppress popular liberty" See page 19.

125   "avoid erecting . . ." *Federal and State Constitutions,* Thorpe (ed.), Vol. V, p. 2772.

126   "until the Statute . . ." Harrington, *Oceana* (1700), p. 40.

126   "rules of precedency" *The Fundamental Constitutions of Carolina* (London, 1670), last page.

126   "the noble government . . ." H. F. Russell Smith, *Harrington and His Oceana* (Cambridge: Cambridge University Press, 1914), p. 161.

126   "imitating . . ." M. Eugene Sirmans, *Colonial South Carolina* (Chapel Hill: University of North Carolina Press, 1966), p. 69.

126   "so disrespectfully . . ." Charles M. Andrews, *The Colonial Period of American History,* 4 vols. (New Haven: Yale University Press, 1936), Vol. III, p. 220.

127   "just and . . ." *The Poetical Works of Robert Herrick,* edited by L. C. Martin (Oxford: Clarendon Press, 1956), p. 252.

127   "cities, towns . . ." *Federal and State Constitutions,* Thorpe (ed.), Vol. V, p. 2544.

127   "The father of . . ." Hazard, *Historical Collections* (1794), Vol. II, p. 571.

128   "The Quakers . . ." Same, Vol. II, p. 581.

128   "the spirit . . ." Roger Williams, *Complete Writings,* Vol. V, p. 41.

128   "wilderness . . ." John E. Pomfret, *The Province of West New Jersey, 1609–1702* (Princeton: Princeton University Press, 1956), p. 60.

128   "no little labor . . ." *Documents Relating to the Colonial History of the State of New Jersey,* edited by William A. Whitehead, Vol. I, 1631–1687 (Newark, 1880) [New Jersey Historical Society Archives, Series 1, Vol. I], pp. 232–33.

129   "both the King . . ." *The Diary of Samuel Pepys,* edited by Henry B.

Wheatley, 10 vols. (London: G. Bell and Sons, Ltd., 1928–1935), Vol. II, p. 19.

129   "he was pleased . . ." William Penn, "Fragments of an Apology for Himself," *Memoirs of the Historical Society of Pennsylvania* (Philadelphia, 1834), Vol. III, Part Two, p. 242.

129 *fn.*   "he had seen . . ." Same, pp. 241–42.

130   "preparing" John E. Pomfret, "The Problem of the West Jersey *Concessions* of 1676/7," *William and Mary Quarterly* (January 1948), p. 104.

130   "We lay . . ." *Documents Relating to . . . New Jersey,* Whitehead (ed.), Vol. I, p. 228.

130   "extinguish . . ." Pomfret, "Problem of the West Jersey *Concessions,*" *William and Mary Quarterly* (January 1948), p. 98.

131   "be guilty . . ." William A. Whitehead, *New Jersey under the Proprietary Governments* (Newark, 1846), p. 311.

131   "Lest any . . ." Same, p. 268.

131   "one rose . . ." Samuel M. Janney, *The Life of William Penn, with Selections from his Correspondence* (Philadelphia, 1852), p. 187.

132   "after many waitings . . ." Same, p. 156.

132   "You shall be governed . . ." Same, p. 159.

132   "As my understanding . . ." Same, p. 163.

132   "a considerable . . ." Same, p. 183.

133   "a certain part . . ." Julius F. Sachse, "Benjamin Furly," *The Pennsylvania Magazine of History and Biography* (October 1895), p. 299.

133   "the virtue . . ." "The Fundamental Constitutions of Pennsylvania," *The Pennsylvania Magazine of History and Biography,* Vol. XX, no. 3 (1896), p. 285.

133   "Since it hath . . ." Same, pp. 287–88.

133   "assent . . ." *Federal and State Constitutions,* Thorpe (ed.), Vol. V, p. 3057.

134   "there being nothing . . ." Same, Vol. V, p. 3053.

134   "stage plays . . ." Same, Vol. V, p. 3063.

134   "I far prefer . . ." Sachse, "Benjamin Furly," *Pennsylvania Magazine of History and Biography* (October 1895), pp. 303–304.

134   "the power of making . . ." Same, p. 304.

134   "a divesting . . ." Same.

134   "For the people . . ." Same.

134   "the very root . . ." Gary B. Nash, "The Framing of Government in Pennsylvania; Ideas in Contact with Reality," *William and Mary Quarterly* (April 1966), p. 199.

134   "not a debating . . ." Same.

134   "glorious river" *A Letter from William Penn . . . to the Committee of the Free Society of Traders* (London, 1683), p. 8.

135   "They have . . ." William Penn, *A further account of the province of Pennsylvania and its improvements* (London [?], 1685), p. 14.

135   "a certain foundation . . ." Sachse, "Benjamin Furly," *Pennsylvania Magazine of History and Biography* (October 1895), p. 304.

135   "concord . . ." *A Letter from William Penn . . . to the Committee of the Free Society of Traders* (1683), p. 8.

136   "powers and privileges . . ." *Federal and State Constitutions,* Thorpe (ed.), Vol. V, p. 3078.

136   "Ye shall hallow . . ." *Leviticus* 25:10.

136   "those three preposterous . . ." *Correspondence between William Penn and*

James Logan, Secretary of the Province of Pennsylvania, and Others, 1700–1750, edited by Edward Armstrong, 2 vols. (Philadelphia: The Historical Society of Pennsylvania, 1870–1872), Vol. I, p. 375.

136   "As a father . . ." Same, Vol. I, pp. 373–74.

136   "the just order . . ." Same, Vol. I, pp. 374–75.

137   "decline into . . ." Same, Vol. II, p. 365.

137   "to such as value . . ." Same.

137   "Before any one family . . ." Janney, *Life of William Penn*, p. 516.

137   "due proportion . . ." Same.

137   "Seeing the frame . . ." Same, p. 517.

137   "the law of Nature" O'Callaghan, *History of New Netherland*, Vol. II, p. 252.

137   "right belonging . . ." Albert Edward McKinley, *The Suffrage Franchise in the Thirteen English Colonies in America* (Philadelphia: Ginn and Company, 1905), p. 242.

138   "No nation . . ." *The American Heritage Pictorial Atlas of United States History* (New York: American Heritage Publishing Company, Inc., 1966), p. 55.

Chapter Seven

139   "the mouth of equal liberty" See page 19.

139   "every man . . ." See page 17.

139   "what freeman . . ." *The Statutes at Large: Being a Collection of All the Laws of Virginia, from the First Session of the Legislature in the Year 1619*, edited by William Waller Hening, 13 vols. (Richmond, etc., 1810–1823), Vol. I, p. 334.

140   "I conceive . . ." *Puritanism and Liberty*, Woodhouse (ed.), p. 83.

140   "Do but follow . . ." *Journals of the House of Burgesses of Virginia*, McIlwaine (ed.), Vol. I, p. 76.

140   "We conceive . . ." *Statutes at Large . . . of Virginia*, Hening (ed.), Vol I, p. 403.

140 fn.   "four of our . . ." Pepys, *Diary*, Wheatley (ed.), Vol. I, p. 330.

141   "manslaughters . . ." See page 16.

141   "people of small . . ." *Select Documents of English Constitutional History*, Adams and Stephens (eds.), p. 190.

141   "Whereas . . ." *Statutes at Large . . . of Virginia*, Hening (ed.), Vol. II, p. 280.

141   "the inordinate . . ." *Records of the Virginia Company*, Kingsbury (ed.), Vol. I, p. 413.

141   "some restraint . . ." Hazard, *Historical Collections* (1794), Vol. II, p. 609.

141   "six parts . . ." Wilcomb E. Washburn, *The Governor and the Rebel, A History of Bacon's Rebellion in Virginia* (Chapel Hill: University of North Carolina Press, 1957), p. 31.

141   "Gentlemen . . ." Richard L. Morton, *Colonial Virginia*, 2 vols. (Chapel Hill: University of North Carolina Press, 1960), Vol. I, p. 241.

142   "protected . . ." Bacon's Manifesto, *Settlements to Society, 1584–1763*, edited by Jack P. Greene (New York: McGraw-Hill Book Company, 1966), p. 180.

142   "the benefit . . ." Same, p. 181.

142   "There were said . . ." "Bacon's Rebellion," *William and Mary Quarterly* (July 1900), p. 10.

142   "At this new . . ." Report of the commissioners, *Narratives of the Insurrec-tions, 1675–1690,* edited by Charles M. Andrews (New York: Charles Scrib-ner's Sons, 1915), p. 113.

142   "and supposing . . ." Washburn, *The Governor and the Rebel,* p. 41.

142   "we ought not . . ." *Statutes at Large . . . of Virginia,* Hening (ed.), Vol. II, p. 342.

142   "unlawful assemblies . . ." Same, Vol. II, p. 353.

142   "Be it enacted . . ." Same, Vol. II, p. 356.

143   "the darling . . ." "The History of Bacon's and Ingram's Rebellion," *Nar-ratives of the Insurrections,* Andrews (ed.), p. 55.

143   "leveling" "Bacon's Rebellion," *William and Mary Quarterly* (July 1900), p. 9.

143   "We find them . . ." Same.

143   "Three young men . . ." Washburn, *The Governor and the Rebel,* p. 69.

143   "with all its wealth . . ." *Narratives of the Insurrections,* Andrews (ed.), p. 136 fn.

143   "the old fool . . ." Same, p. 40.

143   "no hero . . ." Aphra Behn, *The Widdow Ranter or The History of Bacon in Virginia* (London, 1690), p. 4.

143   "dear prize . . ." Same, p. 51.

144   "elected . . ." *Statutes at Large . . . of Virginia,* Hening (ed.), Vol. II, p. 425.

144   "What man . . ." McKinley, *Suffrage Franchise in the Thirteen English Colonies,* p. 65.

144   "of ten shillings" Stephen Foster, "The Massachusetts Franchise in the Seventeenth Century," *William and Mary Quarterly* (October 1967), p. 618.

145   "a house and land . . ." *Federal and State Constitutions,* Thorpe (ed.), Vol. V, p. 2575.

145   "every freeholder . . ." Charles Z. Lincoln, *The Constitutional History of New York,* 5 vols. (Rochester, 1906), Vol. I. p. 97.

145   "By freeholders . . ." Same.

145   "persons in whom . . ." See page 110.

145   "a permanent fixed interest" See page 110.

145   "Yet I found . . ." William Penn, "Fragments of an Apology," *Memoirs of the Historical Society of Pennsylvania* (1834), Vol. III, Part Two, p. 235.

146   "to disable . . ." Carolyn Andervont Edie, "Succession and Monarchy: The Controversy of 1679–1681," *American Historical Review* (January 1965), p. 350.

146   "This book . . ." Caroline Robbins, *The Eighteenth-century Common-wealthsman* (Cambridge: Harvard University Press, 1959), p. 43.

147   "He freely . . ." Michael Garibaldi Hall, *Edward Randolph and the Ameri-can Colonies, 1676–1703* (Chapel Hill: University of North Carolina Press, 1960), pp. 24–25.

148   "like to live . . ." David S. Lovejoy, "Equality and Empire. The New York Charter of Libertyes, 1683," *William and Mary Quarterly* (October 1964), p. 512.

149   "He has a strange . . ." F. C. Turner, *James II* (London: Eyre & Spot-tiswoode, 1950), p. 64.

150   "abridged . . ." Barnes, *Dominion of New England,* p. 50.

150   "If I had a place . . ." Edward Corbyn Obert Beatty, *William Penn as Social Philosopher* (New York: Columbia University Press, 1939), p. 39.

150 "sometimes . . ." *Glorious Revolution in America*, Hall, Leder, and Kammen (eds.), p. 95.

150 "that the judgment . . ." *The Revolution in New England Justified* (Boston, 1691), p. 43.

150 "people . . ." Hall, *Edward Randolph and the American Colonies*, p. 94.

151 "taxes . . ." Barnes, *Dominion of New England*, p. 86 fn.

151 "considering that . . ." Clinton Rossiter, *Seedtime of the Republic* (New York: Harcourt, Brace and Company, 1953), p. 208.

151 "factious . . ." Barnes, *Dominion of New England*, p. 88.

152 "I die . . ." Douglass Adair, "Rumbold's Dying Speech, 1685, and Jefferson's Last Words on Democracy, 1826," *William and Mary Quarterly* (October 1952), p. 530.

152 "our constitution . . ." Charlwood Lawton, "A Memoir of Part of the Life of William Penn," *Memoirs of the Historical Society of Pennsylvania* (1834) Vol. III, Part Two, pp. 216–17.

152 "trumpeters . . ." David Lindsay Keir, *The Constitutional History of Modern Britain, 1485–1951* (London: Adam and Charles Black, 1953), p. 266.

153 "I do not expect . . ." Turner, *James II*, p. 442.

153 "when my subjects' eyes . . ." Same, p. 454.

153 "according to . . ." Lucile Pinkham, *William III and the Respectable Revolution* (Cambridge: Harvard University Press, 1954), p. 220.

153 "having endeavored . . ." Same, p. 225.

154 "those silly . . ." Pieter Geyl, *The Netherlands in the Seventeenth Century, Part One, 1609–1648* (New York: Barnes & Noble, Inc., 1961), p. 258.

154 "This was not . . ." "A Particular Account of the Late Revolution, 1689," *Narratives of the Insurrections*, Andrews (ed.), p. 196.

154 "It was in the month . . ." *Glorious Revolution in America*, Hall, Leder, and Kammen (eds.), p. 39.

154 "the noble undertaking . . ." Same, p. 45.

154 "from the horrible . . ." Same.

155 "no cause . . ." Report of Sir Edmund Andros, *Narratives of the Insurrections*, Andrews (ed.), p. 232.

155 "The Honorable . . ." *Glorious Revolution in America*, Hall, Leder, and Kammen (eds.), p. 52.

155 "freemen . . ." Barnes, *Dominion of New England*, p. 245.

155 "By the encouragement . . ." Andros report, *Narratives of the Insurrections*, Andrews (ed.), p. 234.

156 "If New England . . ." *Glorious Revolution in America*, Hall, Leder, and Kammen (eds.), p. 67.

156 "they esteeming . . ." Andros report, *Narratives of the Insurrections*, Andrews (ed.), p. 235.

156 "seeking opportunities . . ." C. V. Wedgwood, *William the Silent* (New Haven: Yale University Press, 1944), p. 224.

157 "We have a king . . ." "Increase Mather's Brief Account," *Narratives of the Insurrections*, Andrews (ed.), p. 282.

157 "the agents . . ." Same, p. 283.

158 fn. "To give Mr. Penn . . ." The Autobiography of Increase Mather," edited by M. G. Hall, *Proceedings of the American Antiquarian Society* (October 1961), p. 326.

159 "our great restorer . . ." John Locke, *Two Treatises of Government*, edited by Peter Laslett (Cambridge: Cambridge University Press, 1960), p. 155.

159   "The state of Nature . . ." Locke, *Two Treatises of Government*, Laslett (ed.), p. 289.
159   "Men being . . ." Same, p. 348.
159   "That which begins . . ." Same, p. 351.
159   "There are no instances . . ." Same.
159   "government is . . ." Same, p. 352.
160   "for the mutual . . ." Same, p. 368.
160   "if it be thought . . ." Cranston, *John Locke*, p. 425.
161   "follow . . ." See page 131.
161   "the poorest he . . ." See page 109.
161   "It may be . . ." McKinley, *Suffrage Franchise in the Thirteen English Colonies*, p. 155.
161   "Men of no great . . ." Same, p. 211.
162   "freeholder . . ." Same, p. 454.
162   "eldest son . . ." Same.
162   "to the value . . ." *Federal and State Constitutions*, Thorpe (ed.), Vol. III, p. 1879.
162   "Those persons . . ." McKinley, *Suffrage Franchise in the Thirteen English Colonies*, pp. 253–54.
163   "either . . ." Robert E. Brown and B. Katherine Brown, *Virginia, 1705–1786: Democracy or Aristocracy?* (East Lansing: Michigan State University Press, 1964), p. 128.
163   "on his said lot . . ." J. Franklin Jameson, *The American Revolution Considered As a Social Movement* (Boston: Beacon Press, 1964), p. 40.
165   "You cannot plant . . ." Harrington, *Oceana* (1700), p. 192.

Chapter Eight

167   "There is an excess . . ." Penn, *Correspondence*, Armstrong (ed.), Vol. I, p. 374.
168   "the prerogative . . ." Richard Walsh, "Christopher Gadsden: Radical or Conservative Revolutionary?" *The South Carolina Historical Magazine* (October 1962), p. 197.
168   "The Assembly . . ." Jack P. Greene, *The Quest for Power* (Chapel Hill: University of North Carolina Press, 1963), p. 1.
169   "unhinged . . ." *Settlements to Society*, Greene (ed.), p. 359.
169   "levelers . . ." John C. Miller, *Origins of the American Revolution* (Boston: Atlantic Monthly Press, 1943), p. 40.
170   "that it was not safe . . ." See page 65.
170   "that no taxes . . ." See page 151.
170   "very indecent . . ." Edmund S. Morgan, *Prologue to Revolution: Sources and Documents on the Stamp Act Crisis, 1764–1766* (Chapel Hill: University of North Carolina Press, 1959), p. 47.
170   "young, hot . . ." Same.
171   "I returned . . ." Same, pp. 46–47.
171   "shall . . . be reputed . . ." See page 54.
171   "This . . . is the place . . ." *Letters of Benjamin Rush*, edited by L. H. Butterfield, 2 vols. (Princeton: Princeton University Press, 1951), Vol. I, p. 68.
171   "A contest . . ." *Diary and Autobiography of John Adams*, edited by L. H. Butterfield, 4 vols. (New York: Atheneum, 1964), Vol. III, p. 276.

171   "No man . . ." Morgan, *Prologue to Revolution,* p. 101.

172   "a false . . ." George Rudé, *Wilkes and Liberty* (Oxford: Clarendon Press, 1962), p. 33.

173   "the just . . ." Jack P. Greene, "Bridge to Revolution: The Wilkes Fund Controversy in South Carolina, 1769–1775," *The Journal of Southern History* (February 1963), pp. 26–27.

173   "seditious . . ." Same, p. 27.

173   "insensibility" *Autobiography of Thomas Jefferson* (New York: Capricorn Books, 1959), p. 22.

174   "the machinations . . ." Rush, *Letters,* Butterfield (ed.), Vol. I, p. 84.

174   "undone . . ." Same.

175   "That province . . ." Robert H. Woody, "Christopher Gadsden and the Stamp Act," *Proceedings of the South Carolina Historical Association,* 1939, p. 4.

175   "given under . . ." *Journals of the Continental Congress, 1774–1789,* 34 vols. (Washington: Government Printing Office, 1904–1937), Vol. I, p. 17.

176   "a general meeting . . ." Same, Vol. I, p. 24.

177   "The spirit . . ." Belknap, *History of New-Hampshire* (1784), Vol. III, p. 432.

177   "by duly certified . . ." *Journals of the Continental Congress,* Vol. I, p. 19.

177   "the freeholders . . ." Same, Vol. I, p. 21.

177   "the next most proper . . ." Same, Vol. I, p. 22.

178   "The sense of . . ." Adams, *Diary and Autobiography,* Butterfield (ed.), Vol. II, p. 98.

178   "Doubtless . . ." *Letters of Members of the Continental Congress,* edited by Edmund C. Burnett, 8 vols. (Washington, D.C., 1921–1936), Vol. I, p. 9.

178   "There is . . ." Adams, *Diary and Autobiography,* Butterfield (ed.), Vol. II, p. 150.

178   "All its councils . . ." *The Adams-Jefferson Papers,* edited by Lester J. Cappon, 2 vols. (Chapel Hill: University of North Carolina Press, 1959), Vol. II, p. 452.

179   "nibbling . . ." Adams, *Diary and Autobiography,* Butterfield (ed.), Vol. II, p. 156.

179   "most ardently . . ." *Journals of the Continental Congress,* Vol. I, p. 16.

179   "as Englishmen . . ." Same, Vol. I, p. 67.

179   "That they are . . ." Same.

179   "Speaker . . ." Belknap, *History of New-Hampshire* (1784), Vol. III, p. 444.

180   "express . . ." Same, Vol. III, p. 445.

180   "I told them . . ." Same, Vol. III, p. 447.

180   "I hope . . ." John Richard Alden, *General Gage in America* (Baton Rouge: Louisiana State University Press, 1948), p. 220.

181   "true and authentic . . ." *Journals of the Continental Congress,* Vol. II, p. 42.

181   "It is the united . . ." Same, Vol. II, p. 27.

182   "the unhappy . . ." *Life, Journals and Correspondence of Rev. Manasseh Cutler,* 2 vols. (Cincinnati, 1888), Vol. I, p. 51.

182   "Neighbor . . ." Richard B. Morris, "Class Struggle and the American Revolution," *William and Mary Quarterly* (January 1962), p. 20.

182   "for taking . . ." *Letters of Members of the Continental Congress,* Burnett (ed.), Vol. I, p. 18.

182   "language . . ." David Ogg, *England in the Reign of Charles II,* 2 vols. (Oxford: Clarendon Press, 1934), Vol. II, p. 610.

182   "dropped . . ." Same.

183   "We will show . . ." John Sanderson, *Biography of the Signers of the Declaration of Independence,* revised and edited by Robert T. Conrad (Philadelphia, 1847), p. 718.

183   "I will not complain . . ." Lawrence Shaw Mayo, *John Wentworth, Governor of New Hampshire, 1767–1775* (Cambridge: Harvard University Press, 1921), p. 157.

183   "the sudden . . ." *Federal and State Constitutions,* Thorpe (ed.), Vol. IV, p. 2452.

184   "utmost . . ." Adams, *Diary and Autobiography,* Butterfield (ed.), Vol. III, p. 354.

184   "This subject . . ." Same, Vol. III, p. 351.

184   "ought to recommend . . ." Same, Vol. III, p. 315.

184   "truly Ciceronial . . ." *Letters of Members of the Continental Congress,* Burnett (ed.), Vol. I, p. 246.

184   "establish . . ." *Journals of the Continental Congress,* Vol. II, p. 319.

184   "By this time . . ." Adams, *Diary and Autobiography,* Butterfield (ed.), Vol. III, p. 357.

185   "to continue . . ." *Federal and State Constitutions,* Thorpe (ed.), Vol. IV, p. 2452.

186   "No danger . . ." Richard Francis Upton, *Revolutionary New Hampshire* (Hanover: Dartmouth College Publications, 1936), p. 175.

Chapter Nine

187   "wisely . . ." David Duncan Wallace, *The History of South Carolina,* 4 vols. (New York: The American Historical Society, Inc., 1934), Vol. II, p. 123.

188   "Lord William . . ." *Federal and State Constitutions,* Thorpe (ed.), Vol. VI, p. 3243.

188   "carried off . . ." Same.

188   "a clear right . . ." Wallace, *History of South Carolina,* Vol. II, p. 153.

188   "traitor . . ." Arthur M. Schlesinger, *Prelude to Independence: The Newspaper War on Britain, 1764–1776* (New York: Alfred A Knopf, 1958), p. 127.

188   "Resolved . . ." *Journals of the Continental Congress,* Vol. IV, p. 342.

189   "an epocha . . ." Adams, *Diary and Autobiography,* Butterfield (ed.), Vol. III, p. 383.

189   "We are . . ." John Adams, *Works,* edited by Charles Francis Adams, 10 vols. (Boston: Little, Brown and Company, 1850–1856), Vol. IX, p. 391.

189   "under the protection . . ." *Federal and State Constitutions,* Thorpe (ed.), Vol. V, p. 2598.

189   "Many true friends . . ." J. R. Pole, "Suffrage Reform and the American Revolution in New Jersey," *Proceedings of the New Jersey Historical Society* (July 1956), p. 185.

189   "All inhabitants . . ." *Federal and State Constitutions,* Thorpe (ed.), Vol. V, p. 2595.

190   "our worthy . . ." *The Proceedings of the Convention Held at Richmond in the County of Henrico, on the 20th Day of March, 1775* (Williamsburg, 1775), p. 19.

190   "with that prudence . . ." Same, p. 6.

190   "a permanent . . ." *The Letters of Richard Henry Lee,* edited by James Curtis Ballagh, 2 vols. (New York: The Macmillan Company, 1911–1914), Vol. I, p. 205.

190 "mighty . . ." Same, Vol. I, p. 207.

190 "a disinterested . . ." Carter Braxton, *An Address to the Convention of the Colony and Ancient Dominion of Virginia* . . . (Philadelphia, 1776), p. 15.

191 "unless impeached . . ." *The Papers of Thomas Jefferson,* edited by Julian P. Boyd, 17 vols. to date (Princeton: Princeton Universtity Press, 1950–1965), Vol. I, p. 489.

191 "seemed . . ." Same.

191 "If anyone . . ." Locke, *Two Treatises of Government,* Laslett (ed.), p. 380.

191 "by this breach . . ." Same, p. 430.

191 "to resume . . ." Same.

191 "That all men . . ." *Federal and State Constitutions,* Thorpe (ed.), Vol. VII, p. 3813.

191 "That all power . . ." Same.

192 "all men having . . ." Same.

192 "a local . . ." *Puritanism and Liberty,* Woodhouse (ed.), p. 62.

192 "The right . . ." *Federal and State Constitutions,* Thorpe (ed.), Vol. VII, p. 3816.

192 "disputed . . ." *The Writings of Thomas Jefferson,* edited by Paul Leicester Ford, 10 vols. (New York: G. P. Putnam's Sons, 1892–1899), Vol. X, p. 342.

192 "It was not recollected . . ." Chilton Williamson, *American Suffrage from Property to Democracy, 1760–1860* (Princeton: Princeton University Press, 1960), p. 114.

193 "the lady . . ." *The Pennsylvania Magazine: Or, American Monthly Museum* (Philadelphia, January 1775), Vol. I, p. 98.

193 "naturally brave . . ." Same (January 1776), Vol. III, p. 36.

193 "still hoping . . . Those who have . . ." Same (January 1776), Vol. III, p. 45.

193 "to put . . . the unhappy . . ." Same (January 1776), Vol. III, p. 46.

193 "both of them . . ." *Life and Works of Thomas Paine,* 10 vols. (New Rochelle: Thomas Paine National Historical Association, 1925), Vol. I, p. 462.

193 "readily assented . . ." *The Autobiography of Benjamin Rush,* edited by George W. Corner (Princeton: Princeton University Press, 1948), p. 114.

194 "a great and glorious . . ." "Diary of James Allen," *The Pennsylvania Magazine of History and Biography* (1885), Vol. IX, p. 185.

194 "totally foreign . . ." Same, Vol. IX, p. 186.

194 "A long habit . . ." Thomas Paine, *Common Sense,* first edition (Philadelphia, January 1776), from the Introduction.

194 "There is something . . ." Same, p. 9.

194 "These proceedings . . ." Same, p. 79.

195 "It is dangerous . . ." Thomas Paine, *Dissertation on First-Principles of Government* (London, 1795), p. 20.

195 "the right . . ." Same, p. 21.

195 "In a political view . . ." Same, p. 22.

196 "It is certain . . ." Adams, *Works,* C. F. Adams (ed.), Vol. IX, p. 375.

196 "Harrington . . ." Same, Vol. IX, p. 376.

196 "Depend upon it . . ." Same, Vol. IX, p. 378.

196 "to confound . . ." Same.

196 "disastrous . . ." Adams, *Diary and Autobiography,* Butterfield (ed.), Vol. III, p. 330.

197 "totally foreign . . ." See page 194.

197 "utterly reject . . ." William S. Hanna, *Benjamin Franklin and Pennsylvania Politics* (Stanford: Stanford University Press, 1964), p. 195.

197   "A set . . ." Paine, *Common Sense,* first edition (January 1776), p. 75.
197   "By great . . ." Hanna, *Benjamin Franklin and Pennsylvania Politics,* p. 101.
198   "They still have . . ." Same, p. 157.
198   "under the authority . . ." *Journals of the Continental Congress,* Vol. IV, p. 358.
198   "Before we are . . ." David Hawke, *In the Midst of a Revolution* (Philadelphia: University of Pennsylvania Press, 1961), p. 121.
198   "We stared . . ." James Allen, "Diary," *Pennsylvania Magazine of History and Biography* (1885), p. 187.
198   "vehemently . . ." Same.
199   "We are resolved . . ." J. Paul Selsam, *The Pennsylvania Constitution of 1776* (Philadelphia: University of Pennsylvania Press, 1936), p. 205.
199   "the worst . . ." Zoltán Haraszti, *John Adams & the Prophets of Progress* (Cambridge: Harvard University Press, 1952), p. 329.
200   "perfectly acquainted . . ." Hugh Williamson, *What is sauce for a goose is also sauce for a gander* (Philadelphia, 1764), p. 4.
200 fn. "general use . . ." Benjamin Franklin, *Works,* edited by John Bigelow, 12 vols. (New York: G. P. Putnam's Sons, 1904), Vol. IX, p. 444.
201   "rather too much . . ." Rush, *Letters,* Butterfield (ed.), Vol. I, p. 115.
201   "It has substituted . . ." Same, Vol. I, p. 148.
201   "They call it . . ." Same, Vol. I, p. 244.
201   "His hatred . . ." Rush, *Autobiography,* Corner (ed.), p. 149.
201   "in battle . . ." Same, p. 162.
201   "It is a fact . . ." Franklin, *Works,* Bigelow (ed.), Vol. X, p. 416.
201   "unless . . ." Same, Vol. XI, p. 205.
201   "now expedient" Robert L. Brunhouse, *The Counter-Revolution in Pennsylvania, 1776–1790* (Harrisburg: Pennsylvania Historical Commission, 1942), p. 180.
202   "His demeanor . . ." Alexander Graydon, *Memoirs of a Life Chiefly Passed in Pennsylvania* (Harrisburg, 1811), p. 267.
202   "supposed . . ." Franklin, *Works,* Bigelow (ed.), Vol. XII, p. 180.
202   "The combinations . . ." Same, Vol. XII, p. 181.
202   "the rich . . ." Same.
202   "at least six months . . ." *Federal and State Constitutions,* Thorpe (ed.), Vol. V, p. 3096.

Chapter Ten

204   "I am convinced . . ." *Letters of Members of the Continental Congress,* Burnett (ed.), Vol. I, p. 421.
204   "without any adjustments . . ." Same.
204   "that the delegates . . ." *The Proceedings of the Convention of Delegates, Held at the Capitol, in the City of Williamsburg . . . on Monday the 6th of May, 1776* (Williamsburg, 1776), p. 32.
205   "the formation . . ." Lee, *Letters,* Ballagh (ed.), Vol. I, p. 203.
205   "Though a silent . . ." Adams, *Works,* C. F. Adams (ed.), Vol. II, p. 514fn.
205   "a solid . . ." Adams, *Diary and Autobiography,* Butterfield (ed.), Vol. II, p. 100.
205   "dove-like . . ." Rush, *Autobiography,* Corner (ed.), p. 151.
206   "as Homer . . ." Jefferson, *Autobiography* (Capricorn Books), p. 22.

206   "which, judging . . ." Jefferson, *Papers,* Boyd (ed.), Vol. I, p. 19.

207   "Being a younger . . ." Nathan Schachner, *Thomas Jefferson,* 2 vols. (New York: Appleton-Century-Crofts, Inc., 1951), Vol. I, p. 70.

207   "His Lordship's . . ." Lee, *Letters,* Ballagh (ed.), Vol. I, pp. 30–31.

207   "dancing . . ." Jefferson, *Papers,* Boyd (ed.), Vol. I, p. 11.

207   "the very few . . ." Jefferson, *Autobiography* (Capricorn Books), p. 22.

208   "rummaged . . ." Same, p. 24.

208   "The Governor . . ." Same.

208   "The effect . . ." Same, p. 25.

208   "stopped . . ." Same.

208   "a very handsome . . ." Adams, *Diary and Autobiography,* Butterfield (ed.), Vol. III, p. 335.

208   "The most . . ." Same.

209   "to recall . . ." Jefferson, *Papers,* Boyd (ed.), Vol. I, p. 292.

209   "It is a work . . ." Same.

209   "on the day . . ." Jefferson, *Writings,* Ford (ed.), Vol. X, p. 342.

209   "I was for extending . . ." Jefferson, *Papers,* Boyd (ed.), Vol. I, p. 504.

209   "at a committee . . ." Same, Vol. I, p. 491.

209   "You have lived . . ." Same, Vol. I, p. 504.

210   "enrolled . . ." Same, Vol. VI, p. 296.

210   "This constitution . . ." Thomas Jefferson, *Notes on the State of Virginia* (Paris, 1785), p. 211.

210   "The majority . . ." Same.

210   "All men . . ." See page 191.

211   "appointed . . ." Adams, *Diary and Autobiography,* Butterfield (ed.), Vol. III, p. 336.

211   "You can write . . ." Adams, *Works,* C. F. Adams (ed.), Vol. II, p. 514fn.

211   "The committee of five . . ." Jefferson, *Writings,* Ford (ed.), Vol. X, p. 267.

211   "The committee consisted . . ." Adams, *Diary and Autobiography,* Butterfield (ed.), Vol. II, pp. 391–92.

212   "No state . . ." Lee, *Letters,* Ballagh (ed.), Vol. I, p. 178.

212   "the United . . ." Edward Winslow, *Hypocrisie Vnmasked* (London, 1646), p. 88.

212   "Not to find . . ." Jefferson, *Writings,* Ford (ed), Vol. X, p. 343.

212   "We hold . . ." Jefferson, *Autobiography* (Capricorn Books), p. 36.

213   "All men are by nature . . ." See page 191.

213   "All men are born . . ." (Pennsylvania constitution), *Federal and State Constitutions,* Thorpe (ed.), Vol. V, p. 3082.

213   "All men are born . . ." (first Vermont constitution), Same, Vol. VI, p. 3739.

213   "All men are born . . ." (second Vermont constitution), Same, Vol. VI, p. 3751.

213   "a long train . . ." Locke, *Two Treatises of Government,* Laslett (ed.), p. 433.

213   "long train . . ." Jefferson, *Autobiography* (Capricorn Books), p. 36.

213 *fn.*   "We hold . . ." Jefferson, *Papers,* Boyd (ed.), Vol. I, p. 423.

214   "Resolved . . ." *Journals of the Continental Congress,* Vol. V, p. 507.

214   "The abolition . . ." Jefferson, *Papers,* Boyd (ed.), Vol. I, p. 130.

215   "He has waged . . ." Jefferson, *Autobiography* (Capricorn Books), p. 39.

215   "Their people . . ." Same, p. 35.

215   "The second . . ." Adams, *Works,* C. F. Adams (ed.), Vol. IX, p. 420.

216   "May it be . . ." Jefferson, *Writings,* Ford (ed.), Vol. X, pp. 391–92.

216   "Proclaim liberty . . ." *Leviticus* 25:10.
217   "an expression . . ." See page 212.

Chapter Eleven

218   "that it be . . ." *Journals of the Continental Congress,* Vol. V, p. 510.
218   "awful silence . . ." Rush, *Letters,* Butterfield (ed.), Vol. II, p. 1090.
219   "a set of men . . ." Bernhard Knollenberg, *Origin of the American Revolution, 1759–1776* (New York: The Macmillan Company, 1960), p. 191.
219   "every taxable . . ." Philip A. Crowl, *Maryland During and After the Revolution* (Baltimore: The Johns Hopkins Press, 1943), p. 30.
219   "by a majority . . ." Same.
220   "democratical . . ." Same, p. 31.
220   "The Senate . . ." Same, pp. 39–40.
220   "to counteract . . ." Same, p. 40.
221   "All male . . ." *Federal and State Constitutions,* Thorpe (ed.), Vol. II, p. 779.
221   "very democratical . . . power . . ." Williamson, *American Suffrage from Property to Democracy,* p. 105.
221   "the good people . . ." Fletcher M. Green, *Constitutional Development in the South Atlantic States, 1776–1860* (Chapel Hill: University of North Carolina Press, 1930), p. 66.
222   "the tumult . . ." Robert L. Ganyard, "Radicals and Conservatives in Revolutionary North Carolina: A Point at Issue, the October Elections, 1776," *William and Mary Quarterly* (October 1967), p. 572.
222   "many-headed . . ." Green, *Constitutional Development in the South Atlantic States,* p. 68.
222   "to preserve . . . evinced . . ." Same, p. 76.
222   "All freemen . . ." *Federal and State Constitutions,* Thorpe (ed.), Vol. V, p. 2790.
223   "To institute . . ." William Jay, *The Life of John Jay,* 2 vols. (New York, 1833), Vol. I, p. 43.
223   "Wilson will remember . . ." Staughton Lynd, "Who Should Rule at Home? Dutchess County, New York, in the American Revolution," *William and Mary Quarterly* (July 1961), p. 342.
223   "the mass . . ." William Jay, *Life of John Jay,* Vol. I, p. 246.
223   "a favorite . . ." Same, Vol. I, p. 70.
223   "The Convention . . ." Same, Vol. I, p. 68.
224   "a freehold . . ." *Federal and State Constitutions,* Thorpe (ed.), Vol. V, p. 2630.
225   "The general . . ." *Journals of the Provincial Congress . . . of the State of New-York,* 2 vols. (Albany, 1842), Vol. I, p. 892.
225   "to give . . ." Same, Vol. I, p. 898.
225   "absolutely necessary . . ." *Federal and State Constitutions,* Thorpe (ed.), Vol. VI, p. 3739.
225   "our British . . . their chief . . ." Jefferson, *Autobiography* (Capricorn Books), p. 40.
225   "They have hired . . ." *Federal and State Constitutions,* Thorpe (ed.), Vol. VI, p. 3738.
226   "of a quiet . . ." Same, Vol. VI, p. 3742.
226   "Every freeman . . ." Same, Vol. VI, p. 3747.

226   "Freemen are such . . ." See page 124.

226   "Patrick Henry . . ." Rush, *Autobiography,* Corner (ed.), pp. 145–46.

227   "to take them . . ." Same, p. 142.

227   "straggling" Paine, *Common Sense,* first edition (January 1776), p. 53.

227   "simple ignorance . . . dreaded . . ." Adams, *Diary and Autobiography,* Butterfield (ed.), Vol. III, p. 331.

227   "to form . . ." John Adams, *Thoughts on Government: Applicable to the Present State of the American Colonies* (Boston, 1776), p. 16.

228   "in times . . ." Same, p. 7.

228   "The enclosed . . ." Lee, *Letters,* Ballagh (ed.), Vol. I, p. 179.

228   "The sentiments . . ." George Morgan, *Patrick Henry* (Philadelphia: J. B. Lippincott Company, 1929), p. 263.

228   "sick of politics . . ." George Dangerfield, *Chancellor Robert R. Livingston of New York, 1746–1813* (New York: Harcourt, Brace and Company, 1960), p. 87.

229   "until a governor . . ." *Journals of the Continental Congress,* Vol. II, p. 84.

229   "a great and general . . ." *The Journals of the Provincial Congress of Massachusetts in 1774–1775,* edited by William Lincoln (Boston, 1838), p. 359.

230   "and multitudes . . ." Robert J. Taylor, *Western Massachusetts in the Revolution* (Providence: Brown University Press, 1954), p. 86.

230   "impose . . ." Same.

230   "by no means . . ." *Sources and Documents Illustrating the American Revolution, 1764–1788, and the Formation of the Federal Constitution,* edited by Samuel Eliot Morison (Oxford: Clarendon Press, 1962), p. 177.

230   "I am very uneasy . . ." Thomas C. Amory, *Life of James Sullivan,* 2 vols. (Boston, 1859), Vol. I, p. 96.

230   "in favor . . ." Same.

230   "the framing . . ." Theophilus Parsons, *Result of the Convention of Delegates Holden at Ipswich in the County of Essex . . .* [Essex Result] (Newburyport, 1778), p. 4.

230   "the true principles . . ." Same, p. 6.

231   "For as the executive . . ." Same, p. 57.

231   "The man . . ." Same, p. 10.

232   "goodness . . ." *Federal and State Constitutions,* Thorpe (ed.), Vol. III, p. 1889.

232   "those democratical . . ." Adams, *Diary and Autobiography,* Butterfield (ed.), Vol. III, p. 305.

232   "All men are born equally . . ." Adams, *Works,* C. F. Adams (ed.), Vol. IV, p. 220.

232   "All men are born free . . ." *Federal and State Constitutions,* Thorpe (ed.), Vol. III, p. 1889.

232   "that the word . . ." *Journal of the Convention for Framing a Constitution of Government for the State of Massachusetts Bay . . .* (Boston, 1832), p. 43.

233   "designed . . ." Same, p. 50.

233   "collective . . . general . . ." Same, p. 49.

234   "free . . ." E. Francis Brown, *Joseph Hawley, Colonial Radical* (New York: Columbia University Press, 1931), p. 174.

234   "We must . . ." William Tudor, *The Life of James Otis of Massachusetts* (Boston, 1823), p. 256.

234   "If taxes . . ." Alden, *General Gage in America,* p. 110.

234 "precisely . . ." *The Popular Sources of Political Authority, Documents on the Massachusetts Constitution of 1780,* edited by Oscar and Mary Handlin (Cambridge: The Belknap Press of Harvard University Press, 1966), p. 584.

235 "Shall we . . ." Same, pp. 584–85.

235 "The hands . . ." Mary Catherine Clune, "Joseph Hawley's Criticism of the Constitution of Massachusetts," *Smith College Studies in History,* Vol. III, no. 1, p. 49.

235 "main issue . . ." Same, p. 47.

235 "You may perhaps . . ." Same, p. 46.

235 "the first . . ." Same.

236 "The decree . . ." Adams, *Works,* C. F. Adams (ed.), Vol. IX, p. 387.

236 "No government . . ." Page Smith, *John Adams,* 2 vols. (New York: Doubleday & Company, Inc., 1962), Vol. I, p. 464.

Chapter Twelve

237 "The eyes . . . whose memory . . ." Sanderson, *Biography of the Signers of the Declaration of Independence,* Conrad (ed.), p. 656.

237 "Saxon . . ." Jefferson, *Papers,* Boyd (ed.), Vol. I, p. 495.

238 "under apprehensions . . ." Jefferson, *Writings,* Ford (ed.), Vol. X, p. 118.

238 "each state . . ." *Federal and State Constitutions,* Thorpe (ed.), Vol. I, p. 11.

239 "by standing . . ." Jefferson, *Papers,* Boyd (ed.), Vol. VIII, p. 579.

239 "could not realize . . ." George Richards Minot, *The History of the Insurrections, in Massachusetts . . .* (Worcester, 1788), p. 17.

239 "With such . . ." Same.

239 "This meeting . . ." Same, p. 34.

239 "the existence . . ." Same, p. 35.

240 "awake . . ." *Adams–Jefferson Letters,* Cappon (ed.), Vol. I, p. 159.

240 "Ignorant . . ." Same, Vol. I, p. 168.

240 "deluded . . ." See page 193.

240 "What, gracious God. . ." *The Writings of George Washington,* edited by John C. Fitzpatrick, 39 vols. (Washington: U.S. Government Printing Office, 1931–1944), Vol. XXIX, pp. 125–26.

240 "When this spirit . . ." Same, Vol. XXIX, p. 122.

241 "I do not conceive . . ." *Sources and Documents Illustrating . . . the Formation of the Federal Government,* Morison (ed.), p. 216.

241 "awful crisis" Washington, *Writings,* Fitzpatrick (ed.), Vol. XXIX, p. 77.

241 "the darling . . ." Same, Vol. XXIX, p. 153.

241 "I believe . . ." Same.

242 "I seem . . ." Franklin, *Works,* Bigelow (ed.), Vol. XI, p. 333.

242 "an activity . . ." *The Records of the Federal Convention of 1787,* edited by Max Farrand, 4 vols. (New Haven: Yale University Press, 1937), Vol. III, p. 91.

242 "I am mortified . . ." Same, Vol. III, p. 26.

242 "We have not . . ." Adams, *Diary and Autobiography,* Butterfield (ed.), Vol. II, p. 97.

243 "I never before . . ." *Records of the Federal Convention,* Farrand (ed.), Vol. III, pp. 32–33.

243 "the double object . . ." Same, Vol. III, p. 98.

244 "The whole . . ." *Adams–Jefferson Letters,* Cappon (ed.), Vol. II, p. 453.

244	"a gentleman . . ." *Records of the Federal Convention,* Farrand (ed.), Vol. III, p. 95.
244	"the best informed . . ." Same, Vol. III, p. 94.
244	"In a very able . . . all the beauties . . . their situation . . ." Same, Vol. I, p. 110.
244	"every western wind . . ." Adams, *Works,* C. F. Adams (ed.), Vol. IX, p. 623.
244	"of the blood . . ." Same.
244	"Mr. Adams' book . . ." Rush, *Letters,* Butterfield (ed.), Vol. I, p. 418.
245	"a source . . ." *Records of the Federal Convention,* Farrand (ed.), Vol. I, p. 234.
245	"In New Hampshire . . ." Same, Vol. II, p. 402.
245	"so little . . ." Same, Vol. I, p. 218.
245	"The constitution . . ." Same.
245	"The great Montesquieu . . ." Same, Vol. I, p. 391.
246	"The people are gradually . . ." Same, Vol. I, p. 301.
246	"hitherto silent . . ." Same, Vol. I, p. 282.
246	"vast and expensive . . ." Same, Vol. I, p. 287.
246	"The people . . ." Same, Vol. I, p. 299.
246	"hold their places . . ." Same, Vol. I, p. 289.
246	"gentlemen . . ." Same.
246	"the governor . . ." Same, Vol. I, p. 293.
246	"to shock . . ." Same, Vol. I, p. 287.
247	"Great zeal . . ." Broadus Mitchell and Louise Pearson Mitchell, *A Biography of the Constitution of the United States* (New York: Oxford University Press, 1964), p. 64.
247	"In the beginning . . ." *Records of the Federal Convention,* Farrand (ed.), Vol. I, pp. 451–52.
247	"When a broad table . . ." Same, Vol. I, p. 488.
247	"Will you crush . . ." Same, Vol. I, p. 501.
247	"Something . . ." Same, Vol. I, p. 515.
248	"to devise . . ." Same, Vol. I, p. 511.
248	"I *almost* despair . . ." Washington, *Writings,* Fitzpatrick (ed.), Vol. XXIX, pp. 245–46.
248	"now occupied . . ." Manasseh Cutler, *Life, Journals and Correspondence,* Vol. I, p. 262.
248	"Everything . . ." Same, Vol. I, p. 270.
248	"I am fully . . ." Washington, *Writings,* Fitzpatrick (ed.), Vol. XXIX, p. 261.
249	"democracy" *Stuart Constitution,* Kenyon (ed.), p. 21.
249	"Our chief . . ." *Records of the Federal Convention,* Farrand (ed.), Vol. I, pp. 26–27.
249	"He observed . . ." Same, Vol. I, p. 51.
249	"such a refining . . ." Same, Vol. I, p. 136.
250	"Mr. Wilson . . ." Same, Vol. I, p. 68.
250	"A government . . ." Same, Vol. II, p. 31.
251	"because in a new country . . ." Same, Vol. I, p. 398.
251	"In England . . ." Same, Vol. I, p. 431.
251	"to protect . . . overbalanced . . ." Same.
251	"increase . . ." Same, Vol. I, p. 422.
251	"Symptoms . . ." Same, Vol. I, p. 423.

347

251 "the grand depository . . ." Same, Vol. I, p. 48.
251 "Mr. Sherman . . ." Same.
252 "This part . . ." Same, Vol. II, p. 201.
252 "he found himself . . ." Same, Vol. II, p. 237.
252 "one of the most galling . . ." Same, Vol. II, p. 244.
252 "against abridging . . ." Same, Vol. I, p. 375.
252 "The qualifications . . ." Same, Vol. II, p. 178.
253 "substituted . . ." Same, Vol. II, p. 201.
253 "the right of suffrage . . ." Same.
253 "There is no right . . ." Same.
253 "Mr. Dickinson . . ." Same, Vol. II, p. 202.
253 "The time . . ." Same.
253 "Nine-tenths . . ." Same, Vol. II, p. 203.
253 "In future times . . . would be . . ." Same, Vol. II, pp. 203–204.
253 "a system . . ." Same, Vol. I, p. 422.
254 "Dr. Franklin . . ." Same, Vol. II, p. 210.
254 "that we should not . . ." Same, Vol. II, p. 204.
254 "quoted as arbitrary . . ." Same, Vol. II, p. 205.
254 "he had never seen . . ." Same, Vol. II, p. 215.
254 "the elections . . ." Same, Vol. II, p. 216.
254 "The people . . ." Same.
255 "he would sooner . . ." Same, Vol. II, p. 479.
255 "It was reported . . ." Jefferson, *Papers,* Boyd (ed.), Vol. XII, p. 229.
255 "to allay . . ." Same.
255 "I don't know . . ." *Records of the Federal Convention,* Farrand (ed.), Vol. II, p. 642.
255 "Mr. President . . ." Same, Vol. II, pp. 641–43.
256 "Mr. Gouverneur Morris . . ." Same, Vol. II, p. 645.
256 "No man's ideas . . ." Same.
256 "Now at length . . ." Same, Vol. II, p. 648.
256 "to meditate . . ." Same, Vol. III, p. 81.
256 "of obviating . . ." Same, Vol. II, p. 92.
256 "assemblies . . ." Same, Vol. II, p. 88.
256 "Great confusion . . ." Same, Vol. II, p. 90.
256 "in Massachusetts . . ." Same, Vol. II, p. 647.
257 "the mutual . . ." Same, Vol. II, p. 584.
257 "The city . . ." Jefferson, *Papers,* Boyd (ed.), Vol. XIII, p. 370.
257 "To have reduced . . ." *The Federalist,* edited by Benjamin Fletcher Wright (Cambridge: The Belknap Press of Harvard University, 1961), p. 360.
258 "The time to guard . . ." Jefferson, *Papers,* Boyd (ed.), Vol. VI, p. 310.
258 "These observations . . ." *Records of the Federal Convention,* Farrand (ed.), Vol. III, p. 450.
258 "Confining . . ." Same, Vol. III, p. 453.

Chapter Thirteen

259 "We may . . ." Washington, *Writings,* Fitzpatrick (ed.), Vol. XXX, p. 22.
260 "played . . ." Franklin, *Works,* Bigelow (ed.), Vol. XI, p. 433.
260 "the grand depository . . ." See page 251.
260 "His Highness . . ." *The Journal of William Maclay* (New York: Albert and Charles Boni, 1927), p. 25.

260 "His Excellency . . ." *Federal and State Constitutions,* Farrand (ed.), Vol. IV, p. 2462.

261 "more solicitous . . ." *Works of Fisher Ames,* edited by Seth Ames, 2 vols. (Boston: Little, Brown and Company, 1854), Vol. I, p. 62.

261 "high-sounding . . ." Same.

261 "I think . . ." Same, Vol. I, p. 42.

261 "Madison . . ." Same, Vol. I, p. 127.

261 "The best part . . ." See page 81.

261 "All communities . . ." *Records of the Federal Convention,* Farrand (ed.), Vol. I, p. 299.

261 "played . . ." See page 260.

261 "most of the important . . ." *The Papers of Alexander Hamilton,* edited by Harold C. Syrett and Jacob E. Cooke, 13 vols. to date (New York: Columbia University Press, 1961–1967), Vol. XI, p. 442.

261 "the good will . . ." Same, Vol. IV, p. 275.

262 "A love and veneration . . ." *The Debates and Proceedings in the Congress of the United States,* 42 vols. (Washington, 1834–1856), Second Congress, October 24, 1791, to March 2, 1793, p. 510.

262 "a proper stability . . ." See page 243.

262 "When I accepted . . ." Hamilton, *Papers,* Syrett and Cooke (eds.), Vol. XI, p. 427.

262 "It was not . . ." Same, Vol. XI, p. 429.

263 "step by step . . ." Jefferson, *Writings,* Ford (ed.), Vol. VI, p. 103.

263 "system . . ." Same, Vol. VI, p. 102.

263 "The existence . . ." Roy Swanstrom, *The United States Senate, 1787–1801* (Washington: U.S. Government Printing Office, 1962), p. 283.

263 "We are *all* . . ." *Washington's Farewell Address,* edited by Victor Hugo Paltsits (New York: The New York Public Library, 1935), pp. 15–16.

264 "a disease . . ." Walsh, "Christopher Gadsden," *South Carolina Historical Magazine* (October 1962), p. 195.

264 "tumult . . ." Same, p. 202.

264 "the factious . . ." Ames, *Works,* Vol. I, p. 123.

264 "drawn . . ." Manasseh Cutler, *Life, Journals and Correspondence,* Vol. I, p. 238.

265 "Man was born . . ." Jean Jacques Rousseau, *The Social Contract,* edited by Henry J. Tozer (London: George Allen and Unwin, Ltd., 1895), p. 100.

265 "It is beyond doubt . . ." Jacques Godechot, *France and the Atlantic Revolution of the Eighteenth Century, 1770–1799* (New York: The Free Press, 1965), p. 230.

265 "Twenty-six . . ." Charles Downer Hazen, *Contemporary American Opinion of the French Revolution* (Baltimore: Johns Hopkins Press, 1897), p. 149.

265 "the freedom . . ." United States Congress, *Debates and Proceedings,* Second Congress (1791–1793), p. 107.

265 "the wisdom . . . the most perfect . . ." Same, p. 456.

266 "He removeth . . ." *Daniel* 2:21.

266 "hell . . ." W. D. Robson-Scott, *German Travellers in England, 1400–1800* (Oxford: Basil Blackwell, 1953), p. 78.

267 "Should . . ." Hazen, *Contemporary American Opinion of the French Revolution,* p. 192.

267 "the spirit . . . the pride . . ." Same.

267 "inequality . . . it would . . ." Timothy Ford, *The Constitutionalist* (Charleston, 1794), p. 33.

267   "general . . ." Walter R. Fee, *The Transition from Aristocracy to Democracy in New Jersey, 1789–1829* (Somerville: Somerset Press, Inc., 1933), p. 43.

267   "Some grumbletonians . . ." George D. Luetscher, *Early Political Machinery in the United States* (Philadelphia, 1903), p. 39.

267   "Till this period . . ." Same, p. 61.

268   "hellish . . ." Eugene Perry Link, *Democratic–Republican Societies, 1790–1800* (New York: Columbia University Press, 1942), p. 175.

268   "the genius . . ." *The Federalist,* Wright (ed.), p. 144.

268   "on several occasions . . ." United States Congress, *Debates and Proceedings,* Third Congress, December 2, 1793 to March 3, 1795, p. 61.

268 fn.   "had not been . . ." Same, p. 59.

268 fn.   "every man . . ." Same, p. 52.

269   "be useful . . ." *The Speech of Albert Gallatin . . . in the House of Representatives of the General Assembly of Pennsylvania* (Philadelphia, 1795), p. 14.

269   "The conduct . . ." William Miller, "The Democratic Societies and the Whiskey Insurrection," *Pennsylvania Magazine of History and Biography* (July 1938), p. 331.

269   "without rigor . . ." Irving Brant, *James Madison, Father of the Constitution, 1787–1800* (Indianapolis: The Bobbs-Merrill Company, 1950), p. 416.

270   "I consider . . ." Washington, *Writings,* Fitzpatrick (ed.), Vol. XXXIII, pp. 475–76.

270   "My mind . . ." Same, Vol. XXXIV, pp. 3–4.

270   "fomented . . ." Same, Vol. XXXIV, pp. 34–35.

270   "Our anxiety . . ." United States Congress, *Debates and Proceedings,* Third Congress (1793–1795), p. 794.

270   "not strictly . . ." Same, p. 899.

270   "We cannot . . ." Same.

271   "our enemies . . ." Same, p. 796.

271   "Any attempts . . ." Fee, *Transition from Aristocracy to Democracy in New Jersey,* p. 48.

271   "Mr. Ames . . ." Ames, *Works,* Vol. I, p. 22.

271   "Sedition . . ." *Short Story of . . . the Antinomians* (1644), pp. 52–53.

271   "What will you do . . ." See page 73.

272   "Let us ask . . ." United States Congress, *Debates and Proceedings,* Third Congress (1793–1795), p. 930.

272   "The question is . . ." Same, p. 931.

272   "Besides . . ." Same, p. 922.

272   "the innovations . . ." J. C. de Roulhac Hamilton, "A Society for Preservation of Liberty," *American Historical Review* (April 1927), p. 550.

272   "being convinced . . ." Same.

272   "Opinions . . ." United States Congress, *Debates and Proceedings,* Third Congress (1793–1795), p. 934.

272   "If we advert . . ." Same.

273   "Will it be . . ." *Washington's Farewell Address,* Paltsits (ed.), p. 253.

273   "Let me . . . caution . . ." Same, p. 189.

273   "Let me . . . warn . . ." Same, p. 148.

273   "There is an opinion . . ." Same, p. 150.

273   "very criminal . . . the President . . ." Adams, *Works,* C. F. Adams (ed.), Vol. I, p. 473.

273   "great sticklers . . ." Adams, *Diary and Autobiography,* Butterfield (ed.), Vol. III, p. 265.

273   "carried . . ." Same.
274   "Too many . . ." Adams, *Works,* C. F. Adams (ed.), Vol. IX, p. 564.
275   "Never shall . . ." *The Speech of Albert Gallatin, Delivered in the House of Representatives of the United States on the First of March, 1798* (Philadelphia, 1798), p. 30.
275   "If you think . . ." Same.
275   "Behold . . ." David Hackett Fischer, *The Revolution of American Conservatism* (New York: Harper & Row, 1965), p. 360.
275   "subversive . . ." United States Congress, *Debates and Proceedings,* Fifth Congress, May 15, 1797, to March 3, 1799, p. 2110.
275   "that whoever . . ." Same.
275   "shall write . . ." James Morton Smith, *Freedom's Fetters: The Alien and Sedition Laws and American Civil Liberties* (Ithaca: Cornell University Press, 1956), p. 441.
276   "unseemly . . ." See page 12.
276   "as unconquerable . . ." Ames, *Works,* Vol. I, p. 228.
276   "You never felt . . ." *Adams–Jefferson Letters,* Cappon (ed.), Vol. II, p. 346.
276   "reign . . ." Jefferson, *Writings,* Ford (ed.), Vol. VII, p. 265.
276   "To preserve . . ." Adrienne Koch and Harry Ammon, "The Virginia and Kentucky Resolutions: An Episode in Jefferson's and Madison's Defense of Civil Liberties," *William and Mary Quarterly* (April 1948), p. 152.
276   "No government . . ." Jefferson, *Writings,* Ford (ed.), Vol. VI, p. 108.
277   "took upon . . ." Adams, *Works,* C. F. Adams (ed.), Vol. X, p. 113.
277   "I have sacrificed . . ." Page Smith, *John Adams,* Vol. II, p. 1000.
277   "At the present . . ." J. R. Pole, "Jeffersonian Democracy and the Federalist Dilemma: New Jersey, 1798–1812," *Proceedings of the New Jersey Historical Society* (October 1956), p. 283.
277   "all the wealth . . ." "Maryland Politics in 1797 Shown in Letters Selected from the Correspondence of James McHenry," *Publications of the Southern History Association,* Vol. X (1906), p. 32.
277   "contest . . ." Fee, *Transititon from Aristocracy to Democracy in New Jersey,* p. 107.
278   "Long . . ." Adams, *Works,* C. F. Adams (ed.), Vol. IX, p. 579.
278   "the strongest . . ." Jefferson, *Writings,* Ford (ed.), Vol. VIII, p. 3.
278   "If there be . . ." Same.
278   "The revolution . . ." Same, Vol. X, p. 140.

Chapter Fourteen

279   "who had distinguished . . ." Paine, *Life and Works* (New Rochelle), Vol. V, p. 82.
280   "If you subvert . . ." Paine, *Dissertation on First-Principles of Government* (London, 1795), p. 47.
281   "torn asunder . . ." Fee, *Transition from Aristocracy to Democracy in New Jersey,* p. 123.
281   "If the western . . ." *Records of the Federal Convention,* Farrand (ed.), Vol. I, p. 583.
281   "to limit . . ." Same, Vol. II, p. 3.
282   "All free . . ." *Federal and State Constitutions,* Thorpe (ed.), Vol. III, p. 1269.
282   "Every freeman . . ." Same, Vol. VI, p. 3418.

282 "wisdom . . ." Same, Vol. III, p. 1694.

282 "My family . . ." *Memoir of Roger Brooke Taney,* edited by Samuel Tyler (Baltimore, 1872), pp. 81–82.

283 "I am astonished . . ." Williamson, *American Suffrage from Property to Democracy,* p. 146.

283 "some of the wealthiest . . ." Same.

283 "the wise principle . . ." *Votes and Proceedings of the House of Delegates of the State of Maryland* (Annapolis), November session, 1800, p. 85.

283 "When we reflect . . ." Same, p. 89.

283 "We do not consider . . ." Same, p. 91.

284 "We extend . . ." Same.

284 "an act . . ." *Votes and Proceedings of . . . Maryland,* November session, 1802, p. 119.

284 "that every . . ." *Federal and State Constitutions,* Thorpe (ed.), Vol. III, p. 1705.

284 "Such has been . . ." Julian A. C. Chandler, *The History of Suffrage in Virginia* (Baltimore: Johns Hopkins Press, 1901), p. 25.

285 "paid a tax . . ." *Federal and State Constitutions,* Thorpe (ed.), Vol. VI, p. 3259.

286 "maturity . . ." *Pennsylvania Magazine,* Vol. III (July 1776), p. 337.

286 "I do not believe . . ." *Diary of Thomas Robbins, D.D.,* 2 vols. (Boston, 1886), Vol. I, p. 114.

287 "charming . . . We grow . . ." Harry A. Warfel, *Noah Webster, Schoolmaster to America* (New York: The Macmillan Company, 1936), p. 282.

287 "We have defeated . . ." Richard J. Purcell, *Connecticut in Transition, 1775–1818* (Washington: American Historical Association, 1918), p. 235 fn.

287 "The principles of corruption . . ." Same.

287 "principle of admitting . . ." Warfel, *Noah Webster,* pp. 280–81.

287 "Our pious . . ." Alfred Owen Aldridge, *Man of Reason, the Life of Thomas Paine* (Philadelphia: J. B. Lippincott Company, 1959), p. 273.

288 "passion . . ." Paine, *Life and Works* (New Rochelle), Vol. I, p. 466.

288 "Property . . ." William A. Robinson, *Jeffersonian Democracy in New England* (New Haven: Yale University Press, 1916), p. 123.

288 "While the billows . . ." Purcell, *Connecticut in Transition,* p. 279.

289 "a good . . ." *Federal and State Constitutions,* Thorpe (ed.), Vol. I, p. 544.

289 "the criterion . . ." William Griffith, *Eumenes* (Trenton, 1799), p. 50 fn.

289 "all inhabitants . . ." *Federal and State Constitutions,* Thorpe (ed.), Vol. V, p. 2595.

289 "I verily believe . . ." Gladys G. Pidcock, *Constitutional Reform in New Jersey, 1776–1844* (1941), p. 15.

289 "the most preposterous . . ." Griffith, *Eumenes,* p. 44.

289 "he valued . . ." Same, p. 44 fn.

289 "every vagabond . . ." Same, p. 35 fn.

289 "The great . . ." Same, p. 33.

290 "admitted . . ." Same.

290 "voted . . ." Edward Raymond Turner, "Women's Suffrage in New Jersey, 1790–1807," *Smith College Studies in History* (1916), Vol. I, no. 4, p. 182.

291 "every free . . ." *Federal and State Constitutions,* Thorpe (ed.), Vol. IV, p. 2152.

291 "excepting . . ." Same, Vol. III, p. 1649.

292 "gained . . ." *Life and Letters of Joseph Story,* edited by William W. Story, 2 vols. (Boston, 1851), Vol. I, p. 395.

292 "In the absence . . ." *Journal of Debates and Proceedings in the Convention of Delegates, Chosen to Revise the Constitution of Massachusetts Begun and Holden at Boston, November 15, 1820, and Continued by Adjournment to January 9, 1821* (Boston: Boston Daily Advertiser, 1821), p. 243.

292 "a minority . . ." Story, *Life and Letters,* Vol. I, p. 395.

292 "Have you . . ." *Journal of Debates and Proceedings . . . to Revise the Constitution of Massachusetts* (1821), p. 121.

292 "was so ardently . . ." Same.

292 "he recollected . . . if a man . . ." Same, p. 123.

292 "The present constitution . . ." Same, p. 124.

293 "where there are . . ." Same, p. 136b.

293 "It was in the nature . . . that men . . ." Same, p. 121.

293 "In that case . . ." Same, p. 122.

293 "I dislike . . ." Ames, *Works,* Vol. I, p. 61.

293 "the part . . ." *Journal of Debates and Proceedings . . . to Revise the Constitution of Massachusetts* (1821), p. 244.

293 "content . . ." Same, p. 186.

293 "The French . . ." Same, pp. 134–35.

294 "In the course . . ." Adams, *Works,* C. F. Adams (ed.), Vol. X, p. 397.

294 "A letter . . ." *Adams-Jefferson Letters,* Cappon (ed.), Vol. II, p. 291.

294 "So we have . . ." Same.

Chapter Fifteen

295 "whirlpool . . ." Williamson, *American Suffrage from Property to Democracy,* p. 196.

295 "The radicals . . ." *Reports of the Proceedings and Debates of the Convention of 1821, Assembled for the Purpose of Amending the Constitution of the State of New-York* (Albany, 1821), p. 221.

296 "the duty . . ." Williamson, *American Suffrage from Property to Democracy,* p. 204.

296 "To me . . ." *Reports of the Proceedings and Debates of the Convention . . . of New-York,* p. 179.

297 "notion . . ." Same, p. 221.

297 "formed . . ." Same, p. 219.

297 "free and independent . . . By the report . . ." Same, p. 220.

297 "When our constitution . . ." Same, p. 241.

297 "Our community . . ." Same, p. 243.

297 "The provision . . ." Same, p. 242.

297 "There is . . ." Same, p. 360.

297 "vast mass . . ." Same, p. 362.

297 "which the wisdom . . ." Same, p. 215.

298 "Without . . ." Lincoln, *Constitutional History of New York,* Vol. II, p. 4.

298 "We stand . . ." *Reports of the Proceedings and Debates of the Convention . . . of New-York,* p. 222.

299 "The country . . ." Arthur M. Schlesinger, Jr., *The Age of Jackson* (Boston: Little, Brown and Company, 1950), p. 7.

299 "General Jackson . . ." Alexis de Tocqueville, *Democracy in America,* edited by Phillips Bradley, 2 vols. (New York: Alfred A. Knopf, Inc., 1945), Vol. I, p. 299.

300 "I look . . ." Same, Vol. I, p. 300 fn.

300   "general . . . I am not . . ." Jefferson, *Writings,* Ford (ed.), Vol. X, p. 41.

301   "The basis . . ." Same, Vol. X, p. 303.

301   "of incomparably . . . noble . . ." *Proceedings and Debates of the Virginia State Convention of 1829–30* (Richmond: Ritchie & Cook, 1830), p. 908.

302   "democracy . . ." Chandler, "Representation in Virginia," *Johns Hopkins . . . Political Studies* (1896), p. 22 fn.

302   "those who . . ." *Proceedings and Debates of the Virginia State Convention of 1829–30* (Richmond), p. 150.

302   "The Old Dominion . . ." Same, p. 119.

302   "They alone . . ." *Democracy, Liberty, and Property: The State Constitutional Conventions of the 1820's,* edited by Merrill D. Peterson (Indianapolis: The Bobbs–Merrill Company, Inc., 1966), p. 386.

302   "Your memorialists . . ." Same, p. 382.

302   "All men . . ." See page 191.

302   "This is a position . . ." *Proceedings and Debates of the Virginia State Convention of 1829–30* (Richmond), p. 120.

303   "Locke . . ." Same, p. 161.

303   "It appeared . . ." Same, p. 339.

303   "This limitation . . ." Same, p. 340.

303   "I tell you . . ." Same, p. 692.

303   "I am too old . . ." Same, p. 321.

304   "pot-boilers . . . We have been taught . . ." Same, p. 358.

304   "No government . . ." Same, p. 162.

304   "reared . . ." Same, p. 255.

304   "In case . . ." *Federal and State Constitutions,* Thorpe (ed.), Vol. VII, p. 3826.

Chapter Sixteen

307   "the evil . . ." Arthur May Mowry, *The Dorr War* (Providence, 1901), p. 29 fn.

307   "Whatever . . ." Williamson, *American Suffrage from Property to Democracy,* p. 247.

308   "did military . . ." Same, p. 250.

308   "I am . . ." Mowry, *Dorr War,* p. 63.

308   "all free . . ." *Articles of a Constitution Adopted by the People's Convention Held October 4, 1841* (Providence, 1841), p. 3.

309   "A Cataline . . ." C. C. Jewett, *The Close of the Late Rebellion in Rhode-Island* (Providence, 1842), p. 7.

309   "on that awful night . . ." Jacob Frieze, *A Concise History of the Efforts To Obtain an Extension of Suffrage in Rhode Island* (Providence, 1842), p. 89.

309   "fort . . ." Mowry, *Dorr War,* p. 215.

309   "What I did . . ." *Report of the Trial of Thomas Wilson Dorr for Treason* (Providence, 1844), p. 70.

309   "It was of great importance . . ." Same, p. 74.

309   "There are . . ." Same, p. 70.

310   "The servants . . ." Same, p. 70.

310   "The great question . . ." *Address of John Whipple to the People of Rhode-Island on the Approaching Election* (Providence, 1843), p. 16.

310   "the rights of property . . ." *Mr. Goddard's Address to the People of Rhode-Island, Delivered at Newport on Wednesday, May 3, 1843* (Providence, 1843), p. 28.

310   "noble bosoms . . ." Same, p. 47.

311   "long desired . . ." Williamson, *American Suffrage from Property to Democracy,* p. 265.

312   "I cannot see . . ." Emory G. Evans, "A Question of Complexion," *Virginia Magazine of History and Biography* (October 1963), p. 413.

312   "with insolence . . . to fix . . . preserve . . . After all . . ." Same, p. 414.

312   "anchor . . ." *Reports of the Proceedings and Debates of the Convention of 1821 . . . of New-York,* p. 285.

312   "Although property . . ." Same, p. 369.

313   "of peril . . ." *Proceedings and Debates of the Virginia State Convention of 1829–30* (Richmond), p. 382.

313   "All political power . . ." *Federal and State Constitutions,* Thorpe (ed.), Vol. I, p. 537.

313   "what our fathers . . ." Leon F. Litwack, *North of Slavery* (Chicago: University of Chicago Press, 1961), p. 86.

314   "Be so good . . . In this country . . ." de Tocqueville, *Democracy in America,* Bradley (ed.), Vol. I, p. 271 fn.

314   "Public attention . . ." Kirk Harold Porter, *A History of Suffrage in the United States* (Chicago: University of Chicago Press, 1918), p. 222.

314   "The right . . ." *The New York Times,* September 14, 1962.

314   "women . . ." J. Thomas Scharf, *History of Maryland,* 3 vols. (Baltimore, 1879), Vol. II, p. 610.

315   "your Portia" *Letters of Members of the Continental Congress,* Burnett (ed.), Vol. I, p. 311.

315   "laws . . ." *Letters of John Adams, Addressed to his Wife,* edited by Charles Francis Adams, 2 vols. (Boston, 1841), Vol. I, p. 97 fn.

315   "responsible . . ." Porter, *History of Suffrage in the United States,* p. 141.

315   "men of . . ." Same, p. 142.

315   "in the field . . ." Same.

315   "All power . . ." *Federal and State Constitutions,* Thorpe (ed.), Vol. VII, p. 4117.

315   "The rights of citizens . . ." Same, Vol. VII, p. 4132.

316   "metaphysical . . ." *Reports of the Proceedings and Debates of the Convention of 1821 . . . of New-York,* p. 191.

355

Index

Aristotle, 212
Arminianism, 53, 54, 68
army, in English revolution, 102, 103–104, 106–14
Arnold, William, 90, 91
Articles of Confederation (New England), 86; (United States), 238–39, 241, 246, 247, 250
Ashley, Lord, *see* Shaftesbury, Earl of
Asia, passage to, 4, 9, 117
assemblies, legislative, American, *see individual states;* English, *see* Parliament; French, *see* France
Athenaeum, the, 291
Attorney Generals, 48, 78, 100, 101, 149, 157
Avalon, 25, 26, 49
Aylesbury (Eng.), 17*fn.*
Azores, 6

Bacon, Nathaniel, 141–43, 303
Bacon's Rebellion, *see* Virginia, 17th century
Baltimore, Lord, *see* Calvert
Baltimore (Md.), 283, 284
Baltimore and Ohio Railroad, 299
Baltimore Republican Club, 269
Baptists, 113
Barclay, Robert, 130–31
Barebones Parliament, *see* Parliament
Barebones, Praisegod, 113
Bargrave, John, 18–19, 27, 29, 30, 35, 99, 124, 125, 139, 287
Barrow, Henry, 30, 31, 86
Bastille, 265, 279
Baxter, George, 119–20, 121, 137
Baxter, Richard, 103–104, 105, 106, 107
Bedford, Gunning, 247
Behn, Aphra, 143
"Belinda," 207
Bellamy, John, 40, 41
Berkeley, John, Lord, 126–27
Berkeley, Sir William, 140, 141, 142, 143–44; *The Lost Lady,* 140*fn.*
Bible, 15, 60, 94, 103; *see also individual books*
Bill of Rights in state constitutions, Maryland, 220; Massachusetts, 232, 233, 235; Pennsylvania, 200, 213; Virginia, 191–92, 200, 210, 213, 302, 303; as Declaration of Rights, 313, 315

Birmingham (Eng.), 172
Bishop, Abraham, 285, 286
Bland, Mr., 143
Bloch, Adrian, 97
Bloody Tenet, The, see Williams, Roger
Board of Trade, 160, 168, 170, 173, 312
Bonhunt, Mr., 108
borough voting, *see* voting in England
Boston (Eng.), 60, 62
Boston (Mass.), church of, 61, 62, 67–69, 70, 87, 93; 17th century, 62–63, 69–70, 93, 121, 148, 154–55, 156; 18th century, 174, 176, 180, 181, 182, 234, 254, 266, 267, 274; constitutional conventions in, 233, 236, 291
Boston Massacre, 173
Boston Port Bill, 174, 208
Boston Tea Party, 174, 208
Botetourt, Baron de, 207, 208
Bourne, Nehemiah, 102
Bowdoin, James, 232
Bradford, John, 36
Bradford, William, 32, 33, 36, 38, 41, 44, 102; in England and Holland, 31, 34, 36; as Governor of Plymouth, 40, 41, 42, 43, 44, 45, 52, 87, 118*fn.*
Bradford, William (of Philadelphia), 179, 198
Bradstreet, Simon, 59–60, 63, 150, 155, 231
Braintree (Mass.), 231
Braxton, Carter, 190, 204
Breed's Hill, 229, 234
Brent, Margaret, 314
Brewster, Fear, 31
Brewster, Jonathan, 31, 34
Brewster, Patience, 31
Brewster, William, 30, 31, 34, 35, 36, 42, 43, 44
Bridget, *see* Lincoln, fourth Countess of
Bright, Francis, 52
Brissot, Jacques Pierre, 273
Bristol (Eng.), 4, 6, 106, 108, 172
Brook, Richard, 96*fn.*
Brooke, Lord, 76, 77
Brooklyn (N.Y.), 312
Browne, John, 50, 52–53
Browne, Robert, 30, 33
Browne, Samuel, 50, 52–53
Brownists, 29–30, 31, 32–33, 35, 60–61, 86, 103; *see also* Pilgrims
Buckingham, Duke of, 46, 47
Bucks County (Pa.), 197

Buel, David, 297
Bull, William, 169, 173, 176, 187
Bunker Hill, Battle of, 183, 187, 240; *see also* Breed's Hill
Burden, George, 17*fn.*
Burgesses, Hall of, 301
Burgesses, House of, *see* Virginia
Burnet, Bishop, 149
Butler, Pierce, 253
Byllynge, Edward, 127, 128, 130

cabildo, the, 28
Cabot, John, 4
Calvert, George, first Lord Baltimore, 25–26; Cecilius, second Lord Baltimore, 26, 27–28, 132; Charles, third Lord Baltimore, 144
Calvert, Leonard, 28, 314
Calvert County (Md.), 282
Cambridge Agreement, 58, 59
Cambridge (Mass.), 80, 231
Cambridge, University of, 31, 56, 71
Campbell, Lord William, 187, 188
Canterbury, Archbishop of, 152; *see also* Abbot, George *and* Laud, William
Cape Ann, 47
Cape Cod, 37, 37*fn*, 38, 39
Cape Henry, 7
Cape James, 37*fn.*
Carlisle, Earl of, 84
Carolina, 25, 49, 50, 123, 124–26; "Concessions and Agreements," 123, 127; Fundamental Constitutions, 125–26, 131; *see also* North Carolina *and* South Carolina
Carpenters' Hall, 182, 199, 201, 218*fn.*
Carroll, Charles, 219, 220, 282, 285
Carter, Charles, 163
Carteret, Sir George, 126–27, 128, 129, 130
Carteret, Lady, 127
Carver, John, 34, 36, 38, 39
Charity, the, 42
Charles I, King of England, 24, 26, 78, 100, 102, 104, 107, 112; political theories, 51, 53, 54, 104, 112–13; relation to Parliament, *see* Parliament; execution, 110, 112, 115, 183*fn., 266
Charles II, King of England, 115, 116, 121, 145–49; relation to America, 116, 120, 121–23, 141, 143, 144, 147–49, to Parliament, *see* Parliament, to Penn, *see* Penn, William

Charles River, 48, 75
Charleston (S.C.), 161, 168, 174, 182, 187, 188, 266, 267, 285
Charleston Democratic Club, 274
Charter of Liberties and Privileges, *see* New York
Charter of Privileges, *see* Pennsylvania
charters, granting of English: Avalon (1623), 25; Carolina, first (1629), 25, second (1663), 122–23; Connecticut (1662), 121–22; Maryland (1632), 26; Massachusetts Bay, first (1629), 48, second (1691), 157; New Albion (1634), 25; New England (1620), 25; New York (1664), 116; Pennsylvania (1681), 131–32; Rhode Island, first (1643), 97, second (1663), 122; Virginia, first (1606), 6, second (1609), 10, third (1612), 11
Chaucer, Geoffrey, 16
Chesapeake Bay, 5, 6–7, 26, 28
Chester County (Pa.), 197
Chesterfield County (Va.), 304
Chestnut Street, 135, 211
Child, Robert, 71–72
Chinese, 312
Church of England, as a political force, 32, 51, 53, 100; becomes Presbyterian, 102
Cicero, 212
City Hall (N.Y.C.), 241, 259, 264
City Tavern, 256
Civil War, American, 311, 313, 315; English, *see* revolution, first English
Clarke, John, 93, 122
Clarke, William, 107, 109
Clinton, De Witt, 296, 298
Coddington, William, 60, 61, 93–95, 96, 98, 122
Coke, Sir Edward, 86–87
Coleman Street, 83, 84, 85*fn.*
Colleton, Sir Peter, 125
colonies, *see individual listings*
Columbus, Christopher, 4
Commission for Foreign Plantations, 99, 100
Committee of Detail, 252, 254
Committee of the Whole, in England, 172, 178; in America, 178, 188, 192, 209, 214, 242, 293
Common Sense, see Paine, Thomas
Commons, House of, *see* Parliament

214–15; signed, 218–19, 299; reprinted, 218, 225

Declaration of Rights, American, 179; English, 154, 158, 212; French, 280; *see also* Bill of Rights

Declaratory Act, 172

Defense of the Constitutions, see Adams, John

Delaware, 131, 169, 220, 247, 249–50, 298; legislative assembly, 177, as Convention, 177; constitution (1776), 220; voting, 162, 220

Delaware Bay, 26, 93, 131

Delaware River, 134

Delegates, House of, *see* Maryland

"democracy," in 17th century, 22–23, 27, 77, 78, 96, 97, 137; in 18th century, 201, 232, 271, 277; at Constitutional Convention, 246, 249, 251, 257, 260; in 19th century, 284, 293, 295, 302, 303; word becomes respectable, 299, 305

Democracy in America, see Tocqueville, Alexis de

democratic clubs or societies, 267–68, 269–72, 273

Democratic Party, 299

Democratic Society of Pennsylvania, 266–67, 270

Devon County (Eng.), 25

Deuteronomy, Book of, 81, 85

D'Ewes, Sir Simonds, 61–62, 78

Dickinson, John, 249–50, 253

Directory, *see* France

Discourses Concerning Government, see Sidney, Algernon

Dissertation on First Principles, see Paine, Thomas

Dominion, under Charles II, 148–49, under James II, 149–51, 158*fn.*, under William III, 154–56; in New England, 148, 149–51, 154–55, 157; elsewhere, 149, 151, 155, 156, 157

Donne, John, 14, 22

"Dorchester" (Conn.), 80

Dorchester (Eng.), 47, 55

Dorchester (Mass.), 79

Dorchester Company, 47, 49, 60

Dorchester County (Md.), 284

Dorr, Thomas, 307–10, 311

Dorr War, *see* Rhode Island

Dover (Del.), 250

Downing, Emmanuel, 56–57

Downing, George, 104, 116

Downing, Lucy, 56, 57

Drayton, William Henry, 188

Dudley, Thomas, 59, 60–61, 63, 67, 67*fn.*

Dunmore, Lord, 190, 208

Dutch East India Company, 117

Dutch West India Company, 117, 118, 119, 120

Dutton, Warren, 293

Dyer, Mary, 127

East India Company, 9, 174

East Jersey, *see* New Jersey

Eaton, Anne, 86, 119

Eaton, Theophilus, 84, 85, 94, 118*fn.*, 122

Edinburgh, 152

Edward I, King of England, 151

Edwards, Thomas, 103

electoral college, 220, 250, 263, 298

Eliot, Sir John, 54, 57, 76, 171, 176

Elizabeth I, Queen of England, 3, 20, 30, 32, 33, 101

Elizabeth (N.J.), 127, 131, 290

Ellsworth, Oliver, 253

Endecott, John, 48, 50, 51, 52–53, 63, 119, 128

"England's Great Interest," *see* Penn, William

Era of Good Feelings, 302

Essay Concerning Human Understanding, see Locke, John

Essex County (Eng.), 50

Essex County (Mass.), 151, 230

Essex County (N.J.), 290

Essex Result, 231, 235

Eumenes, see Griffith, William

"Excellent Privilege, The," *see* Penn, William

Exchequer, Chancellor of the, 170

Exchequer, Court of, *see* Court of Exchequer

Exclusion Bill, 146

Exeter (Eng.), 6, 127

Exeter (N.H.), 92, 176, 179, 183, 185, 307

Exeter, Earl of, 9

Fairfax, Thomas, 108, 112

Family of Love, 33

Faneuil Hall, 266, 311

see Penn, William, to other friends, 127, 131

James River, 8

Jamestown (Va.), church, 12, 14, 143; town of, 7–8, 12–13, 14, 18, 23, 26, 37, 139, 143, 190; as political unit, *see* Virginia, 17th century

Jay, John, 201, 223, 224, 241, 257, 295, 296

Jefferson, Thomas, general career, 205–17, 276–78, 300–301; in Continental Congress, 205, 214, 238; on committees, 205, 207, 209, 211, 237; writes Declaration of Independence, 211–14, 225, 316; abroad, 240; as Secretary of State, 262, 264, 276; as Vice President, 276; presidential campaign, 277, 281, 285, 286; as President, 278, 281; views on religion, 208–209, 277; on Virginia constitution, 209, 210, 257, 300–301; on voting, 209–10, 300–301; on slavery, 214–15; on education, 216, 287, 300; on government, 206–207, 210–11, 216, 219, 262–63, 276, 277, 278, 294; *Notes on the State of Virginia,* 210; *A Summary View,* 205, 208, 214; relation to Adams, *see* Adams, John, to Madison, *see* Madison, James

Jeffreys, George, 146, 151

Jersey, island of, 127

Jews, 312

Johnson, Isaac, 55, 56, 58, 59, 60

Jones, Christopher, 37

Kennebec River, 9

Kennedy, John Fitzgerald, 314

Kent County (Del.), 220

Kent, James, 295, 296, 297, 298, 307, 310

Kentucky, 268, 281

Kentucky County, 282

Kentucky Democratic Society, 268

Kieft, Willem, 118–19, 120

King, Rufus, 242, 256, 296

King, Samuel Ward, 308, 309

King's College, 223

Kingsbridge (N.Y.), 223

Kingston (N.Y.), 224

Kirke, Percy, 148–49, 150, 151

Knox, Henry, 241, 248

Lafayette, Marquis de, 201, 240, 265, 279

Langdon, John, 245

Laud, William, Bishop of London and Archbishop of Canterbury, 51, 53, 62, 68, 77, 99, 100, 102, 174

Law and Order Party, 310

Lawrence, Margaret, 5

Laws Divine, Moral and Martial, 12, 13

Lee, Richard Henry, 190, 204, 205, 207, 212, 214, 228, 237

Leicestershire, 51

Leigh, Benjamin Watkins, 303, 304

Leisler, Jacob, 155–56

Levant Company, 9

Leveler Party, 105–107, 111, 112, 130, 140, 163

Leverett, John, 102

Leviticus, Book of, 85, 136, 216

Lexington and Concord, battles of, 181, 182, 229

Leyden, 34, 117

Liberty Bell, 136, 216

Lichfeld, Thomas, 17*fn.*

Lilburne, John, 105, 106–107, 192

Lincoln, Bridget, fourth Countess of, 55, 60, 61, 76

Lincoln, Elizabeth, third Countess of, 35, 55

Lincoln, Theophilus, fourth Earl of, 55, 59

Lincolnshire, 52, 55, 60, 61, 68

Littleton (Mass.), 292

Livingston, Peter R., 225

Livingston, Robert R., 205, 219, 223, 228, 259; as "Mr. R," 211

Lloyd, David, 136, 137

Lloyd, Edward, 283

Lloyd, James, 275

Locke, John, career, 125–26, 126*fn.,* 158–59; relation to Shaftesbury, 125, 145, 158; political theories, 159–60, 191, 212, 213, 292; effect on America, 161, 191–92, 212–13, 228, 303; *Essay Concerning Human Understanding,* 126*fn.,* 303; *Two Treatises of Government,* 159–60, 303

Logan, James, 137

London, as center of colonization, 6, 9, 49, 55, of radicalism, 104–105, 111, 146–47, 180–81; mayors of, 10, 58, 146, 181; Bishop of, *see* Laud, William

Long Island, 93, 118, 119, 120, 137, 257

Long Parliament, *see* Parliament

Lords, House of, *see* Parliament

Lords of Trade, 149, 156, 168

Rhodes, Isle of, 97
Richardson, Joseph, 292
Richmond (Va.), 190, 208, 301, 302, 304
Rittenhouse, David, 267
Roanoke Colony, 5-6
Roanoke, island of, 4, 5
Robinson, John (minister), 30, 31, 34, 35, 36-37, 40, 42, 45, 77, 117
Robinson, John, 210*fn.*
Robinson, Widow, 284
Rolfe, John, 31
Roman Catholicism, fear of, 152, 154; *see also* Parliament
Rotterdam, 132
Rousseau, Jean Jacques, 265
Royal Exchange, 22, 40, 167
Royal Society, 125
Rumbold, Richard, 151-52, 216
Rush, Benjamin, 171, 174, 193-94, 201, 218-19, 226, 244, 294
Rushworth, John, 107, 107*fn.*, 208
Russia, 9
Rutledge, John, 178, 249

Sagadahoc, the, 9
Sagadahoc colony, 9, 50
St. Augustine (Fla.), 4, 28
St. George's County (Md.), 219
St. Lawrence Jewry, 85*fn.*
St. Mary's (Md.), 26, 27, 156
St. Stephen's, chapel, 14; church, 85*fn.*
Salem, early history, 48, 50, 52; church of, 52, 61, 68, 70, 87, 115, 119; town of, 60, 68*fn.*, 88, 90, 119, 176, 180, 291
Saltonstall, Sir Richard, 58, 59, 60
Sandys, Sir Edwin, 19-21, 30-31; in Parliament, 12, 20-21, 28, 53, 158; relation to King James, 20-21, to Pilgrims, 29, 30, 35, 37, to Virginia, 22, 23*fn.*, 29, 141, to Virginia Company, 10, 12, 21-23, 35
Sandys, Sir Samuel, 31
Sanford, Nathan, 296, 298
Saratoga County (N.Y.), 316
Savannah (Ga.), 221
Saybrook (Conn.), 76-77, 79, 80, 101
Saye and Sele, Lord, 55, 76, 77, 78, 79, 100, 101, 122
Schuylkill River, 134
scot and lot, 136
Scotch-Irish, 197-98
Scotland, 100, 115, 130, 174, 198, 225, 252

Scrooby (Eng.), 31, 33
secret ballot, 21, 66, 97
Secretary of State, 26, 35, 270, 276, 278, 301; *see also* Jefferson, Thomas
Secretary of the Treasury, 278; *see also* Hamilton, Alexander
Sedition Bill and Act, 275-76, 277
Seekers, 104
Seekonk (Mass.), 88, 90
Seekonk River, 88
Sempringham, 55, 56, 58, 60, 88
Senate, federal, *see* Constitutional Convention *and* Congress, U.S.; state, *see individual listings*
Separatists, 33, 51, 52, 60-61, 103, 104
Sergeant at Arms, 13, 14, 17, 54
Sexby, Edward, 108
Shaftesbury, Anthony Ashley Cooper, Lord Ashley, later Earl of, 124-25, 126, 145, 146, 158, 182; relation to Locke, *see* Locke, John
Shakespeare, William, 21, 183, 228
Shays, Daniel, 240
Shays' Rebellion, *see* Massachusetts, 18th and 19th centuries
Sherman, Roger, 205, 211, 226, 251
ship-money case, 78, 101, 172
Sidney, Algernon, 132, 146, 148, 212, 228; *Discourses Concerning Government,* 146
Skelton, Samuel, 52, 61, 87, 93
slavery, Negro, 214-15, 292, 312
Slocum, Elihu, 292
Smith, John, 7, 8-9, 22, 24, 37*fn.*, 39
Smith, Ralph, 51, 87
Smith, Samuel S., 281
Smythe, Sir Thomas, 9, 10-11, 12, 13, 21, 23*fn.*, 35, 66, 67
Society of Friends, *see* Quakers
South Carolina, 168, 173, 176, 187-88, 215, 285, 298; legislature as Commons House of Assembly, 126, 169, 173, 176, 187, as Provincial Congress, 187, 188, as General Assembly, 188, 285; constitution of 1776, 188, 190, 194, of 1778, 188, 249; delegation to Constitutional Convention, 242, 249, 253; voting, 161, 188, 285; for early history *see* Carolina
Southampton (Eng.), 36, 59, 60
Southampton, Earl of, 21, 23, 40
Southwark (Eng.), 10
Spain, 4, 5, 8, 20, 28, 34, 117, 138, 150, 285

Speaker of the House, 15, 17, 54, 56, 101, 145, 178, 179, 206, 230, 260; *see also individuals*
Speedwell, 36
Spencer, Ambrose, 297
Stamp Act Congress, 175, 205
Stamp Act and Stamp Tax, 170–72, 179, 191, 205–206, 219, 234, 268
Standish, Miles, 118*fn*.
Stansbury, Arthur, 301
State House, in Philadelphia (Independence Hall), 136, 182, 198–99, 200, 218, 241–42, 248, 260; in Boston, 291
State House Yard, 199, 216
Staten Island, 257
Staunton (Va.), 300
Stoke House, 87
Story, Joseph, 291, 292–93
Stoughton, Israel, 102, 108–109
Strand, the, 9, 125
Stuyvesant, Peter, 119, 120, 121, 137
Suffolk County (Eng.), 8, 57, 141
suffrage, *see* voting
Sullivan, James, 196, 230, 233
Sullivan, John, 176, 180, 186
Summary View, A, see Jefferson, Thomas
Supreme Court, of U.S., 291, 301; of Connecticut, 288
Sussex County (Del.), 220
Sussex County (Eng.), 8
Sweden, 131
Sydenham, Thomas, 125

Talleyrand, Charles Maurice de, 274
Taney, Michael, 282–83
Taney, Roger Brooke, 282–83
Tangier, 149
Tattershall (Eng.), 55
Taunton (Mass.), 151
taverns for political meetings, 54, 176, 207
taxation without representation, in England, 53–54, 78, 78*fn*., 152, 172; in America (17th century), 42, 65–66, 71, 148, 150–51 (18th century), 170–72, 189, 191, 234 (19th century), 313
Taylor, Senator, 263
Tennessee, 281, 282, 299
Thanksgiving, first, 40
Thomson, Charles, 178, 184, 214, 218, 219, 243

Thoughts on Government, see Adams, John
Three Cranes, the, 54
Tocqueville, Alexis de, 299–300, 314; *Democracy in America,* 299
Tories, 182, 221, 223, 230, 264, 288*fn*.
Trinidad, 6
Turgot, Anne Robert Jacques, 244
Two Treatises of Government, see Locke, John
Tyler, John, 301, 308

Ulster, 198
Ulster County (N.Y.), 224
United Provinces, *see* Netherlands
Upshur, Abel, 301

Valley Forge, 226
Van Buren, Martin, 296, 298, 305, 312
van der Donck, Adriaen, 118, 119, 120
Vane, Henry, 68–69, 70, 79
Vane, Sir Henry, 69
Verin, Jane, 90
Verin, Joshua, 90
Vermont, relation to New York, 225, 253, 281; admitted to Union, 281; constitution of 1777, 213, 225–26, of 1786, 213; voting, 225–26, 313
Verrazano, Giovanni da, 97
veto, use of, 75–76, 215, 246
Virginia, 17th century, early history, 4–6; charter of 1606, 6, 7 (for other charters, *see* Virginia Company); founding of Jamestown, 7–9, 21–22, 50, 276; subsequent history, 12–17, 22–24, 139–44; first legislature (House of Burgesses), 13–15, 23*fn*., 49, 139, 158; later assemblies, 24, 28, 139–41, 161; Bacon's Assembly, 142–43; Bacon's Rebellion, 143, 161; voting, 17–18, 139–40, 141, 142, 144, 161, 282, 311, 312
Virginia, 18th and 19th centuries, for revolutionary activity, *see individuals;* legislature as House of Burgesses, 163, 170, 171, 206, 207–208, 302, 312, as Convention, 178, 190–92, 204, 205, 208, 209, Senate, 191, 249; delegation to Constitutional Convention, 242, 243, 249, 250, 251, 255, 256; constitution of 1776, 190–92, 205, 209–10, 218, 228, 243, 301